EVOLUTIONARY PSYCHOLOGY
Alternative Approaches

EVOLUTIONARY PSYCHOLOGY
Alternative Approaches

edited by

Steven J. Scher
Eastern Illinois University
Charleston, Illinois

Frederick Rauscher
Michigan State University
East Lansing, Michigan

KLUWER ACADEMIC PUBLISHERS
Boston / Dordrecht / New York / London

Distributors for North, Central and South America:
Kluwer Academic Publishers
101 Philip Drive
Assinippi Park
Norwell, Massachusetts 02061 USA
Telephone (781) 871-6600
Fax (781) 681-9045
E-Mail: kluwer@wkap.com

Distributors for all other countries:
Kluwer Academic Publishers Group
Post Office Box 322
3300 AH Dordrecht, THE NETHERLANDS
Telephone 31 786 576 000
Fax 31 786 576 474
E-Mail: services@wkap.nl

 Electronic Services < http://www.wkap.nl >

Library of Congress Cataloging-in-Publication Data

Evolutionary psychology: alternative approaches / edited by Steven J. Scher, Frederick Rauscher.
   p. cm.
  Includes bibliographical references.
ISBN: 1-4020-7279-1 (alk. paper)
   1. Generic psychology. I. Scher, Steven J., 1962- II. Rauscher , Frederick, 1961-

  BF701 .E97 2002
  155.7—dc21

                      2002034083

TABLE OF CONTENTS

ACKNOWLEDGMENTS

We would like to thank the many people who helped this book come to fruition. First of all, the contributors to this volume deserve our thanks for providing the meat of the book and for putting up with our nagging.

We are grateful to Delores Rauscher and Grant Sterling for many useful discussions about evolutionary psychology. We would also both like to thank Delores & Konrad Rauscher for their emotional and nutritional support during an intense summer work period. Sarah Ward and Joe Slowik provided valuable work editing the chapters.

The idea for this project grew out of a symposium on Alternative Approaches to Evolutionary Psychology that was presented at the 1999 Meetings of the American Psychological Association. We would like to express our gratitude to Bill Addison for helpful advice on the organization of the symposium, and to the participants: Linnda Caporael, Gilbert Gottlieb, and Sheldon Solomon.

CONTRIBUTORS

William Bechtel
Department of Philosophy, 0119
University of California, San Diego
9500 Gilman Drive
La Jolla, CA 92093

Linnda Caporael
Department of Science and Technology Studies
Rensselaer Polytechnic Institute
Troy, NY 12180

Niles Eldredge
Committee on Evolutionary Processes & Division of Paleontology
American Museum of Natural History
Central Park West at 79th St.
New York, NY 10024

Paul E. Griffiths
Department of History and Philosophy of Science
1017 Cathedral of Learning
University of Pittsburgh
Pittsburgh, PA 15260

Sarah Blaffer Hrdy
Anthropology Department
University of California
Davis, CA, 95616

Timothy J. Ketelaar
Department of Psychology
New Mexico State University
Las Cruces, NM 88003

Jennifer Mundale
University of Central Florida
Department of Philosophy
CNH 411
Orlando, FL 32816

Dominic Murphy
Division of the Humanities and Social Sciences
California Institute of Technology
Pasadena CA 91125

Domenico Parisi
Research Group on Artificial Life
Institute of Cognitive Science and Technologies
Italian National Research Council
Viale Marx, 15
00137 Rome
Italy

Steven R. Quartz
Division of the Humanities and Social Sciences
California Institute of Technology
Pasadena CA 91125

Frederick Rauscher
Department of Philosophy
Michigan State University
503 South Kedzie Hall
East Lansing, MI 48824

Steven J. Scher
Department of Psychology
Eastern Illinois University
Charleston, IL 61920

Karola Stotz
Center for Philosophy of Science
University of Pittsburgh
817 Cathedral of Learning
Pittsburgh, PA 15260

David Sloan Wilson
Department of Biological Sciences
Binghamton University
Binghamton, NY 13902

FREDERICK RAUSCHER AND STEVEN J. SCHER

ALTERNATIVE APPROACHES TO EVOLUTIONARY PSYCHOLOGY

Introduction

The idea for this book had its genesis as the approach we call ''narrow evolutionary psychology" first began to appear. "Narrow evolutionary psychology" refers to the specific program of research described and defended by scholars such as Buss (1995, 1999), Dennett (1995), Pinker, (1997), Symons (1979, 1987), and Tooby and Cosmides (1992; Cosmides & Tooby, 1997). This approach, however, is only one particular method among many that could be used to apply evolutionary concepts to psychology. We use the term 'narrow evolutionary psychology' to contrast it with the general question of how one would address psychological evolution, without specifying any particular approach ("broad evolutionary psychology" or simply "evolutionary psychology"). "Narrow evolutionary psychology" is a description meant to be evaluatively neutral, in essence meaning only the term "evolutionary psychology", narrowly construed to refer to one particular approach. By using this term, we mean to indicate only that this perspective operates with a narrower range of assumptions than the whole field of evolutionary psychology, broadly construed. The term "narrow evolutionary psychology" was independently arrived at by the editors and by one of the chapter authors (Wilson). For all other chapters, its insertion was instigated by the editors.[1]

In the late 1980's and early 1990's, a number of papers using this approach appeared in the empirical psychology literature. For example, Cosmides' (1989) exhaustive examination of the Wason Selection Task argued for a Darwinian approach to reasoning; Buss' (1989; Buss et al., 1990) large cross-cultural study of preferences in mates argued for a set of universal gender differences; and Kenrick & Keefe's (1992) exploration of age and gender differences in mate preferences added life-history ideas to the tools appearing in the psychological literature.

---

[1] Previously, narrow evolutionary psychology has been called "inclusive fitness psychology" (Caporael, 2001), "cognitive adaptationism" (Scher, 2001), and, (tongue firmly in cheek), the "Standard Selectionist pSychology Model (SSSM; Scher, 1999b). Heyes (2000, p. 3) refers to what we are calling "broad evolutionary psychology" as "evolutionary psychology in the round".

Steven J. Scher & Frederick Rauscher (eds.). Evolutionary Psychology: Alternative Approaches, xi-xviii

At that time, one of us (Scher) joined the many other psychologists who reacted to this growing literature with doubts about its plausibility. Never doubting that humans were evolved creatures, these critics nevertheless questioned whether Darwinian concepts could be usefully applied to human psychology. Spurred by this skepticism, Scher began to read the more conceptual literature coming from the narrow evolutionary psychology camp (e.g., Buss, 1995; Crawford & Anderson, 1989; Kenrick, 1989; Tooby & Cosmides, 1990, 1992).

These conceptual articles were persuasive. They made a strong case that Darwinism did have something useful to say about human psychology. Furthermore, it was clear that many of the criticisms that were being leveled at (narrow) evolutionary psychology were inappropriate, based on stereotyped or outdated ideas about sociobiology. At the same time, a great many questions and criticisms still seemed to apply.

Meanwhile, Rauscher, a philosopher, had developed an interest in evolution as a result of his interest in the possibility of naturalism in ethics. While working on the nature of ethics in such Eighteenth-Century philosophers as David Hume and Immanuel Kant — one an early naturalist, the other a famous critic of naturalism — Rauscher noticed a similarity between debates about naturalism in ethics then and now. The philosophical debate on naturalism was highly critical of sociobiology (Kitcher, 1985) while at the same time holding out promise for some use of evolutionary theory to understand human behavior (Kitcher, 1993, 1994). Rauscher (1997) showed how evolutionary concepts are compatible with Kant's ethical ideas. A chance meeting between Scher & Rauscher (at a performance of African drumming) further broadened both author's exposure to approaches to applying evolutionary science to human affairs.

Meeting weekly (along with another philosopher, Grant Sterling) to read about and discuss issues in evolution and human behavior, we quickly became aware that despite the impression given off by authors such as Tooby & Cosmides, Buss, Pinker (1997), and Dennett (1995), there were a wide variety of ways in which one could think about the evolution of human (and non-human) psychology.

This lead directly to a symposium at the 1999 meetings of the American Psychological Association on alternative approaches to evolutionary psychology (Scher, 1999), and to the development of this book. In this book, we seek to add to the growing literature (e.g., Caporael, 2001; Heyes & Huber, 2000) which points out the variety of ways in which evolution and psychology might interact. As we described the book when we contacted potential chapter authors, our purpose is not to be critical of narrow evolutionary psychology but to offer positive alternatives to further the general field of evolutionary psychology. We are aiming to publicize a host of different methodologies for studying human psychology from an evolutionary perspective — some of which might be incompatible with each other. Our purpose is not to endorse any of them; rather, we wish to make them more widely known, in order to enhance the scholarly debate surrounding evolutionary psychology. We are happy to say that the contributions to the book not only meet this challenge, but in many cases exceed our expectations. These chapters do not merely raise questions about some aspects of the narrow approach to evolutionary psychology, more importantly they offer distinct viable alternatives.

In our chapter, we present a historical overview of the ideas that came together to become evolutionary psychology, with a particular emphasis on the ideas that led up to narrow evolutionary psychology. We then provide a detailed discussion of the assumptions that define that approach, and we discuss how those assumptions represent the combination of particular approaches to psychology and to evolutionary biology. This allows us to consider how alternative approaches can be formed by adopting either alternative assumptions about psychology, alternative assumptions about biology, or alternative assumptions about the unique combination of these two disciplines.

Tim Ketelaar offers a defense of evolutionary psychology construed in the narrow sense against the challenges offered by opponents of the approach. He argues that most opponents of narrow evolutionary psychology are too quick to reject the entire approach when they discover one or two specific problems in its application. He links this tendency to a Popperian philosophy of science centered on falsifiability of theories. In its place he advocates an approach to alternatives more in line with a Lakatosian philosophy of science in which narrow evolutionary psychology is viewed as a layered set of hypotheses and predictions arranged around a core set of basic theoretical assumptions. When specific hypotheses or predictions are challenged, they may be modified without affecting the basic theoretical assumptions. Critics of narrow evolutionary psychology, he then concludes, must convince psychologists that the basic theoretical assumptions themselves are inherently flawed rather than merely citing disagreements with particular applications. For an alternative approach to be successful, it must show that its theoretical assumptions are superior on scientifically relevant criteria. (In light of Ketelaar's argument, we have attempted in our chapter to provide an organizational structure for alternative approaches by describing various places for alternatives within the larger theory of evolutionary psychology, broadly construed.)

In his chapter, David Sloan Wilson discusses a large number of particular methodological alternatives to narrow evolutionary psychology. He argues in favor of a broader role for group selection, culture/gene interaction, genetic variability, various other types of evolutionary processes, and behavioral plasticity in evolutionary psychology. His focus on morality and the human capacity for change and flexibility highlights how these issues are interrelated. The narrow evolutionary psychology stress on individual selection overlooks the recent success in using group selection models to explain altruistic behavior. But groups of altruists do not necessarily share a genetic determinant of their altruistic behavior; rather, shared social norms might explain their behavioral uniformity, at least in interaction over generations with genetic evolution. Within the group, and certainly within the human species, genetic variation might also explain aspects of human psychology — a line of research, he claims, overlooked by narrow evolutionary psychology with its focus on the universality of the architecture of the human mind. Wilson also stresses that the process of evolutionary change appears to be both very rapid and very diverse, operating beyond simply hard-wired behavioral determinations acquired during the Environment of Evolutionary Adaptedness (EEA). Plasticity of behavior allowing for flexibility in novel environments can also explain the rapid change in recent human cultural evolution and can explain different cultural and social norms operating on the basis of genetic components.

Like Wilson, Linnda Caporael urges evolutionary psychology to move beyond inclusive fitness theory with its exclusive focus on genetic inheritance. Inheritance is expanded, she notes, if we consider the way in which traits are assembled from a diverse collection of resources that include both elements internal to organisms (e.g., genes, proteins, hormones) and elements external to organisms (e.g., conspecifics, elements of the physical environment, cultural norms). This perspective points toward multi-level theories of evolution and selection. Wherever interaction between a particular entity and its environment reliably recreates some object, be it at the gene, cell, organism, group, or other level, selection and replication of particular entities can occur. Caporael refers to replicated objects as "repeated assemblies". A vocabulary of repeated assembly fits Darwin's emphasis on descent with modification better than a vocabulary of inclusive fitness, although the genes described by inclusive fitness are themselves among the entities which repeatedly assemble. Caporael stresses that the entities chosen for study as repeated assemblies are independent of any ontology, that is, she is not making metaphysical claims about the proper way to carve nature at its joints; rather, repeated assembly is a functional concept applied to any aspect of experience involving such replication and selection. The focus of evolutionary psychology ought to include the multiple levels of analysis within which objects repeatedly reassemble rather than exclusively discuss genetic selection.

Niles Eldredge objects to the adaptationist focus on reproduction in narrow evolutionary psychology. Reproductive functions, that is, those concerning behavior aimed at passing on genetic information to new generations, ought to be distinguished from what he calls "economic" functions, that is, those concerning behavior aimed at matter/energy transfers to sustain the individual organism's life. Although interdependent, these two types of functions lead to parallel, distinct hierarchical structures of organisms. In human beings (and possibly bonobos) there is further a third category of behavior because sex is disconnected from its merely reproductive function. These three components of human behavior interact in human culture (learned behavior), which Eldredge traces back to the Pleistocene era of accelerated human evolution. Thus Eldredge concludes that merely linking an observed behavior to its perceived reproductive function is not enough to determine that it is an adaptation; he cites rape in contemporary society as an example. Evolutionary psychology must instead turn from a focus on reproductive behavior to a more complex interplay among all types of behavior in human beings.

The context of adaptation is stressed by Sarah Blaffer Hrdy. She argues that rather than focussing strictly on the EEA as advocated by Buss and other proponents of narrow evolutionary psychology, evolutionary psychology ought to take into account the history of a possible adaptation. This history includes not only the context of origin for an adaptation, but also its subsequent expression in different contexts which might reveal any inherent flexibility in the adaptive behavior. Hrdy offers the example of female mate preferences. Human females exhibit varying degrees of polyandrous behavior in different contexts. Cultural variations are only one possible explanation; the broader social environment and various levels of resources must also be taken into account during periods of possible acquisition of the adaptation. Hrdy's alternative focus on history not only expands the time period to be studied as the "Environment of Evolutionary Adaptedness" but also challenges the narrow modularity resulting from overlooking the context of an adaptation in practice.

Karola Stotz and Paul Griffiths offer a framework for any successful evolutionary psychology. Explanations in such a naturalistic psychology must (a) be causally explainable in reference to mechanistic physical entities, (b) be consistent with an historical account of the emergence of the features in response to unique circumstances (and not necessarily providing universal laws of nature), and (c) provide an understanding of the developmental processes which lead to the trait — both in terms of its ontogeny and its original appearance as an "evolutionary novelty". According to Stotz and Griffiths, narrow evolutionary psychology lacks these components because it relies on inadequate information about proposed specific historical niches and possible developmental pathways occupied by early humans. It is thus unable to identify psychological functions to the degree of certainty necessary for subsequent hypotheses about psychological mechanisms. Stotz and Griffiths recommend a study not of the past adaptive environment of human beings but of their current environment. For Stotz and Griffiths, this focus serves the goal of properly identifying the functional breakdown of the mind, independent of an analysis solely of the adaptive function. This approach fills in the information missing in narrow evolutionary psychology's approach. In order to naturalize evolutionary psychology, then, Stotz and Griffiths stress, like Caporael, the concept of extended inheritance — the concept that the development of phenotypic features involves a variety of resources both internal and external to the organism. They suggest that these resources are put together by a developmental system, which operates in part through a process of self-organization. Such an approach gives an active role to the organism in the process of selection, and shifts the focus of evolutionary psychology from the products of processes to the processes themselves.

Dominic Murphy's chapter begins with a defense of narrow evolutionary psychology's reliance on hypotheses about the distant past against charges that such hypotheses are unverifiable speculation. To do this he describes two types of adaptationism: backward-looking adaptationism and forward-looking adaptationism; the former begins with a current trait and postulates its origin in the environment of evolutionary adaptedness while the latter begins with speculation about the environment of evolutionary adaptedness and deduces hypotheses about current mental modules. Forward-looking adaptationism in particular, Murphy argues, can usefully provide testable hypotheses about current human psychology. But what this method provides is evidence of particular psychological capacities.   Not all psychological capacities, however, are discrete modules: they may overlap one another or exist in multiple modules, or they may be part of domain-general systems, for example.   Like Stotz and Griffiths, Murphy further asserts that we can best understand psychological capacities and their underlying cognitive architecture if we attend to the developmental systems which create the capacities. Simply viewing them as innate structures does not provide adequate insight. Murphy thus holds out the hope that a developmental perspective advanced in light of hypotheses from forward looking adaptationism can provide a methodology for evolutionary psychology.

Steven Quartz also questions whether narrow evolutionary psychology can generate reasonable hypotheses about human cognitive architecture. He contends that a reasonable evolutionary psychology must integrate developmental cognitive neuroscience and developmental biology into an alternative he calls developmental evolutionary psychology.   In particular, Quartz rejects narrow evolutionary psychology's *massive modularity hypothesis* as inconsistent with knowledge about the evolution and ontogenetic development of neural structures. He offers, instead, a view stressing the systematic effects that alterations to one step in a developmental program can have to the development of a complete neural system. As a result, possible evolutionary changes are constrained. Any possible cognitive evolution must thus be based on this deep structure of neural development; narrow evolutionary psychology's view of modules must be replaced with a behavioral systems view giving pride of place to neural development. Quartz concludes by reviewing arguments that the environment in which the hominid brain evolved was far more variable then is normally proposed by narrow-school evolutionary psychologists, and suggests that this variability is (a) more consistent with his approach, and (b) may underlie the capacity for complex cultural learning.

William Bechtel also objects to the characterization of modules in narrow evolutionary psychology, and also contends that they are inconsistent with our knowledge of the brain. By pairing psychological modules with postulated domains corresponding to certain tasks such as mate acquisition, the narrow approach makes modules too large. That is, they are rather coarse grained in comparison to the finer grained operations revealed by neuroscience. Coarse grained functions utilize many finer grained information processing operations distributed throughout the human brain. Further, coarse grained functions overlap one another by utilizing identical finer grained functions. The cognitivist model underlying narrow evolutionary psychology could therefore more usefully be replaced with a model incorporating finer resolution of specific mental processes and their interconnections. Such a model could still employ evolutionary reasoning regarding the coarse modules, but to do so it would require the input of neuroscientific and phylogenetic information. New coarse-grained modules may evolve through the incorporation of increasingly specialized fine-grained operations, or through the reorganization of pre-existing components. Study of modules in light of their neuroscientific structure, and their phylogenetic history would reveal the constraints acting upon coarse modules conforming to the actual structure of primate brains and their possible relations through evolution. Coarse modules could then be seen as arising as adaptations through incremental changes among relations of the finer modules.

Like Quartz and Bechtel, Jennifer Mundale questions narrow evolutionary psychology's model of cognitive architecture. She stresses that evolutionary psychology ought to avoid undue reliance on functionalist accounts of psychological mechanisms. Information processing models of the mind which assume multiple realizability of cognitive structures in different possible materials prevent the proper integration of evolutionary psychology with other, lower level sciences (particularly neuroscience). Since integration with other sciences, particularly biology, is a goal of narrow evolutionary psychology, Mundale advocates rejecting this aspect of that approach in favor of an approach which stresses the concrete results of biology, neuroscience, and similar disciplines. Information processing accounts can be retained by invoking them at different levels, retaining the very general multiply realizable level while adding lower levels with more detail, such as claims about specific brain systems or neural pathways. The more specific information processing accounts could be derived from adaptive claims corresponding to very specific domains, even more specialized than those currently hypothesized in narrow evolutionary psychology, such as particular steps in a psychological task for a particular species. Neurobiology can be integrated with evolutionary psychology at this level, avoiding some of the problems associated with overreliance on functionalist information processing accounts.

Domenico Parisi advocates two closely-linked methods for evolutionary psychology. First, he argues that connectionism offers a better model for mental behavior than cognitivism. Connectionism's use of neural networks and similar devices more closely match the physical structure of the brain, and the emphasis on physical structure makes evolutionary psychology more easily integrated with the physical sciences it purports to apply to human psychology. Second, Parisi wants to expand the sources of particular hypotheses and methods used to confirm them by adding computer simulations of selective environments and adaptations. These two methods are united in "Artificial Life" computer simulations, which allow particular modeled sets of neural networks to respond to extended artificial environments over many generations, thus providing a proving ground for various hypotheses within evolutionary psychology. In his chapter, Parisi discusses a number of such simulations as examples, including models which incorporate both learning and innate knowledge. This approach allows tests of claims about the way in which cognitive abilities have evolved.

The twelve chapters in this book provide a heterogenous set of approaches to doing evolutionary psychology. Since evolutionary psychology is still a young field, highlighting these variations can only enhance it by allowing all methods to be explored and compared.

Michigan State University
Eastern Illinois University

1. REFERENCES

Buss, D.M. (1989). Sex differences in human mate preferences: Evolutionary hypotheses tested in 37 cultures. *Behavioral and Brain Sciences, 12*, 1-49.

Buss, D. M. (1995). Evolutionary psychology: A new paradigm for psychological science. *Psychological Inquiry, 6*, 1-30.

Buss, D.M. (1999). *Evolutionary Psychology: The New Science of the Mind.* Needham Heights, MA: Allyn & Bacon.

Buss, D.M. et al. (1990). International preferences in selecting mates: A study of 37 cultures. *Journal of Cross-cultural Psychology, 21*, 5-47.

Caporael, L. R. (2001). Evolutionary psychology: Toward a unifying theory and a hybrid science. *Annual Review of Psychology, 52*, 607-628.

Cosmides, L. (1989). The logic of social exchange: Has natural selection shaped how humans reason? Studies with the Wason selection task. *Cognition, 31*, 187-276.

Cosmides, L. & Tooby, J. (1997). Evolutionary psychology: A primer. [online] Available at http://www.psych.ucsb.edu/research/cep/primer.html

Crawford, C. B. & Anderson, J. L. (1989). Sociobiology: An environmentalist discipline? *American Psychologist. 44*, 1449-1459

Dennett, D.C. (1995). *Darwin's Dangerous Idea: Evolution and the Meanings of Life.* NY: Simon & Schuster.

Heyes, C. (2000). Evolutionary psychology in the round. In C. Heyes & L. Huber (Eds.). *The Evolution of Cognition.* Cambridge, MA: MIT Press.

Heyes, C. & Huber, L. (Eds.). (2000). *The Evolution of Cognition.* Cambridge, MA: MIT Press.

Kenrick, D.T. & Keefe, R.C. (1992). Age preferences in mates reflect sex differences in reproductive strategies. *Behavioral and Brain Sciences, 15*, 75-133.

Kenrick, D. T. (1989). Bridging social psychology and sociobiology: The case of sexual attraction. In R.W. Bell, & N.J. Bell (Eds). *Sociobiology and the social sciences.* (pp. 5-23). Texas Tech University Press.

Kitcher, P. (1985). *Vaulting Ambition*, Cambridge, MA: MIT Press.

Kitcher, P. (1993). The evolution of human altruism. *Journal of Philosophy, 90*, 497-516.

Kitcher, P. (1994). Four ways of biologicizing ethics. In E. Sober, (Ed)., *Conceptual Issues in Evolutionary Biology*, (pp. 439 – 450). Cambdridge, MA: MIT Press.

Pinker, S. (1997). *How the Mind Works.* NY: WW Norton & Co.

Rauscher, F. (1997). How a Kantian can accept evolutionary metaethics. *Biology and Philosophy, 12*, 303-326.

Scher, S.J. (1999, August). Evolutionary psychology: Dinosaurs and mammals (Introduction). In S.J. Scher (Chair), *Evolutionary Psychology: Alternative Approaches.* Symposium conducted at the meeting of the American Psychological Association, Boston, MA.

Scher, S.J. (2001, May). What is evolutionary psychology? Paper presented at Aalborg University, Aalborg, Denmark.

Symons, D. (1979). *The Evolution of Human Sexuality.* NY: Oxford University Press.

Symons, D. (1987). If we're all Darwinians, what's the fuss about? In C.B. Crawford, M.F. Smith, & D. Krebs (Eds.). *Sociobiology and psychology: Ideas, Issues, and Applications.* (pp. 121-146). Hillsdale, N.J.: Lawrence Erlbaum and Associates.

Tooby, J. & Cosmides, L. (1990). On the universality of human nature and the uniqueness of the individual: The role of genetics and adaptation. *Journal of Personality, 58*, 17-68.

Tooby, J. & Cosmides, L. (1992). The psychological foundations of culture. In J.H. Barkow, L. Cosmides, & J. Tooby (Eds.). *The Adapted Mind: Evolutionary Psychology and the Generation of Culture.* (pp. 19-136). Oxford, Eng.: Oxford University Press.

STEVEN J. SCHER AND FREDERICK RAUSCHER

NATURE READ IN TRUTH OR FLAW

Locating Alternatives in Evolutionary Psychology

Evolutionary psychology is a powerful new methodology in psychology. Its practitioners claim success in reading human nature where previous methods in psychology have failed. But whether nature is read in truth or with flaws depends in part on a serious study of the exact methods used in evolutionary psychology.

Currently, one particular approach to evolutionary psychology is associated with the field. This has led many — proponents and critics alike — to debate the soundness of evolutionary psychology in reference only to this well-publicized approach. In this paper, we will trace the recent history of attempts to apply Darwin's theory of evolution by natural selection to psychology, and then we will discuss in detail the assumptions of the particular

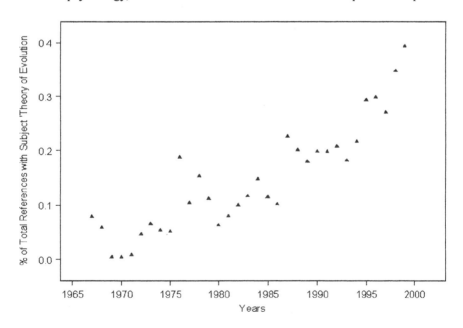

Figure 1. Percent of References to 'Theory of Evolution' in the PsycInfo Database (1967-1999)

Steven J. Scher & Frederick Rauscher (eds.). Evolutionary Psychology: Alternative Approaches, 1-29

approach which now dominates the field of evolutionary psychology (narrow evolutionary psychology[1]).

Some scholars assume that this method is the only possible way to practice evolutionary psychology. However, many other approaches are being developed and used successfully by researchers in psychology, philosophy, neuroscience, anthropology, biology, linguistics, and other fields. We will argue below that there is a legitimate place for a variety of alternative approaches to the application of evolutionary science to the study of mind and behavior, and we will show where the assumptions of some of these alternatives fit within a conceptual structure for evolutionary psychology, broadly construed.

1.   THE ROOTS OF EVOLUTIONARY PSYCHOLOGY[2]

Evolutionary psychology emerged during the 1980s and grew exponentially during the 1990s, seeping out of academia and into the popular understanding of social science. The scholarly literature grew rapidly throughout that time period. Figure 1 shows the percent of all abstracts in the PsycInfo database that were classified under the subject heading `Theory of Evolution' from 1967 to 1999. The steep increase in such citations throughout the 1990's is evidence of the influence of the evolutionary psychologists on contemporary psychology. This influence was an outgrowth of a series of historical developments that can be traced at least to the beginning of the twentieth century.

1.1.   The Modern Synthesis.

At the turn of the twentieth century, geneticists studying the mechanisms of heredity, and naturalists studying organisms existing in the wild, had very little in common. They used different research methods, with naturalists concentrating on the measurement of variability among organisms in the wild, and geneticists on experimental studies of heredity in the lab; growing personal animosity further deepened the separation (Bowler, 1989).

The experimental biologists used genetics to refute the evolutionary significance of Lamarckianism and other mechanisms. They studied mutations and discontinuous variation among organisms because these were most amenable to their methodology. A

---

1 EDITOR'S NOTE: In this book, the term 'narrow evolutionary psychology' signifies the approach to evolutionary psychology developed by Cosmides, Tooby, Buss, et al. This term was chosen not to imply that this approach has an inappropriately narrow point of view, but merely to suggest that the approach adopts a narrower range of assumptions than 'broad evolutionary psychology' (or, just 'evolutionary psychology'). This latter term signifies evolutionary psychology generally, practiced with any of a very broad range of assumptions possible within the general framework of evolutionary approaches to psychology. For more detail on this terminology, see the editor's introduction, p 1

2 Theories of the growth and evolution of mind and behavior have a long history. At least since the earliest explications of Darwin's theory of natural selection, evolutionists have been applying the theory to human thought and emotion (e.g., Darwin, 1871, 1872). Here, we briefly review the history of these ideas in the twentieth century as they have influenced the development of the dominant school of evolutionary psychology. For general treatments of the history of evolutionary thought, see Bowler, 1989; Ruse, 1996. For histories of the application of Darwinism in psychology and the other social sciences, see Degler, 1991; Richards, 1987. Our historical sketch is largely based on these sources.

focus on single-gene action, compatible with a Mendelian analysis of heredity, fit with a rejection of natural selection (which depended on the presence of continuous variation).

The field naturalists, on the other hand, saw continuous variability in their observations of populations of organisms in the wild. Their interest in evolution led eventually to a greater acceptance of natural selection as a mechanism for the production of adaptation and to theoretical ideas emphasizing geographical isolation as the cause of speciation.

As early as 1902, G.U. Yule had argued that if traits were affected by more than one gene, they could appear to have continuous variation, but still operate according to the laws of Mendelian genetics. Although it took some time for this position to break through the personal and professional barriers dividing the naturalists and the geneticists, the mathematical treatments by Ronald A. Fisher, J.B.S. Haldane, and Sewell Wright were eventually adopted by the naturalists (although few could understand the actual mathematics: Bowler, 1989; Richards, 1987). The geneticists, likewise, could now accept natural selection as a viable principle in the shaping of the gene pool. Theodosius Dobzhansky's publication, in 1937, of *Genetics and the Origin of Species* "trigger[ed] an explosion of activity that initiated the modern synthesis during the 1940s" (Bowler, 1989, p. 314).

Part of this process involved a push to professionalize the study of evolution (Ruse, 1996). In the early decades of the century, the study of evolution was relegated to a second-class status within biology. Positions in universities, research funding, and journal publication space were limited for researchers working on questions of evolution. The modern synthesis can be read as an attempt to gain respectability for the study of evolution by making it less speculative, and by making it amenable to theoretical models which more closely emulated the abstract models of sciences that were considered more objective. This was accomplished by a move to restrict evolutionary mechanisms to elaborations of those Mendelian effects that could be demonstrated experimentally. It was also accomplished through the establishment of journals and professional societies, along with the promotion of evolutionists for positions in larger scientific bodies and the promotion of evolutionary research in funding competitions.

1.2. Behaviorism and the Cognitive Revolution.

Curiously, American academic psychology was almost simultaneously going through a similar professionalization process. In 1913, John B. Watson published "Psychology as the Behaviorist Views It" in an attempt to move psychology beyond what he saw as its speculative, introspective, and metaphysical roots. Like the modern synthesis, it took some time for these ideas to be widely adopted, but by mid-century, behaviorism had cast a wide net over American psychology. Behaviorists sought to raise the scientific status of psychology by modeling it after their view of physical science; they imported ideas from logical positivism, and argued for the study of observable behaviors, for an objectification of the subject of study, and for the reduction of behavior to "chained sequences of atomic bits of behavior" (Richards, 1987, p. 539).

The prominence of B.F. Skinner's radical behaviorism in the mid-Twentieth century, which rejected any notion of intervening variables or mentalistic concepts, was of limited duration (and, moreover, was a uniquely American phenomenon). The behaviorism of Clark Hull (e.g., 1943), and especially of Edward Tolman (e.g., 1932), had significant cognitive components. By the late 1950s, the so-called 'Cognitive Revolution' was beginning. Chomsky's (1959, 1966) review of Skinner's work (1957) on verbal behavior serves as a marker for the transition from behaviorism to cognitivism. Chomsky's criticisms were taken up eagerly by many psychologists, even though Chomsky's specific ideas (e.g., regarding the existence of a nativist language module) did not exert an impact on most of cognitive psychology until several decades had passed.

As the cognitive revolution began, psychologists began to move away from models of stimulus and response, and toward models of information-processing. These models continued psychology's quest for reflected respectability by incorporating ideas from engineering – most notably Information Theory (Shannon and Weaver, 1949) – and by holding up the computer as the physical realization of the concepts of information structures and operations that were at the center of their theories. By the late sixties, cognitivism was well established. For example, Ulric Neisser, in his well known book on cognitive psychology, published in 1967, felt no need to defend his approach against the behaviorist position (Leahey, 1997, p. 433).

Cognitivism was, in fact, only a minor break from behaviorism, especially considering the behaviorism of theorists such as Hull, Spence, and Tolman (Leahey, 1997; Mills, 1998). Cognitive psychology retained behaviorism's focus on associationism (with the emphasis shifted from associations between simuli and responses to association among cognitive representations), on operationalism, and on materialism. Perhaps most importantly for the current discussion, cognitivists initially retained three further behavioristic ideas (a) that complex behavior could be conceptualized as the piecing together of strings of simple behaviors (i.e., atomism), (b) that there is a continuity of mental processes between humans and other animals, and (c) that the processes of learning and thinking were produced by a general mechanism, independent of the content of the information or behavior to be learnt/thought about.

This last idea, however, was already being somewhat undermined as the cognitive revolution got underway. Garcia's research (e.g., Garcia, Ervin and Koelling, 1966; Garcia and Koelling, 1966) showing that the laws of Pavlovian conditioning did not apply to certain types of learning (specifically, to the association of sensory stimulation to nausea and other internal states) started a process of reevaluation of the *tabula rasa* view that had held center stage because of behaviorism (and, especially in anthropology and sociology, because of the influence of Franz Boas; cf., Degler, 1991; Richards, 1987). (As mentioned above, Chomsky also rejected the *tabula rasa* view, but his ideas were not widely adopted by psychologists in the early days of the cognitive revolution).

By the 1980s, the ecological approach to cognition, which situated cognition in more realistic settings, was well underway (if not universally accepted). This research formed part of the argument for a modular view of cognition, which described mental processes as operating by different mechanisms in different domains (e.g., Hirschfield & Gelman, 1994).

This modularization of the mind was also spurred on by another legacy of behaviorism. The view of behaving organisms as machines paved the way for the development of the computer metaphor for cognition, and the parallel development of artificial intelligence. Attempts to program computers to think and behave like living organisms required the programming of subroutines; furthermore, the difficulty involved in actually creating a machine that even approximated a living organism led directly to the notion that the subroutines of the mind must contain 'preprogrammed' content.

At this point, Chomsky's ideas began to have more of an influence on psychologists. Chomsky's nativist concept of language acquisition is now often cited as the prototypical example of a domain-specific module: an in-born mechanism which contains the content (in this case rules of universal grammar) needed to abstract the required environmental input into a working psychological function (in this case, language).

1.3. Adaptationism, Inclusive Fitness, and Selfish Genes.

Most of the major figures in the development of the modern synthesis in biology gave a central role to natural selection operating on individual organisms to select for adaptive features; however, most also espoused a pluralistic perspective on the mechanisms of evolution (especially macroevolution – the creation of new species; this is contrasted with microevolution – the production of changes within a species).

In the early days of the synthesis, emphasis was placed on arguing that "evolution at all scales, particularly macroevolution, could be explained by the genetic mechanisms observed in laboratories and local populations" (Gould, 1983, p. 71). These mechanisms certainly included natural selection, but they could also include genetic drift and group-level selection (cf., Gould, 1983; Provine, 1983; Richards, 1987; Ruse, 1996).

Gould (1983) has argued, however, that the synthesis hardened in the late 1940s, with all the major synthetic theorists coming to insist that "cumulative natural selection leading to adaptation be granted pride of place as *the* mechanism of evolutionary change" (p. 75). This hardened synthesis reached its apotheosis in the 1960s. Hamilton's (1964) exposition of the concept of *inclusive fitness* or *kin selection* (the idea that one gains fitness by increasing a genetic relative's chances of reproducing) formalized previous ideas about kin altruism as a form of natural selection. Two years later, Williams (1966) published his *tour de force, Adaptation and Natural Selection*. This book criticized the idea that group selection could play a significant role in evolution, and for many scientists it was viewed as a strong defense of what Gould and Lewontin (1979; see also Mayr, 1983) call the "adaptationist programme". It set firmly in cement the notion that "life, in both physical form and behavior, is adaptive. It is produced by natural selection and is generally as good ('optimized') as possible. This is as much the tool of ... research as the hypothesis under examination" (Ruse, 1999, pp. 179-180).

Hamilton's (1964) development of inclusive fitness as an important tool in explaining behavior forced a subtle shift in thinking about natural selection. It was the final step in reducing evolution to a "minimalist genetics" (Richards, 1987, p. 541) – both microevolution and macroevolution occurred through a form of genic selection. No longer was the emphasis on the survival and reproduction of individuals; what mattered now was that copies of one's geneotype survived. Geneotypes could be thought of as selfish because even when they promoted apparently altruistic acts for the individual who possessed the gene, they did so to enhance the possibility that they (the genes) would be represented in the next generation. Thus, the "selfish gene" (Dawkins, 1989) became a central element in the study of evolution.

1.4. Sociobiology.

This shift in thinking from *individual* selection to *genic* selection was only one consequence of the success of Hamilton's and Williams' ideas. A second shift was that evolutionists began to think "as readily about the importance of what animals do as about what they are" (Ruse, 1996, p. 459).

This increasing emphasis on behavior was to take debates on evolutionary theory out of the obscurity of technical journals and professional meetings, and into the limelight. E.O. Wilson's 1975 book *Sociobiology* made bold claims about the usefulness of evolutionary thinking to solve "centuries old questions, which hitherto had wonderfully perplexed intellects in the humanities," but "could now be given a simple solution, one that had the authority of modern biology and mathematical genetics" (Richards, 1987, p. 542).

As Wilson (1978) put it, "sociobiology ... is a ... hybrid discipline that incorporates knowledge from ethology (the naturalistic study of whole patterns of behavior), ecology (the study of the relationships of organisms to their environment), and genetics in order to derive general principles concerning the biological properties of entire societies" (p. 16). Sociobiology was an attempt to apply the adaptationist program to the study of behavior — particularly social behavior. In fact, the quote from Ruse (1999) four paragraphs above, used there to describe aspects of adaptationism generally, was written as a description of Wilson, specifically.

As sociobiology developed, its application to the study of non-human animals came to be called "behavioral ecology" (e.g., Krebs & Davies, 1997). Here, several methods, drawn from sociobiology's parent disciplines (ethology, ecology, genetics) were used to develop and test hypotheses about the adaptive basis of behavior. Behavioral ecologists use comparisons of the behavior of different species and studies of variation in behavior and its relationship to variations in fitness within a species to learn about potential behavioral adaptations.

Wilson (1975, 1978) proposed the same methods for the study of humans. These principles, he contended, could be used to discern the genetically determined bases of human behavior. Sociobiologists rejected the behaviorist idea that there is a "simplicity and equipotentiality in learning" (Wilson, 1978, p. 65), and the similar idea that humans have a universal cultural flexibility. Rather, sociobiologists held that individuals were endowed with different psychological traits genetically. "The question of interest is no longer whether human social behavior is genetically determined; it is to what extent" (Wilson, 1978, p. 19).

Sociobiology faced strong opposition both inside and outside academia. Many regarded some of the initial hypotheses of sociobiology as politically motivated and rejected the application of evolutionary thinking to human nature (Caplan, 1978). Others criticized the particular methods used by human sociobiology while allowing that evolution could yet be applied to human psychology using some other method (Kitcher, 1985).

1.5. Sociobiology becomes Evolutionary Psychology.

As sociobiology developed in the 1980's and responded to its critics, it focused on exploring the evolutionary roots of overt behavior and social organization. As early as the late seventies, however, certain changes were creeping into the literature on the application of evolutionary ideas to human behavior. In his 1978 book expanding his arguments for human sociobiology, Wilson described the human mind as "an autonomous decision-making instrument, an alert scanner of the environment that approaches certain kinds of choices and not others in the first place, then innately leans toward one option as opposed to others and urges the body into action according to a flexible schedule" (p. 67). This cognitive description reflected changes that had already occurred in psychology (i.e., the cognitive revolution) and foreshadowed the more explicitly cognitive approach that we call narrow evolutionary psychology.

Donald Symons' book on human sexuality, published in 1979, is widely cited as the first work of narrow evolutionary psychology. It introduces nearly all of the emphases that would be developed by later theorists and researchers. Symons defends a cognitive approach to the evolution of the mind; he stresses the role of natural selection acting on genes as a unit of selection and leading to the evolution of species-typical adaptations, which are "designed to solve the specific problems that have been important in the evolutionary history of a species" (Symons, 1979, p. 5). As we will discuss in detail in the next section, these assumptions (i.e., cognitivism, adaptationism, modularity, genetic selection, and species-typicality) form the basis of narrow evolutionary psychology.

This approach to the application of evolutionary ideas and methods to human psychology[3] grew over the next decade. By the end of the eighties, important empirical publications like Daly & Wilson's work on homicide (1988) and child abuse (1981, 1985), Cosmides' work on logical reasoning (1989), and Buss' work on mate selection preferences (1989) had begun to attract attention.

The use of the term "evolutionary psychology" to refer to this approach seems to have first appeared in print in 1987 (Cosmides & Tooby; Daly & Wilson). It was apparently used, however, in a 1985 talk given by Irven DeVore and John Tooby. DeVore (1988) and Tooby (1988) produced written versions of each part of the talk separately; DeVore refers in his talk to "human sociobiology," while Tooby's chapter is entitled "The Emergence of Evolutionary Psychology."

This approach to evolutionary psychology represents the merger of a particular metatheoretical approach to evolution, and a particular metatheoretical approach to psychology. It is "the modern descendent of sociobiology" (Sterelny and Griffiths, 1999, p. 315), modified to adapt to the cognitive revolution in psychology and to the problems

---

3 This brand of evolutionary psychology, along with the other alternatives discussed in this book, focuses primarily (although not exclusively) on human psychology. However, evolutionary psychology most broadly construed can also include a focus on the behavior and cognition of non-human animals. See the papers in Heyes and Huber, 2000, for further discussion.

caused by the fact that the current range of environments in which humans live probably bear little resemblance to the environments in which we evolved.

From psychology, advocates of this approach adopt the metatheoretical assumptions of the cognitive revolution. From evolution, they adopt most of the metatheoretical assumptions of sociobiology. Specifically, "evolutionary psychology can be thought of as the application of adaptationist logic to the study of the architecture of the human mind" (Cosmides and Tooby, 1997, p. 13). Sociobiologists put an emphasis on "ultimate causation — the adaptive significance of observed traits ... on the other hand sociobiologists paid relatively little attention to proximate causation" (Wilson, 1984, p. 1).

Narrow evolutionary psychology places an emphasis on using adaptationist reasoning to elucidate the proximate mechanisms which produce behavior, and the way in which those mechanisms function in the current environment (cf., Crawford, 1998; Cosmides & Tooby, 1987). These proximate mechanisms are assumed to be cognitive or information-processing modules, which provide the missing link between evolution and behavior (Cosmides & Tooby, 1987).

One important implication of this change in emphasis is a rejection of a methodology used by some sociobiologists: looking at differences in people's behavior, and correlating those differences with differences in fitness (measured by the number of descendents, or some proxy for number of descendents; see Alexander, 1979; Betzig, Mulder, & Turke, 1988; Changon & Irons, 1979; Turke, 1990; for examples and discussion). Narrow-school evolutionary psychologists argue that this research strategy — sometimes called "Darwinian Anthropology" (Symons, 1989), "Darwinian Social Science" (Barkow, 1990; Symons, 1992), or "the adaptiveness program" (Symons, 1990) — grows out of "a view of humans as 'fitness maximizers' or 'fitness strivers' or that humans act 'as if' they were inclusive-fitness maximizers" (Buss, 1995, p. 9).

Buss and other proponents of narrow evolutionary psychology reject this methodology, firstly, because they seek to identify adaptations which are species-typical (i.e., nearly universal within the species; see below), and secondly, because "selection operates over thousands of generations, ... our brains are adapted to that long-vanished way of life, not to brand-new agricultural and industrial civilizations" (Pinker, 1997, p. 42). Thus, "our modern skulls house a stone age mind" (Cosmides & Tooby, 1997, p. 11). As a result, a psychological mechanism that may have worked effectively in the past (i.e., in the environment of our evolutionary adaptedness [EEA]) will not necessarily work effectively now.

This exception notwithstanding, practitioners of narrow evolutionary psychology otherwise adopt many of the metatheoretical assumptions of sociobiology, and adapt them to metatheoretical assumptions of cognitive psychology. Ketelaar & Ellis (2000, p. 1) provide a succinct description of what they call the central assumption of narrow evolutionary psychology: "the human brain is comprised of a large number of specialized mechanisms that were shaped by natural selection over vast periods of time to solve the recurrent information-processing problems faced by our ancestors ... The field of evolutionary psychology focuses on explicating the nature of the specific information-processing problems encountered during human evolutionary history, and on developing and testing models of the psychological adaptations (mechanisms and behavioral strategies) that may have evolved as solutions to these problems".

This approach reached a landmark with the 1992 publication of *The Adapted Mind* (Barkow, Cosmides, & Tooby); the chapters in that book were designed "to introduce the newly crystallizing field of evolutionary psychology to a wider scientific audience" and "to clarify how this new field ... supplies the necessary connection between evolutionary biology and the complex, irreducible social cultural phenomena studied by anthropologists, sociologists, economists, and historians" (Cosmides, Tooby, & Barkow, 1992, p. 3). *The Adapted Mind* became a manifesto for evolutionary psychology, and is still frequently cited as a central text in the field.

The maturity of evolutionary psychology is now demonstrated, 15 years after the term was first introduced, by the appearance of a handbook of evolutionary psychology (Crawford and Krebs, 1998) and the appearance of several textbooks for courses in evolutionary psychology (Badcock, 2000; Barrett, Dunbar, & Lycett, 2002; Buss, 1999; Palmer & Palmer, 2002) or textbooks written with an evolutionary approach for use in introductory psychology courses (Gaulin & McBurney, 2001).

2. THE NATURE OF NARROW EVOLUTIONARY PSYCHOLOGY

> When I first encountered the term 'evolutionary psychology, I thought it referred to the study of how mind and behavior have evolved. But I was mistaken. In the last decade, evolutionary psychology has come to refer exclusively to research on human mentality and behavior, motivated by a very specific nativist-adaptationist interpretation of how evolution operates (Heyes, 2000, p.3).

We identify five major metatheoretical assumptions or commitments that are generally accepted by the narrow evolutionary psychology school, which we will discuss in detail below. This discussion is intended to lay out the assumptions specific to narrow evolutionary psychology; other possible evolutionary psychologies may or may not share any of these assumptions. We will refrain from assessing these assumptions, leaving that work to other contributors to this volume as well as other evolutionary psychologists.

The five major assumptions characteristic of narrow evolutionary psychology are:

a. *cognitivism*: A commitment to a functionalist information-processing model of psychology; that is, to a description of psychological mechanisms in the form of decision rules or computational models without regard to their physical manifestation.

b. *adaptationism*: The empirical assumption that complex features of modern organisms are adaptations to selective pressures in the past (i.e., the EEA), the explanatory assumption that apparent design and the relation of organisms to the environment are the important questions and natural selection the only answer, and the methodological commitment to the use of design analysis to search for these adaptations.

c. *modularity*: A commitment to a cognitive architecture which views the mind as consisting of many domain-specific and informationally-encapsulated information processing modules.

d. *inclusive fitness*: A commitment to the gene as the unit of selection (i.e., inclusive fitness models of selection).

e. *species-typicality*: A commitment to the universality of psychological adaptations; a commitment to the search for a universal human nature.

2.1. Cognitivism: From Behaviors to Psychological Mechanisms.

> Natural selection implies (at least to some scientists and philosophers) that were mind functionless it would long ago have withered away, not become more elaborate, as it obviously has (Symons, 1979, p. 39).

Symons provides one part of the justification for focusing evolutionary psychology on a cognitive or information-processing level. This move from a prediction of the evolution of adaptive *behaviors*, to the evolution of adaptive *cognition* forms a central component of modern narrow evolutionary psychology.

Cognitivism's focus on internal mental states stresses a functionalist understanding of mental processes. A functionalist philosophy of mind focuses on causal relations among environmental inputs, mental states, and behavioral outputs. A particular mental state is identified solely by its place in an information-processing chain; the mental state receives input from the environment or other states which precede it in the chain and sends output to states later in the chain, and ultimately to behavior. For example, fear of heights is part of an information processing chain which starts with sensory input such as the sight of a cliff, includes calculations involving other mental states such as the desire to avoid death or injury and the belief that falling from a cliff can cause them, and results in behavioral output, such as avoiding the edge. For the functionalist, this information-processing description is the proper level for understanding psychology. It is meant to describe the mind independently of any particular manifestation of these processes in a physical system, such as computer hardware, the brain, or silicon-based alien life-forms.

Cosmides and Tooby (1997) quite explicitly adopt the computer metaphor of cognition that provides a central conceptual principle of information-processing psychology. They write that "the brain is a physical system. It functions as a computer. Its circuits are designed to generate behavior that is appropriate to your environmental circumstances" (p. 4). Likewise, Pinker (1997) writes that "without the computational theory, it is impossible to make sense of the evolution of the mind … The typical imperative from biology is not 'Thou shalt …,' but 'If … then … else' " (Pinker, 1997, p. 27).

Tooby and Cosmides (1992) argue that the cognitive (information processing) level is the appropriate level for the description of adaptations, preferable to both the behavioral and the neurobiological levels. First, this level is better than a focus on behavior because, "the evolutionary function of the brain is the adaptive regulation of behavior and physiology on the basis of information derived from the body and from the environment," and because, "adaptations are usually species-typical. Consequently, to capture evolved functional organization, one needs a language that can describe what is invariant across individuals and generations ... behavior is not a phenomenon *sui generis*. It is the product of mechanisms that process information" (p. 64). Second, the information processing level is sufficient to capture what is important about the functioning of the mind, so neurobiological study of the particular implementation of these processes is unnecessary

2.2. Adaptationism: Designing the Mind.

> The output of an evolved psychological mechanism is directed toward the solution of a specific adaptive problem (Buss, 1999, p. 49).

Buss identifies the connection that links narrow evolutionary psychology to adaptationism. Evolutionary psychologists following this research program seek to identify adaptations: "goal directed (i.e., functionally designed), phenotypic features" of the mind (Thornhill, 1998, p. 546). When narrow-school evolutionary psychologists use the term "functional" in this sense they mean that the feature serves a particular purpose, specifically the one which provided a reproductive benefit as a consequence of which the feature was selected. (This should not be confused with the philosophical account of functionalism described above). Adaptations are identified predominantly by positing a hypothetical problem that existed in the environment in which the species under study (usually humans) is assumed to have evolved (i.e., in the EEA).

    All three types of adaptationism identified by Godfrey-Smith (2001) — empirical, explanatory, and methodological — form part of the metatheoretical assumptions of narrow evolutionary psychology. *Empirical adaptationism* asserts that "to a large degree, it is possible to predict and explain the outcome of evolutionary processes by attending only to the role played by selection. No other evolutionary factor has this degree of causal importance" (Godfrey-Smith, 2001, p. 336). As Tooby and Cosmides (1992) express their empirical adaptationism, "important and consequential aspects of organismic architectures are shaped by selection. By the same token, those modifications that are so minor that their consequences are negligible on reproduction are invisible to selection and, therefore are not organized by it" (p. 52).

    Explanatory adaptationism suggests that the important questions to be answered revolve around the design of organisms, and the relationships between organisms and their environments. Furthermore, according to this view, natural selection is the key to answering these questions. It is this type of adaptationism which Mayr (1997) refers to when he writes that "For each characteristic, the questions that must be asked are: Was the evolutionary emergence of this characteristic favored by natural selection, and what was its survival value that has led to its being favored by natural selection? This is the so-called adaptational program" (p. 191). Godfrey-Smith describes a strong form of explanatory adaptationism as holding "that selection is the *only possible* naturalistic and non-theological solution to the problem of design" (p. 337); Buss (1995), at least, adopts this point of view when he writes that "evolution by natural selection is the only known causal process capable of producing complex physiological and psychological mechanisms" (p. 2).

Methodological adaptationism, according to Godfrey-Smith, is the view that "the best way for scientists to approach biological systems is to look for features of adaptation and good design. Adaptation is a good 'organizing concept' for evolutionary research" (p. 337). Cosmides and Tooby (1997) make the latter point by writing that "knowledge of adaptive function is necessary for carving nature at the joints" (p. 14); Buss (1995) makes the same point when he writes that "a central premise of evolutionary psychology is that the main nonarbitrary way to identify, describe, and understand psychological mechanisms is to articulate their functions — the specific adaptive problems they were designed to solve" (p. 6).

Methodological adaptationism suggests more than just the idea that adaptation is an organizing principle. It also suggests specific methodologies to use in studying organisms. Cosmides & Tooby (1997) write: "engineers figure out what problems they want to solve, and then design machines that are capable of solving these problems in an efficient manner. Evolutionary biologists figure out what adaptive problems a given species encountered during its evolutionary history, and then ask themselves, 'What would a machine capable of solving these problems well under ancestral conditions look like?'" (p. 15).

The narrow evolutionary psychology version of this research strategy (so-called forward-looking adaptationism; cf., Murphy, this volume) starts with hypotheses about the EEA, and about the adaptive problems our ancestors would have faced in that environment. The next step in the narrow evolutionary psychology research strategy is to hypothesize design features that would effectively and efficiently solve the adaptive problem. Empirical evidence that these design features exist in modern organisms (again, usually humans) is taken as support for the presence of the particular adaptation under study, and, indirectly, for the hypothesis about the EEA which led to the design features being hypothesized in the first place.

The EEA is a related concept of narrow evolutionary psychology worthy of some attention. Adaptationists studying non-human species generally view the adaptive problems that the organisms faced previously as being the same ones they face currently. Their assumption is that non-human plants and animals are adapted to the environment in which they live, that is, that the EEA for these species has not changed in evolutionarily relevant ways (at least for those living in their natural environment). As already mentioned (1.5), however, the narrow evolutionary psychology of humans operates on the assumption that the environment to which humans are adapted (usually identified as the African savannah, during the Pleistocene) was quite different from current human environments. Some of the adaptations specific to the EEA are even treated as maladaptive to current human environments.

Narrow-school evolutionary psychologists defend their reliance on adaptationism both by citing its use in evolutionary biology and by direct reference to psychological traits. The biological argument stresses the dominance of adaptationist thinking in evolutionary theory. The success of explanatory adaptationism in biology gives adaptationist reasoning a privileged status. "This system of description has some warrant on being considered a privileged frame of reference because the complex functional organization that exists in the design of organisms was injected into them through the construction of adaptations by natural selection. Adaptations are the accumulated output of selection, and selection is the single significant anti-entropic or ordering force orchestrating functional organic design (Dawkins, 1986). So if one is interested in uncovering intelligible organization in our species-typical psychological architecture, discovering and describing its adaptations is the place to begin" (Tooby & Cosmides, 1992, p. 55). Complex functional organization, it is thought, can result only from selection pressures and not from other factors; it is "the single significant" ordering force operating on the human mind. The success evolutionary biology has had by using adaptationist thinking as the explanation for the functional design of organisms' traits, as opposed to other possible explanations such as spandrels, is cited, for example, by Dennett (1995, pp. 229ff).

Regarding psychological traits, adaptationism is defended as merely an extension of its proven success in the extra-mental traits of organisms such as the vertebrate eye (Pinker 1997, pp. 36-37). Since the mind is a part of an organism whose other important traits are explained by adaptationist thinking, the mind itself must be subject to such explanation as well. The mind's architecture and functions are no more likely to be by-products of other traits or to be created by genetic drift than are eyes and other traits clearly identified as adaptations.

Adaptationism is further defended by contrasting it with the more general approach used by some sociobiologists of explaining the existence of a behavior in reference to its fitness-maximizing potential. The error of the sociobiologists is said to be their avoidance of the intermediate step of psychological mechanisms which themselves maximized fitness in the EEA by solving particular adaptive problems and can — but need not — cause specific behavior today. The missing focus on specific functions of these mechanisms, based on the assumption that functions of traits reflect particular answers to particular problems, allows the researcher to narrow in on the cognitive architecture required for that function and thus provides a more useful psychology (Tooby & Cosmides, 1992, pp. 54-55.). Thus, adaptationism goes hand in hand with modularity because functions correspond to parts of the mind.

2.3. Modularity: The Atomization of the Mind.

> The mind, I claim, is not a single organ but a system of organs, which we can think of as psychological faculties or mental modules. The entities now commonly evoked to explain the mind — such as general intelligence, a capacity to form culture, and multipurpose learning strategies — will surely go the way of protoplasm in biology and of earth, air, fire, and water in physics (Pinker, 1997, p. 27).

In narrow evolutionary psychology, cognitive (information-processing) adaptations are conceptualized as mental modules, and the mind is said to be made up of many modules. Modularity is central to narrow evolutionary psychology. Cosmides and Tooby (1997) write "on this view, all normal human minds reliably develop a standard collection of reasoning and regulatory circuits that are functionally specialized and, frequently, domain-specific. " (p. 3). Buss (1997) writes that "at the core of evolutionary psychology is a firm position on the modularity or domain specificity of evolved psychological mechanisms" (p. 397). The flexibility of the mind stems not from a flexible, domain-general, mechanism, but from many specific modules. Although the exact number is unknown, evolutionary psychologists of this school generally assume that most, if not all, mental function is carried out by separate modules.

The narrow evolutionary psychology idea of modularity draws from the work of philosopher Jerry Fodor (1983), whose book *Modularity of Mind* provided a basis for this research program. Fodor characterized modules in terms of nine properties (cf., Bechtel, this volume); however, two of the properties are most central to the concept of modules as used within narrow evolutionary psychology: modules are said to be *domain-specific* and *informationally encapsulated* (see also Murphy, this volume).

In general, a domain is a subset of the environment in which an organism operates. A domain is the problem for which a module is the solution; modules in the mind are said to correspond to domains outside the mind. A domain can be identified in terms of a particular adaptive problem that had to be solved in the EEA. Narrow evolutionary psychology assumes that these problems are circumscribed narrowly rather than broadly: "Because adaptive problems are specific, their solutions tend to be specific as well" (Buss, 1999, p. 52). This assumes that there is a one-to-one correspondence between domains and modules. Narrow domains lead to narrow modules. For example, instead of hypothesizing a broad domain of interpersonal behavior with a correspondingly general module for social interaction, or a set of several narrow domains related to interpersonal behavior all encompassed by one broad, general module for social interaction, an evolutionary psychologist of the narrow school would focus on a narrow domain of mating behavior and its correspondingly narrow module in the mind.

Narrow-school evolutionary psychologists claim that modules can be differentiated from one another because they require qualitatively different rules for the solution to their corresponding adaptive problems. For example, Cosmides and Tooby (1997) compare modules for choosing food and choosing a mate: "To solve the adaptive problem of finding the right mate, our choices must be guided by *qualitatively different standards* than when choosing the right food, or the right habitat." (p. 8; emphasis in original). Likewise, Pinker (1997), describing the use of stereo vision to generate images of depth perception and three-dimensionality from two-dimensional images on the retina, writes that it "imposes particular demands on the wiring of the brain, and it *depends on principles specific to its problem* (p. 241, emphasis added).

Because they require different types of standards, domains place further constraints on the nature of modules. In order to solve specific problems, one needs specific knowledge. That is, one mechanism can solve a problem that another mechanism cannot because the former has available to it knowledge which is not available to the latter. This is what Pinker (1997) is referring to when, in discussing how the visual system turns stimulation of the retina into recognition of three-dimensional objects, he argues that to perform this feat of inverse optics, "*the brain supplies the missing information*, information about the world we evolved in and how it reflects light" (p. 28, emphasis in original) or what Cosmides and Tooby (1997) are discussing when they write that "biological machines are calibrated to the environments in which they evolved, and they embody information about the stably recurring properties of these ancestral worlds … Evolved problem-solvers … are equipped with crib sheets: they come to a problem already 'knowing' a lot about it" (p. 9). There must be information in the module (i.e., modules are not *tabula rasa*): "Each of the major engineering problems solved by the mind is unsolvable without built-in assumptions about the laws that hold in that arena of interaction with the world" (Pinker, 1997, pp. 31-32). Modules contain information.

Other than the information inside the module, the only information available to a module comes from a narrow range of inputs related to the specific adaptive problem the module is designed to solve. "An evolved psychological mechanism is designed to take in only a narrow slice of information … the input of an evolved psychological mechanism tells an organism the particular adaptive problem it is facing;" (Buss, 1999, pp. 48). Drawing all these features together, one might define the domain specificity of modules as their orientation toward sensory input concerning specific adaptive problems requiring particular information and rules for processing and decision making.

The other important aspect of modules for narrow evolutionary psychology, information encapsulation, involves modules' relative independence from other modules for information. The informationally-encapsulated nature of psychological modules means that the information needed to transform inputs into appropriate output must be within the module. (Thus providing a second argument for the idea that modules contain specific knowledge). Modules may receive inputs from other modules' outputs, but are still said to process those inputs according to the isolated mechanism of the module itself and the information contained within the module.

The modularity of the mind is justified by several sorts of arguments. One justification comes from an analogy between physical organs and so-called "mental organs." Anatomists and physiologists have divided the body up into different physical organs, based largely on the identified function of the organ (although also on the physical nature and spatial contiguity of the organ). As Cosmides and Tooby (1997) write

> Our body is divided into organs, like the heart and the liver, for exactly this reason. Pumping blood through the body and detoxifying poisons are two very different problems. Consequently, your body has a different machine for solving each of them. The design of the heart is specialized for pumping blood; the design of the liver is specialized for detoxifying poisons. Your liver can't function as a pump, and your heart isn't any good at detoxifying poisons. For the same reason, our minds consist of a large number of circuits that are *functionally specialized*. (p. 8).

Moreover, the analogy between physical and mental organs isn't meant to be solely metaphorical. Evidence about the modularity of the brain is offered as a second justification for modularity of the mind. "Taking an evolutionary approach to the explanation of cognitive function follows naturally from the growing body of neuroscientific evidence showing that the mind is divisible … By recognizing the modularity of mind, however, it is possible to see how human mentality might be explained by the gradual accretion of numerous special function pieces of mind" (Cummins & Allen, 1998, p. 3).

However, the similarity between mental organs and physical organs is limited. Some of these cognitive-level "organs" may be relatively easy for neuroscientists to identify; these can then be used as above as evidence of modules in the mind. Most modules, however, are probably not generated by anatomically contiguous regions of the brain. They "are not likely to be visible to the naked eye as circumscribed territories on the surface of the brain, like a flank steak and the rump roast on the supermarket cow display. A mental module probably looks more like roadkill, sprawling messily over the bulges and crevasses of the brain. Or it may be broken into regions that are interconnected by fibers that make the regions act as a unit ... the circuitry underlying a psychological module might be distributed across the brain in a spatially haphazard manner" (Pinker, 1997, pp. 30-31).

The commitment to the search for adaptations — complexly-designed solutions to prehistoric problems — provides a third justification for the modular perspective. "Because specific problems require specific solutions, numerous specific problems will require numerous specific solutions ... Because a large number of different adaptive problems cannot be solved with just a few mechanisms, the human mind must be made up of a large number of evolved psychological mechanisms" (Buss, 1999, p. 53). Furthermore, each of these "large number of evolved psychological mechanisms" presumably has an independent evolutionary history. Therefore, it is important that the mechanism operate relatively independently from other adaptations (psychological or otherwise). Thus, the modules should be domain-specific and informationally encapsulated.

Methodological adaptationism points to one final justification of modularity. "Those who study species from an adaptationist perspective adopt the stance of an engineer;" they search for elements which solve problems with "reliability, efficiency, and economy." "Finding that an architectural element solves an adaptive problem with 'reliability, efficiency, economy' is prima facie evidence that one has located an adaptation (Williams, 1966)." (Above quotes from Cosmides & Tooby, 1997, p. 14). Those who apply this methodology to the mind can rely on more than just speculation. Artificial intelligence is a scientific endeavour aimed at programming computers to mimic minds. Those adopting the assumptions of narrow evolutionary psychology can refer to attempts to simulate mental function in computers as a method for generating hypotheses about the nature of the mind. Artificial intelligence programmers have generally found it necessary to include domain-specific, content-laden subroutines in their programs. Psychologists pursuing narrow evolutionary psychology argue, therefore, that the human mind must also contain such subroutines. "Given the vastness of the possible solution space, an organism needs mechanisms to guide it to the minuscule pockets that actually provide successful solutions. Domain-general mechanisms, by failing to provide guides through design space, get paralyzed by combinatorial explosion" (Buss, 1997, p. 397).

2.4. Inclusive Fitness: The Gene as the Unit of Selection.

To claim that a trait is an adaptation is to claim that there are genes in the species' gene pool specifically *for* the trait. (Symons, 1990, p. 428, emphasis in original).

There must be genes for an adaptation because such genes are required for the passage of the adaptation from parents to offspring (Buss et al., 1998, p 535)

Narrow evolutionary psychology assumes that selection operates on genes (and, only genes). A psychological mechanism will be selected for if it reliably generates behavior which increases the likelihood that copies of the gene for the mechanism will be produced. Inclusive fitness, as Hamilton (1964) famously argued, holds that selection does not focus on individual organisms leaving direct descendents but on copies of the organism's genes surviving in other organisms. A gene which is typically expressed by traits that favor the survival of copies of itself is the unit of selection. The gene is selected no matter which organism possesses that gene; a copy of a gene in a particular individual organism is as good as a copy of that gene in any other particular organism. Narrow-school evolutionary psychologists do not consider selection operating at other levels (e.g., individual organisms or groups) or on other material (e.g., cultural beliefs) to be useful for the study of the mind.

The focus on genes has two aspects. First, selection is said to operate on individual genes which themselves have a role in the development of corresponding modules. In this manner, the module itself is claimed to be adaptive (see the Symons quote above). If natural selection operated at another level, for example, groups of genes in the organism or groups of organisms, the module itself would not be subject to isolated selection pressures and thus might not be itself adaptive: it could, for instance, be a maladaptive part of an adaptive, unified whole at the higher level of selection. Second, the gene is said to be the only method by which information can be transmitted from one generation to another to allow adaptations to be inherited (see the Buss quote above). Genes are thought to encode information for the generation of particular modules.

There is, however, very little (if any) discussion in narrow evolutionary psychology of the exact developmental relationship between genes and psychological mechanisms. Because the mechanisms were presumably produced by natural selection (i.e., they are adaptations), and because adaptations, it is assumed, can only be produced by genic selection, there must be some genetic basis for the mechanism. In this sense, genes are considered abstractly as information carriers between generations without reference to the physical process of gene expression, much in the same way that the philosophically functionalist account of mind considers mental processes without reference to their physical manifestation. In practice, the assumption of the genetic origin of psychological mechanisms plays very little role in the empirical work of narrow evolutionary psychology. The assumption of genic selection is important in narrow evolutionary psychology as a way to connect it to modern-synthesis style adaptationism, and as a conceptual tool to limit the complexity of the questions that must be answered about a psychological adaptation.

Furthermore, despite their focus on the gene, evolutionary psychologists in this camp are not genetic determinists. They acknowledge the interactive nature of development; however, the role of everything non-genetic is given secondary status in narrow evolutionary psychology. The environment (both the immediate environment in which a mechanism is activated, and the ontogenetic environment in which the organism developed) has its most central role in shaping and activating a species-universal psychological mechanism in a particular individual at a particular time. The assumption is that at the root of these evolved psychological mechanisms are genes (see Stotz & Griffiths, this volume, for further discussion of the primacy of genetics in narrow evolutionary psychology).

The focus on genetic selection is defended by many arguments, including several mentioned above such as a belief that transmittal of adaptations between generations is possible (at least in the EEA) only through genes and that there is a direct correspondence between modules and genes. Largely, however, narrow-school evolutionary psychologists support their genic focus by an appeal to its perceived dominance in evolutionary biology (Pinker, 1997, p. 43; Tooby, 1987; Buss, 1999). Specifically, inclusive fitness theory is held as the standard model for evolutionary biology.

2.5. Species-Typicality: The Universal Nature of Psychological Adaptations.

The development of [the cognitive] architecture is buffered against both genetic and environmental insults, such that it *reliably develops* across the (ancestrally) normal range of human environments ... The genetic basis for the human cognitive architecture is universal, creating what is sometimes called the *psychic unity of humankind*. (Cosmides & Tooby, 1997, p. 16)

One method used by behavioral ecologists when studying adaptations is to examine either natural or experimentally induced variability in a feature, and to observe whether or not this variability corresponds with variability in reproductive success (or, alternatively, inclusive fitness). As already mentioned, this method is not used as part of the methodology of narrow evolutionary psychology for two reasons: because adaptations are said to have evolved in response to a long-ago EEA and are not necessarily fit (at least in humans) to the current environment (see above), and because "our basic psychological mechanisms are likely to be species typical, shared by most or all humans" (Buss, 1995, p. 11).

Species-typicality means that the adaptive psychological mechanisms will appear in all normally developing members of the species. Barring some interruption to normal development, for example, human children will be born with four fingers and an opposable thumb on each of two hands. This configuration is species-typical for humans. Although not strictly universal, species-typical features are treated as invariant within the species.

This is not to say that individuals within a species do not vary. Rather, the variation among individuals, differences between genders[4], cultural differences, etc, are said to be the result of universal psychological mechanisms producing different output. Understanding individual, cultural, and gender differences from the narrow evolutionary psychology perspective involves understanding how these mechanisms operate to produce difference. "Individual differences cannot be understood apart from human nature mechanisms any more than differences in the turning radius and stopping ability of cars can be understood apart from the basic car-nature mechanisms such as steering wheels and brakes" (Buss, 1995, p. 11). All types of variability are seen as a result of, but not a cause of, human evolved psychology. This view on individual variation is contrasted with a behavioral genetics view, which seeks to answer the question "given a large population of people in a *specific* environment, to what extent can *differences* between these people be

4 Some narrow-school evolutionary psychologists seem to imply, at times, that males and females may have different modules for some domains (for example, Tooby & Cosmides, 1992, p. 45). These modules can be said to be gender-typical, rather than species-typical.

accounted for by *differences* in their genes?" (Cosmides and Tooby, 1997, p. 16). Narrow-school evolutionary psychologists do not concern themselves with the question of heritability, in the behavior genetics sense, because heritability indexes the amount of variation in the trait that corresponds to genetic variation. For the traits of interest to narrow-school evolutionary psychologists, there is no variability to index.

One reason given for the focus on species-typicality is methodological. Cosmides and Tooby (1987) claim that "sciences prosper when researchers discover the level of analysis appropriate for describing and investigating their particular subject: when researchers discover the level where invariance emerges, the level of underlying order" (p. 278). The appropriate level of analysis in psychology is universal psychological mechanisms. Further, the way to identify universal psychological mechanisms is to identify adaptations: "Because humans are the product of the evolutionary process, the explanation for their characteristics must be sought in the evolutionary process: for a science of human behavior, the level of underlying order is to be sought in an evolutionary approach" (p. 278).

A second argument supporting species-typicality in narrow evolutionary psychology is imposed by the commitment to adaptationism. Adaptations are defined as complex solutions to adaptive problems. They are solutions that have presumably evolved to fixation in the EEA. Because empirical adaptationism (see above) implies that "there are few constraints ... on the biological variation that fuels" natural selection (Godfrey-Smith, 2001, p. 336), adaptationism implies that if there were a better solution to be had to a problem, then the organism would have found it. If something is variable, therefore, it is not the best solution to some problem; therefore, it is not an adaptation.

A third argument for species-typicality rests on the assumption that mechanisms are transmitted via genetic inheritance. "Essentially, all complex mechanisms require dozens, hundreds, or thousands of genes for their development. Sexual recombination, by shuffling genes with each new generation, makes it exceedingly unlikely that complex mechanisms could be maintained if genes coding for complex adaptations varied substantially between individuals. Selection and sexual recombination tend to impose relative uniformity in complex adaptive design" (Buss, 1995, p. 11; cf., Tooby & Cosmides, 1990).

3.   METATHEORY AND ALTERNATIVE APPROACHES TO EVOLUTIONARY PSYCHOLOGY

> I would offer this advice to those who oppose evolutionary psychology: Articulate a compelling alternative metatheory and demonstrate in the arena of empirical testing that the alternative is superior by the normal standards of science — superior in accounting for known facts, superior in generating new facts, and superior in providing a heuristic to important domains of inquiry (Buss, 1995, p. 85).

With these words, Buss challenges critics of narrow evolutionary psychology to offer their own alternatives. He asserts that alternatives must offer what he calls alternative "metatheories," by which he means the general theoretical assumptions basic to a research program in a science. He suggests that the only alternatives to evolution as metatheories for the origin of life are creationism and seeding theory (life originating from beyond earth). But Buss apparently equates the metatheory of evolution with specific assumptions of narrow evolutionary psychology, such as inclusive-fitness theory (Buss, 1995, p. 2).

In this section, we will argue that Buss' position as well as similar points of view held by other evolutionary psychologists coming from the same perspective assume too much, namely that narrow evolutionary psychology is the only possible evolutionary psychology as well as that it stems directly from general evolutionary theory. This constricted view of viable metatheories for evolutionary psychology leads narrow-school evolutionary psychologists to reject the possibility that other viable evolutionary psychologies exist. We will show that there is a place for alternatives short of rejecting general evolutionary theory.

At the same time we acknowledge the uphill battle facing any particular alternative to the narrow approach. As Ketelaar argues (this volume), the narrow approach has generated a series of flourishing research programs which solidify its theoretical basis. Any evolutionary psychologist now entering the field is faced with established practices supported by detailed theoretical arguments. An ever growing amount of experimental data generated by particular hypotheses serves to buttress the claim that the currently dominant approach to evolutionary psychology has it right. Alternative approaches must prove themselves not by objecting to current approaches but by successfully proving themselves in practice. We endorse Ketelaar's main point that alternative approaches cannot ignore the flexibility of the narrow approach in dealing with potential objections. But we also hold that any specific approach to evolutionary psychology must be able to defend its theoretical assumptions on their own terms.

As a theory, narrow evolutionary psychology employs the assumptions we detailed in the section above. If an alternative set of assumptions is more successful in generating useful empirical hypotheses and confirming them, then evolutionary psychology ought to be open to change toward that approach. Or, if alternative assumptions unite existing data to explain the mind more coherently, more succinctly, or better by other standards of science, then the very foundations of evolutionary psychology ought to be altered. That evolutionary psychology has a place for such changes is the argument of this section. Whether this is considered simply an evolution of the narrow approach, or a replacement with something else, is immaterial.

3.1. A Context for Alternative Evolutionary Psychologies

In his textbook on evolutionary psychology, Buss (1999) devotes a chapter to describe "the logic and methods of the science of evolutionary psychology" (p. 34). Buss's description makes clear that he sees the approach using the particular assumptions we outlined in Section 2 as constituting evolutionary psychology as a whole; his discussion covers cognitivism (pp. 48-49), adaptationism (pp. 36-39), modularity (pp. 47-54), inclusive fitness theory (p. 39), and species-typicality (pp. 46-47), although not necessarily using those terms .

But rather than identifying this approach to evolutionary psychology as one among many possible approaches, Buss (and most other narrow-school evolutionary psychologists) treat it as if it is the only subset of general evolutionary theory relevant to psychology. In other places in his textbook, Buss mentions possible alternative assumptions such as group selection (Buss, 1999, p. 387-388) but these are neither given prominence there nor hinted at in the chapter on the nature of evolutionary psychology. When he discusses the concept of alternative approaches in the chapter devoted to laying out the logic of evolutionary psychology, they are all alternative possible applications of the assumptions of narrow evolutionary psychology not alternatives at the higher theoretical level; Buss discuss alternative middle-level evolutionary theories (e.g., Trivers's theory of parental investment and sexual selection),   alternative particular hypotheses, and alternative predictions at still lower levels (Buss, 1999, pp. 40-46). Only in applying evolutionary psychology, but not in evolutionary psychology itself, does Buss allow for alternatives.

The second assumption can be revealed by noting the absence of any general *psychological* theory in Buss's account. Evolutionary psychology is treated as an evolutionary theory but not a psychological theory, even though Buss discusses the particular assumptions used in the narrow-school approach. The psychology side of evolutionary psychology, with its attendant assumptions operating in the same way as assumptions within general evolutionary theory, does not appear to have the same weight; evolutionary psychology is seen as derived from general evolutionary theory rather than general psychological theory or some combination of both.

Both of these assumptions combine to create the illusion that no alternatives to narrow evolutionary psychology exist save the scientifically unacceptable creationism and seeding theories noted by Buss. But when one alters these unwarranted assumptions, one realizes that alternatives to narrow evolutionary psychology are possible. To see this clearly, one must make two alterations to the taxonomy of evolutionary psychology depicted by Buss.

First, a place must be found for evolutionary psychology. Since evolutionary psychology is not equivalent to general evolutionary theory, it ought to be treated as a distinct application of evolutionary theory. Narrow evolutionary psychology is derivative of evolutionary theory using particular assumptions. Even broad evolutionary psychology should be distinguished from evolutionary theory in general. The application of evolutionary thinking to the mind is one of many ways that evolutionary thinking can be applied.

Second, one must make explicit that evolutionary psychology draws not only from general evolutionary theory, it draws equally from what may be called "general psychological theory". After all, narrow evolutionary psychology itself claims to be a union of psychology and evolution, and many psychologists pursue their work using the same psychological metatheory adopted by narrow evolutionary psychology but without an evolutionary focus. As a discipline, psychology does have certain assumptions which operate at the level of theory. Tooby and Cosmides (1992) claim that what they call the Standard Social Science Model operates at this level for psychology, and they hope to replace it with (narrow) evolutionary psychology. The assumptions of the cognitive revolution have generally been accepted by most scientific psychologists for the past 25 years (although that unanimity has been breaking down recently). Cosmides and Tooby note, correctly, that evolutionary psychology uses methods of cognitive science, "informed" by evolutionary considerations (Cosmides, Tooby & Barkow, 1992, p. 7). Pinker also sees evolutionary psychology as a combination of cognitive theory and evolutionary biology (1997, p. 23). Evolutionary psychology is thus not exclusively a general evolutionary theory; rather, it is a combination of elements of a specific evolutionary approach and a specific psychological approach.

Our version of the nature of evolutionary psychology (Figure 2) explicitly includes both assumptions of evolutionary theory and assumptions of psychological theory. Within evolutionary theory, we make explicit the assumptions of inclusive fitness and adaptationism. Moreover, there are alternative assumptions one could make. (In the figure, assumptions listed in the same row are related, but they are not necessarily mutually exclusive).

As with evolutionary theory, there are multiple assumptions which one could make within the general context of psychological theory. Psychologists taking the narrow-school approach have focused on a functionalist and modular cognitivism; as indicated in the figure, however, other alternatives are possible.

Additional assumptions may be made when assumptions from evolutionary theory are combined with assumptions from psychological theory to form a particular evolutionary psychology. The narrow evolutionary psychology assumption of species-typicality is at this level.

From this perspective, we can see that narrow evolutionary psychology is but one possible alternative within broad evolutionary psychology (the general claim that psychology is best explained in reference to evolution). Narrow evolutionary psychology is the particular school of evolutionary psychology which adopts the particular set of assumptions discussed in the previous section: cognitivism, adaptationism, modularity, inclusive fitness, and species-typicality. The space for alternatives to narrow evolutionary psychology is clear: to the extent that different methodologies and assumptions are available in general evolutionary theory and general psychological theory, different alternative evolutionary psychologies are always possible. *Any particular evolutionary psychology is a combination of particular assumptions drawn from both evolutionary theory and psychological theory.*

3.2. Locating the Alternatives

Most of the other chapters in this volume offer such alternative approaches to evolutionary psychology. In order to place these alternatives in a broader framework, it is useful to review possible alternative assumptions which can be drawn together for alternative

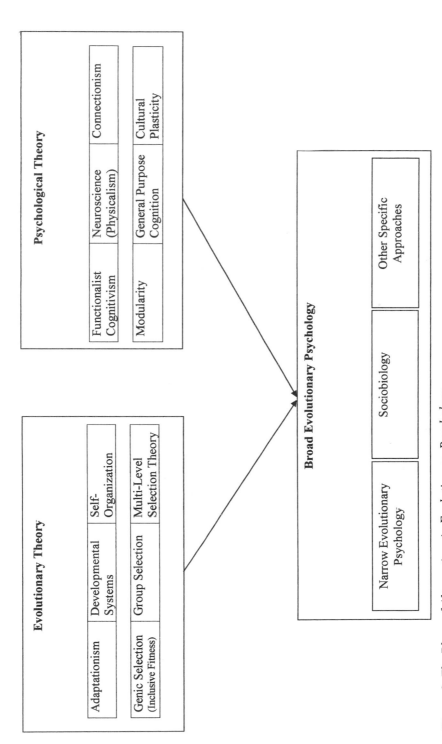

Figure 2. The Place of Alternatives in Evolutionary Psychology.

evolutionary psychologies. The list below is not meant to be exhaustive but only to cover alternatives used by other contributors to this volume. We indicate in the list which contributors adopt which alternative assumptions. There are three types of assumptions: those of general evolutionary theory (which can be used by any evolutionary biologist, whether discussing mental or non-mental traits of organisms), those of general psychological theory (which can be used by any research psychologist whether or not in reference to evolutionary considerations), and those peculiar to the union of these in an evolutionary psychology (which are not typically used within either evolutionary or psychological theory, but can be used in viewing psychological attributes in light of evolution).

A. *General Evolutionary Theory*. There are differences in assumptions and methods within general evolutionary theory. As discussed in the previous section, narrow evolutionary psychology assumes a strong form of adaptationism and a gene-centered selection process. These are not, however, the only assumptions used in evolutionary theory. Alternatives include:

  a. A developmental systems approach, which stresses interactions among genes, organisms, and environment without assigning any of them priority. Developmental systems theory entails that genetic selection falsely isolates genes and correspondingly distorts actual evolutionary processes and transmission of traits between generations (Stotz and Griffiths, Caporael).

  b. Multilevel selection theory, which holds that selection operates at many levels, including on sets of individuals (group selection). Multilevel selection operates more widely than inclusive fitness theory, even subsuming inclusive fitness theory as a case of selection of a group of genes (Wilson, Caporael, Eldredge).

B. *General Psychological Theory*. The general assumptions used by narrow evolutionary psychology in the metatheory of psychology are cognitivism and modularity as discussed in our previous section. Alternatives to these assumptions include:

  a. Connectionism, which uses simulated neural networks to model psychological processes (Parisi).

  b. A related view which rejects modules as too broad and postulates many more, small mental processes used in multiple larger processes. This view holds that broad mental tasks performed by modules are not informationally encapsulated but share many of the smaller mental processes, and that these mental processes are highly interconnected (Mundale, Bechtel, Murphy).

  c. Plasticity of mind, which rejects modules as too narrow because they impose rigid rules on a constricted range of inputs and behavioral outputs, and which replaces this assumption with variability in both neural architecture and behavioral responses (Hrdy, Wilson).

d. A stress on neuroscience, which stresses the explanation of mental processes at the neuronal level: the actual physical mechanisms and states of the brain (Quartz, Mundale, Bechtel).

C. *Broad Evolutionary Psychology.* Some assumptions of evolutionary psychology do not seem to come clearly from either general evolutionary theory or general psychological theory. Although these assumptions may be related to assumptions from one of evolutionary psychology's parent disciplines, they are not assumptions typically made by practitioners in those parent disciplines. These assumptions seem to be made within evolutionary psychology itself, that is, only when one unifies evolutionary and psychological considerations into a single theory. One such assumption in narrow evolutionary psychology discussed in the previous section is that only species-typical traits are of interest to evolutionary psychologists. Other assumptions used in the narrow-school are that the environment of evolutionary adaptedness for human psychological processes is a relatively environmentally stable Pleistocene Era (an assumption related to adaptationism; see section 2.2 above) and that human culture is the result of but not a cause of the human evolved psychology (an assumption related to genic selection; see section 2.4). Alternatives are:

a. Species-variability, which holds that variations among human beings rather than only species typical traits are important for evolutionary psychology (Wilson).

b. Alternatives concerning the EEA, which are offered for many particular aspects of a stress on an EEA: The period after the EEA is equally important for identifying the scope of adaptations (Hrdy); the EEA was not as stable as assumed (Quartz); the EEA is only a heuristic device (Murphy); rather than a focus on a distant EEA, research can utilize computer simulations to test hypotheses about the evolution of particular traits (Parisi) or should look at current human niches (Stotz and Griffiths)

c. Ontogenesis, which studies psychological mechanisms as the result of the development of neural architecture over time as a result of the interaction of environmental and genetic influences (Quartz)

d. Non-genetic evolution, which holds that human culture must be seen as contributing to the development of human psychology independently of the reproductive (adaptive) value of traits (Wilson, Eldredge)

Any particular theorist who wants to understand psychology in light of evolution, then, must pick and choose among variations within the general theories of each discipline. These alternatives to narrow evolutionary psychology — and narrow evolutionary psychology itself — will of course only be as successful as their theoretical assumptions. In the course of scientific practice, some metatheoretical assumptions will be shown superior to others; evolutionary psychology will itself evolve as these assumptions change.

3.3. The Broad Spectrum of Evolutionary Psychology

By adopting an alternative psychological metatheory and/or an alternative evolutionary metatheory, evolutionary psychologists can arrive at dramatically different ways of doing evolutionary psychology. Many of the approaches noted above, including narrow evolutionary psychology itself, will continue to evolve, and other approaches will certainly be developed.

As discussed above (and in Ketelaar, this volume), the value of a metatheory depends on how successfully it provides a narrative structure to explain past findings, and how successfully it guides future research through the stimulation of theoretical ideas and the generation of new hypotheses. Many evolutionary psychologists (e.g., Buss, 1999; Ketelaar, this volume) have argued that narrow evolutionary psychology has been particularly successful in this regard. In part, this success is a reflection of the success of the evolutionary metatheory (adaptationism) from which narrow evolutionary psychology is derived. But, narrow evolutionary psychology has also successfully generated research hypotheses (e.g., Cosmides, 1989) that most likely would not have been generated under alternative approaches to psychology.

Other approaches to evolutionary psychology are newer or less developed, and have so far had less widespread application or success. Some of the approaches will flourish, and others will wither; new approaches will be developed, and they, too, will have to stand the test of scientific success. This does not mean that there will inevitably be a "winner" — an approach to evolutionary psychology that can be declared the "right" approach, or the most successful approach; the coronation of a single approach to evolutionary psychology should not be a desideratum of the discipline. There may be room within the broad spectrum of evolutionary psychology for adherents of different approaches to contribute to our understanding of the mind.

Eastern Illinois University
Michigan State University

4.   REFERENCES

Alexander, R.D. (1979). *Darwinism and Human Affairs*. Seattle: University of Washington Press.
Badcock, C. (2000). *Evolutionary psychology: A Critical Introduction*. Malden, MA: Blackwell.
Barkow, J.H. (1990). Beyond the DP/DSS controversy. *Ethology and Sociobiology, 11*, 341-351.
Barkow, J.H., Cosmides, L., & Tooby, J. (Ed.). (1992). *The Adapted Mind*. Oxford, Eng.: Oxford University Press.
Barrett, L., Dunbar, R., & Lycett, J. (2002). *Human Evolutionary Psychology*. Princeton, NJ: Princeton University Press
Betzig, L.L., Mulder, M.B., & Turke, P.W. (Eds). (1988). *Human Reproductive Behavior: A Darwinian Perspective*. Cambridge, Eng.: Cambridge University Press.
Bowler, P.J. (1989). *Evolution: The History of an Idea*. (Revised Edition. First edition published, 1983). Berkeley: University of California Press.
Buss, D.M. (1989). Sex differences in human mate preferences: Evolutionary hypotheses tested in 37 cultures. *Behavioral & Brain Sciences, 12*, 1-49
Buss, D. M. (1995). Evolutionary psychology: A new paradigm for psychological science. *Psychological Inquiry, 6*, 1-30.
Buss, D.M. (1997). The emergence of evolutionary social psychology. In J.A. Simpson and D.T. Kenrick (Eds.). *Evolutionary Social Psychology*. (pp. 387-400). Mahwah, NJ: Lawrence Erlbaum and Associates.
Buss, D.M. (1999). *Evolutionary Psychology: The New Science of the Mind*. Needham Heights, MA: Allyn & Bacon.
Buss, D.M., Haselton, M.G., Shackelford, T.K., Bleske, A.L. & Wakefield, J.C. (1998). Adaptations, exaptations, and spandrels. *American Psychologist, 53*, 533-548.
Caplan, A. (Ed.). (1978). *The Sociobiology Debate*. New York: Harper.
Changon, N. & Irons, W. (Eds.). (1979). *Evolutionary Biology and Human Social Behavior: An Anthropological Perspective*. North Scituate, MA: Duxbury Press.
Chomsky, N. (1959). Review of B.F. Skinner's *Verbal behavior*. *Language, 35*, 26-58.
Chomsky, N. (1966). *Cartesian Linguistics*. NY: Harper & Row.
Cosmides, L. (1989). The logic of social exchange: Has natural selection shaped how humans reason? Studies with the Wason selection task. *Cognition, 31*, 187-276.
Cosmides, L. & Tooby, J. (1987). From evolution to behavior: Evolutionary psychology as the missing link. In J. Dupre, (Ed). *TheLatest on the Best: Essays on Evolution and Optimality*. (pp. 276-306). Cambridge, MA: The MIT Press.
Cosmides, L., & Tooby, J. (1997). Evolutionary psychology: A primer. [Online} Available: http://www.psych.ucsb.edu/research/cep/primer.html.
Cosmides, L., Tooby, J., & Barkow, J. H. (1992). Introduction: Evolutionary psychology and conceptual integration. In J.H. Barkow, L. Cosmides, & J. Tooby (Eds.). *The Adapted Mind: Evolutionary psychology and the generation of culture*. NY: Oxford University Press.
Crawford, C. (1998). The theory of evolution in the study of human behavior: An introduction and overview. In C. Crawford & D. L. Krebs (Eds). *Handbook of Evolutionary Psychology: Ideas, Issues, and Applications*. Mahwah, NJ: Lawrence Erlbaum Associates.
Crawford, C. & Krebs, L. (1998). (Eds). *Handbook of Evolutionary Psychology: Ideas, Issues, and Applications*. Mahwah, NJ: Lawrence Erlbaum Associates.
Cummins, D.D. & Allen, C. (1998). Introduction. In D.D. Cummins & C. Allen (Eds.). *The Evolution of Mind* (pp. 3-8). Oxford, England: Oxford University Press.
Daly, M. & Wilson, M. (1981). Abuse and neglect of children in evolutionary perspective. In R.D. Alexander & D.W. Turke (Eds). *Natural Selection and Social Behavior*. NY: Chiron Press.
Daly, M. & Wilson, M. (1985). Child abuse and other risks of not living with both parents. *Ethology and Sociobiology, 6*, 197-210.
Daly, M. & Wilson, M. (1987) The Darwinian psychology of discriminative parental solicitude. *Nebraska Symposium on Motivation. 35* 91-144
Daly, M. & Wilson, M. (1988). *Homicide*. Hawthorne, NY: Aldine de Gruyter.
Darwin, C. (1871). *The Descent of Man and Selection in Relation to Sex*. London: John Murray.
Darwin, C. (1872). *The Expression of the Emotions in Man and Animals*. London: John Murray.

Dawkins, R. (1986). *The Blind Watchmaker*. New York: W. W. Norton & Co
Dawkins, R. (1989). *The Selfish Gene*. (New Edition. Originally published in 1976). Oxford, Eng.: Oxford University Press.
Degler, C. N. (1991). *In Search of Human Nature: The Decline and Revival of Darwinism in American Social Thought*. NY: Oxford University Press.
Dennett, D.C. *Darwin's Dangerous Idea: Evolution and the Meanings of Life*. NY: Simon & Schuster.
Devore, I. (1988). Prospects for a synthesis in the human behavioral sciences. In D. Pines (Ed.). *Emerging Syntheses in Science*. (pp. 85-105) Redwood City, CA: Addison-Wesley Puslishing Co., Inc.
Dobzhansky, T. (1937). *Genetics and the origin of species*. NY: Columbia University Press.
Fodor, J. (1983). *The Modularity of Mind*. Cambridge, MA: MIT Press.
Foley, R. (1996). The adaptive legacy of human evolution: A search for the environment of evolutionary adaptedness. *Evolutionary Anthropology, 4*, 194-203.
Garcia, J., Ervin, F. R., & Koelling, R. A. (1966). Learning with prolonged delay of reinforcement. *Psychonomic Science. 5*, 121-122.
Garcia, J. & Koelling, R. A. (1966). Relation of cue to consequence in avoidance learning. *Psychonomic Science. 4*, 123-124.
Gaulin, SJC & McBurney, DH (2001). *Psychology: An Evolutionary Approach*. Upper Saddle River, NJ: Prentice-Hall.
Godfrey-Smith, P. (2001). Three kinds of adaptationism. In S.H. Orzack & E. Sober (Ed.) *Adaptationism and Optimality* (pp. 335-357).
Gould, S.J. (1983). The hardening of the modern synthesis. In M. Grene (Ed.), *Dimensions in Darwinism: Themes and Counterthemes in Twentieth-Century Evolutionary Theory* (pp. 71-93).
Gould, S.J. & Lewontin, R. C. (1979). The spandrels of San Marco and the Panglossian program: A critique of the adaptationist programme. *Proceedings of the Royal Society of London, 250*, 281-288.
Hamilton, W.D. (1964). The genetical evolution of social behavior. *Journal of Theoretical Biology, 7*, 1-16, 17-52.
Heyes, C. & Huber, L. (Eds.). (2000). *The Evolution of Cognition*. Cambridge, MA: MIT Press.
Heyes, C. (2000). Evolutionary psychology in the round. In C. Heyes & L. Huber (Eds.). *The Evolution of Cognition*. Cambridge, MA: MIT Press.
Hirschfeld, L. & Gelman, S. (1994). *Mapping the Mind: Domain Specificity in Cognition and Culture*. NY: Cambridge University Press.
Hull, C.L. (1943). *Principles of Behavior*. NY: Appleton-Century-Crofts.
Ketelaar, T. & Ellis, B. (2000) Are evolutionary explanations unfalsifiable?: Evolutionary psychology and the Lakatosian philosophy of science, *Psychological Inquiry 11*, 1-21.
Kitcher, P. (1985). *Vaulting Ambition*. Cambridge, MA: MIT Press.
Krebs, J.R. & Davies, N.B. (Eds.). (1997). *Behavioural Ecology : An Evolutionary Approach* (4th ed.). Malden, MA : Blackwell Science.
Leahey, T.H. (1997). *A History of Psychology: Main Currents in Psychological Thought* (4 ed.). Upper Saddle River, N.J.: Prentice-Hall.
Mayr, E. (1983). How to carry out the adaptationist program. *The American Naturalist, 121*, 324-334.
Mayr, E. (1997). *This is Biology*. Cambridge, MA: Harvard University Press
Mills, J.A. (1998). *Control: A History of Behavioral Psychology*. NY: New York University Press.
Palmer, J.A. & Palmer, L.K. (2002). *Evolutionary psychology: The ultimate origins of human behavior*. Needham Heights, MA: Allyn & Bacon
Pinker, S. (1997). *How the Mind Works*. NY: WW Norton & Co.
Provine, W.B. (1983). The development of Wright's theory of evolution: systematics, adaptation, and drift. In M. Grene (Ed.), *Dimensions in Darwinism: Themes and Counterthemes in Twentieth-Century Evolutionary Theory* (pp. 43-70). NY: Cambridge University Press.
Richards, R.J. (1987). *Darwin and the Emergence of Evolutionary Theories of Mind and Behavior*. Chicago: University of Chicago Press.
Ruse, M. (1996). *Monad to Man: The Concepts of Progress in Evolutionary Biology*. Cambridge, MA.: Harvard University Press.
Ruse, M. (1999). *Mystery of Mysteries: Is Evolution a Social Construction?* Cambridge, MA: Harvard University Press.
Shannon, C.E. & Weaver, W. (1949). *The Mathematical Theory of Communication*. Urbana, IL: University of Illinois Press.

Skinner, B.F. (1957). *Verbal Behavior*. NY: Appleton-Century-Crofts.

Sterelny, K. & Griffiths, P.E. (1999). *Sex and Death: An Introduction to Philosophy of Biology*. Chicago: University of Chicago Press.

Symons, D. (1979). *The Evolution of Human Sexuality*. NY: Oxford University Press.

Symons, D. (1989). A critique of Darwinian anthropology. *Ethology and Sociobiology, 10*, 131-144.

Symons, D. (1990). Adaptiveness and adaptation. *Ethology and Sociobiology, 11*, 427-444.

Symons, D. (1992). On the use and misuse of Darwinism in the study of human behavior. In J.H. Barkow, L. Cosmides, & J. Tooby (Eds.). *The Adapted Mind: Evolutionary Psychology and the Generation of Culture*. (pp. 137-159). New York: Oxford University Press.

Thornhill, R. (1998). Darwinian aesthetics. In C.B. Crawford & D.L. Krebs (Eds). *Handbook of Evolutionary Psychology: Ideas, Issues, and Applications*. Mahwah, N.J.: Lawrence Erlbaum and Associates.

Tolman, E. C. (1932). *Purposive Behavior in Animals and Men*. NY: Appleton-Century-Crofts.

Tooby, J. (1988). The emergence of evolutionary psychology. In D. Pines (Ed.). *Emerging Syntheses in Science*. Redwood City, CA: Addison-Wesley Puslishing Co., Inc.

Tooby, J. & Cosmides, L. (1990). On the universality of human nature and the uniqueness of the individual: The role of genetics and adaptation. *Journal of Personality, 58*, 17-68.

Tooby, J. & Cosmides, L. (1992). The psychological foundations of culture. In J.H. Barkow, L. Cosmides, & J. Tooby (Eds.). *The Adapted Mind: Evolutionary Psychology and the Generation of Culture*. (pp. 19-136). Oxford, Eng.: Oxford University Press.

Turke, P.W. (1990). Which humans behave adaptively, and why does it matter? *Ethology and Sociobiology, 11*, 305-339.

Watson, J. B. (1913). Psychology as the behaviorist views it. *Psychologist Review, 23*, 158-177.

Williams, G. (1966). *Adaptation and Natural Selection: A Critique of Some Current Evolutionary Thought*. Princeton, NJ: Princeton University Press.

Wilson, E.O. (1975). *Sociobiology: The New Synthesis*. Cambridge, MA: Harvard University Press.

Wilson, E.O. (1978). *On Human Nature* Cambridge, MA: Harvard University Press.

Wilson, E.O. (1984). Human sociobiology: A preface. *Journal of Human Evolution, 13*, 1-2. [Reprinted in J. Wind (1985). (Ed.). *Essays in Human Sociobiology*. London: Academic Press.]

Wynne-Edwards, V.C. (1962). *Animal Dispersion in Relation to Social Behavior*. NY: Hafner.

Yule, G.U. (1902). Mendel's laws and their probable relations to intra-racial heredity, *New Phytologist, 1*, 193-207, 222-38

TIMOTHY KETELAAR

THE EVALUATION OF COMPETING APPROACHES WITHIN HUMAN EVOLUTIONARY PSYCHOLOGY

A central assumption of human evolutionary psychology is that the brain is comprised of many specialized psychological mechanisms that were shaped by natural selection over vast periods of time to solve the recurrent information-processing problems faced by our ancestors (Buss, 1995, 1999; Barkow, Cosmides, & Tooby, 1992; Gaulin & McBurney, 2000; Ketelaar & Ellis, 2000; Symons, 1995). Although this so-called "narrow" approach to evolutionary psychology[1] shares many features with the broader meta-theoretical perspective of evolutionary biology, this approach can be considered just one application (among many) of the basic principles and knowledge of evolutionary biology, rather than the *sine qua* non of all "evolutionary psychology". In this manner, the term "narrow" merely reflects a focus on a particular set of core assumptions (inclusive fitness, gene-centered selection, adaptationism), rather than a limited or necessarily myopic application of evolutionary biology. Paradoxically, some researchers have argued that what is referred to here as the "narrow" approach to evolutionary psychology actually represents the ascendent view in much of human evolutionary psychology (see Ketelaar & Ellis, 2000; Ellis & Ketelaar, in press). The aim of this chapter is to illustrate how researchers can evaluate competing evolutionary explanations at all levels of analysis ranging from the most basic assumptions lying at the hard core of the meta-theory to the strong and weak predictions lying in the protective belt of auxiliary hypotheses that surrounds the hard core.

1. A LAKATOSIAN PERSPECTIVE ON EVALUATING ALTERNATIVE EXPLANATIONS

Although this chapter presents an explicitly *descriptive* framework (the Lakatosian Model) for articulating how researchers evaluate alternative explanations in human

---

[1] EDITOR'S NOTE: In this book, the term 'narrow evolutionary psychology' signifies the approach to evolutionary psychology developed by Cosmides, Tooby, Buss, et al. This term was chosen not to imply that this approach has an inappropriately narrow point of view, but merely to suggest that the approach adopts a narrower range of assumptions than 'broad evolutionary psychology' (or, just 'evolutionary psychology'). This latter term signifies evolutionary psychology generally, practiced with any of a very broad range of assumptions possible within the general framework of evolutionary approaches to psychology. For more detail on this terminology, see the editors' introduction, p 1

Steven J. Scher & Frederick Rauscher (Eds.). Evolutionary Psychology: Alternative Approaches, 31-54.

evolutionary psychology, it will employ one normative argument. Specifically, it is argued that pitting two competing (evolutionary) alternative explanations against one another is a more reasonable (i.e., defensible, efficient) research strategy than the alternative strategy of Popperian null hypothesis testing whereby the researcher pits a plausible alternative hypothesis against its logical opposite (often framed as an implausible null hypothesis). Although the Popperian method of falsification is useful for evaluating the scientific status of specific statements (predictions & hypotheses), it is argued that falsificationism is an inappropriate strategy for *directly* evaluating the theories and meta-theoretical assumptions that generate such statements. In this chapter a case is made for the claim that the Lakatosian criterion of progressivity provides a better guide than Popperian Falsification for evaluating competing evolutionary explanations, including those that occur at the level of basic meta-theoretical assumptions.

There are two central features of Lakatos' philosophy of science that provide a basis for constructing and evaluating alternative explanations, including alternative explanations generated by the same theory (see Ketelaar & Ellis, 2000). The first feature is that competing research programs are judged as "progressive" or "degenerative", rather than as "false" or "not-yet-falsified" as a strict Popperian might contend. The second feature is the recognition that meta-theoretical research programs — such as "narrow" evolutionary psychology — are comprised of several levels of analysis centered on a "hard core" of basic assumptions surrounded by a "protective belt" of auxiliary hypotheses that connect these basic assumptions to observable data.

2.   PROGRESSIVITY (RATHER THAN FALSIFICATION) AS A MEANS OF COMPARING ALTERNATIVE EVOLUTIONARY EXPLANATIONS

It is not uncommon to hear critics of the so-called "narrow" evolutionary psychology invoke "Falsificationism" and the ghost of Sir Karl Popper in one breath when they charge that:

> the rejection of one adaptive story usually leads to its replacement by another, rather than
> to a suspicion that a different kind of explanation might be required (Gould and Lewontin,
> 1979, pp. 587-88).

Contrary to this Popperian rhetoric, the history of science suggests that one does not suspect that an alternative meta-theoretical framework is needed simply because a singular explanation generated from that framework has been refuted. For example, when a horrific and tragic explosion destroyed the Space Shuttle Challenger in 1986, scientists did not question the basic laws and assumptions of physics. Rather, they questioned how they had applied those laws and assumptions to the construction of the O-rings which sealed the shuttle's booster rockets (Feynman & Leighton, 1988). Lakatos (1978, p. 48) points out that it is typically the auxiliary hypotheses that surround one's basic assumptions, and not the basic assumptions themselves, that bear the burden of empirical tests and are "adjusted and re-adjusted, or even replaced, to defend the thus hardened-core" of the research program. Although this Popperian notion that *one should reject an entire theory like a house of cards once a single prediction has failed* is not an uncommon refrain in the social sciences, Falsificationism as a general research strategy can be challenged on both descriptive and normative grounds.

On normative grounds, the Popperian strategy of accumulating negative knowledge about what the mind does *not* do and then inferring positive knowledge by considering the explanations that are left unrefuted has been challenged as an inefficient and statistically problematic strategy akin to null hypothesis testing (Newell, 1973; 1990; Meehl, 1978; Gigerenzer & Murray, 1987). At a descriptive level, where one is concerned largely with depicting what scientists *actually* do when they construct and evaluate explanations, it becomes quite clear that while many scientists "talk the talk" of Karl Popper, they certainly do not "walk the walk" when it comes to evaluating explanations (Meehl, 1978). Newell (1990, p. 14) argued:

> ...we are not living in the world of Popper (Popper, 1959), as far as I'm concerned, we are living in the world of Lakatos (Lakatos, 1970). Working with theories is not like skeet shooting–where theories are lofted up and bang, they are shot down with a falsification bullet, and that's the end of the story. Theories are more like graduate students -- once admitted you try hard to avoid flunking them out...Theories are things to be nurtured and changed and built up. One is happy to change them to make them more useful.

This is not to say that falsification is an invariably poor tool for acquiring scientific knowledge, but rather that science simply does not — and some would argue, should not — operate via falsification alone. It was in this spirit that Newell (1990; see also Meehl, 1978) called for psychology to recognize the utility of the Lakatosian philosophy of science as an addendum to Popper. Among the most important contributions of the Lakatosian approach is its description of how competing research programs are judged as "progressive" or "degenerative" based on their explanatory and predictive power, rather than as "false" or "not-yet-falsified" (as a strict Popperian might contend). Lakatos (1976, p. 11) argued that when a research program begins to contribute only marginally to the advancement of knowledge because it is employed primarily in dealing with anomalies, this explanatory system is viewed as degenerative rather than progressive:

> A research programme is said to be *progressing* as long as its theoretical growth anticipates its empirical growth, that is, as long as it keeps predicting novel facts with some success (*'progressive problemshift'*); it is *stagnating* if its theoretical growth lags behind its empirical growth, that is, as long as it gives only *post hoc* explanations either of chance discoveries or of facts anticipated by, and discovered in, a rival programme (*'degenerative problemshift'*).

Rather than simply searching for confirmatory (or disconfirmatory) evidence, the Lakatosian framework suggests that the process of evaluating evolutionary explanations involves sorting through a set of plausible alternative accounts. In this manner, the Lakatosian approach to science emphasizes the process of establishing acceptable claims to knowledge (rather than "truth" per se) through methods analogous to construct validation (e.g., Cronbach & Meehl, 1955; Ellis & Ketelaar, 2000; Hooker, 1987; Meehl, 1990). To establish construct validity, it is necessary for an evolutionary explanation of a given phenomenon to specify the meaning of a construct (e.g., to specify the functional design of a proposed adaptation), distinguish it from other constructs, and generate precise, testable predictions about how measures of the proposed construct should and should not relate to other variables (Ellis & Ketelaar, 2000). In this manner, well-validated evolutionary explanations can count as acceptable knowledge claims; that is, these explanations can be corroborated (or falsified), even though they cannot be directly verified (see Salmon, 1967, 1990, 1992 for detailed discussion of verification and inductive reasoning in science). The notion that alternative evolutionary explanations should be evaluated in terms of their progressivity rather than simply in terms of whether or not they have been falsified has important implications for evaluating alternative explanations in evolutionary psychology. This is the case because, as Lakatos (1970) first pointed out, many theory-driven research programs consist of several levels of analysis and it is not always possible to reject an entire research program simply because an explanation at one level of analysis has been empirically refuted or called into question.

3.   LEVELS OF ANALYSIS IN META-THEORETICAL RESEARCH PROGRAMS: HARD CORE ASSUMPTIONS AND THE PROTECTIVE BELT

Although the Lakatosian model of science describes two levels of analysis (the hard core of basic assumptions and a protective belt of auxiliary hypotheses), the protective belt in "narrow" evolutionary psychology can actually be broken down into three separate levels of analysis (middle-level theories, hypotheses, and predictions, see below). In this manner, narrow evolutionary psychology can be described in terms of four levels of analysis as depicted in Figure 1 (see Buss, 1995; 1999; Ketelaar & Ellis, 2000). These four levels correspond to:

1) *the meta-theory level*: the most basic assumptions and guiding metaphors (sometimes quite abstract) of a "paradigm" or "research program".

2) *the middle level theory level*: specific applications of a particular set of meta-theoretical assumptions to a particular content domain.

3) *the hypothesis level*: general statements about the state of the world that one expects to observe if the particular middle-level theory that generated them is true

4) *the predictions level*: more precise statements about the state of the world that one expects to observe if the particular hypothesis that generated them is true.

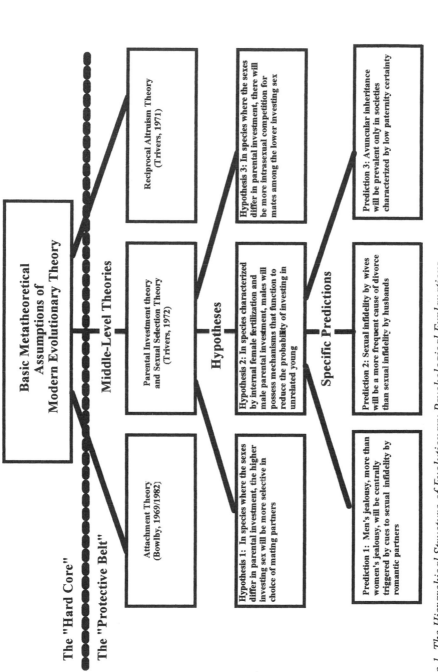

Figure 1. The Hierarchical Structure of Evolutionary Psychological Explanations. (Adapted from Ketelaar & Ellis, 2000, based on Buss, 1995).

3.1. The Hard Core of Basic Assumptions.

Scientists typically rely on basic (though usually implicit) meta-theoretical assumptions when they construct and evaluate theories. Once these basic assumptions have been empirically established, they are often not directly tested thereafter. Instead these assumptions are used as a starting point for further research. Lakatos (1970) referred to these basic, a priori assumptions as the "hard core" of a meta-theoretical research program. Newton's laws of motion form the meta-theory for classical mechanics, the principles of gradualism and plate tectonics provide a meta-theory for geology. Much of what is referred to (in this volume) as "narrow evolutionary psychology" draws its core assumptions from the adaptationist program in evolutionary biology. These meta-theoretical assumptions consist of the general principles of genetical evolution drawn from modern evolutionary theory, as outlined by W. D. Hamilton (1964) and instantiated in more contemporary "selfish gene" theories of genetical evolution via natural and sexual selection (see Cronin [1991], Dawkins [1976, 1982, 1986], Dennett [1995], Mayr [1983], Tooby & Cosmides [1992], and Williams [1966, 1992] for accessible overviews). The underlying logic of the adaptationist program can be stated quite simply: Random variation (i.e., mutation) exists in the genetic material of individuals. This variation (together with environmental inputs during ontogeny) produces differences between individuals in their manifest attributes (i.e., in their phenotypes). Each generation, natural selection acts like a sieve on this variation (Dawkins, 1996). Whereas most genetic variants are either selectively neutral or produce phenotypic effects that detract from the organism's ability to survive and reproduce (and thus are eventually filtered out), other genetic variants produce phenotypic effects that contribute to the organism's survival and reproduction (and thus pass through the sieve, becoming more prevalent in future generations). Through this filtering process, natural selection (a) produces small incremental modifications of preexisting phenotypes and (b) leads to accumulation of phenotypic characteristics that are organized for reproduction (specifically gene reproduction). These characteristics are referred to as "adaptations" because they served specific functions (such as a change in color increasing an organism's ability to avoid detection by predators) that, during their period of evolution, recurrently promoted the survival of the genes that direct their construction. Adaptations are reliably developing characteristics of species that, over long periods of evolutionary time, interacted with the physical, social, or internal environment of individuals in ways that recurrently solved problems of survival and reproduction (Dawkins, 1976, 1982; Tooby & Cosmides, 1990, 1992; Williams, 1966, 1992).

This reliance on a set of basic meta-theoretical assumptions gives scientific explanation a markedly Bayesian flavor whereby certain auxiliary assumptions (lying in the protective belt, see below) are seen as more or less plausible (than other assumptions) by virtue of holding these a priori meta-theoretical assumptions about the way the world works (see Salmon [1990] for a nice discussion of this Bayesian approach to science). For example, most scholars adopting the meta-theoretical perspective of narrow evolutionary psychology would be quite skeptical of the hypothesis that risk of interpersonal violence is largely determined by frequency of contact between individuals (i.e., the "mutual access hypothesis"). This hypothesis has been suggested by criminologists to explain why the family is the single most common locus of all types of interpersonal violence: "It cannot be surprising that more violence is directed against those with whom we are in more intimate contact. We are all within easy striking distance of our friends and spouses, for a goodly part of the time" (Goode, 1969, p. 941). The mutual access hypothesis suggests that children who are most often "within easy striking distance" of their parents are at the greatest risk for physical abuse, regardless of whether those children are steprelations or biological offspring. For most 'narrow' evolutionary psychologists, however, the existence of such a general mechanism would constitute *an a priori null hypothesis* (see Ketelaar & Ellis, 2000). This is the case because natural selection favors psychological mechanisms that function to promote the survival and reproduction of one's direct descendants and close relatives. Accordingly, a basic meta-theoretical assumption for these evolutionary psychologists, is that natural selection favors nepotism: the inclination to discriminate in favor of genetic relatives. Given identical levels of physical proximity and social interaction, parents should be much more inhibited against harming or killing their own biological children than against harming or killing stepchildren (Daly & Wilson, 1988). If this supposition was shown to be false (i.e., if the psychological mechanisms underlying family violence were not nepotistically biased but instead followed a general "easy striking distance" rule that applied equally across different genetic relationships), then it would call into question a basic meta-theoretical assumption of modern evolutionary theory. In this manner, one can think of these meta-theoretical assumptions lying at the hard core of the meta-theory as a set of powerful methodological heuristics: "Some tell us what paths to avoid (negative heuristic), and others what paths to pursue (positive heuristic)" (Lakatos, 1970, p. 47).

3.2. The Protective Belt of the Meta-theory.

According to the Lakatosian approach to science, the hard core of the meta-theory is surrounded by a protective belt of auxiliary hypotheses (theoretical models, hypotheses and predictions) consistent with those core assumptions. The function of this protective belt is to provide an empirically verifiable means of linking the more basic meta-theoretical assumptions to observable data. The protective belt serves as the problem solving machinery of the meta-theoretical research program because it is used to provide indirect evidence in support of the meta-theory's most basic assumptions (Lakatos, 1970). Lakatos (1970) argued that any revolutionary meta-theory, by definition, begins within a sea of anomalies and counter-examples. Scientists then proceed to accommodate these anomalies by reevaluating old "facts" and creating new middle-level theories and auxiliary hypotheses within the protective belt of their adopted meta-theory. For example, when Newton's theory of classical mechanics was first introduced, it was immediately called into question by current measurements of the earth's circumference (in other words, existing data appeared to directly refute Newton's theory). In the case of early counter-examples to Newtonian meta-theory, new measurements of the earth's circumference were made and the original measurements were shown to be false. In this manner it could be shown that the initial test of Newtonian theory was based upon incorrect facts, and when the original figures on which he had based his initial tests of his theory were replaced by the corrected figures, these calculations agreed with the Newtonian account of planetary motion (Reichenbach, 1951; c.f. Lakatos, 1970). Recalculating the circumference of the earth is an instance of reevaluating an old "fact," digesting it, and in this case turning it into positive evidence. Calculating the position, mass, and velocity of a previously unknown planet in order to explain an anomaly in the motion of a known planet would be an example of a generative auxiliary hypothesis used to protect the hard core of the meta-theory (see Churchland, 1986, pp. 261-262). As one philosopher notes: "As long as the adding of auxiliary assumptions led to fruitful new discoveries and explanations, the program was progressive; when the auxiliary assumptions needed to protect the core began contributing only marginally to the advancement of learning, the program 'degenerated' and was discarded" (Galison, 1988, p. 204).

The protective belt does more, however, than just protect the hard core of meta-theoretical assumptions: it uses these assumptions to extend our knowledge of particular domains. For example, a group of physicists who adopt a Newtonian meta-theory may construct several competing middle-level theories concerning a particular physical system, but none of these theories would violate Newton's laws of mechanics. Each physicist designs his or her middle-level theory to be consistent with the basic assumptions of the meta-theory, even if the middle-level theories are inconsistent with each other. These alternative middle-level theories then compete to achieve the best operationalization of the core logic of the meta-theory as it applies to that particular domain. The competing wave and particle theories of light (generated from a quantum physics meta-theory) are excellent contemporary exemplars of this process (see Gribbin, 1984). In this manner, the use of a meta-theory places logical restrictions (boundaries) on the range of plausible explanations that one can generate in the protective belt, yet empirical evidence is the final arbiter in determining which of these alternative explanations is best (see Ketelaar & Ellis, 2000). The research agenda becomes a process of using empirical evidence (the *data* aspect of science) to sort through the set of alternative explanations that are deemed theoretically plausible (the *logic* aspect of science). In the next section, examples from contemporary evolutionary biology and current research in human evolutionary psychology are used to illustrate how competing models and hypotheses are developed and tested at each level of analysis within this four-tiered framework.

4.   COMPARING ALTERNATIVE EVOLUTIONARY EXPLANATIONS AT FOUR DIFFERENT LEVELS OF ANALYSIS

4.1. Competing Meta-theoretical Assumptions in Human Evolutionary Psychology.

Competing approaches within evolutionary psychology can occur at all levels of analysis including the basic assumptions lying at the hard core of the meta-theory. For example, there is currently a debate among evolutionary psychologists about whether group-level adaptations are theoretically possible and, if so, over how viable a force group selection is in nature (see Cronk, 1994; Dawkins, 1976, 1994; Ellis & Ketelaar, 2000 Sober & Wilson, 1998; Wilson & Sober, 1994; Wilson, this volume). Some theorists have even argued that the gene selectionist approach that forms part of the meta-theory for narrow evolutionary psychology should be replaced by a different meta-theoretical assumption involving multilevel selection (Caporael, this volume; Caporael & Brewer, 2000). Whereas the gene selectionist view (roughly speaking, inclusive fitness theory) conceptualizes genes or individuals as the units of selection (see Dawkins, 1976; Hamilton, 1964; Williams, 1966), multi-level selection theory (MLST) is based on the premise that natural selection is a hierarchical process that can operate at many levels, including genes, individuals, groups within species, or even multi-species ecosystems. A number of evolutionary scientists have employed multilevel selection principles to explain existing puzzles such as female-biased sex ratios (see below) and decreased parasite virulence (see Lenski & May, 1994) and to solve practical problems such as increasing egg production in multi-hen cages (Muir, 1996; see Ellis & Ketelaar, 2000 for a brief review). In this manner, MLST is often conceptualized as an elaboration of inclusive fitness theory (adding the concept of group-level adaptation) rather than an alternative to it (Wilson & Sober, 1994; Sober & Wilson, 1998).

The Lakatosian philosophy of science provides an excellent framework for understanding why multi-level selection theory has not replaced gene level selection as a basic meta-theoretical assumption for most human evolutionary psychologists. Consider, for example, the issue of female-biased sex ratios. Individual-level selection within a population tends to favor even sex ratios because each offspring has one male and one female parent; thus, whichever sex is less common tends to produce more offspring per individual, resulting in frequency-dependent selection for greater numbers of the less common sex (Fisher, 1958). Although the assumption of gene (or individual) level selection generally favors a 1:1 sex ratio, there are many examples in nature of deviations from this ratio. Drawing on the meta-theoretical principles of inclusive fitness theory, a series of important middle-level evolutionary theories (e.g., Fisher, 1958; Hamilton, 1967; Trivers & Willard, 1973; van Scheik & Hrdy, 1991) have been developed to explain these deviations. However, MLS theorists have developed an alternative set of meta-theoretical assumptions — involving group selection — to explain these deviations as well (Colwell, 1981). Specifically, MLS theorists have hypothesized that group-level selection between populations may favor female-biased sex ratios because it enables greater total production of offspring. Accordingly, group-level adaptations are most likely to arise when members of a group have a high degree of "shared fate," when there is a highly subdivided population structure, when there are low levels of reproductive competition within groups, and when there is differential survival and reproduction between groups.

To date, however, only the gene-centered middle-level theories have proved useful in predicting the conditions under which individuals adjust offspring sex ratios (Trivers, 1985, chapter 11; Ridley, 1993). As one proponent of the gene-centered view (Trivers, 1985, p. 271) notes: "Our ability to explain the facts concerning the primary sex ratio in dozens of contexts and hundreds of species is one of the great achievements of modern evolutionary biology and one that gives strong support to a whole host of assumptions." According to a Lakatosian perspective, in order for a multilevel selection approach to supersede the gene-centered approach as an explanation for female-biased sex ratios, it must both account for the empirical successes of the inclusive fitness based middle-level theories and successfully predict novel facts about the occurrence of female-biased sex ratios -- facts which have not been (and ideally cannot be) accounted for by a selfish gene approach. If, for example, the conditions which ostensibly facilitate group selection (see above) successfully anticipated the distribution of female-biased sex ratios, then many skeptics might be convinced.

From a Lakatosian perspective, however, MLST needs to demonstrate its progressivity by successfully predicting novel facts, rather than simply providing *post hoc* explanations of facts already anticipated by, or equally well explained by, rival meta-theoretical assumptions (e.g., the gene-centered view of evolution). If group selection has been an important force in human evolution, then it would have tremendous implications for personality and social psychology and "group-level adaptations" would be apparent in studies of the human brain/mind. Some proponents of MLST (Wilson and Sober, 1994; Sober & Wilson, 1998; Wilson, 1997) argue that such adaptations are apparent, and they have applied group selectionist analyses to a variety of known human psychological phenomena (e.g., selfless behavior in Hutterite communities, cooperative team behavior, group-level decision making processes such as "groupthink"). These post hoc explanations of known phenomena, however, are not enough. As Lakatos (1970, 1978) has shown, it is relatively easy to stretch theories to accommodate known facts. The key question, as in the sex ratio example, is whether group selection models can predict facts about human psychology that were not known in advance and are not easily explained by a selfish gene account.

By comparison, the gene-centered view that lies at the hard core of the "narrow" evolutionary psychology program has established a successful early track record of empirical discoveries that were not anticipated by rival approaches (Ketelaar & Ellis, 2000). The core concept of inclusive fitness (Hamilton, 1964), for example, has enabled evolutionary biologists to formulate hypotheses concerning how eusocial insects should distribute their reproductive effort toward sisters, half-sisters, brothers, and offspring. These hypotheses have been tested and confirmed (e.g., Frumhoff & Baker, 1988; Trivers & Hare, 1976). Moreover, inclusive fitness has provided a strong account of numerous anomalous cases of apparent altruism, such as the alarm calls given in prey species which appear to benefit kin by alerting them of danger, but which put the caller at greater risk for predation (see Cronin, 1991). In sum, inclusive fitness theory (Hamilton, 1964) has not only defended the hard core of the narrow evolutionary psychology meta-theory from refutation, but it has also enabled this meta-theoretical perspective to turn a series of apparent counter-examples (e.g., eusociality, predator alarm calls) into positive evidence (see Ketelaar & Ellis, 2000; Ellis & Ketelaar, in press). By contrast, multi-level selection models have (thus far) been less progressive as tools of discovery. As of yet, there has not been a single new discovery about human cognition or behavior that has been directly guided by multi-level selection models (Ellis & Ketelaar, in press). Although an important debate continues about the technical merits of these different views of the evolutionary process (e.g., Caporael, this volume; Laland, Odling-Smee, & Feldman, 2000; Wilson & Sober, 1994; Wilson, this volume), it is rather premature to suggest that multi-level selection models should replace the currently dominant, gene-centered adaptationist program that has become the ascendent view in much of evolutionary psychology (see Ellis & Ketelaar, 2000; in press). When and if MLST begins to contribute significantly to the growth of knowledge in psychology by anticipating new facts and resolving old puzzles, then it would naturally become a more central part of human evolutionary psychology's meta-theory.

Just as competing meta-theoretical research programs are often evaluated indirectly in terms of the progressivity vs. degenerativity of their middle-level theories, so too competing middle-level evolutionary theories are most often evaluated indirectly through the performance of their derivative hypotheses and predictions. The next section provides a brief illustration of how the Lakatosian approach aids us in evaluating competing evolutionary explanations that occur at the level of middle-level theories.

4.2. Competing middle-level theories in human evolutionary psychology.

Following the Lakatosian philosophy of science, different middle-level theories (even those generated from the very same meta-theory) can compete to provide the best explanation for a particular phenomenon. Accordingly, these competing middle-level evolutionary theories are evaluated in terms of their relative success in applying the core assumptions of the meta-theory to a given domain. One theory may be judged as more useful than another because it possesses greater *explanatory power*; that is, it solves more of the existing puzzles and accounts for a wider range of known facts, including apparently anomalous findings. In addition to this ability to account (post hoc) for what is known, one middle-level theory may be judged as more useful than another because it possesses greater *predictive power*; that is, it better anticipates the data by specifying (a priori) previously unobserved phenomena (Lakatos, 1970, 1978).

Despite this competition, different middle-level theories can be firmly grounded in the very same meta-theoretical assumptions. For example, both the theory of parental investment and sexual selection (Trivers, 1972) and the theory of reciprocal altruism (Axelrod & Hamilton, 1981; Trivers, 1971; Williams, 1966) have been applied to the question: Why do adult males interact with infants?

Working within these different frameworks, evolutionary scientists have generated competing models about the evolution of male parental behavior. These two evolutionary models produce competing hypotheses about the social contexts in which male parental care is most likely to occur (see below). Yet, at a meta-theoretical level, both models share the assumption that the evolution of male parental care is predicated on a selective history of fitness benefits to the fathers who engaged in it. For example, neither model would expect a general "paternal instinct" to evolve, but rather a tendency to affiliate with and invest in infants in particular contexts that historically promoted male reproductive success.

Rather than reflecting scientific impropriety, the existence of alternative middle-level evolutionary theories of the very same phenomenon merely reflects the fact that scientists can disagree about how to apply the shared "higher level" assumptions to particular phenomena at "lower levels" of analysis. Consistent with the Lakatosian approach to science, different scientists can subscribe to the same set of meta-theoretical assumptions and still accept that science is the process of sorting through *multiple alternative* (competing) models of phenomena. Just as competing research programs are rarely evaluated through direct tests of basic meta-theoretical assumptions, so too competing middle-level evolutionary theories are rarely evaluated on the basis of a single crucial test of their central assumptions. Instead competing middle level theories are most often evaluated indirectly through the relative performance of their derivative hypotheses and predictions. In this manner, the middle level theory that displays the greatest progressivity is often judged as providing the best approximation of the truth.

5.   COMPETING HYPOTHESES IN HUMAN EVOLUTIONARY PSYCHOLOGY

Because the basic assumptions of one's meta-theory can be combined with an array of auxiliary assumptions, it follows that a wide number of hypotheses can be derived from a single middle-level theory. These hypotheses typically vary along a continuum of confidence ranging from "firm hypotheses" (such as the relation between relative parental investment and mate selection; see below) that are clear and unambiguous derivations from an established middle-level evolutionary theory to more typical formulations — hypotheses that are merely inferred from a middle-level theory but not directly derived from it (Ellis & Ketelaar, 2000; Ellis & Symons, 1990). This distinction can be illustrated by considering the issue of paternity uncertainty in the context of male parental investment in offspring. The supposition that in species characterized by both internal female fertilization and substantial male parental investment, selection will favor the evolution of male mechanisms for reducing the probability of expending that investment on unrelated young is a firm hypothesis that can be directly derived from the theory. What form these mechanisms will take, however, cannot be directly derived from the theory because natural and sexual selection underdetermine specific phylogeny. Selection could favor the evolution of sexual jealousy, or it could favor the evolution of sperm plugs to block the cervix of female sexual partners following copulation. Given the universal occurrence of jealousy in humans (Daly, Wilson, & Weghorst, 1982), evolutionary psychologists have hypothesized that men's jealousy should be centrally triggered by cues to sexual infidelity while women's jealousy should be centrally triggered by cues to loss of commitment and investment. This hypothesis is reasonably inferred from the theory but cannot be directly deduced from it. We refer to this type of hypothesis as an "expectation." This hypothesis was originally proposed by Daly et al. (1982) and has since received considerable empirical support (Buss et al., 1992, 2000; Buunk, Angleitner, Oubaid, & Buss, 1996; DeSteno & Salovey, 1996; Wiederman & Allgeier, 1993).

As one moves farther down the continuum of confidence, into the area where inferences from middle-level theories are drawn farther from their core, "expectations" grade insensibly into "interesting questions" or "hunches." At this level, different interpretations of the theory can and often do generate directly competing hypotheses. For example, Buss and Shackelford (1997) have proposed two competing evolutionary hypotheses concerning the effects of unequal attractiveness between romantic partners on women's mate retention behavior. The first hypothesis suggests that individuals (women and men) married to others who are perceived as more attractive than the self will devote *more* effort to mate retention than individuals married to others who are perceived as equal to or less attractive than the self. The logic behind this hypothesis is that individuals who are married to relatively attractive partners are at greater risk of losing them. The second hypothesis suggests the opposite, but only for females: women married to men who are perceived as more attractive than the self will relax their mate retention efforts. The logic behind this hypothesis focuses on the greater ability of men to fractionate their reproductive investment among multiple partners. For example, a man can simultaneously beget and raise children with three different women (a phenomenon that is quite common in polygynous societies), whereas it would take a woman several years to bear and raise children with three different men. As a consequence of the male ability to partition investment, women may face the trade-off of obtaining a fraction of the attention and resources of a highly attractive male or the full attention and resources of a less attractive male. Buss and Shackelford (1997) suggest that women in unevenly matched marriages might devote *less* effort to mate retention, an implicit acknowledgment of the potential costs involved in trying to prevent the more attractive partner from devoting some of his resources to outside relationships.

Competing evolutionary hypotheses can also be generated from different middle-level theories. This generation of opposing hypotheses exemplifies what narrow evolutionary psychology has been most criticized for: its apparent ability to explain anything and its opposite. This criticism unfortunately conflates the distinction between the *process* of scientific inquiry (the process of hypothesis generation and evaluation) and the *products* of scientific inquiry (the nearly consensual facts about why and how the world works the way it does). The process of scientific inquiry often begins with a host of initially viable, alternative hypotheses generated by competing theoretical models. The generation of alternative (competing) hypotheses within a single evolutionary framework is in principle no different (see Daly & Wilson, 1988; Mayr, 1983). For example, the paternity certainty and reciprocity models generate competing hypotheses about variations in levels and specificity of paternal investment. The paternity certainty model predicts that male parental investment — paternal behaviors that benefit young at some cost to the male — will be overwhelmingly directed toward a male's own offspring rather than the offspring of unrelated males (Trivers, 1972); thus, the degree of male parental investment should vary as a function of paternity certainty, both across- and within-species (e.g., Alexander & Noonan, 1979). By contrast, the reciprocity model suggests that male care of young is likely to arise in the context of a "mutually advantageous, reciprocal exchange of benefits between males and females" (Smuts, 1985, p. 257); it predicts that the quality of the relationship between the male and the infant's mother, rather than the degree of genetic relatedness between the male and the infant, will be the most important determinant of paternal investment. In contrast to the paternity certainty model, the reciprocity model posits that substantial male parental investment will sometimes evolve in species where paternity certainty is low. The generation of competing evolutionary explanations is defensible to the extent that they are rigorously formulated so that they produce clear, testable hypotheses. Vague explanations that do not have testable consequences represent poor science no matter what theoretical perspective they come from. The next section provides a quick overview of the level of analysis where the battle between competing hypotheses, and thus competing middle-level theories and meta-theories, is fought: the level of specific predictions.

6.   COMPETING PREDICTIONS IN HUMAN EVOLUTIONARY PSYCHOLOGY

Predictions correspond to specific statements about the state of the world that one would expect to observe if the hypothesis was in fact true. The performance of evolution-based predictions provides the basis for evaluating the more general hypotheses from which they are drawn. In essence, predictions represent explicit, testable instantiations of hypotheses. For example, a number of specific predictions have been derived from the evolutionary hypothesis that men (more so than women) will be intensely concerned about the sexual fidelity of reproductive age partners. Some of these predictions include: (1) sexual infidelity by wives will be a more frequent cause of divorce than sexual infidelity by husbands (Betzig, 1989); (2) the use or threat of violence by husbands to achieve sexual exclusivity and control of wives will vary as a function of wives' reproductive value, which peaks in the late teens and declines monotonically thereafter (Wilson & Daly, 1996); and (3) in the context of competing for romantic partners, the tactic of spreading rumors that a same-sex rival is sexually promiscuous will be more effective when performed by women than by men (because it raises the specter of cuckoldry; see Buss & Dedden, 1990). The fact that the first two predictions have been supported by extensive cross-cultural data whereas the third prediction has not been supported factors into one's evaluation of the more general hypothesis from which these predictions were generated. That two of the three predictions garnered strong support provides indirect support for the hypothesis. That the third prediction was rejected raises questions about the hypothesis. Ultimately the value of the more general hypothesis and theoretical model is judged by the cumulative weight of the evidence.

In evolutionary psychology, as in the rest of science, specific theoretical models and hypotheses are proposed, developed, revised, and replaced on evidential grounds. When the data fail to support a prediction it is back to the drawing board, either to attempt a better translation of the hypothesis (into a specific prediction) or to actually modify or reject the hypothesis altogether. In the preceding case of spreading rumors about same-sex rivals, the predictive failure led to a rethinking of the problem of paternity uncertainty and to the recognition of an error in the original conceptualization: the failure to distinguish between long-term and short-term mating contexts (see Schmitt & Buss, 1996). Although men want sexual exclusivity in long-term mates, they may consider sexual promiscuity desirable in potential short-term mates because it signals sexual availability and less chance of entanglement. Schmitt and Buss (1996) thus predicted and subsequently found a moderating effect of temporal context: In the context of competing with other women for long-term mates, spreading rumors that a same-sex rival was *sexually promiscuous* was judged to be an effective means of reducing that rival's attractiveness; but in the context of competing with other women for short-term mates, spreading rumors that a same-sex rival was *sexually unavailable* was judged to be an effective means of reducing that rival's attractiveness.

At a more general level, Buss and Schmitt (1993) recognized that a limitation of Trivers' (1972) theory of parental investment and sexual selection was its failure to explicitly distinguish between short-term and long-term mating contexts. Buss and Schmitt (1993) proposed an extension of parental investment and sexual selection theory — sexual strategies theory — that specifically incorporated this temporal dimension. Sexual strategies theory generated a multitude of new predictions about between- and within-sex variation in mating strategies. It enabled the parent theory (parental investment and sexual selection) to digest a series of anomalous findings and turn them into positive evidence. The process began with a set of predictive failures at the lowest level of the hierarchy, which in turn led to reevaluation of more general hypotheses and ultimately to an adjustment of the middle-level theory. This adjustment spawned a host of new research (e.g., Cramer, Schaefer, & Reid, 1996; Gangestad & Simpson; 2000; Landolt, Lalumiere, & Quinsey, 1995; Schmitt & Buss, 1996) that has significantly advanced our understanding of human mating strategies. Consistent with Lakatos' (1970) description of scientific progress, the feedback process between theory and data was critical to the acquisition of knowledge.

This example demonstrates why, in most cases, falsifying a specific evolutionary prediction does not directly falsify evolutionary meta-theory (unless that prediction directly tests a hard core meta-theoretical assumption, such as nepotism; see earlier discussion of family violence). This is because the generation of predictions depends on the specification of appropriate auxiliary assumptions. These auxiliary assumptions are part of the middle-level theory, which applies the basic assumptions of the meta-theory to a particular content domain. If a middle-level theory fails to specify some important auxiliary assumption (e.g., the distinction between short-term and long-term mating contexts), then the falsification of a lower-level hypothesis or prediction does not directly call into question the higher-level (meta-theoretical) assumptions from which the middle-level theory was drawn (see Figure 1). Instead, the middle-level theory itself is questioned. This logic is consistent with (among others) the Lakatosian philosophy of science and illustrates how middle-level theories, hypotheses, and predictions provide a "protective belt" which insulates the basic assumptions at the hard core of a meta-theory from direct refutation (Lakatos, 1970, 1978).

        To summarize, evolutionary psychological explanation of phenomena such as sexual jealousy and male parental investment involves multiple levels of analysis. Because the basic assumptions of one's meta-theory can be combined with an array of auxiliary assumptions, several hypotheses can be derived from a single middle-level theory and these hypotheses might differ from those generated by competing theories, even if both theories share many of the same meta-theoretical assumptions. For example, the theory of parental investment and sexual selection draws upon many of the same basic assumptions as reciprocal altruism theory, and yet both theories provide competing hypotheses about male parental investment. These hypotheses vary on a continuum of confidence, ranging from firm to speculative. At the speculative end of the continuum, different interpretations of a single middle-level theory can and do generate competing hypotheses (Ellis & Ketelaar, 2000; Ellis & Symons, 1990). The existence of competing hypotheses generated from a single evolutionary theory (explaining anything and its opposite) is defensible only to the extent that explanations (hypotheses) are formulated so that they generate specific, testable predictions. When a prediction fails, it calls into question the more general hypothesis from which it was drawn, and this may in turn lead to revision or abandonment of the middle-level theory that generated it. At each level of analysis, evaluation is based on the cumulative weight of the evidence. These standards and procedures for evaluating evolutionary explanations are "normal paradigm science" (Kuhn, 1962).

7. WHY COMPARING ALTERNATIVE (EVOLUTIONARY) EXPLANATIONS IS GENERALLY MORE INFORMATIVE THAN NULL HYPOTHESIS TESTING

        It is not uncommon to call into question the scientific status of a theory that purports to explain something and its opposite. This plaint has been a common criticism levied against competing explanations of the same phenomenon in narrow evolutionary psychology (Gould & Lewontin, 1979). From a naïve Popperian perspective, the mere existence of competing hypotheses generated from the same theory is often taken as evidence that the theory itself cannot be falsified and is therefore unscientific. In the social sciences, alternatives to this Popperian view (such as Lakatos's philosophy of science) are relatively uncommon (see Ketelaar & Ellis, 2000; Meehl, 1978; Newell, 1990). As a result, researchers have historically been leery of generating competing explanations from the same theory. Following a line of reasoning first introduced by Allen Newell (1973, 1990), it can be argued, however, that the comparison of alternative explanations (even competing explanations generated from the same theory) is logically and statistically more defensible as a general research strategy, than a strictly Popperian strategy of pitting a plausible alternative hypothesis against an implausible null hypothesis.

7.1. Null Hypothesis Testing as a Perilous Game of Twenty Questions.

It was almost thirty years ago at a conference on information processing that cognitive psychologist Allen Newell first made the point that the field of psychology suffers from a slow rate of progress as a result of its emphasis on a decidedly Popperian strategy of null hypothesis testing. Newell was asked to comment on the papers presented at a symposium. Newell's (1973) comments — published under the title "You can't play twenty questions with nature and win" — have obtained a certain notoriety because they have come to be interpreted as Newell's observation that the field of psychology was, and still is (see Newell, 1990), in trouble. Specifically Newell (1973) was critical of the lack of a coherent unifying theory to guide research in psychology. Newell (1990, p. 293) wrote:

> What I wanted was for these excellent pieces of the experimental mosaic to add up to the psychology that we had all wished to foresee. They didn't, not because of any lack of excellence locally, but because most of them seemed part of a pattern of psychological activity that didn't seem able to cumulate.

Newell argued that because researchers were operating without a larger theoretical framework to guide the construction and evaluation of alternative explanations, they had no explicit guidelines for separating the a priori plausible (alternative) explanations from the a priori implausible (null) explanations (see Ketelaar & Ellis, 2000 for further elaboration of this point).

In Newell's (1973, p. 287) eyes, this resulted in a sort of twenty questions strategy in which many scientific findings were being cast in terms of their support or refutation of binary oppositions: "We worry about nature versus nurture, about central versus peripheral, about serial versus parallel, and so on." To take a more contemporary example, in judgment and decision-making research human performance is often compared to a particular normative standard (e.g., an optimal Bayesian reasoner). When performance falls short of this proposed standard, researchers conclude that the human mind "does not work that way" (e.g., as an optimal Bayesian reasoner). Often these deviations from the normative standard are interpreted as evidence for a specific set of alternative procedures (typically labeled as 'heuristics' or 'biases'). Newell argued that this sort of research strategy whereby one claims support for a particular hypothesis by ruling out its apparent opposite (e.g., Bayesian reasoner vs. Non-Bayesian reasoner), has the appearance of a game of twenty questions in which the essential structure of the mind is revealed by 1) accumulating negative knowledge about what the mind does not do and then 2) inferring positive knowledge about how the mind operates by considering the explanations that are left unrefuted. Newell (1990, p. 2) observed that "what psychologists mostly did for theory was to go from dichotomy to dichotomy....Theoretical life in psychology seemed just a forever-long sequence of dichotomies."

Obviously the twenty questions research strategy does not characterize all psychological research programs; however, the use of a Popperian twenty questions research strategy is symptomatic of a concern that is pervasive in psychology: the common failure to identify an explicit set of basic meta-theoretical assumptions that can then be used to distinguish a priori null hypotheses from a priori alternative hypotheses (see Ketelaar & Ellis, 2000). In essence, Newell's plea to stop playing twenty questions can be translated into a call for psychology to abandon its emphasis on the statistically questionable Popperian strategy of Null hypothesis testing in favor of the more acceptable Neyman-Pearson approach to alternative hypothesis testing (see Gigerenzer & Murray, 1987).

7.2. The Problematic Popperian Strategy of Null Hypothesis Testing.

Recently, several statistically inclined psychologists have observed that much of modern psychological research can be characterized as an attempt to reject a null hypothesis in which one has never believed (see Gigerenzer & Murray, 1987; Meehl, 1978). For example, what should you conclude about the structure of the mind if you observe that decision-makers do not appear to be using Bayes Theorem to solve a particular reasoning task? Should you conclude that the human mind did not evolve to use Bayes theorem? Would such findings suggest that humans are not Bayesian reasoners after all? The Popperian twenty questions strategy of indirectly supporting an hypothesis by rejecting its binary opposite (Bayesian vs. non-Bayesian reasoning) is clearly a version of the Fisherian approach to null hypothesis testing (Fisher, 1937; see Gigerenzer & Murray, 1987). The Fisherian approach typically proceeds by: 1) setting up a null hypothesis that a set of observations corresponds to a hypothetical population with a known distribution, 2) collecting data and calculating a sample statistic (e.g., a mean), 3) determining whether the sample statistic deviates from the mean of the hypothetical population by more than a set criterion — the alpha level — of significance, and 4) rendering a verdict of "rejected" or "not rejected." Null hypothesis testing has a decidedly Popperian flavor.

A central problem with adopting this sort of null hypothesis testing strategy is that it does not allow for statistical inference concerning the validity of the research hypothesis of interest, that is, the alternative hypothesis (see Gigerenzer & Murray, 1987). Specifically, null hypothesis testing only allows the researcher to calculate the probability of rejecting the null hypothesis when it is in fact true (Type I error, α). Consider the set of appropriate conclusions that can be drawn after one has rejected the null hypothesis that individuals use Bayesian reasoning to solve a medical decision task involving conditional probabilities. Observing that individuals do not employ Bayesian reasoning in this context does not provide strong evidence for any particular type of non-Bayesian reasoning (e.g., neural network models, multiple regression, guessing, etc). In fact, recent research that employs a strategy of alternative hypothesis testing (see below) rather than null hypothesis testing, has actually pitted two competing Bayesian explanations against one another (see Hoffrage & Gigerenzer, 1998)! This research reveals that although individuals do not use Bayesian reasoning when the decision task is framed in terms of probabilities, they are more likely to use Bayesian reasoning to solve the same task if it is framed in terms of relative frequencies (see Hoffrage & Gigerenzer, 1998; also Brase, Cosmides, & Tooby, 1998). These sorts of empirical findings highlight how the research strategy of null hypothesis testing (e.g., Bayesian vs. non-Bayesian reasoning) is problematic. If only one interpretation of Bayesian reasoning is rejected, this does not automatically allow the researcher to point to one particular alternative explanation (even a non-Bayesian explanation) as the correct explanation. Rejecting one explanation (framed as a null hypothesis) only allows one to *indirectly* infer that its binary opposite is true, it does not tell us which of the myriad plausible alternative explanations is the best explanation (see Gigerenzer & Murray, 1987).

7.3. The more useful strategy of alternative Hypothesis testing.

Because differing auxiliary assumptions and hypotheses can often lead different researchers to generate competing explanations within a single (evolutionary) meta-theory, an alternative to the Popperian strategy of null hypothesis testing is clearly needed in human evolutionary psychology. Newell argued that the problematic twenty questions strategy of null hypothesis testing could be avoided if only scientists could somehow identify a unifying meta-theory to guide them in distinguishing a priori *alternative* explanations from a priori *null* explanations (Ketelaar & Ellis, 2000). In this manner researchers could focus on comparing plausible alternative explanations, rather than simply rejecting implausible null explanations. Fortunately, such an alternative strategy exists: it is known as the Neyman-Pearson strategy of alternative hypothesis testing.

By contrast with the Popperian/Fisherian approach, the Neyman-Pearson strategy of alternative hypothesis testing allows the researcher to actually calculate — not indirectly infer — the probability that the research hypothesis of interest is true (Gigerenzer & Murray, 1987). The Neyman-Pearson approach typically proceeds by: 1) specifying two alternative hypotheses (H_0 and H_1) and their hypothetical distributions, 2) determining two types of error corresponding to "the probability of incorrectly rejecting H_0" (type I error) and "the probability of incorrectly rejecting H_1" (type II error), 3) collecting data and calculating a sample statistic, 4) determining whether--given the sample size and error--the sample statistic falls to the left or the right of the decision criterion (dictated a priori by the α and β), and 5) rendering a verdict of whether to accept H_0 or H_1. Because this alternative hypothesis testing strategy allows the researcher to calculate the probability of rejecting the research hypothesis (H_1) when it is in fact true (Type II error, β), the researcher can directly calculate the power ($1 - \beta$) of a test — the probability of accepting the research hypothesis if it is true — by taking into account sample size, error, and the α (alpha) criterion prior to the test (see Gigerenzer & Murray, 1987). This allows the researcher to directly infer whether the research hypothesis of interest has been supported.

By relying on a particular set of meta-theoretical assumptions to distinguish plausible and implausible alternative explanations, researchers could focus on comparing plausible alternative explanations, rather than simply rejecting implausible null explanations. In this light, it would appear that the philosophy of science articulated by Imre Lakatos provides an excellent framework (see Ketelaar & Ellis, 2000) for describing how researchers can utilize a single (evolutionary) meta-theory to construct and evaluate plausible alternative (evolutionary) explanations. Armed with an understanding of this alternative (Lakatosian) philosophy of science, both the critics and the consumers of evolutionary psychology have additional tools (beyond mere Popperian falsification) in their toolbox of strategies for evaluating competing approaches in evolutionary psychology (Ketelaar & Ellis, 2000).

8.   CONCLUSIONS

Because human evolutionary psychology is a meta-theoretical research program consisting of multiple levels of analysis it makes sense to evaluate alternative explanations at each level of analysis ranging from core evolutionary assumptions to specific predictions derived from competing middle-level evolutionary theories. Although much of the action in narrow evolutionary psychology occurs in the protective belt of the meta-theoretical research program (e.g., when alternative middle level models compete to explain particular phenomena, see Ketelaar & Ellis, 2000), alternative evolutionary explanations can also occur at the level of basic meta-theoretical assumptions (e.g., group selection vs. gene selection). Rather than suggesting that the existence of competing evolutionary explanations reflects scientific impropriety, the Lakatosian approach to science illustrates how the existence of alternative explanations may simply reflect the fact that scientists can disagree about how to apply the shared "higher level" assumptions to particular phenomena at "lower levels" of analysis. Moreover, evolutionary psychologists do sometimes disagree about the most appropriate starting assumptions (see Caporael, this volume; Wilson, this volume). In this light, the Lakatosian philosophy of science provides an excellent description of how evolutionary psychologists (appropriately) spend most of their research efforts sorting through *alternative* (competing) "evolutionary" explanations, rather than attempting to reject a priori null explanations (see Ketelaar & Ellis, 2000). Thus, contrary to some critics of narrow evolutionary psychology (e.g., Gould and Lewontin, 1979) rejecting a particular evolutionary explanation does not logically suggest that one should look for a different type of explanation, nor does it provide support for any particular alternative hypothesis, including a non-evolutionary account. Central to both the Lakatosian model and the narrow evolutionary psychology research program is the idea that alternative hypothesis testing as a general research strategy can be useful to researchers who are interested in developing and testing evolutionary explanations that are deductively consistent with certain a priori basic assumptions and inductively consistent with empirical observation.

New Mexico State University

9.   AUTHOR NOTES

Portions of this chapter have been adapted from Ketelaar, T. & Ellis, B. (2000) "Are evolutionary explanations unfalsifiable?: Evolutionary psychology and the Lakatosian philosophy of science" which appeared in *Psychological Inquiry*, 2000, volume 11, pp. 1-21 and Ellis, B. & Ketelaar T. "On the natural selection of alternative models: Evaluation of explanations in evolutionary psychology" which appeared in *Psychological Inquiry*, 2000, volume 11, pp. 56-68.

10. REFERENCES

Alexander, R. D., & Noonan, K. M. (1979). Concealment of ovulation, parental care, and human social behavior. In N.A. Chagnon & W. Irons (Eds.), *Evolutionary biology and human social behavior* (pp. 145-180). North Scituate, MA: Duxbury Press.

Axelrod, R. & Hamilton, W. D. (1981). The evolution of cooperation. *Science, 211,* 1390-1396.

Barkow, J. H., Cosmides, L. & Tooby, J. (Eds.) (1992). *The Adapted Mind: Evolutionary Psychology and the Generation of Culture.* New York: Oxford University Press.

Betzig, L.L. (1989). Causes of conjugal dissolution: A cross-cultural study. *Current Anthropology, 30,* 654-676.

Brase, G. L., Cosmides, L. & Tooby, J. (1998). Individuation, counting, and statistical inference: The role of frequency and whole-object representations in judgment under uncertainty. *Journal of Experimental Psychology: General,* 127, 3-21.

Buunk, B.B., Angleitner, A., Oubaid, V., & Buss, D.M. (1996). Sex differences in jealousy in evolutionary perspective: Tests from the Netherlands, Germany, and the United States. *Psychological Science, 7,* 359-363.

Buss, D. M., (1995). Evolutionary psychology: A new paradigm for psychological science. *Psychological inquiry, 6,* 1-30.

Buss, D. M. (1999). *Evolutionary Psychology: The New Science of the Mind.* Boston: Allyn and Bacon.

Buss, D. M. & Dedden, L. (1990). Derogation of competitors. *Journal of Social and Personal Relationships, 7,* 395-422.

Buss, D. M., Larsen, R. J., Weston, D. & Semmelroth, J. (1992). Sex differences in jealousy: Evolution, physiology, and psychology. *Psychological Science, 3,* 251-255.

Buss, D. M. & Shackelford, T.K. (1997). From vigilance to violence: Mate retention tactics in married couples. *Journal of Personality and Social Psychology, 72,* 346-351.

Buss, D. M., Shackelford, T.K., Kirkpatrick, L.A., Choe, J., Hasegawa, M., Hasegawa, T., & Bennett, K. (2000). Jealousy and the nature of beliefs about infidelity: Tests of competing hypotheses about sex differences in the United States, Korea, and Japan. *Personal Relationships, 7,* 235-243.

Buss, D.M., & Schmitt, D.P. (1993). Sexual strategies theory: A contextual evolutionary analysis of human mating. *Psychological Review, 100,* 204-232.

Caporael, L. R.; Brewer, M. B. (2000). Metatheories, evolution, and psychology: Once more with feeling. *Psychological Inquiry, 11,* 23-26.

Cartwright, N. (1983). *How the Laws of Physics Lie.* New York: Clarendon Press.

Colwell, R.K. (1981). Group selection is implicated in the evolution of female-biased sex ratios. *Nature, 290,* 401-404.

Churchland, P. S. (1986). *Neurophilosophy: Toward a Unified Science of the Mind-Brain.* Cambridge, Ma.: The MIT Press.

Cramer, R.E., Schaefer, J.T. & Reid, S. (1996). Identifying the ideal mate: More evidence for male-female convergence. *Current Psychology: Developmental, Learning, Personality, Social, 15,* 157-166.

Cronbach, L. J.; Meehl, P. E. (1955). Construct validity in psychological tests. *Psychological Bulletin, 52,* 281-302.

Cronin, H. (1991). *The Ant and the Peacock: Altruism and Sexual Selection from Darwin to Today.* New York: Cambridge University Press.

Cronk, L. (1994). Group selection's new clothes. *Behavioral and Brain Sciences, 17,* 615-616.

Daly, M. & Wilson, M. (1988). *Homicide.* Hawthorne, NY.: Aldine de Gruyter.

Daly, M., Wilson, M., & Weghorst, S. J. (1982). Male sexual jealousy. *Ethology and Sociobiology, 3,* 11-27.

Dawkins, R. (1976). *The Selfish Gene.* New York: Oxford University Press.

Dawkins, R. (1982). *The Extended Phenotype.* San Francisco: W. H. Freeman.

Dawkins, R. (1986). *The Blind Eatchmaker.* New York: W. W. Norton &

Dawkins, R. (1994). Burying the vehicle. *Behavioral and Brain Sciences, 17,* 616-617.

Dennett, D. C. (1995). *Darwin's Dangerous Idea: Evolution and the Meanings of Life.* New York: Simon & Schuster.

DeSteno, D.A., & Salovey, P. (1996). Evolutionary origins of sex differences in jealousy? Questioning the "fitness" of the model. *Psychological Science, 7,* 367-372.

Ellis, B. & Ketelaar T. (2000). On the natural selection of alternative models: Evaluation of explanations in evolutionary psychology, *Psychological Inquiry, 11,* 56-68.

Ellis, B. J. & Ketelaar, T. (in press). Clarifying the foundations of evolutionary psychology: A reply to Lloyd and Feldman. *Psychological Inquiry.*

Ellis, B.J., & Symons, D. (1990). Sex differences in sexual fantasy: An evolutionary psychological approach. *Journal of Sex Research, 27,* 527-556.

Feynman, R. & Leighton, R. V. (1988). *What Do You Care What Other People Think?* New York: W. W. Norton.

Fisher, R.A. (1958). *The Genetical Theory of Natural Selection* (2nd revised ed.). New York: Dover Press.

Frumhoff, P.C., & Baker, J. (1988). A genetic component to division of labour within honey bee colonies. *Nature, 333,* 358-361.

Galison, P. L. (1988). History, philosophy, and the central metaphor. *Science in Context, 2,* 197-212.

Gangestad, S. W. & Simpson, J. A. (2000). The evolution of human mating: Trade-offs and strategic pluralism.. *Behavioral & Brain Sciences, 23,* 573-644.

Gaulin, S. J. C. & McBurney, D. H. (2001). *Psychology: An Evolutionary Approach.* New Jersey: Prentice Hall.

Gigerenzer, G. & Murray, D. J. (1987). *Cognition as Intuitive Statistics.* Hillsdale, NJ: Lawrence Erlbaum Associates.

Goode, W. (1969). Violence among intimates. In D.J. Mulvihill & M.M. Tumin (Eds.), *Crimes of Violence. Report to the National Commission on the Causes and Prevention of Violence* (Vol. 13, pp. 941-977). Washington, D.C.: U.S. Government Printing Press.

Gould, S. J., & Lewontin, R. C. (1979). The spandrels of San Marco and the Panglossian paradigm: A critique of the adaptationist programme. *Proceedings of the Royal Society, B205,* 581-598.

Gribbin, J. (1984). *In Search of Shroedinger's Cat: Quantum Physics and Reality.* New York: Bantam Books.

Hamilton, W. D. (1964). The genetical evolution of social behavior. *Journal of Theoretical Biology, 7,* 1-52.

Hamilton, W.D. (1967). Extraordinary sex ratios. *Science, 156,* 477-488.

Hoffrage, U. & Gigerenzer, G. (1998). Using natural frequencies to improve diagnostic inferences. *Academic Medicine, 73,* 538-540.

Hooker, C.A. (1987). *A Realistic Theory of Science.* Albany, NY: SUNY Press.

Ketelaar, T. & Ellis, B. (2000) Are evolutionary explanations unfalsifiable?: Evolutionary psychology and the Lakatosian philosophy of science, *Psychological Inquiry 11,* 1-21.

Kuhn, T. S. (1962). *The Structure of Scientific Revolutions.* Chicago: University of Chicago Press.

Lakatos, I. (1970). Falsificationism and the methodology of scientific research programmes. In I. Lakatos & A. Musgrave (Eds.), *Criticism and the Growth of Knowledge* (pp. 91-196). Cambridge, Eng.: Cambridge University Press.

Lakatos, I. (1976). History of science and its rational reconstructions. In C. Howson (Ed.), *Method and appraisal in the physical sciences* (pp. 1-39). Cambridge, Eng.: Cambridge University Press.

Lakatos, I. (1978). *The Methodology of Scientific Research Programmes: Philosophical Papers, Volume 1,* J. Worral & G. Currie (Eds.). Cambridge, Eng.: Cambridge University Press.

Laland, K.N., Odling-Smee, J., & Feldman, M.W. (2000). Niche construction, biological evolution, and cultural change. *Behavioral and Brain Sciences, 23,* 131-175.

Landolt, M.A., Lalumiere, M.L., & Quinsey, V.L. (1995). Sex differences in intra-sex variations in human mating tactics: An evolutionary approach. *Ethology and Sociobiology, 16,* 3-23.

Lenski, R. E., & May R.M. (1994). The evolution of virulence in parasites and pathogens: Reconciliation between two competing hypotheses. *Journal of Theoretical Biology, 169,* 253-265.

Mayr, E. (1983). How to carry out the adaptationist program. *American Naturalist, 121,* 324-334.

Meehl, P. E. (1978). Theoretical risks and tabular asterisks: Sir Karl, Sir Ronald, and the slow progress of soft psychology. *Journal of Consulting and Clinical Psychology, 46,* 806-834.

Meehl, P. E. (1990). Appraising and amending theories: The strategy of Lakatosian defense and two principles that warrant it. *Psychological Inquiry, 1,* 108-141.

Muir, W. M. (1996). Group selection for adaptation to multiple-hen cages: Selection program and direct responses. *Poultry Science, 75,* 447-458.

Newell, A. (1973). You can't play 20 questions with nature and win: Projective comments on the papers in this symposium. In W. G. Chase (Ed.), *Visual Information Processing.* New York: Academic Press.

Newell, A. (1990). *Unified Theories of Cognition.* Cambridge, MA: Harvard University Press.

Popper, K. R. (1959). *The Logic of Scientific Discovery.* New York: Hutchinson Education.

Reichenbach, H. (1951). *The Rise of Scientific Philosophy*. Los Angeles: University of California Press.

Ridley, M. (1993). *The Red Queen: Sex and the Evolution of Human Nature*. New York: Macmillan.

Salmon, W. C. (1967). *The Foundations of Scientific Inference*. Pittsburgh: University of Pittsburgh Press.

Salmon, W. C. (1990). Rationality and objectivity in science, or Tom Kuhn meets Tom Bayes. In C. W. Savage (Ed.), *Minnesota Studies in the Philosophy of Science* (Vol. 14, pp. 175-204). Minneapolis: University of Minnesota Press.

Salmon, W. C. (1992). Epistemology of natural science. In J. Dancy & E. Sosa (Eds.), *A Companion to Epistemology* (pp. 292- 296). Oxford, Eng.: Blackwell Publishers Ltd.

Schmitt, D.P. & Buss, D.M. (1996). Strategic self-promotion and competitor derogation: Sex and context effects on the perceived effectiveness of mate attraction tactics. *Journal of Personality and Social Psychology, 70*, 1185-1204.

Smuts, B.B. (1985). *Sex and Friendship in Baboons*. New York: Aldine de Gruyter.

Sober, E., & Wilson, D.S. (1998). *Unto Others: The Evolution and Psychology of Unselfish Behavior*. Cambridge, MA: Harvard University Press.

Symons, D. (1995). Beauty is in the adaptations of the beholder: The evolutionary psychology of human female sexual attractiveness. In P. Abramson & S. Pinkerton (Eds.), *Sexual Nature/Sexual Culture* (pp. 80-118). Chicago: University of Chicago Press.

Tooby, J., & Cosmides, L. (1990). On the universality of human nature and the uniqueness of the individual: The role of genetics and adaptation. *Journal of Personality, 58*, 17-67.

Tooby, J., & Cosmides, L. (1992). The psychological foundations of culture. In J. H. Barkow, L. Cosmides, & J. Tooby (Eds.), *The Adapted Mind: Evolutionary Psychology and the Generation of Culture* (pp. 19-136). New York: Oxford University Press.

Trivers, R.L. (1971). The evolution of reciprocal altruism. *Quarterly Review of Biology, 46*, 35-57.

Trivers, R. L. (1972). Parental investment and sexual selection. In B. Campbell (Ed.), *Sexual Selection and the Descent of Man: 1871-1971* (pp. 136-179). Chicago: Aldine.

Trivers, R.L. (1985). *Social Evolution*. Melon Park, CA: Benjamin/Cummings.

Trivers, R.L., & Willard, D.E. (1973). Natural selection of parental ability to vary the sex ratio of offspring. *Science, 179*, 90-92.

van Scheik, C.P., & Hrdy, S. B. (1991). Intensity of local resource competition shapes the relationship between maternal rank and sex ratios at birth in cercopithecine primates. *Amercian Naturalist, 138*, 1555-1562.

Wiederman, M.W., & Allgeier, E.R. (1993). Gender differences in sexual jealousy: Adaptationist or social learning explanation? *Ethology and Sociobiology, 14*, 115-140.

Williams, G. C. (1966). *Adaptation and Natural Selection*. Princeton, NJ: Princeton University Press.

Williams, G.C. (1992). *Natural Selection: Domains, Levels, and Challenges*. New York: Oxford University Press.

Wilson, D.S. (1997). Incorporating group selection into the adaptationist program: A case study involving human decision making. In J.A. Simpson & D.T. Kenrick (Eds.), *Evolutionary Social Psychology* (pp. 345-386). Mahwah, NJ: Lawrence Erlbaum.

Wilson, D.S., & Sober, E. (1994). Reintroducing group selection to the human behavioral sciences. *Behavioral and Brain Sciences, 177*, 585-654.

Wilson, M., & Daly, M. (1996). Male sexual proprietariness and violence against wives. *Current Directions in Psychological Science, 5*, 2-7.

DAVID SLOAN WILSON

EVOLUTION, MORALITY AND HUMAN POTENTIAL

In the minds of many people, the theory of evolution seems to threaten the fabric of human life. After all, words such as 'bestial' refer to the very worst things that people do to each other. If we are mere beasts, what is to prevent us from behaving in a bestial fashion?

Sophisticated evolutionary biologists tend to smile at the naivete of this question. They know that the real theory of evolution can explain benign behaviors such as cooperation in addition to despicable behaviors such as rape. However, those of us who write books and teach courses on evolution and human behavior know that education is not sufficient to solve the problem. Even the newest research and theory provokes an allergic reaction, no less than Darwin's original theory.

Two major issues impede the acceptance of the theory of evolution: morality and human potential.

Morality: The conventional view of morality is founded upon the idea of common welfare. Moral rules such as the Ten Commandments and the golden rule are manifestly adaptive at the level of whole groups. In other words, societies that abide by moral rules are likely to prosper, even in the biological currency of survival and reproduction. The problem with moral conduct is its vulnerability to exploitation within groups. The word "selfish" in everyday language is often reserved for immoral behaviors. When people who think in conventional moral terms encounter the subject of evolution, they enter a strange world in which "for the good of the group" is somehow taboo and "the selfish gene" somehow accounts for everything that evolves. The collision between what they already believe and what they are being asked to accept should be obvious.

Human potential. Many people like to think that the future can be much better than the present or past. Individuals have the potential to be happier and more effective and societies can be changed to eliminate injustices. Social activism of all sorts, including religious inspiration, draws from this kind of optimism. When people who think this way encounter the subject of evolution, they often learn that human nature evolved in the stone age and remains fixed because the tortoise of genetic evolution is no match for the hare of environmental change. Even the advent of agriculture and civilization has not altered the genetic architecture of our minds. Once again, what many people believe and strongly want to believe appears to be denied by the theory of evolution they are being asked to accept.

Steven J. Scher & Frederick Rauscher (eds.). Evolutionary Psychology: Alternative Approaches, 55-70.

At this point, I imagine a cacophony of reactions among readers who are already knowledgeable about evolution and human behavior. Some will agree with my characterization and will conclude that the problem resides in our current knowledge of evolution, or at least in the way it is presented. Others will agree with my characterization but will conclude that the problem resides in those learning about evolution, who must remove their rose-colored glasses before they can see the truth. There is among evolutionary biologists a strong tradition that regards human nature as fundamentally immoral and unable to change. My favorite example is a passage from Ghiselin (1974, p. 247, quoted in Sober and Wilson, 1998, p. 5) that ends "scratch an altruist and watch a hypocrite bleed." Still others will disagree with my characterization, regarding their view of evolution to be more compatible with conventional views of morality and human potential.

These differences of opinion reveal that evolutionary biologists themselves disagree on the very same issues that trouble the newcomer to evolution. Indeed, despite very substantial gains in knowledge, the study of human behavior from an evolutionary perspective is in far greater disarray than most outsiders realize. Before we can make progress on the questions of morality and human potential, we must understand the nature of the discord among evolutionary biologists.

1.   TRIBAL SCIENCE

The human sciences are famous for fragmenting into a number of isolated disciplines with little intellectual rhyme or reason. Most anthropologists feel little need to study psychology (much less biology!) and visa versa. The major disciplines are themselves fragmented into subject areas that are isolated and in some cases downright hostile toward each other. Subject areas emerge and fade as if they are fads like the hula hoop or the miniskirt. To pick an example with which I am familiar, Machiavellianism was a popular subject in social psychology during the 1970's and 1980's. The fad began with a single research group that became interested in studying the kind of personality that Machiavelli represents (Christie and Geis, 1970), "caught on" among other labs, and then simply went out of fashion. Nowadays it is lucky to receive more than a single paragraph in social psychology textbooks. When my colleagues and I decided to study Machiavellianism from an evolutionary perspective (Wilson, Near and Miller 1996, 1998), more than one psychologist warned that we would appear as silly as wearing bell bottoms and granny glasses. They did not seem to realize that we had decided to study Machiavellianism for important theoretical reasons, rather than picking a subject out of a hat. When we started to review the literature, we discovered that it was isolated from closely related subject areas even within the field of social psychology, such as sociopathy (reviewed from an evolutionary perspective by Mealey 1995).

Of course, biology and the physical sciences are also divided into many subject areas. For practical reasons alone, research communities must focus their efforts on topics of manageable size. However, the subject areas of biology and the physical sciences are better integrated than the subject areas of the social sciences.

Biologists do feel a need to study chemistry and physics, in contrast to the anthropologist who does not feel a need to study psychology and biology. Even if individual biologists become too specialized to reach outside their narrow subject areas, the subject areas themselves are so integrated that discrepancies quickly become the focus of attention and repair. A theory of genetic recombination that violates the laws of chemistry or a theory of animal population regulation that violates the laws of evolution would die a quick death.

Part of the glamour of studying human behavior from an evolutionary perspective is the promise of this kind of integration for the human sciences. Tooby and Cosmides (1992) begin their discourse on evolutionary psychology with this theme. More recently, E.O. Wilson (1998) adopted the term *consilience* and devoted a whole book to the subject. One must always be wary of the promotional hype associated with new movements, in science as elsewhere. In this case, however, there is something genuine about the claim that the human sciences are not integrated in their current form and can become much more so in the future. Evolutionary psychologists are impelled to study anthropology, biology and other far-flung branches of knowledge because it is the only way to understand the mind as an organ (or collection of organs) of survival and reproduction that evolved in ancestral environments. Returning to the subject of Machiavellianism, social life in many species is an eternal struggle between cooperation and exploitation. Individual differences in cooperation/exploitation will always be an important subject in evolutionary social psychology and will receive as much space in textbooks 100 years from now as in the present. The emerging evolutionary literature on Machiavellianism, sociopathy, and related subjects provides a good example of how evolutionary thinking can reorganize and revitalize specific subjects with a long history of study in the human sciences (in addition to the above cited references, see Byrne and Whiten 1988, Whiten and Byrne 1997).

Given the genuine potential for integration, it is disturbing that the study of human behavior from an evolutionary perspective is in the process of fragmenting into isolated and even hostile subject areas, just like the rest of the human sciences. Of special concern is a school of thought that calls itself evolutionary psychology, which earnestly tries to achieve the kind of integration that I have outlined above. Nevertheless, despite important insights that I will acknowledge below, it has arrived at a narrow conception of human nature that is not even integrated with the facts of evolutionary biology, much less other fields of knowledge. In the process, it has alienated a large number of evolutionary biologists; not just famous critics such as Stephen Jay Gould and Richard Lewontin, but dozens of others who themselves are working to understand the psychology of humans and other species from an evolutionary perspective. As one example, a recent edited volume entitled *Evolution and Cognition* (Heyes and Ludwig, 2000) begins with the following statement (Heyes, 2000 p.3):

> When I first encountered the term 'evolutionary psychology', I thought it referred to the study of how mind and behavior have evolved. But I was mistaken. In the last decade, evolutionary psychology has come to refer exclusively to research on human mentality

and behavior, motivated by a very specific nativist-adaptationist interpretation of how
evolution operates.

It is not my purpose to hurl insults at narrow evolutionary psychology[1],
thereby contributing to the fragmentation process. I like much of the work that has
emerged from this school and I am willing to praise it in some contexts as strongly
as I criticize it in others. Nevertheless, the reason that biology and the physical
sciences are integrated is because discrepancies immediately become the focus of
attention and repair. It is in this spirit that we must examine narrow evolutionary
psychology for discrepancies with wider bodies of knowledge.

With sufficient care, it is possible to catch narrow evolutionary psychology
in the act of jettisoning large portions of evolutionary theory to reach its specific
conclusions. Consider a world-wide web article entitled "Evolutionary Psychology:
A Primer" by Cosmides and Tooby (1997). It begins (p. 2) by quoting Einstein's
comment that "it is the theory that decides what we can observe" to emphasize the
novelty of their perspective against the background of the so-called standard social
science model (SSSM). If we take Einstein's comment seriously, we might conclude
that human behavior is highly contingent upon what people believe, which in turn is
highly variable among cultures. However, this is a road not taken as far as narrow
evolutionary psychology is concerned and in fact is more typical of the SSSM that is
being rejected.

Later (p. 7), we are invited to think of the individual mind as like the
federal government, with consciousness as the president of the United States. Just as
the President makes a few executive decisions while remaining unaware of most of
the vast machinery of the federal government, the conscious mind makes a few
executive decisions while remaining unaware of most of the vast adaptive machinery
of the individual mind. If we take this metaphor seriously, we might conclude that
human society, including an enormous modern society such as the United States of
America, is organized adaptively and can even be compared to a single mind. Some
evolutionary biologists do think along these lines but it is definitely a road not taken
as far as narrow evolutionary psychology is concerned!

Further in Cosmides & Tooby's 'primer' (p. 13), we are told that two of the
most important evolutionary principles accounting for the characteristics of animals
are common descent and adaptation driven by natural selection. The former
characterizes what Cosmides & Tooby call the 'phylogenetic approach,' while the
latter characterizes the 'adaptationist approach'. Next, we are told (p. 14) that
"evolutionary psychology can be thought of as the application of adaptationist logic

---

[1] EDITOR'S NOTE: In this book, the term 'narrow evolutionary psychology' signifies the approach to
evolutionary psychology developed by Cosmides, Tooby, Buss, et al.   This terminology was
independently arrived at by the author of the present chapter and the editors. The term was chosen not
to imply that narrow evolutionary psychology takes an inappropriately narrow point of view, but merely
to suggest that the approach adopts a narrower range of assumptions than 'broad evolutionary psychology'
(or, just 'evolutionary psychology'). This latter term signifies evolutionary psychology generally,
practiced with any of a very broad range of assumptions possible within the general framework of
evolutionary approaches to psychology. For more detail on this terminology, see the editor's
introduction, p 1

to the study of the architecture of the human mind." Shockingly, and by the authors' own admission, narrow evolutionary psychology is defined to exclude one of the most important evolutionary principles accounting for the characteristics of animals!

Some adaptations evolve to fixation while others are maintained in the population as genetic polymorphisms. Surely, the science of evolutionary psychology should acknowledge the possibility of genetic polymorphisms that influence mind and behavior. Not according to Cosmides and Tooby (p. 17):

> In fact, evolutionary psychology and behavior genetics are animated by two radically different questions:
>
> 1. What is the universal, evolved architecture that we all share by virtue of being humans (evolutionary psychology).
> 2. Given a large population of people in a specific environment, to what extent can differences between these people be accounted for by differences in their genes (behavior genetics).

Once again, by the authors' own admission, a subject as evolutionary as behavior genetics is excluded from the definition of evolutionary psychology.

Human behavior is determined largely by processes of social transmission that we refer to broadly as culture. Evolutionary psychology must offer a predictive theory of culture to itself count as a comprehensive theory of human nature. Unfortunately, although Cosmides and Tooby use the word "culture" several times while describing the SSSM that they reject, they manage to describe their own framework without using the word 'culture' once. In other papers they make a distinction between "evoked culture", which is an expression of individual phenotypic plasticity, and "transmitted culture", which is actually passed from one person to another. This distinction is important because most people assume that behavioral differences among groups of people are caused by transmitted culture without considering the possibility of evoked culture. Remember that I agree with certain elements of narrow evolutionary psychology and I am happy to give credit where it is due. Even after we acknowledge the importance of evoked culture, however, we are left with the task of explaining transmitted culture from an evolutionary perspective. It is here that narrow evolutionary psychology fails deeply. Other highly qualified scientists are studying transmitted culture from an evolutionary perspective, but for narrow evolutionary psychology it is a road not taken. As one symptom of this neglect, Cosmides and Tooby (p. 19) refer to reading as a byproduct of human cognition because it is a recent cultural invention that cannot be explained as a genetically evolved adaptation. I will return to this peculiar interpretation of reading and its broader implications below.

I have both praised and criticized narrow evolutionary psychology in more detail elsewhere (Wilson 1993, 1994, 1999b). As an evolutionary biologist with a strong interest in human behavior, it is clear to me that narrow evolutionary psychology offers many insights but is in danger of interfering with the process of integration when it presents itself as the one and only theory of human nature from an evolutionary perspective. Labels are important and the term "evolutionary psychology" should be reserved for "the study of psychology from an evolutionary perspective", broadly construed, not a particular narrow school of thought. I am an evolutionary psychologist even when I disagree with Cosmides and Tooby, Buss (1999) and others at a fundamental level. This volume and others such as Heyes and Huber (2000) are performing an important service by restoring the term evolutionary psychology to its proper broad meaning.

2.   BEYOND PLATITUDES

While remaining broad, it is also important to avoid meaningless platitudes such as "every trait reflects the role of both genes and environment" A trait such as eye color is importantly different than a trait such as table manners. If we say that both reflect a gene-environment interaction, we have obscured a distinction that needs to be made elsewhere to have an explanatory theory. There is a constructive aspect to a narrow school of thought such as narrow evolutionary psychology. By making so many specific assumptions, it becomes a nimble theoretical tool for making specific predictions. The gamble of making the assumptions pays off when the predictions are confirmed but there must be a willingness to go back to the drawing board when the predictions fail. Those who object to narrow evolutionary psychology must provide theoretical tools of their own with specific predictions that are equally consistent with evolutionary theory and other branches of knowledge. With these broad considerations in mind, let us now return to the troublesome issues of morality and human potential.

3.   MORALITY

I stated earlier that moral rules such as the ten commandments are manifestly adaptive at the group level and pose a problem for evolutionary theory only because of their disadvantage relative to immoral behaviors within groups. Darwin proposed the concept of group selection as a solution to this problem. Very simply, immoral individuals may best moral individuals within groups, but moral groups best immoral groups. A process of natural selection operating at the group level allows the interpretation of morality as something that exists for the good of the group to be accepted at close to face value.

The widespread rejection of group selection in the 1960's turned morality into a paradox. Alexander (1987) claimed that folk psychology is completely wrong on the subject of morality, which must be explained without recourse to altruism and only on the basis of genetic self-interest. Williams (1996; see also Paradis and Williams 1989) declared mother nature a wicked old witch and portrayed morality as just about the only thing that cannot be explained by evolution. Dawkins' (1976) concept of memes has been used to portray moral systems such as religions as downright parasitic on their human hosts (Blackmore 1999). Narrow evolutionary psychology tends to ignore the subject of morality altogether; the word doesn't even appear in Buss's (1999) undergraduate textbook, which is also a comprehensive review of the narrow evolutionary psychology literature. Is there any reason to wonder why those who value the standard view of morality are as repelled by evolutionary theory as their counterparts in Darwin's day?

I certainly don't mean to imply that evolutionary biologists who reject the standard view of morality are bad people. To pick one example, Alexander (1987) is as passionate as any preacher about the need to solve the same range of problems that concern all moralists. Furthermore, it is possible that folk psychology is completely wrong on the subject of morality and that resisting the evolutionary truth is just a sign of intellectual weakness. However, it is also possible that Einstein's comment "it is the theory that decides what we can observe" applies to evolutionary biologists in addition to other folk. As we have seen, narrow evolutionary psychology and other narrow schools of evolutionary thought make a large number of questionable assumptions on their way to their specific conclusions. Before we reject an explanation of morality based on "the good of the group", we need to carefully check the assumptions upon which the rejection is based.

Despite earlier skepticism, multilevel selection theory has rejoined mainstream evolutionary biology. In an article describing recent developments (Dicks 2000), theoretical biologist Joel Peck stated "There is no doubt that we were way too hasty in trashing group selection. The theoretical models of the 60's and 70's were very oversimplified and should be taken with a pinch of salt." Even early critics such as John Maynard Smith (1998, Maynard Smith & Szathmary, 1995) have warmed to the possibility of group selection as a strong force in human evolution.

This newfound plausibility can be attributed in part to a new generation of theoretical models that dovetail nicely with what anthropologists know about hunter-gatherer societies. Earlier group selection models made a simplifying assumption, common to many evolutionary models, that behaviors are coded directly by genes. For example, models of altruism typically assume two alleles at a single locus that code for altruism and selfishness respectively. This assumption makes behavioral variation within and among groups directly proportional to genetic variation. The only way for a group to be behaviorally uniform is for it to be genetically uniform. If groups are composed of genetically unrelated individuals, most of the genetic (and behavioral) variation exists within groups rather than between groups. This is the reasoning that made genetic relatedness appear so essential for the evolution of altruism and made group selection appear unlikely in the case of our own species.

Genes certainly do influence behavior but the connection is usually indirect, especially in the case of our own species. In particular, human groups can be behaviorally uniform even when they are genetically diverse. In a random sample of world cultures, Sober and Wilson (1998 Ch. 5) encountered many descriptions such as the following for the Mbuti (Turnbull 1965, p 118): "Even the most insignificant and routine action in the daily life of the family is potentially a major concern to the band as a whole...It is important that there should be a pattern of behavior that is generally accepted, and which covers every conceivable activity."

This kind of behavioral uniformity within groups (and differences among groups) can be attributed, not to shared genes, but to shared social norms — another subject that receives scant attention within narrow evolutionary psychology (Wilson 1998). Before we can even begin to assess the importance of group selection in human evolution, we must abandon the simplifying assumption of strict genetic determinism and model the evolution of social norms and other factors known to influence the partitioning of behavioral variation within and among human groups. Genes still have a role to play in these models, but their effect on behavior is indirect rather than direct. Every multilevel selection model that has been built along these lines has indicated a strong role for group selection in human evolution (e.g., Boyd and Richerson 1985, Wilson and Kniffin 1999).

In the same vein, anthropologists such as Boehm (1993, 1999) and Knauft (1994) have described hunter-gatherer societies as strongly egalitarian but not in the romantic form imagined by Rousseau and others. Hunter-gatherers have roughly the same proclivity to dominate their fellows as nonhuman primate species and human members of larger societies. However, the balance of power is such that no single individual or coalition can oppose the majority. The result is a guarded egalitarianism that strongly enforces social norms agreed upon by consensus but otherwise resists the power of any individual to tell any other individual what to do. According to Boehm, human social groups have been moral communities for much of their evolutionary history, with all the behavioral prescriptions, social monitoring and punishment of deviance implied by the word moral. This time span is sufficient for genetic evolution to have shaped the psychological traits associated with moral systems, which in turn shape the more rapid process of cultural evolution that determines the specific content of social norms. It is toward this conception of gene-culture evolution that we must turn to ascertain the importance of group selection in human evolution.

This view of human evolution falls within the orbit of Darwinian theory at least as firmly as narrow evolutionary psychology and other schools of thought. Yet, true to Einstein's comment, it radically changes the way we view morality from an evolutionary perspective. The phrase "for the good of the group" is as acceptable for describing the outcome of group-level selection as the phrase "for the good of the individual" is acceptable for describing the outcome of individual-level selection. Moral systems in particular can be explained in terms of their group-level benefits, exactly as Darwin proposed. Yet, explaining morality as a product of group selection does not require us to don rose-colored glasses. The morality that evolves by group selection operates within groups and often is directed against other groups in ways that are highly immoral from a broader perspective. The mechanisms that enforce morality within groups are often highly coercive. There is room for explaining features of moral systems and even entire moral systems that are dysfunctional at the group level, since evolution always involves the production of failures in addition to successes. Any successful theory of morality must explain the complexity that is inherent in the subject. Multilevel selection theory makes a good start at explaining the complexity rather than painting a naïve portrait of universal niceness.

Earlier I said that biology and the physical sciences are integrated because discrepancies immediately become the focus of attention and repair. The yawning discrepancies among the various evolutionary theories of morality provide a poor model of integration. They cannot all be right so work is required to weed out the faulty assumptions until a more consistent picture emerges. The assumption of narrow genetic determinism (genes coding directly for behaviors) clearly requires attention. Most evolutionary biologists would not try to defend this assumption but their intuition rests upon it more than they know. The assumption that a selfish gene explanation constitutes an argument against group selection also requires attention. By now even Dawkins (1982) and Williams (1992) have acknowledged that this assumption confuses the concept of genes as replicators with the question of whether groups qualify as vehicles of selection. This confusion allows Alexander (1987) to marginalize group selection in his own mind while stressing the paramount importance of between-group competition in human evolution (see Wilson 1999a for a detailed analysis). Elsewhere (Wilson 2000) I have jestingly described the wholesale rejection of group selection as like someone who faces directly away from an object, bends over, looks between his legs, and claims to see a new object. Evolutionary biologists must clean up their own act before they can be taken seriously outside their own field on the subject of morality.

I began this essay by taking the perspective of a newcomer to evolutionary theory who feels threatened by its implications. Imagine such a person learning that individuals should be impelled to maximize their inclusive fitness, even when this involves great harm to other individuals. The "should" in this statement is not a moral injunction, of course, but merely a factual prediction. However, it is not counterbalanced by any other "shoulds" or even a discussion of why the word "should" should ever acquire a moral dimension. The result is an allergic reaction that I have observed many times in students encountering evolution for the first time. Now imagine such a student learning that behaviors can be evolutionarily successful in two ways--by increasing the fitness of individuals relative to others within their group, or by increasing the fitness of groups relative to other groups. Humans are psychologically adapted to employ both pathways with great flexibility. In addition to individual flexibility, it is also reasonable to expect important individual differences that reflect either genetic differences or developmental trajectories that are flexible early in life and later become fixed. Moral systems are biologically and culturally evolved adaptations that are designed to limit within-group selfishness and enhance the fitness of the group. Moral systems include psychological processes that are genetically evolved but they also include a strong cultural component that define the actual behaviors that count as moral or immoral in a particular time and place. Building and abiding by moral systems can be evolutionarily successful, just as subverting moral systems can be evolutionarily successful. That is why morality is a subject of such passion and ambivalence. Finally, what appears highly moral within a given social group can appear highly immoral from other perspectives. Forms of morality that transcend group boundaries remain highly problematical from an evolutionary perspective, as they are in real life.

I submit that the second account of morality from an evolutionary perspective is both closer to the truth and far less threatening to my imagined newcomer without requiring the donning of rose-colored glasses. Katz (2000) provides a useful review of the full spectrum of views on morality from an evolutionary perspective.

4.   HUMAN POTENTIAL

The Oxford English Dictionary defines "potential" as "possible, as opposed to actual." Human potential means the capacity for change, at the level of both individuals and societies. Ever since Darwin, evolutionary theory has been interpreted as a denial of human potential. After all, how is change possible when our behaviors are programmed by our genes? Despite the naivete of this question and the misconceptions upon which it often rests, simple education does not make it go away.

Evolutionary theory can explain a capacity for change in humans or any other species in two different ways. The first is phenotypic plasticity, which leads to what Cosmides and Tooby call evoked culture. If a species experiences environments A and B repeatedly throughout its evolutionary history, it may evolve the capacity to behave appropriately in either environment. This is a form of potential but one that is limited to the range of environments that existed in the distant past. There is no reason to expect individuals to behave appropriately in a truly novel environment C.

To give credit where it is due, narrow evolutionary psychology has done an excellent job of stressing the importance of this kind of human potential. My favorite example is Wilson and Daly's (1997) study of risk-taking in men, and age of first reproduction in women, in the city of Chicago. Unlike most cities, whose neighborhoods are subject to a rapid turnover of residents, Chicago neighborhoods tend to be demographically stable. They also vary greatly in their quality of life, which is reflected in life expectancies that range from the mid-fifties for the worst neighborhoods to the mid-seventies for the best neighborhoods. Daly and Wilson showed that violent risk-taking in men and age of first reproduction in women correlated very strongly with life-expectancy. Of course, both of these are perceived as social problems. Politicians talk endlessly about reducing violence and teen-age pregnancies, especially in our inner cities. However, when women from the worst neighborhoods were asked why they had children so young, they gave an answer that can only invoke sympathy: They said that they wanted their mothers to see their grand-children and in turn wanted to see their own grandchildren. They used the term "weathering" to refer to the aging process that they observed in themselves and their loved ones all around them. If everyone around you was weathering and dying at an average age of 55, wouldn't *you* want to start having children early (as a female) or take great risks to obtain the status and resources required to reproduce (as a male)?

To rephrase this question as an evolutionary hypothesis, suppose that life history traits such as age of first reproduction are phenotypically plastic. Many fish species live in lakes and streams that might or might not include predators. When predators are absent, they can expect to live a long and happy life. When predators are present, every day might be their last. Few evolutionary biologists would be surprised to discover the ability of a fish to assess the presence of predators in its environment and modify its growth and age of first reproduction accordingly. Wilson and Daly are merely advancing the same kind of hypothesis and providing the same kind of evidence for humans. They propose that low life expectancies in one's environment serve as cues to evoke risk-taking in males and early reproduction in females.

Phenotypic plasticity is a form of genetic determinism that specifies a set of if-then rules rather than a single behavior. It leads to a position that could be called evolutionary environmentalism, which, in terms of social change, is the polar opposite of the standard portrayal of genetic determinism. If a desired behavior is within the repertoire of the if-then rules, the easiest way to produce the behavior is to provide the environment that evokes the behavior (hence the term evoked culture). For example, the easiest way to solve the problem of teen-age pregnancy is to improve life-expectancy in the neighborhood. This is the kind of solution that a self-styled critic of genetic determinism might propose. In general, narrow evolutionary psychology's emphasis on the genetic determination of if-then rules should not be confused with the fixed genetic determination of single behaviors.

The second way that evolutionary theory can explain a capacity for change in humans is by processes that themselves are evolutionary. After all, evolution is all about change, making it ironic that evolutionary theory so often leads to the appearance of incapacity for change in humans. The only way to reach the conclusion that humans cannot change is by focusing exclusively on genetic evolution as a process that is hopelessly slow relative to the time scale of environmental change. Narrow evolutionary psychology is deeply committed to this position but many other possibilities are firmly within the orbit of Darwinian theory.

In the first place, genetic evolution is not always a slow process. Selection pressures are often so great and phenotypic variation is often sufficiently heritable to produce significant genetic change in a single generation and certainly in ten generations. The discovery that natural selection is a process strong enough to directly observe is one of the most important developments in modern evolutionary biology, as eloquently described by Weiner (1994) in his Pulitzer prize-winning book *The Beak of the Finch*.

Human populations are not exempt from strong selective pressures and most human traits appear to have a strong heritable component. The concept of gene-culture coevolution, in which a cultural invention such as the spear selects for genetic traits such as limb proportions and musculature best adapted for throwing spears, has a long history of study (Brues 1959). Some of the hypotheses are speculative but others have been documented in impressive detail, such as lactose tolerance as a genetic adaptation to milk as an adult resource (reviewed by Durham

1991). Proponents of narrow evolutionary psychology such as Cosmides and Tooby engage in elaborate verbal stage-setting to minimize the possibility and importance of rapid genetic evolution in humans (see Wilson 1994 for a detailed analysis), as the exclusion of behavior genetics from their definition of evolutionary psychology attests.

More importantly, there is more to evolution than genetic evolution. Any process that includes blind variation and selective retention counts as evolutionary, as the late social psychologist and evolutionary epistemologist Donald Campbell (1960, 1974, 1994) never tired of pointing out. Learning, development, culture, and even important aspects of brain development may all qualify as rapid evolutionary processes, capable of adapting to modern environments that were never encountered in our ancestral past. Nevertheless, all of these open-ended processes are marginalized within narrow evolutionary psychology along with rapid genetic evolution. Learning, like culture, is discussed far more in the negative account of the SSSM than the positive account of narrow evolutionary psychology. The brain is envisioned as a collection of pre-evolved modules adapted to solve the most important problems encountered in ancestral environments, which excludes the possibility of open-ended neurobiological process (Deacon 1998). Development is envisioned as the mere switching on or off of innate modules during various points in the life cycle. And culture, as we have already seen, is reduced to an expression of individual phenotypic plasticity. Narrow evolutionary psychology marginalizes all open-ended evolutionary processes, making adaptation to ancestral environments (however flexible) the only game in town. Just as Einstein said, it is truly the theory that decides what can be observed.

Once again, narrow evolutionary psychology can be roundly criticized for some of its assumptions without being rejected altogether. It is the middle ground that we are trying to achieve, not one set of provincial assumptions over another. The concept of modularity that is the hallmark of narrow evolutionary psychology has much to recommend it. Some basic features of human psychology are universally shared and can be regarded as fixed for all intents and purposes. However, we can acknowledge and make use of these insights without agreeing with the long chain of inferences that cause proponents of narrow evolutionary psychology to reach their specific conclusions. The immune system provides a good example of how innateness and modularity can facilitate rather than prevent an open-ended evolutionary process. If our immune systems can adapt our bodies to truly novel disease environments, then why can't similar systems adapt our minds and societies to truly novel environments?

The concept of moral systems outlined above provides an especially plausible scenario for cultural evolution as an open-ended evolutionary process. The psychological mechanisms that establish and enforce social norms may include genetically innate components but the specific contents of the norms are free to vary. Groups that are genetically identical nevertheless can differ dramatically in the behaviors that are actually practiced and transmitted from one person to another. Evolution is about heritable phenotypic variation, not about genes. Even heritability is defined as a phenotypic correlation between parents and offspring, which may or may not involve genetic variation as a mechanism. Social norms established and maintained by moral systems provide ample phenotypic variation and heritability for rapid evolution to take place during the course of human history, adapting human groups to their current environments.

The work of Richard Nisbett and his collaborators provides a good example of how cultural evolution can be integrated with the valid components of narrow evolutionary psychology. During much of his career Nisbett was a distinguished social psychologist who did not attempt to incorporate evolution into his framework (e.g., Nisbett and Ross 1980). Later, an interest in cultural differences in violence between regions of the United States (Nisbett and Cohen 1996) brought him into contact with evolutionary psychology, especially the work of Daly and Wilson (1988). Nevertheless, his evolutionary perspective has not prevented him from also appreciating cultural differences so fundamental that western psychologists are in danger of mistaking culturally specific aspects of their mentality for universal human nature (Fiske et al. 1998; Nisbett et al., 2001).

Group size provides one example of a culturally evolved adaptation that falls far outside the range of responses to the ancestral environment. There is little doubt that we are psychologically adapted as a species to interact in small face-to-face groups of no more than a few hundred individuals (Dunbar 1996). Despite this genetic constraint, functionally organized human groups have become larger and larger over the course of human history. Group size almost certainly is adaptive in between-group competition, as long as larger groups have the internal organization to act in a coordinated fashion. However, getting large numbers of people to do the right thing at the right time and preventing them from undermining the group for their own gain is no easy task. The devices that have evolved to accomplish this task are cultural in nature (Wilson 2002). They use elements of our ancestrally evolved innate psychology as building blocks, which are used to build new adaptive structures that solve problems that never existed in the ancestral past. This has always been the way of evolution, which Jacob (1977) aptly described as a tinkerer that builds new structures out of old parts.

Reading provides another example of a cultural innovation that has changed the course of human evolution. Prior to the written word, virtually all of the information in a culture had to be contained within human heads (although there is an interesting sense in which other cultural artifacts can be regarded as externally stored information; Donald 1991; Hutchins 1995). Much of human thought may have been structured around this constraint. The advent of writing may have initiated a cognitive revolution by relaxing the memory constraint, freeing the mind to engage in other kinds of cognitive tasks. People and societies did not need to evolve genetically to capitalize on this cultural innovation. Given the open-ended nature of brain development, it may even have resulted in neurobiological changes. According to Ong (1982), the written word has changed the way we think so profoundly that people from preliterate cultures strike us as mentally retarded. Just as the printing press changed the course of human history by making printed information widely available, computers and the internet are ushering a new revolution. When the words "history" and "revolution" are understood in more detail, "evolution" will prove to be the better word. For Cosmides and Tooby to call reading a byproduct because it does not represent a genetically evolved adaptation merely reveals how much can be rendered invisible by a narrow school of thought.

5.   CONCLUSION

I began this essay by taking the perspective of a newcomer to evolution who feels threatened by its implications for morality and human potential. Evolutionary biologists must do more than smile indulgently at such a response and regard themselves as superior for being able to grasp uncomfortable truths. A theory that cannot provide a coherent account of human morality and the potential of individuals and societies to adapt to their current environments has only itself to blame for widespread skepticism and rejection. In addition, evolutionary biologists are failing at their own goal of extending the kind of integration that marks the physical and biological sciences to the human sciences. The study of humans from an evolutionary perspective must become internally integrated before it can provide a model for the rest of the human sciences.

Binghamton University

6. REFERENCES

Alexander, R. D. (1987). *The Biology of Moral Systems.* New York: Aldine de Gruyter.

Blackmore, S. (1999). *The Meme Machine.* Oxford,UK: Oxford University Press.

Boehm, C. (1993). Egalitarian society and reverse dominance hierarchy. *Current Anthropology, 34,* 227-254.

Boehm, C. (1999). *Hierarchy in the Forest.* Cambridge, MA: Harvard University Press.

Boyd, R., & Richerson, P. J. (1985). *Culture and the Evolutionary Process.* Chicago: University of Chicago Press.

Brues, A.M. (1959). The spearman and the archer. *American Anthropologist, 61,* 458-469.

Buss, D. M. (1999). *Evolutionary Psychology.* Boston: Allyn and Bacon.

Byrne, R. W., & Whiten, A. (Ed.). (1988). *Machiavellian Intelligence: The Evolution of Intellect in Monkeys Apes and Humans.* Oxford, Eng.: Claredon Press.

Campbell, D. T. (1974). Evolutionary epistemology. In P. A. Schilpp (Eds.), *The Philosophy of Karl Popper* (pp. 413-63). LaSalle, ILL: Open court publishing.

Campbell, D. T. (1994). How individual and face-to-face-group selection undermine firm selection in organizational evolution. In J. A. C. Baum & J. V. Singh (Eds.), *Evolutionary Dynamics of Organizations* (pp. 23-38). New York: Oxford University Press.

Campbell, T. D. (1960). Blind variation and selective retention in creative thought and other knowledge processes. *Psychological Review, 67,* 380-400.

Christie, R., & Geis, F. (Ed.). (1970a). *Studies in Machiavellianism.* New York: Academic Press.

Cosmides, L., & J., T. (1997). *Evolutionary psychology: A primer.* [Online] Available at: *http://www.psych.ucsb.edu/research/cep/primer.html.*

Dawkins, R. (1976). *The Selfish Gene* (1st ed.). Oxford, Eng.: Oxford University Press.

Dawkins, R. (1982). *The Extended Phenotype.* Oxford, Eng.: Oxford University Press.

Daly, M. & Wilson, M. (1988). *Homicide.* New York: Aldine de Gruyter.

Deacon, T. W. (1998). *The Symbolic Species.* New York: Norton.

Dicks, L. (2000, July 8). All for one! *New Scientist,* 30-35.

Donald, M. (1991). *Origins of the Modern Mind:Tthree Stages in the Evolution of Culture and Cognition.* Cambridge, MA: Harvard University Press.

Dunbar, R. I. M. (1996). *Grooming, Gossip and the Evolution of Language.* Cambridge, Mass: Harvard University Press.

Durham, W. H. (1991). *Coevolution: Genes, Culture and Human Diversity.* Stanford, CA: Stanford University Press.

Fiske, A. P., Kitayama, S., Markus, H. R., & Nisbett, R. E. (1998). The cultural matrix of social psychology. In D. T. Gilbert,S. T. Fiske, & G. Linzey (Eds.), *Handbook of social psychology* (pp. 915-981). Boston: McGraw-Hill.

Ghiselin, M. T. (1974). *The economy of nature and the evolution of sex.* Berkeley: University of California Press.

Heyes, C. (2000). Evolutionary psychology in the round. In C. Heyes & L. Huber (Eds.), *The Evolution of Cognition* (pp. 3-22). Cambridge, MA: MIT Press.

Heyes, C., & Huber, L. (Ed.). (2000). *The Evolution of Cognition.* Cambridge, MA: MIT Press.

Hutchins, E. (1995). *Cognition in the Wild.* Cambridge, Mass: MIT press.

Jacob, F. (1977). Evolution and tinkering. *Science, 196,* 1161-1166.

Katz, L. D. (Ed.). (2000). *Evolutionary Origins of Morality: Cross-disciplinary Perspectives.* New York: Academic Imprint.

Knauft, B. M. (1994). Culture and cooperation in human evolution. In L. E. Sponsel & T. Gregor (Eds.), *The Anthropology of Peace and Nonviolence* (pp. 37-67). Boulder, CO: Lynne Rienner.

Maynard Smith, J. (1998). The origin of altruism. *Nature, 393,* 639-640.

Maynard Smith, J., & Szathmary, E. (1995). *The Major Transitions of Life.* New York: W.H. Freeman.

Mealey, L. (1995). The sociobiology of sociopathy. *Behavioral and Brain Sciences, 18,* 523-599.

Nisbett, R., & Ross, L. (1980). *Human Inference: Strategies and Shortcomings of Social Judgement.* Englewood Cliffs, N.J.: Prentiss Hall.

Nisbett, R. E., & Cohen, D. (1996). *Culture of Honor*. New York: Westview Press.

Nisbett, R. E.,Peng, K.,Choi, I., & Norenzayan, A. (2001). Culture and systems of thought: Holistic vs. analytic cognition. *Psychological Review, 108*, 291-310.

Ong, W. J. (1982). *Orality and Literacy*. New York: Routledge.

Paradis, J., & Williams, G. C. (Ed.). (1989). *Evolution and Ethics*. Princeton, NJ: Princeton University Press.

Sober, E., & Wilson, D. S. (1998). *Unto Others: The Evolution and Psychology of Unselfish Behavior*. Cambridge, Mass.: Harvard University Press.

Tooby, J., & Cosmides, L. (1992). The psychological foundations of culture. In J. H. Barkow,L. Cosmides, & J. Tooby (Eds.), *The Adapted Mind:Evolutionary Psychology and the Generation of Culture* (pp. 19-136). Oxford, Eng.: Oxford University Press.

Turnbull, C. M. (1965). *The Mbuti Pygmies: An Ethnographic Survey*. New York: American Museum of Natural History.

Weiner, J. (1994). *The Beak of the Finch: A Story of Evolution in our Time*. New York: Knopf.

Whiten, A., & Byrne, R. W. (Ed.). (1997). *Machiavellian Intelligence II: Evaluations and Extensions*. Cambridge, Eng.: Cambridge University Press.

Williams, G. C. (1992). *Natural Selection: Domains, Levels and Challenges*. Oxford, Eng.: Oxford University Press.

Williams, G. C. (1996). *Plan and Purpose in Nature*. London: Weidenfeld and Nicolson.

Wilson, D. S. (1993). Review of *The Adapted Mind* (J.H. Barkow, L. Cosmides, and J. Tooby, eds., Oxford University Press). *Quarterly Review of Biology, 68*, 621-623.

Wilson, D. S. (1994). Adaptive genetic variation and human evolutionary psychology. *Ethology and Sociobiology, 15*, 219-235.

Wilson, D. S. (1998). Evolutionary game theory and human behavior. In L. A. Dugatkin & H. K. Reeve (Eds.), *GameTheory and Animal Behavior* (pp. 261-282). Oxford, Eng.: Oxford University Press.

Wilson, D. S. (1999a). A critique of R.D. Alexander's views on group selection. *Biology and Philosophy, 14*, 431-449.

Wilson, D. S. (1999b). Tasty slice--but where is the rest of the pie? (review of *Evolutionary Psychology*, by David Buss). *Evolution and Human Behavior, 20*, 279-289.

Wilson, D. S. (2000). Nonzero and nonsense: Group Selection, nonzerosumness, and the human Gaia hypothesis. *Skeptic, 8*, 84-89.

Wilson, D.S. (2002). *Darwin's Cathedral: Evolution, Religion, and the Nature of Society*.   Chicago: University of Chicago Press.

Wilson, D. S., & Kniffin, K. M. (1999). Multilevel selection and the social transmission of behavior. *Human Nature, 10*, 291-310.

Wilson, D. S., Near, D., & Miller, R. R. (1996). Machiavellianism: A Synthesis of the Evolutionary and Psychological Literatures. *Psychological Bulletin, 199*, 285-299.

Wilson, D. S.,Near, D. C., & Miller, R. R. (1998). Individual differences in Machiavellianism as a mix of cooperative and exploitative strategies. *Evolution and Human Behavior, 19*, 203-212.

Wilson, E. O. (1998). *Consilience*. New York: Knopf.

Wilson, M., & Daly, M. (1997). Life expectancy, economic inequality, homicide, and reproductive timing in Chicago neighborhoods. *British Medical Journal, 314*, 1271-1274.

LINNDA CAPORAEL

REPEATED ASSEMBLY

Prospects for Saying What We Mean

While there is certainly no scientific debate left on whether or not humans evolved, there is still considerable heat over how to make use of that fact. Technically, evolution is defined as changes in population gene frequencies. To the theoretical population biologists who promote this definition, the primary factors of interest are genes and their transmission generation-to-generation. A certain amount of lip service is given to the environment and to development, but these nods to propriety are quickly forgotten. Phenotypic development and interaction with the environment are treated as secondary (Brandon & Antonovics, 1996; Endler, 1986). Yet in the human sciences, development and interaction is all that we can really observe. Proponents of the "gene's-eye" view of evolution anthropomorphize "the gene" and ask how selfish genes made their organisms behave so as to maximize their genetic success (Dawkins, 1976). The phenotype, or observable characteristics of the organism, is assumed to simply mirror the genotype (Grafen, 1984). These strategies work well enough with fruit flies and flour beetles, but the apparent reduction to lower levels of analysis creates major obstacles for evolutionary perspectives on human behavior. The selfish gene is a heuristic device that substitutes a fiction for the complexities of interaction with environment; genes are imbued with the very characteristics that psychologists try to explain.

A vocabulary originating in selfish genes is so limited that even many biologists object (e.g., Eldredge & Grene, 1992). It requires us to make claims and assumptions about genetic causes that cannot be empirically supported, and it makes tacit presuppositions that are difficult to resist. The main goal of this paper is to sketch an alternative vocabulary based on the notion of *recurrence*, which is, after all, one of the primary observations that drives us to seek out evolutionary explanations. While any vocabulary of recurrence is more complex than one of simple cause and effect, the complexity is worthwhile if it helps us to say what we mean and mean what we say.

1. SAYING WHAT WE DON'T MEAN

In order to use the gene's eye view of evolution in any scientifically respectable way, we would have to shoulder certain "burdens of proof" from biology (Lloyd, 1999).

Steven J. Scher & Frederick Rauscher (eds.). Evolutionary Psychology: Alternative Approaches, 71-89.

First, we would have to begin with a well-defined biological trait. In evolutionary biology, a trait such as altruism can be well defined by fiat: altruism is genetic or reproductive self-sacrifice. In psychology, altruism may be operationalized for the purpose of an experiment, as for example "picking up dropped papers" or "willingness to donate kidney" but these are hardly well defined biological traits. Second, we would have to eliminate alternative explanations for the trait. In biology, competing explanations for natural selection include developmental constraints, phenotypic constraints, and random genetic drift. For humans, we would have to add culture to the list of alternatives. Finally, we would have to demonstrate that variations in the phenotypic trait are correlated with variations in reproductive or genetic fitness. For example, to support the claim that a male preference for young and attractive females is a genetically based result of evolution by natural selection, we would have to show that such picky males outreproduced males willing to take any possible copulatory opportunity in the small hunter-gather groups of the evolutionary past.

Proponents of narrow evolutionary psychology[1] have tried to finesse such problems by appealing to complexity of design as evidence of genetic adaptation to the Plio-Pleistocene environment. But we are no better off with this approach. Determining genetic fitness of alternative designs in the past is no easier than determining fitness in the present. Moreover, there are no standard criteria for evaluating complexity in organic design: it's a matter of taste and intuition. For example, as Pacific salmon journey upstream to spawn, their internal organs are absorbed during egg development and the salmon dies after egg laying. Arguably, this is a suboptimal, inefficient and jerrybuilt design—why not survive to reproduce again? The example implies another shortcoming of the argument by design: what rules should we use for imagining possible relevant alternatives that went extinct without a trace or never evolved? As if the empirical deficiencies were not enough, the vocabulary of selfish genes presents insurmountable difficulties for achieving a rapprochement between evolutionary theory and human social, cognitive and behavioral studies. Imbued as "genes for" various dispositions such as altruism, dominance, mate preferences or parenting behavior, "genes-for" might become interesting (especially in popular culture), but they are also harmful fictions, suggesting that the understanding of a phenomena is complete once it can be attributed to genes. An evolutionary discourse couched in the language of "selfish genes" requires that social scientists make claims about genes that are unprovable, and too often just plain mystical.

The evolutionist John Maynard Smith (1987) complained that he sometimes found it difficult to determine when evolutionary theory was being used as myth or science. There is a surreal correspondence between the terminology of

---

[1] EDITOR'S NOTE: In this book, the term 'narrow evolutionary psychology' signifies the approach to evolutionary psychology developed by Cosmides, Tooby, Buss, et al. This term was chosen not to imply that this approach has an inappropriately narrow point of view, but merely to suggest that the approach adopts a narrower range of assumptions than 'broad evolutionary psychology' (or, just 'evolutionary psychology'). This latter term signifies evolutionary psychology generally, practiced with any of a very broad range of assumptions possible within the general framework of evolutionary approaches to psychology. For more detail on this terminology, see the editor's introduction, p 1

evolutionary psychology and Christianity (Table 1). The language of immortal genes, like the language of immortal souls, suggests that there is an essence of the person, more enduring and therefore more worthy of attention than mere mortal flesh. The phenotype, or vehicle of the genes — like the vessel of the soul — is fleeting and transitory. In some instances, the parallels are clearly recognized by biologists. Dawkins' (1987) description of natural selection as a "blind watchmaker" is a deliberate correspondence to the "divine watchmaker" of 19th century natural theology. Incredibly, some biologists (e. g., Dawkins, 1976; Williams, 1989) have urged people to rebel against their genes, much as pastors urge their flocks to resist temptation. When the very notion of "rebelling against your genes" was declared nonsensical, George C. Williams (1989) defended it, arguing that cosmetic technologies proved that people could "correct perceived flaws in development controlled by their own genotypes" (p. 214). In the same way, people could see the moral flaws caused by their selfish genes and similarly correct their behavior.

The real problem with gene-talk is that it imposes tacit and a priori conceptual relationships on evolutionary theorizing, forcing evolutionary ideas into pre-existing molds (Caporael, 1994). The current vocabulary of evolution compels us to make ontological commitments that we may not want to make. These include a thoroughgoing dualism between nature and nurture, biology and culture, and body and mind. The idea of a resident homunculus that struggles with a wayward body recreates, rather than questions, the basic ontology of mind-body dualism. Similarly, losing the Garden of Eden (or natural environment; Symons, 1992) implies the current human condition deviates from a more desirable condition in the mythic past. An interesting problem is why such correspondences exist. Rather than rejecting evolution in the study of human behavior or dismissing the evolution-religion correspondence as ideology or as motivated by religious impulse (Nelkin, 2001), the discourse of narrow evolutionary psychology should be taken as data that can reveal something about the nature of recurrence in the history of ideas. But these speculations will have to be pursued after the main topics.

2. FINDING A TOEHOLD: MULTI-LEVEL EVOLUTIONARY THEORY

Despite the shortcomings of the gene's eye view, narrow-school evolutionary psychologists insist that inclusive fitness theory is *the* modern theory of evolution, and that the only alternatives are seeding from outer space or creationism (Buss, 1995). The section above suggests that there is already a bit too much creationism in the gene's-eye view of evolution and we should be searching for some alternative approaches. The major scientific difficulty, however, is that the gene construct of theoretical population biologists is at a level of analysis different from, and inappropriate for, evolutionary psychology. Most psychologists are not particularly interested in gene frequency turnover in a population. Equally problematic is the reification of abstractions (e.g., altruism, mate preference) as entities evolved by natural selection rather than focusing on concrete, situated behaviors. There is a great deal of difference between altruism as risking life and limb to save another and

Table 1 Parallels Between Biological and Religious Discourse

Biology	Theology
Immortal Genes	Immortal Soul
Phenotypic Vehicle of the Genes	Bodily Vessel of the Soul
Selfish Genes	Original Sin
Man has Lost his Natural Environment	Expulsion from the Garden of Eden
Genes in Future Generations VS. Loss from the Gene Pool	Salvation VS. Damnation
Self-interest → Future Success (Representation in the Gene Pool)	Charitable Acts → Future Success (A Place in Heaven)
Optimization of Design	Perfection of Design
Central Dogma	Dogma
Blind Watchmaker	Divine Watchmaker
Natural Selection	God

altruism as donating spare change. The problem, then, is finding a toehold for an evolutionary vocabulary that does not compel us to cut nature at the same joints as creationism and popular culture; that is at an appropriate level of analysis, and yet is consistent with evolutionary theory. I suspect the interests of most evolutionarily inclined psychologists, are much closer to Darwin's original idea of descent with modification, regardless of the source of heritability, and of fit, meaning the relational properties between the organism and environment (Caporael & Baron, 1997), that makes behavior look adapted.

Fortunately, modern evolutionary theory has expanded beyond the "gene's eye view." Multilevel evolutionary theory acknowledges that the history of life requires multiple levels of analysis that are not reducible to genetic action. Evolutionary processes operate on entities at levels of hierarchical organization— macromolecules, genes, cells, organisms and even sometimes groups of individuals (see Figure 1). These levels represent major transitions in the evolution of life on earth. They are also represented in the bodies of multicellular organisms (Buss, 1987; Maynard Smith & Szathmáry, 1995), and serve as rough guides to levels of analysis. The significance of genes to an explanation depends on levels of analysis and empirical evidence that genes are the difference that makes a difference (Oyama, 1985) in phenotypic variation.

Hierarchically organized entities are concretely situated in specific contexts. The situated environment for genes is the cellular machinery with which DNA and its products interact. The situated environment for humans is the face-to-face group, through which they are able to interact with the habitat. The reason for stressing "situatedness" in a context is that selection results from *relations* between entity and environment (Endler, 1986). Partially, biologists emphasize relations to move away from the insinuation that organisms are passive pieces of clay molded by natural selection. The idea that natural selection "acts on" or "favors" traits hides the very conditions of entity-environment relations that result in natural selection.

Of the many insights from multilevel evolutionary theory, two seem especially relevant for evolutionary psychology. First, "gene-environment" interaction—when "the environment" is taken to mean "everything outside the body"— makes no sense. Again, the environment for the gene is the cell, with its multiple interacting influences, its response and "editing" of incoming products (e.g., hormones), and its complex machinery. The continued replication of genes and other lower level units depends on the balance of conflicts and synergisms at all levels. Second, genes are insufficient for evolutionary explanation. Phenotypes emerge from constructive interactions among multiple recurrent resources, including genes, cellular machinery, social resources, the reliable presence of critical features of the habitat, and the ongoing results of previous development. Whether or not successful genetic transmission occurs depends on phenotypic outcomes.

The repeated assembly of these constructive interactions over generations provides us with what we need: a vocabulary for evolutionary discourse suitable to our level of analysis and our interests. For lack of a better term, let me refer to this vocabulary simply as "repeated assembly." Repeated assembly points to recurrences that we can observe — recurrences from generation to generation as well as

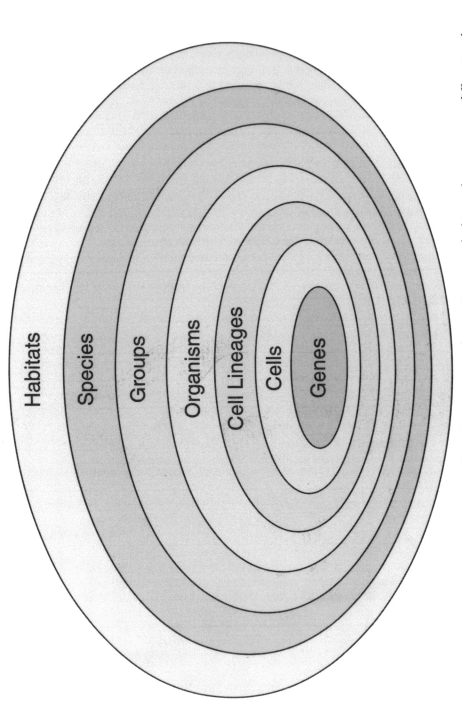

Figure 1. A model of biological hierarchy in multilevel evolutionary theory. Entities in the hierarchy persist over different scales of time and are relationally situated in the specific contexts of higher levels.

recurrence across cultures. Not only do organisms repeatedly assemble, but so also do the products of organisms, including human ideas, artifacts and cultural practices. Repeated assembly enables us to escape the dichotomy of biology and culture, nature and nurture, genes and environment; it does not require us to make commitments about genes in the absence of hard evidence; and it is consistent with the Darwinian model of selection, variation and retention.

3.   REPEATED ASSEMBLY

If the last paragraph celebrated the good news about repeated assembly, this one confesses the bad: a difficult definition. Repeated assemblies are (a) recurrent, (b) entity-environment relations composed of (c) hierarchically organized (d) heterogenous components having (e) different temporal frequencies and scales of replication.

The elements in the definition of repeated assembly have been previously mentioned. *Recurrence* is fairly obvious, although we are most interested in a particular kind of recurrence, that which is recursive, where the seeds of the next cycle are part of a current cycle. *Entity-environment relations* are, at the psychological level, organism-environment relations, where the environment may be features of the physical habitat or configurations of conspecific groupings. *Hierarchical organization* (actually, heterarchical because causal effects may be downward and upward) is built into the evolving, jury-rigged structure of living organisms. *Heterogeneous components* refer to the multiple resources that compose a repeated assembly, although which resources are the objects of research depends on the focus and perspective of the research question.   Components can be heterogeneous partly because they recur over *different time scales*. DNA recurs over macro-evolutionary time; at the other extreme, social rituals can rise and fall within a lifetime (affecting phenotype, but having no systematic selective effects).

Let me put these ideas together in the example of a zygote. A zygote is composed of multiple resources. There are two sources of DNA from the gametes, centrosomes from the sperm, maternal information in the egg cell, and an appropriate setting in the body. If all these resources are in the right place at the right time, a zygote automatically results. There is no genetic program; in fact, the genes are inactive during the first few cell divisions of the fertilized egg. The difference that makes a difference for the differentiation of structure and specialization of tissue is time and space—recall, all DNA in cells are the same. Cells in the zygote adhere to each other, lose adhesion, and migrate to different regions. The cellular activity influences genetic activity, which in turn affects cellular activity.

The zygote is a repeated assembly, and like other repeated assemblies, it is inherently interactionist. It emerges from the constructive interaction of genes, temporal and spatial relations, and the changing cellular machinery. Its continued development and existence depends on the reliable recurrence of appropriate contexts—from cellular machinery to social events to regularities in the habitat to persistent resources such as gravity and atmosphere (Griffiths & Gray, 1994). Genes are always part of the repeated assembly of an organism, but so also (in the human case) are group memberships, customs, artifacts, learned skills, languages and world-views. These resources may vary wildly in their specifics, but are nevertheless critical to human survival and reproduction.

4.   WHAT EVOLVES?

Technically (that is, in the view of theoretical evolutionary biologists), populations evolve; a change in gene frequency marks the evolution of a population (by natural selection or other means, such as genetic drift). But when most people ask, "what evolves?" they want to know what traits are ("genetically-based") species-typical adaptations. There are many lists of the traits of human nature (e.g., Brown, 1991; Wilson, 1978) that come from sociobiological and evolutionary psychological introspection, but they suffer from two difficulties. First, many such traits seem uncomfortably close to folk psychology glossed with evolution. Mate preferences, parental investment and reciprocal altruism are more likely constructed from the observations of everyday life than from genes attempting to launch copies of themselves into the next generation. Second, claims about genetic causes tend to forestall further investigation. The "evidence" for the purportedly adaptive trait seems to be all around us—people marry, care for children (or not), and help their neighbors. Once the causes are believed to be genetic, there does not seem to be much left to investigate.

A different response to "what evolves?" comes from developmental systems theorists (Griffiths & Gray, 1994; Oyama, Griffiths, & Gray, 2000). They argue that the life cycle is what replicates in evolution. A life cycle, or developmental system, "is a series of events which initiates new cycles of itself" (Griffiths & Gray, 1994 , p. 291).   Rather than being the result of genetic blueprints or developmental programs, a developmental system is like ecological succession. A bare area of land will be colonized by grasses. These affect the properties of the soil and are succeeded by shrubs, which are then succeeded by trees. There is no central organizer parallel to the genotype for reforesting bare land. Yet given the reliable resources characteristic of the local area, the outcome --reforestation -- occurs. An important feature of the developmental systems view is the extension of heredity to include all the reliably recurrent resources of a developmental process. Another feature is dissolving the boundary between biology and culture by recognizing culture as evolved resources that interact with development. (An illustration of both points will be given later using language as an example.) Recurrent features of culture are critical for the development of species-typical psychological traits (Fiske, 2000).

Yet another answer to the question of "what evolves?" comes from Hendriks-Jansen (1996). He argues that low-level activity patterns evolve. These activity patterns emerge through interaction with the world. Activity patterns are layered, meaning that at the lowest level we would expect to find reliably associated stimulus-action feedback loops. These enable adaptive activity within specific environmental constraints. For example, walking behavior is a quintessential species-typical behavior often assumed to be under genetic control. Yet, although walking is described at a gross level as having distinct stages, every parent observes that early infant walking involves a lot of flailing around. This is not just noise in the system. Scientific examination shows that walking emerges through the interaction of low level reflexes such as a response to backward foot extension (as when the infant is held on the experimenter's treadmill or "walked" by a parent), alternating patterns of leg swing and other resources including gravity and the infant's own body weight (Thelen & Smith, 1994). The components for walking develop at different rates and depend on context. They repeatedly assemble in evolutionary time, in ontogeny, and in the day-to-day activity of walking, which requires constant adjustment to terrain, the walker's own physical condition, or even the use of artifacts for walking such as canes or crutches.

"The world" in Hendriks-Jansen's (1996) usage is not our ordinary description of the environment, although we may use such descriptions because they are meaningful to us. Rather, it is the ongoing world that emerges through the activity of the organism and its sensory systems. Species-typical activity patterns emerge (a) through an evolutionary history of selection, (b) through developmental processes, and (c) through the execution of low-level activities in interaction with a species-typical environment.

The vocabulary of repeated assembly draws heavily on work on situated activity patterns (Hendriks-Jansen, 1996; Lave, 1988) and on developmental systems theory, but generalizes these approaches to more easily include groups and artifacts (Caporael, 1995; Caporael, 1997b). The unit of analysis is a pattern. In its most conventional sense, that could be the life cycle of the organism in its setting. However, as in the example of ecological successions, organisms can also be "dissolved" into other repeating patterns such as groups (Caporael, 2001b) or the "extended phenotype" (Dawkins, 1982). For example, there is no sense in which a preference for Elvis Presley music, like a specific scar, is a resource in the repeated assembly (developmental system) of humans (Sterelny, Smith, & Dickison, 1996). However, humans are crucial resources for the repeated assembly of Elvis music around the world and through generations. As the example of Elvis music suggests, questions about the ontology of repeated assemblies are independent from identifying them as units of analysis (which is why repeated assembly is a descriptive vocabulary and not a theory). How we carve a repeated assembly from the energy flows surrounding us depends on the perceptual and intellectual tools we have and on the research questions we address.

5.   DARWINIAN CRITERIA

Snowflakes repeatedly assemble, are marvelously designed, have recurrent components (their shape) and presumably have infinite variation. Yet, there is no selection among snowflakes, and one cannot give rise to another. Repeated assembly is consistent with evolutionary theory when it has the potential for selection, variation and retention — the basic properties for Darwinian evolution. Repeated assemblies are not limited to organisms. Cultural products are also repeatedly assembled and frequently show signs of evolutionary dynamics such as path dependencies, early radiation of new forms, and selection processes that are closer to "natural" than "artificial." The role of individual intentionality in the final form an artifact takes is greatly exaggerated (Bijker, 1995; Bucciarelli, 1994). Bijker's (1995) description of the development of the bicycle fits a Darwinian model nicely, with various beliefs about users, gender and the functions of the artifact being critical elements of the selection environment. The following sections concern selection, variation, and retention of repeated assemblies, whether natural or artifactual. I will begin with selection and then turn to variation and retention.

5.1.   Selection

Psychologists pursuing narrow evolutionary psychology make a pan-adaptationist assumption: all traits are adaptations, evolved by natural selection (Barkow, 1989). Evidence of adaptation is assumed to be given in the complexity and optimality of design (Dennett, 1995; Tooby & Cosmides, 1992). However, although some traits of organisms do inspire marvel for their optimality of design (and were used as evidence for God's handiwork by 19th century natural theologians), evolutionary theory is ultimately a theory about the history of use, not design. Ruth Millikan (1984) has developed the most detailed analysis of function based on a history of use in reliably recurrent environments.

Some repeated assemblies have specialized functions. They repeatedly assemble because in the past, some components, in some specific relation to their contexts, contributed to the replication of the assembly (cf., Millikan, 1984). Specialized functions describe what an assembly is "supposed to do" under historically ideal conditions. Millikan (1984) uses the example of a screwdriver. The device is supposed to screw and unscrew screws, although it can be used to pry open paint cans or poke holes in leather. While these other uses can be quite handy, they do not explain why screwdrivers continue to be replicated. Screwdrivers are repeatedly assembled because of their specialized function — use with screws.

Carrying through a function may actually be infrequent. For example, a function of sperm is to fertilize an egg cell. However, ova are rare in the world of sperm, and the vast majority of them fail to fertilize. Nevertheless, it is because some ancestor sperm did find and fertilize ova that sperm are repeatedly assembled. As Millikan (1984) points out, historically ideal conditions are not necessarily statistically average or modal conditions; the function of acorns is to produce oak trees, but most acorns produce humus.

Specialized functions may be quite awkward, inefficient and clumsy, far from optimal design. They reflect the meandering path dependencies that occur in history. Human bipedalism appears to be one such example. An artifactual example of the result of such path dependencies is the QWERTY keyboard. Its design originated as a way of fitting the striking mechanisms for the keys into the machine to reduce jamming by slowing down fast typists (e.g., by separating TH). As the machine constraints were altered, other keyboard designs with better ergonomic features for users were developed. However, these better designs were unable to invade the keyboard niche.

Some repeated assemblies have no function; they repeat but not because of a history of use. Some repeated assemblies can result from illusory contingencies or once useful behavior. Others may have had a function at one time, but become dissociated from it. Langer (1989) reports a friend who would always cut a slice off the end of a roast before placing it in the oven. The friend said she did this because her mother did it; her mother said she did it because *her* mother did it. Finally, grandmother shed light on the practice: the pan she used for roasting was too small to accommodate the whole piece of meat. Of course, such dissociations can occur in evolutionary time (we call these vestiges) or in cultural-historical time, resulting in practices that have no function or are even costly (Boyd & Richerson, 1985).

While a view of function depending on a history of use rather than apparent utility is more consistent with evolutionary theory, paleontologists rarely hand over knowledge of that history to us. Instead, we will have to rely on a combination of fieldwork, experiments and comparative studies. Sometimes history can be guessed because of the continuing constraints imposed by the interaction of morphology and ecology. Presumably the distance humans today can walk are equivalent to those of their ancestors, given similar terrains and caloric requirements. Other times, careful work will be needed to infer lower-level components (including basic stimulus-action feedback loops) that must have evolved in order for higher-level repeated assemblies to occur.

5.2.   Variation

At the genetic level, variation results from mutation and recombination. Repeated assembly broadens the relevant scope of variation. Within historical, ecological, and developmental constraints, repeated assemblies are enormously variable, despite physical, developmental and historical constraints. Change in any repeating component of an assembly, whether genetic or epigenetic, can increase or decrease the probability of future assembly. This is because repeated assemblies are concretely situated in specific flows of interaction. Each instance of a repeated assembly is in some sense unique. Whether we look at the same organism-in-setting at time$_1$ and time$_2$ or different organisms in functionally identical settings, no sequence of behavior is ever identical—and some sequences can make the difference between life or death, success in reproduction or failure. The possibilities for selection are almost endless.

Despite the uniqueness of situated activity, patterns of assemblies bear a family resemblance. Like Eleanor Rosch's (Rosch, 1977) prototypical categories, there are no clear-cut boundaries to repeated assemblies. Components may have varying degrees of membership in a repeated assembly, with some components being more prototypical or central than others. Some common but peripheral components may even be missing. Some natural repeated assemblies such as birds have features recognized cross-culturally as prototypic. Interestingly, they are also those features with longer evolutionary histories of selection (Boster, Berlin, & O'Neill, 1986).

5.3.   Heritability

The third feature of Darwinism is retention or heritability. At the extreme, narrow-school evolutionary psychologists may identify genes as the only heritable components of the phenotype (Williams, 1989). In the vocabulary of repeated assembly, heritability is expanded.   It includes not only genetic products, but also the reliably recurrent resources of previous generations. Heritability itself is thus no indicator of the universality, fixity, or difficulty of changing organism-environment relations.

Instead, repeated assemblies are characterized in terms of scales of time, or persistence, and cycles, the frequency of repetition (see Figure 2).   Some components, such as the DNA code, have been parts of repeated assemblies since the beginning of life. Other components, such as a cultural environment, have a temporal scale measured in historical terms. Still others recur on the scale of a lifetime. "In the past" does not refer to a dichotomy between the Pleistocene and the urban present, as it does in narrow evolutionary psychology. The temporal structure of repeated assemblies may be measured in terms of ontogeny (in "habits of a lifetime"), cultural-historical time (as in "2,000 years of Western civilization"), or geological-evolutionary time (the temporal scale of DNA). Paradoxically, time expands the notion of heritability; we inherit not only genes, but also attitudes, practices, place, nationality, expectations for behavior, and so forth.   Assemblies may persist in evolutionary time, among Americans, in the Smith family, or in J. Smith. There may be change within cycles, but this simply indicates low reliability of repetition.

6.   LANGUAGE AS A REPEATED ASSEMBLY

One of the most important advantages of repeated assembly is that it enables us to say what we mean and mean what we say. We are not forced into the nature-nurture dichotomy, an inescapable consequence of a "genes-eye" vocabulary of evolutionary processes. We can observe this trap close on Tooby and Cosmides (1992). In *The Adapted Mind*, they argued that

- Genes and the environment fully codetermine the phenotype.

- Phenotypes cannot be decomposed into genetically—determined and environmentally-determined components

- Events at one stage of life are contingent upon prior developmental outcomes

- Both genes and environments are products of evolutionary processes.

In other words, Tooby and Cosmides reject nature-nurture dualism and genetic determinism in terms identical to developmental systems theorists (Levins & Lewontin, 1985; Oyama, 1985). However, coming from the gene's-eye view, Tooby and Cosmides (1992) are unable to avoid the traps of genetic determinism.

They use language as an example to illustrate the difference between what they call "evolved" and "manifest characters," an intentional parallel to genotype and phenotype. Tooby and Cosmides posit that all humans have an underlying universal mechanism for learning language. This evolved language acquisition device (LAD) is specified by genetically based developmental programs. The evolved device enables children to learn a language and exhibit a manifest trait: speaking Kikuyu or speaking English. In the special case of a child raised in isolation, Tooby and Cosmides say that the LAD would still develop, but abnormal speech would occur because of the lack of environmental inputs.

No amount of new terminology can alter the underlying conceptual structure of their account, which posits an innate component, the LAD, "filled in" by environmental inputs. This view of language is ancient, and the gene's-eye view has done little to update the picture. Tooby and Cosmides are unable to escape nature-nurture dualism despite their best intentions.

From the perspective of repeated assembly, genes are a necessary component in the development of language, but an equally important resource is a language environment. Both genes and the language environment must be inherited, although the components differ temporally (see Figure 2). One set of resources, which includes genes, is a cycle in evolutionary time. Nested within it is another set — just as critical — which includes the language environment. Both sets are repeatedly assembled, but on different scales of time. The cycle of language environment (English or Kikuyu), in cultural-historical time, is nested within the cycle of other components, including genes, in evolutionary time. Although the frequency and scale of the cycles may be roughly distinguished, it makes little sense to separate language into an innate and an acquired component. The LAD is a fiction, because it construes the development of language from the unique perspective of nature-nurture dualism. Language is a repeatedly assembled from a language environment and genes enabling its utilization. Moreover, other cycles of time, such as generational or cohort time, are nested in evolutionary and cultural-historical time. At the intersection of these different timescales is the situated activity of the organism-in-setting: a child raised in a social environment or in isolation where the conditions for an assembly to be repeated — be it later in the day or in succeeding generations — recur or fail to recur.

7.   WHAT IS NOT A REPEATED ASSEMBLY?

As we look around us, it seems that everything is an example of a repeated assembly. The obvious question is what is *not* repeatedly assembled? The answer will often depend on level of analysis and perspective. Any specific individual — even one of a monozygotic twin set — is unique. No twin has precisely the same experiences as the other. However, organisms in general are repeatedly assembled.

Often the product of a repeated assembly with specialized functions is unique. For example, the collections of devices to allow the healing of wounds are repeated assemblies in organisms. However, the specific scars that result are the unique results of an individual's history.

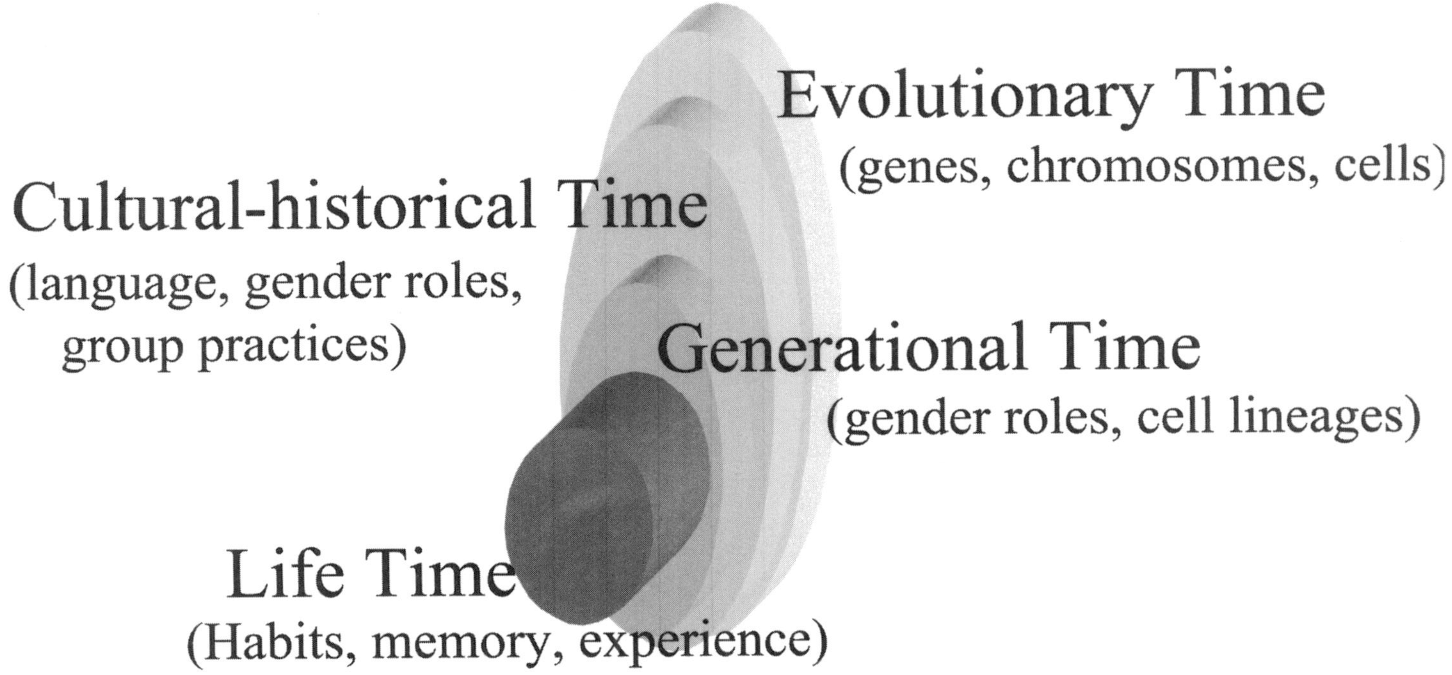

Evolutionary Time
(genes, chromosomes, cells)

Generational Time
(gender roles, cell lineages)

Cultural-historical Time
(language, gender roles,
group practices)

Life Time
(Habits, memory, experience)

Figure 2. Recurring multiple resources having different scales of time contribute to the repeated assembly of unique individuals.

By definition, errors would not be repeated assemblies. Despite considerable redundancy in biological systems, errors do occur in development and produce organisms unable to survive or reproduce. Hence, their lineages cease to repeatedly assemble. At first glance, it seems that there should be few errors repeatedly assembling in artifactual systems because these can be corrected when discovered. However, undesirable outcomes of poor design can repeatedly assemble because of ignorance or even outright deceit, as in the cases of the Ford Pinto's faulty gas tank and the Dalkon shield.

An adaptive response to a novel event may be unique; but even though it is useful, it may fail to repeatedly assemble. In his examination of "cognition in the wild," Hutchins (1996, p. 317ff.) observes a situation that is adaptive, but does not become a repeated assembly. While on board the vessel where he did his fieldwork, the ship's navigational systems failed. The two men who recorded the position and plotted it on a chart had to work out a new procedure for doing joint calculations by hand in order to navigate the ship. Through a process of trial and error, the two men eventually figured out how to modularize the calculations, after which, the problem of plotting location ran smoothly. There was a "Darwinian" trial-and-error adaptation to local circumstances (Skinner, 1966), resulting in a cultural innovation. However, it was an innovation that was not saved in the cultural system. The situation for using the solution again is rare because considerable redundancy is built into the operation of large ships.

8.   CONCLUSION: SAYING WHAT WE MEAN

Narrow evolutionary psychology is too impoverished for evolutionary perspectives at higher levels of analysis. Even if we can agree that "genes for" particular traits can refer to "virtual genes" (Dennett, 1995) or to a chain of differential effects (Dawkins, 1982) rather than the effects of specific DNA structures, we are left without words for connecting the concrete, observable activities of organisms to recurrence in meaningful ways. In contrast, repeated assembly is a term that allows us to see nature as having multiple joints, not necessarily mutually exclusive. Repeated assembly is not a new theory, but it is a vocabulary that enables us to say what we mean and mean what we say without specious claims about genes.

Instead of fictionalizing genes as souls and decision makers, repeated assembly draws on multilevel-evolutionary theory for a view of Darwinism as situated and relational. It emphasizes *context*, be it a cellular medium or a social medium; *contingency,* as the interactive relationship between events, including relationships over different scales of time; and *construction*, through the self-organizing properties of recurrent resources (gametes, organisms, ecosystems, etc.). Some of these resources are genetic, others are non-genetic (zygotic machinery, the social environment for normal psychological development), and yet other resources are the results of previous interactions. Some developmental resources will themselves be repeated assemblies: customs, artifacts, learned skills, languages, world-views and group configurations can all be repeatedly assembled. While their specifics are wildly variable, humans require many of these repeatedly assembled cultural products for survival and reproduction.

The vocabulary for repeated assembly represents a middle way; it suggests how the results of evolution and some processes of change can be studied in the here and now without allusions to a vanished past and a maladapted present (Symons, 1992; Tooby & Cosmides, 1992). Repeated assemblies with an evolutionary history are also repeated in development and in daily life. For example, Caporael (1997a,b) proposed a model of human social cognitive evolution in the context of four core group configurations analogous to those found in hunter-gatherer groups: dyads, small hunting groups (about five individuals), bands (about 30 individuals), and seasonally occurring macrobands (about 300 individuals). These groups are associated with group size and modal tasks, which jointly correspond to specialized functions. Caporael (1997a) observes that, although there are many kinds of group configurations in modern life, these four core groups and their associated specialized functions recur on a daily basis. They also recur in ontogeny as children expand their interdependence to a widening circle of people, from a focal caregiver, to the small groups of family and playgroups, to the larger groups of classroom, schools, and identity groups.

Repeated assembly can also provide a hypothesis to explain the metaphoric correspondences between evolution and religion. A religious peg for hanging the evolutionary hat appears to be repeated through the medium of origin stories. Origin stories are ubiquitous in human cultures. They serve to mediate a group's relationship to its habitat and other groups, reinforce a worldview, regulate gender relations and sexuality, and model the relations of people in a moral community. Darwinism is not only a scientific theory; it is also an origin story for secular culture (Caporael & Brewer, 1991). Genetic explanations provide simple and satisfying explanations for gender differences, sibling rivalry, marriage and divorce, status, ethics and other interesting dilemmas of modern life (e.g., Ridley, 1998; Wright, 1994). Darwinism was, and continues to be, a theory that explains human origins, one purporting to replace an existing creationist theory of origins dealing with the same human dilemmas. Challenging the existing Judeo-Christian claims meant making its same tacit assumptions and responding to its questions and observations. Despite the status of Darwinism as a scientific theory, when transported without reflection into the human realm, it unknowingly adopted the underlying conceptual structure of religious explanations. The old and familiar dualisms and assumptions about human nature repeatedly assembled despite the new vocabulary of genotypes, phenotypes and DNA.

Freyd's (1983) work sheds some light on the possible mechanisms for the repeated assembly of the evolution-religion correspondence. She argues that cognitive and linguistic structures have the forms they do *not* because they are so represented in individual human minds, but rather because they must be shared. In other words, knowledge in language or any other semiotic system is subject to the constraints of "shareability." Freyd (1983) makes two interesting predictions. First, a new term has to fit existing components of shared knowledge if it is to be successfully introduced into a language. Second, attempts to introduce new terms that *nearly* fit pre-existing knowledge will result in distortions of meaning in the direction of prior knowledge. Both predictions appear to be realized in the evolution-religion correspondence. In fact, it is difficult to imagine that it could be any other way. New ideas, like new evolved forms, can never be utterly new under the sun. The history of ideas is also rooted in a history of use.

The critique of narrow evolutionary psychology and its religious metaphor that began this paper is no reason to abandon evolutionary perspectives. On the contrary, it points toward hopeful prospects for a human evolutionary theory. A successful evolutionary psychology will be a hybrid science (Caporael, 2000, 2001a), one acutely aware that scientific practice is a cultural product that requires reflection as much as empiricism, and that scientists are humans, too, and therefore objects and subjects of their own study.

Rensselaer Polytechnic Institute

9.   REFERENCES

Barkow, J. H. (1989). *Darwin, Sex, and Status.* Toronto: University of Toronto Press.
Bijker, W., E. (1995). *Of Bicycles, Bakelite, and Bulbs: Toward a Theory of Sociotechnical Change.* Cambridge, MA: MIT Press.
Boster, J., Berlin, B., & O'Neill, J. (1986). The correspondence of Jivaroan to scientific ornithology. *American Anthropologist, 88,* 569-583.
Boyd, R., & Richerson, P. J. (1985). *Culture and the Evolutionary Process.* Chicago: University of Chicago Press.
Brandon, R., & Antonovics, J. (1996). The coevolution of organism and environment. In R. Brandon (Ed.), *Concepts and Methods in Evolutionary Biology.* New York: Cambridge University Press.
Brown, D. E. (1991). *Human Universals.* Philadelphia: Temple University Press.
Bucciarelli, L. (1994). *Designing Engineers.* Cambridge, MA: MIT Press.
Buss, D. M. (1995). Evolutionary psychology: A new paradigm for psychological science. *Psychological Inquiry, 6,* 1-30.
Buss, L. W. (1987). *The Evolution of Individuality.* Princeton: Princeton University Press.
Caporael, L. R. (1994). Of myth and science: Origin stories and evolutionary scenarios. *Social Science Information, 33,* 9-23.
Caporael, L. R. (1995). Sociality: Coordinating bodies, minds and groups. *Psycoloquy* [on-line serial], *6*(1), Available: *http://www.cogsci.soton.ac.uk/cgi/psyc/newpsy?6.01.*
Caporael, L. R. (1997a). The evolution of truly social cognition: The core configurations model. *Personality and Social Psychology Review, 1,* 276-298.
Caporael, L. R. (1997b). Vehicles of knowledge: Artifacts and social groups. *Evolution and Cognition, 3,* 39-43.
Caporael, L. R. (2000). The hybrid science. *The Journal of the Learning Sciences, 9,* 221-232.
Caporael, L. R. (2001a). Evolutionary psychology: Toward a unifying theory and a hybrid science. *Annual Review of Psychology, 52,* 607-628.
Caporael, L. R. (2001b). Parts and wholes: The evolutionary importance of groups. In C. Sedikides & M. B. Brewer (Eds.), *Individual Self,Relational Self, and Collective Self* (pp. 241-258). Philadelphia, PA: Psychology Press.
Caporael, L. R., & Baron, R. M. (1997). Groups as the mind's natural environment. In J. Simpson & D. Kenrick (Eds.), *Evolutionary Social Psychology* (pp. 317-343). Hillsdale: NJ: Lawrence Erlbaum.
Caporael, L. R., & Brewer, M. B. (1991). The quest for human nature. *Journal of Social Issues, 47,* 1-9.
Dawkins, R. (1976). *The Selfish Gene.* New York: Oxford University Press.
Dawkins, R. (1982). *The Extended Phenotype: The Long Reach of the Gene.* New York: Oxford University Press.
Dawkins, R. (1987). *The Blind Watchmaker.* New York: Norton.
Dennett, D. C. (1995). *Darwin's Dangerous Idea.* New York: Simon & Schuster.
Eldredge, N., & Grene, M. (1992). *Interactions: The Biological Context of Social Systems.* New York: Columbia University Press.
Endler, J. (1986). *Natural Selection in the Wild.* Princeton: Princeton University Press.
Fiske, A. P. (2000). Complementarity theory: Why human social capacities evolved to require cultural complements. *Personality and Social Psychology Review, 4,* 76-94.
Freyd, J. (1983). Shareability: The social psychology of epistemology. *Cognitive Science, 7,* 191-210.
Grafen, A. (1984). Natural selection, kin selection and group selection. In J. R. Krebs & N. B. Davies (Eds.), *Behavioural Ecology* (pp. 62-84). London, Eng.: Blackwell.
Griffiths, P. E., & Gray, R. D. (1994). Developmental systems and evolutionary explanation. *Journal of Philosophy, 91,* 277-304.
Hendriks-Jansen, H. (1996). *Catching Ourselves in the Act.* Cambridge, MA: MIT Press.
Hutchins, E. (1996). *Cognition in the Wild.* Cambridge, MA: MIT Press.
Langer, E. J. (1989). *Mindfulness.* New York: Addison-Wesley.
Lave, J. (1988). *Cognition in Practice.* New York: Cambridge University Press.
Levins, R., & Lewontin, R. (1985). *The Dialectical Biologist.* Cambridge, MA: Harvard University Press.
Lloyd, E. A. (1999). Evolutionary psychology: The burdens of proof. *Biology and Philosophy, 14,* 211-233.

Maynard Smith, J. (1987). Science and myth. In N. Eldredge (Ed.), *The Natural History Reader in Evolution* (pp. 222-229). New York City: Columbia University Press.

Maynard Smith, J., & Szathmáry, E. (1995). *The Major Transitions in Evolution*. New York: W. H. Freeman.

Millikan, R. G. (1984). *Language, Thought, and Other Biological Categories*. Cambridge, MA: MIT Press.

Nelkin, D. (2001). Less selfish than sacred? Genes and the religious impulse in evolutionary psychology. In H. Rose & S. Rose (Eds.), *Alas, Poor Darwin* (pp. 17-32). New York: Harmony Books.

Oyama, S. (1985). *The Ontogeny of Information*. New York: Cambridge University Press.

Oyama, S., Griffiths, P. E., & Gray, R. D. (Eds.). (2000). *Cycles of Contingency: Developmental Systems and Evolution*. Cambridge, MA: MIT Press.

Ridley, M. (1998). *The Origins of Virtue*. New York: Penguin.

Rosch, E. (1977). Human categorization. In N. Warren (Ed.), *Studies in Cross-Cultural Psychology* (pp. 1-49). New York: Academic Press.

Skinner, B. F. (1966). The phylogeny and ontogeny of behavior. *Science, 153*, 1205-1213.

Sterelny, K., Smith, K. C., & Dickison, M. (1996). The extended replicator. *Biology and Philosophy, 11*, 377-403.

Symons, D. (1992). On the use and misuse of Darwinism in the study of human behavior. In J. H. Barkow & L. Cosmides & J. Tooby (Eds.), *The Adapted Mind* (pp. 137-159). New York: Oxford University Press.

Thelen, E., & Smith, L. B. (1994). *A Dynamic Systems Approach to the Development of Cognition and Action*. Cambridge, MA: MIT Press.

Tooby, J., & Cosmides, L. (1992). The psychological foundations of culture. In J. H. Barkow & L. Cosmides & J. Tooby (Eds.), *The Adapted Mind* (pp. 19-136). New York: Oxford.

Williams, G. C. (1989). A sociobiological expansion of *Evolution and Ethics*. In J. Paradis & G. C. Williams (Eds.), *Evolution and Ethics* (pp. 179-214). Princeton: Princeton University Press.

Wilson, E. O. (1978). *On Human Nature*. Cambridge, MA: Harvard University Press.

Wright, R. (1994). *The Moral Animal*. New York: Vintage Books.

NILES ELDREDGE

HUMAN TRIANGLES

Genes, Sex and Economics in Human Evolution

The molecular revolution, triggered by the elucidation of the chemical structure of DNA and RNA a half century ago, has permeated virtually all of biology and made significant inroads in disciplines far beyond biology's traditional borders. Indeed, E.O. Wilson (1998) has called for "consilience" between all avenues of systematic and rational contemplation of the organic world and all phenomena associated with human beings. In that work, Wilson quickly reveals his belief that a unified scholarly approach to the study of all aspects of human behavior involves not so much an innocent and unweighted "jumping together" of disciplines as disparate as biology, psychology, anthropology, sociology, history and economics (to say nothing of the rest of the "humanities"), as it does describing the traditional subject matter of these latter disciplines in the peculiar (and narrowly construed) terms of the first: a gene-centered version of evolutionary biology. Wilson, it seems fair to say, sees it as an eminently plausible and realistic goal that complexities of human behavior can for the most part be reduced to the relatively much simpler terms of (his version of) evolutionary biology. In other words, evolutionary biology wants to eat everyone else's lunch — and claims it has the power to do so.

Wilson, "father" of sociobiology (e.g., Wilson, 1975), based his gene-centered vision of the structure and evolution of social systems in part on the earlier works of such theorists as Hamilton (1964a,b) and Williams (1966). And it was, of course, the metaphor of the "selfish gene" (Dawkins, 1976) that provided most of the rhetorical momentum behind the sociobiological movement. For the last decades of the twentieth century, we have been living in a world dominated by the imagery of selfish genes: not only does life evolve (we are told) through the competition among genes for representation in the next generation, but the answer to almost every *functional* question of the old nature/nurture dichotomy has come down unrelentingly firmly on the side of nature (meaning gene-based behavior) over nurture (meaning learned behavior) — as perusal of virtually any issue of the *New York Times Science Times* faithfully reveals.

No one disputes that today's "broad evolutionary psychology" is a direct outgrowth of sociobiology—though it is fair to say that there is a great deal of difference between Wilson's (1975) famous/infamous Ch. 20, in which he resolutely took the plunge and applied his sociobiological percepts to human beings, and that

Steven J. Scher & Frederick Rauscher (eds.). Evolutionary Psychology: Alternative Approaches, 91-110.

somewhat diverse array of approaches usefully lumped together as "evolutionary psychology" today. I must say at the outset that, as an evolutionary biologist, I am firmly convinced that humans have evolved — in concert with, and through the very same mechanisms as, the rest of all life. Likewise I am persuaded that human cognitive faculties have evolved as well. Further, there is undeniably a genetic component (though surely not absolute 100% determinism) underlying many if not all specifiable components of human behavior — and thus there is very likely an evolutionary basis of them[1].

In other words, I believe it quite possible that certain forms of human behavior — whether adopted or adapted — suitable for life in small hunter-gathering groups on the African savannah hundreds of thousands of years ago persist in modern humans, perhaps as maladaptations in the (seemingly) vastly different "environments" of suburbs and the corporate world. In principle, this could easily be the case. Furthermore, I do not doubt that a comparative psychology of surviving hunter-gatherers, pastoralists, pre-industrial agriculturalists and persons living in today's complex social structures of industrialized nations might shed useful light on these issues.

But I do find difficulties with what I take to be the simplistic and incomplete description of biological systems underlying the entire gene-centered approach of what I have elsewhere termed "ultradarwinism" (e.g., Eldredge, 1995a). Indeed, I have recently concluded (Eldredge, 1999, In press) that most, if not all, evolutionary change is associated with true speciation — and that most speciation events take place in the context of regional ecological upheaval typically involving significant amounts of species-level extinctions. Thus, for most of the history of life, evolution seems triggered primarily by environmental events, and to involve many unrelated lineages (of microbes, fungi, plants and animals) of regional biotas. The empirical patterns of such extinction/speciation "turnovers" (Vrba, 1985) in itself is sufficient to suggest that any version of evolutionary theory that restricts its gaze to single lineages, and assumes that competition among genes alone suffices as a driving mechanism to explain the evolution of life is simply — yet devastatingly — incomplete. It does *not* mean that directional natural selection does not underlie the modification of adaptations—but it does suggest (as I explain more fully below) that the gene's eye view of natural selection is probably not the best way to characterize this, the most central of evolutionary dynamic processes.

If the "selfish gene" is incomplete at best, and misleading at worst, as a metaphorical symbol and descriptor of how the evolutionary process actually works, the further question naturally arises: how appropriate is the gene-centered view to describing the structures, internal dynamics and evolutionary histories of complex entities such as social systems? And how do human social structures compare with colonial and social systems in the rest of the animal kingdom (let alone among protoctistans, fungi and plants)? I have explored these themes in detail with philosopher Marjorie Grene (Eldredge and Grene, 1992). Here, to understand what

---

[1] However, it must be said that demonstration of the genetic basis underlying a structure, a biochemical pathway or a bit of behavior, and understanding its evolutionary origin as an adaptation fashioned thorough natural selection, are two quite different things often difficult to connect rigorously.

alternatives might be taken to the perspectives of narrow evolutionary psychology[2], I will begin by pulling apart the basic components of organismic life and their relation to larger-scale systems found in all the major groups of organisms. I will then derive a conceptualization of natural selection that turns out to be much closer to Darwin's (1859) original formulation than that of authors such as Dawkins (1976). I then turn to a consideration of the general ontological status of biological social systems, based on these preliminary discussions; *human* social systems turn out to be even more complex. I then briefly examine human evolutionary history and current status from an ecological point of view. We will then be in a position to ask the final questions: how plausible in general is it to ask if a certain item of human behavior is really "about" the spread of genes — or at least a vestige from bygone days when it was fashioned by natural selection? And — toughest question of all — how can we "test" any given hypothesis that an item of human behavior is not just "controlled by genes," but represents some form of adaptation to spread those genes?

1. BIOLOGICAL SYSTEMS AND PROCESSES: A BRIEF DECONSTRUCTION

Organisms do two—and only two—kinds of things. They (1) engage in matter/energy transfer processes that enable them to differentiate and develop from a fertilized zygote, grow to adulthood and maintain the soma[3]. And they (2) reproduce. I (Eldredge, 1985, 1986; Eldredge and Grene, 1992) have referred to the first category as the "economic" side of organismic life. While traditional physiology lists "reproduction" as one of 9 or 10 basic organismic functions, all the others (e.g. "respiration," "excretion," etc.) are somatic functions and clearly fall into the "economic" category.

The relationship between the economic and reproductive functions within organisms is asymmetrical: organisms need to engage in matter/energy transfer processes on a moment-to-moment basis simply to exist. They do *not* need to reproduce to live—and it is notorious that reproductive activities are routinely short-circuited under times of physical stress[4]. Put another way, there must be a functioning soma—a body to house the reproductive organs and to supply the requisite energy necessary for reproduction to occur.

Recognition of this simple dichotomy of organismic functional properties has two immediate and very powerful consequences, enabling us to see both (1) the

---

[2] EDITOR'S NOTE: In this book, the term 'narrow evolutionary psychology' signifies the approach to evolutionary psychology developed by Cosmides, Tooby, Buss, et al. This term was chosen not to imply that this approach has an inappropriately narrow point of view, but merely to suggest that the approach adopts a narrower range of assumptions than 'broad evolutionary psychology' (or, just 'evolutionary psychology'). This latter term signifies evolutionary psychology generally, practiced with any of a very broad range of assumptions possible within the general framework of evolutionary approaches to psychology. For more detail on this terminology, see the editor's introduction, p 1

[3] These functions pertain specifically to Metazoans, but the dichotomy between economic and reproductive classes of behaviors holds generally for all organisms.

[4] As when women, in vigorous long term training (for example, for marathon running) commonly cease menstruation.

functional organizing principles underlying a number of kinds of larger-scale biological systems, and (2) the nature of the processes interconnecting those systems—including the fundamental characteristics of natural and sexual selection.

Consider large-scale biological systems — entities such as ecosystems, demes, species, monophyletic taxa and social systems. All of these (save the last — a special case discussed immediately below) flow out of one or the other class of organismic activity, forming twin, parallel hierarchical systems that I (e.g. Eldredge, 1985, 1986; Eldredge and Grene, 1992) refer to as the "economic" and "genealogical" hierarchies (fig. 1). On-going matter-energy transfer processes within animals, for example, means that all individuals must seek energy and nutrient supplies. Interaction (whether cooperatively or competitively) with conspecifics in a local setting creates what Damuth (1985) has usefully dubbed "avatars," i.e., local economic populations as distinct from the local *reproductive* populations — the "demes" of classical evolutionary (population genetics) theory[5]. It is these avatars — these local populations of conspecifics — that play the concerted economic role usually defined as the "niche." And it is the cross-genealogical interaction between avatars that creates the local ecosystem.

In other words, matter-energy transfer processes—the very act of securing energy resources — sets up a system of multiple local avatars, where (ultimately solar) energy flows between avatars in classic food-web fashion. Local ecosystems are both formed and held together by moment-to-moment matter-energy transfer processes every bit as much as individual organisms are formed and held together (i.e. exist, continue to live) by such processes internally. And, as I have discussed elsewhere in the references already cited, local ecosystems are linked by matter/energy flow between them — hooked up into regional biomes, and ultimately, into the entire global biosphere[6].

Reproduction has its own, equally dramatic organizational consequences. Demes are local populations of sexually mature conspecifics. Virtually all evolutionary biologists agree with Wright's (e.g. Wright, 1931, 1932) vision of the internal structure of species, i.e., broken up into localized breeding populations with varying amounts of contact (gene flow); demes are formed by colonization or fragmentation; they also merge and become locally extinct. And demes are parts of

---

[5] Demes and avatars are often quite distinct in terms of their actual composition of local conspecifics. Consider African elephants, where adult (breeding) bulls spend most of the year alone; females and younger elephants, in contrast, form large (and hierarchically organized) herds, while young adult males often form smaller bands of a half dozen or so individuals. Thus the composition of a local African elephant deme is very different from the functional organization of the local ecological avatars; the environmental impact of large herds of elephants is also very different compared with that of isolated bulls.

[6] Chemoautotrophic bacteria convert radioactive decay-generated heat flowing from the earth's crust (ultimately, from the mantle) to provide the energy driving "vent fauna" ecosystems of the deep seas; such endogenously fueled ecosystems are obviously decoupled from the solar-energy-driven global plexus of the remainder of the earth's ecosystems. Yet it is unclear how thorough-going such decoupling may actually be — as potentially utilizable nutrients and bits of organic material raining down from above, and conversely materials disseminated by currents from the vent faunas, no doubt forge some economic links — no matter how tenuous — between these two otherwise very different and decoupled sorts of ecosystems.

species — defined, following the classic formulations of Dobzhansky (1937) and Mayr (1942) as reproductive communities. Actually, I believe H.E.H. Paterson (1985) has said it best when he characterized species as that largest collection of individuals sharing what he called the "Specific Mate Recognition System" ("SMRS") — a set of chemical, physiological, behavioral and structural adaptations that allows individuals to "recognize" each other as potentially appropriate mates[7].

Nor do the consequences of reproduction stop there. Species are derived from antecedent species, usually by a form of fissioning ("speciation"). Thus genera, families etc. all the way up through the highest rungs of the Linnaean hierarchy are simply progressively larger, and more inclusive, sets of species all derived from a single ancestral species[8].

Thus organisms are parts of demes, which are parts of species, which in turn are parts of taxa that themselves form an hierarchically arrayed system. The entire genealogical hierarchy is formed and held together by forms of "more-making": replication of genes, reproduction of organisms, fates of demes, and fissioning of ancestral species to form descendant species. In the end, all the elements of the genealogical hierarchy — organisms, demes, species and monophyletic taxa — emerge as hierarchically arrayed "packages" of genetic information[9].

Thus, in a very abbreviated nutshell, we see that organisms, by dint of each of their two functional categories, automatically set up larger-scale systems of which they are a part: organisms are parts of an avatar, itself a part of a local ecosystem, itself a part of ever-larger, more inclusive geographically delineated economic systems on up to the most inclusive of all: the Biosphere. At one and the same time, every sexually reproducing organism is a member of a deme, which is part of a species, which is a part of larger-scale taxa culminating in the (unnamed!) taxon "All Life."[10] And these systems, and their hierarchical structure, are formed simply because organisms routinely engage in both classes of activity.

---

[7] Paterson's concept of the SMRS embraces all sexually reproducing organisms; for example, many sessile marine invertebrates reproduce by shedding their gametes into the waters above them; it is the chemical affinities of the gametes bumping into one another that supply the "recognition" in such instances.

[8] Meaning that taxa are monophyletic; they are so by the genealogical process of evolution — but just as the "calculated mean" is an estimate of the "true mean" in statistics, not all taxa conventionally recognized may, ultimately, turn out to be monophyletic. Though we may be reasonably certain that all eutherian mammals are monophyletic (i.e., derived from a single common ancestor), arguments persist, for example, on whether or not bats (Order Chiroptera) are monophyletic.

[9] I note in passing the important implication that species, as packages of genetic information, do not in themselves "do" anything in the economy of nature; species, for example, do not have "niches", as species are not dynamic parts of specifiable ecosystems — the way local avatars (of conspecifics) are. The trivial exception to this observation occurs if, and only if, a species is reduced to a single local population — as in fact may happen — especially at the outset of a species' existence, and then again at its end, as it faces extinction.

Also, I note that species make "more of themselves" via speciation — but taxa above the species level do not: genera, families, etc., are strings of ancestral-descendant species. As such, there is no dynamic process in nature of "genusiation" — where a genus can give rise to another genus, etc. — despite the rhetoric of evolutionary theorists of an earlier day.

[10] Meaning that no one, as yet, has cast serious doubt on the monophyly of all life — viz. archaebacteria, eubacteria, "protoctists," fungi, plants and animals.

Having established that economic and genealogical systems exist in their own right[11], we now must examine the dynamic connections that do in fact exist between these two different domains of biological function and hierarchically nested systems. I see the connections at three levels — the organismic and population levels for all organisms, as well as the third, and special, case of social systems[12].

We have already seen that organisms engage in both economic and reproductive functions — and that, in an important, sense, the relationship between them is not reciprocal: organisms need to engage in matter/energy processes, but not in reproduction, in order simply to stay alive. And without such economic activity, there can in any case be no reproduction.

But consider another aspect of the relationship in which the situation is entirely reversed: replicative fidelity followed by gene expression is a (if not *the*) *sine qua non* of reproduction. Genes, to a very large extent, make the (new) organism. What happens to a decipherable piece of genetic information very much matters to the nature of its end-product. But, as Weismann was the first to demonstrate, with few if any exceptions, the converse is simply not true: what happens to the soma in the course of an organism's lifetime does not effect the germ-line. So there is a reciprocal side to the equation, after all, and both statements are simultaneously true: within any individual organism (1) only economic behavior is necessary to live but (2) insofar as reproduction is concerned, the germ-line effects the soma — and there is no reciprocal relationship there.

Up one step, consider populations — in evolutionary theory, the domain of natural selection and other processes affecting gene frequency between generations. The gene-centered view developed by Dawkins and accepted by most sociobiologists and evolutionary psychologists sees selection as an active deterministic process, i.e., that genes are somehow actively competing for representation in the next generation. From this gene-centered point of view, an organism is a "vehicle" to carry around, protect, and supply the technical wherewithal and energetics that allow the gene to do its job. Thus organisms live to reproduce; to do so, they must eat as a necessity in order that the real job gets done: that genes may replicate themselves, and join in the battle to see themselves represented in the next generation[13]. According to ultradarwinians, chickens are an egg's way of making another egg.

This is, of course, a far cry from Darwin's (1859, p. 5) original formulation of natural selection. In and of itself, this is no bad thing — for we expect progress in the growth of knowledge — and it could conceivably be the case that the new

---

11   And, incidentally, we have also established the epistemological corollary that traditionally distinct and often non-communicating biological disciplines such as ecology and evolutionary theory have arisen as a natural reflection of the separate existence of these two sorts of systems.

12   Though my colleague Stanley Salthe (1985) sees connections between the economic and genealogical hierarchies at all levels, I take the far more conservative view that the interactions between the economic and genealogical hierarchies rest with (1) individual organisms — who after all are performing both classes of activity, and (2) at the population level as explained in the text. To my mind, there is no clear-cut evidence that (and thus no reason to posit that), say, a regional ecosystem can have a direct effect on an entire species except through the organismic and population levels.

13   As George Williams (1992) has pointed out, it is not literally the corporeal gene, but rather the information that it conveys, that is alleged to be seeking this transmittal.

knowledge of genetics has changed the picture considerably[14]. Yet, given the foregoing analysis of the nature and structure of economic and genealogical systems, the more balanced view of Darwin's original formulation is easily mapped on — while the position espoused by the ultradarwinian theory of selection as a fallout of genic competition, I would contend, makes considerably less sense.

Here is Darwin's (1859, p.5) statement on natural selection:

> As many more individuals of each species are born than can possibly survive, and as, consequently, there is a frequently recurring Struggle for Existence, it follows that any being, if it vary however slightly in any manner profitable to itself, under the complex and sometimes varying conditions of life, will have a better chance of surviving, and thus be *naturally selected*.

Darwin was, in effect, saying that how an organism fares in its economic life, to the extent that its fate is based on heritable properties, will affect how it fares in the reproductive arena — and thus bias the transmission of genetic information (as we would now put it) to the next generation. In other words, there is a (statistically) deterministic vector from the economic side that biases what goes on the genealogical (reproductive) side of the ledger. Later, he (Darwin, 1871, p. 256) clarified the nature of selection still further with his explicit definition of *sexual* selection as arising from:

> ...the advantage which certain individuals have over other individuals of the same sex and species, in exclusive relation to reproduction.

In other words, Darwin saw that relative success in reproducing might arise, not from "advantages" enjoyed in the economic arena, but rather simply from variation in behavior, physiology or structure of purely reproductive adaptations. This, too, is easily understood with respect to the dual hierarchy scheme discussed here and as shown in Figure 1.

I see this as a much more balanced view: how well an organism fares in its economic life *vis à vis* its conspecifics in the local population (avatar) is expected to have some statistically deterministic effect on how well it fares reproductively *vis à vis* its local conspecifics within its local deme. Among other things, this vision of natural selection says that neither economics nor reproduction is "more important" than the other. Both are simply there as organismic activities — and their interplay is not difficult to analyze. This amounts to saying that an organism eats, not to reproduce, but to live; but there are reproductive consequences to how well it eats.

If natural selection is a vector from the economic to the genealogic side of the ledger, it is fair to ask: Is there no *quid pro quo*? Does the reproductive side of the ledger have any effect on the economic side? And of course it does: ongoing reproduction literally provides the players in the game of life — which takes place in

---

[14]   Dobzhansky (1937), though, pointed out that natural selection is a population-level process, whereas what he called "physiological genetics" goes on at the individual level. In this, the first clear statement of the hierarchical structure of biological systems — and hence of the evolutionary process — Dobzhansky established that no matter how much we learn about inheritance per se, it cannot in principle affect our understanding of how natural selection works. For this reason, I have sometimes (e.g., Eldredge, 1999) referred to the genealogical hierarchy as "Dobzhansky's hierarchy."

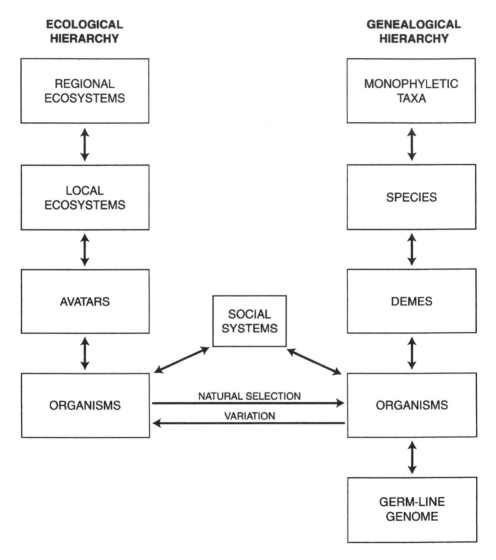

Figure 1. The Economic and Genealogic Hierarchies. (See Text for Explanation).

the arena of the local ecosystem. Nowhere is this better seen than in instances following local environmental degradation and extirpation of local avatars and demes — when recruitment from outlying demes takes over, usually in the context of some form of ecological succession.

What, then, of social systems? In our review of colonial organisms, as well as insect and vertebrate social systems, we (Eldredge and Grene, 1992) concluded that social systems in general arise from complex fusions of economic and reproductive adaptations of organisms (Figure 1). In other words, any form of society, be it a hive of eusocial hymenopterans or a troop of bonobos, has both economic and reproductive features.

Eusocial hymenopterans are "haplo-diploid," so that the females are more closely related to each other than to males and their parents. The discovery of haplo-diploidy thus contributed insight to the age-old conundrum of altruism in evolution (Hamilton, 1964a, 1964b). This is the underlying reason why sociobiology has accepted largely without question that social systems generally are all about reproduction, meaning, ultimately, that social systems reflect complex adaptations for the spread of genes. All economic behavior — as performed by sterile members of a number of different castes — is seen solely in light of what effect they have on the vicarious spreading of their genes through the Queen.

Yet, once again, why assume priority, or greater importance of one function (i.e. reproduction) over another (economics)? Just as selection among organisms can judiciously be seen as an interplay between both classes of activities, so too can social systems be conceived as (often complex) reintegrations of economic and reproductive adaptations. This works even for haplo-diploid hymenopterans: a hive of eusocial bees is clearly as much an avatar, playing a concerted economic role within the local ecosystem, as it is a reproductive cooperative. To assume to the contrary (as sociobiologists routinely do) that reproduction is paramount — what the hive is "really all about" — is to fall into the trap of thinking that, because evolution may reasonably be defined as the fate of genetically-based information, genetic (including reproductive) processes lie alone at the heart of the evolutionary process. But if the fate of genetic information — evolution — is actually a fall-out of a complex interplay between the economic and reproductive aspects of organisms' lives, such an ultradarwinian perspective clearly distorts the process.

Though nothing like haplo-diploidy occurs in the genetics of either social or asocial vertebrates[15], the presumption is nonetheless usually still there that all manner of social behavior is, at base, "about" reproductive success. The countervailing (and, I would claim, more balanced) view is that vertebrate social systems are local populations that arise from the intertwined economic and reproductive activities of their component organisms (Eldredge and Grene, 1992, p. 151). For example, the rather rudimentary social behavior exhibited by Florida scrub jays (Woolfenden and Fitzpatrick, 1984) is routinely assumed to be based on enhanced inclusive fitness

---

[15] Naked mole rats, which exhibit an interesting convergence on hymenopteran social organization (Sherman, Jarvis, & Alexander, 1991) are an interesting exception to this generalization.

enjoyed by helper birds engaged in cooperative breeding[16]. Yet, as Woolfenden and Fitzpatrick (1984) clearly show, such cooperative "helper" behavior is best interpreted as a delaying tactic, so that helpers can eventually find and occupy territory of their own. This they do primarily through (non-genetic!) "inheritance" of all or part of the territory. Territories are tightly defended year-round; and remain more or less constant for years. And it is, of course, in these territories that the Florida scrub jays make their living. The data strongly suggest that Florida scrub jay behavior is at least as much concerned with the economics of survival as it is about vicarious, or even eventual direct, reproductive success.

In more complex vertebrate social systems — such as those of chimpanzees and bonobos (Wrangham, 1986) — the interplay between economic and reproductive behavior is far more intricate. Based on detailed field studies, Wrangham (1986) has argued that a shift in diet between chimpanzees and their collateral (and presumably evolutionarily derived) kin reduced foraging competition in the proto-bonobos, leading to greater social mixing and, perhaps, overall less male-male competition than is the case observed today in modern chimpanzees (Eldredge and Grene, 1992, p. 158). Bonobos live in far larger troops than do chimps, and engage in group foraging behavior; females spend more time with males than is the case with chimps, and "...are sexually receptive for longer, and have more elaborate sexual interactions. Males are less inclined to fight, groom each other less, and are less given to travelling all over the community range than male chimpanzees are." (Wrangham, 1986, p. 376). Though it is relatively easy to see the reproductive consequences of economic behavior (especially when chimps and bonobos are compared) in Wrangham's analysis, it also seems that reproductive — or, in any case, aspects of *sexual* — behavior in bonobos has effects on foraging behavior.

And this raises a crucial point about human social behavior: Bonobos may well be our closest living relatives, and it is in the social behavior of this great ape species that we first see glimmers of a *decoupling* between sexual and reproductive behavior.

2.   THE HUMAN TRIANGLE: ECONOMICS, REPRODUCTION — AND SEX

Tradition holds that prostitution is the "world's oldest profession." Whether it is or not, prostitution starkly highlights the economic implications of sex in human society. The Vatican and sociobiology notwithstanding, human sexual behavior is by no means just about making babies. Sexual behavior is pursued for its own sake in all human societies — and reproduction is but one of its possible consequences. And, that the decoupling of sexual and reproductive behavior is arguably detectable among bonobos, implies that it was present at least in embryonic form before the human lineage diverged from the great apes some 5 million years ago — thus vastly predating the emergence of *Homo sapiens* on the African savannah only some 150,000-250,000 years ago. If there is such a thing as a "human nature," and if we

---

[16]   Interestingly, Woolfenden and Fitzpatrick (1984) do not themselves subscribe to this conclusion — seeing, instead, that by far the greatest contribution to the fitness of helpers lies in their own, albeit delayed, reproductive activities.

are to understand the evolutionary roots of human behavior generally, then we had better realize that (with the possible partial exception of bonobos) humans are absolutely unique among the earth's 10,000,000 species: we have added a third category of behavior to the 3.5 billion year old dichotomy between reproduction and economics. And that category — sex — in many important respects provides the bridge between economics and reproduction within human social systems.

Once again, it is important to see the separateness of the three elements of economics, reproduction and sex in human life simply to be able to analyze the complexities of the interactions between them (Figure 2). Causal vectors connect each pair in each direction, and, additionally, any one category can affect another via the third. I'll give a few examples of each vector simply to establish the validity — and, I believe, potential importance — of seeing this "triangle" of human behavior for the analysis of the evolutionary basis of human behavior. These examples are intended to be illustrative only — harbingers, I would hope, of a much more intense and ultimately rigorous future analysis.

2.1. Economics ↔ Reproduction

Back in the 1980s, the Mayor of Singapore was reported (in the *New York Times*) to have echoed an age-old concern of public officials and governmental policy planners: poor people seemed to be having far more children per capita than more affluent citizens. Malthus (1798), long before Darwin (and indeed, as a direct inspiration to both Darwin and Wallace in their initial formulations of natural selection), noted the tendency of population numbers to increase with improved economic conditions — though ongoing reproduction would, he believed, eventually outstrip food production with eventually disastrous consequences: famine and social upheaval. The notion that Darwin and Wallace derived from Malthus as applicable to all organisms is that food production/availability sets a limit to population size, an

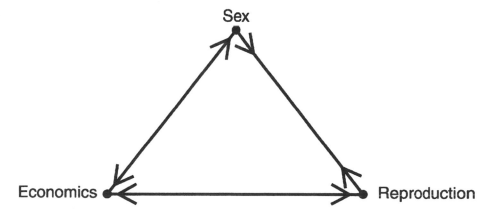

Figure 2. The Human Triangle. (For Explanation, See Text).

obvious and evolutionarily crucial control of economics over reproduction, and a critical cornerstone of their notion of natural selection. But, as the Mayor of Singapore noted, such seems not always to be the case with humans, at least in post-industrial human societies. Rather, the greater the economic resources, frequently the fewer the children produced. If evolutionary success is measured by relative amounts of genes left to the next generation, then the short term economically successful are losing the evolutionary race — particularly if (as the Mayor patently assumed), relatively higher economic success in Singapore reflects greater innate (genetic) talent. How to explain this paradox?

As Marx and others have been saying for a century-and-a-half, children are a form of capital. In other words, there are direct economic ramifications of reproduction in human social life. Children born to the lower classes often have a higher probability of dying (hence more are needed to ensure passage of those genes); but they also have been documented as important cogs in the family economic wheel. Especially in the days before child labor laws, they commonly worked prodigiously long hours — and if for a pittance, nonetheless as important contributors to the family exchequer (see, for example, Pick and Anderton, 1999). In rapidly developing China, the legal restriction of one child per couple[17] is rigidly enforced in cities, but apparently less so in the countryside where it is both harder to monitor and, critically, where children are viewed as important components in the labor force in the often marginal agricultural economy. Crudely put, lower class children are generally "r-selected," (i.e. with relatively larger numbers produced to offset higher mortality rates) — for both reproductive and economic reasons. Upper class children, on the other hand, do not as a rule produce income (they are an economic drain!), have lower mortalities, and so for both economic and reproductive reasons are produced typically in fewer numbers — meaning that they are "K-selected."

In other words, the vector works both ways: there are obvious reproductive consequences to economic behavior (though, in humans, the effect of economic success on reproductive success is at the very least different in aspect and certainly more complex, than in other organisms). But there are, as well, economic consequences to reproductive behavior. The vectorial arrows point both ways.

2.2. Sex ↔ Reproduction.

That, for all but a handful of secondarily asexually reproducing animal species, sex is necessary for reproduction, is of course a no-brainer. But consider the conundrum that homosexuality poses for orthodox ultradarwinian thought: if the game of life is really about maximizing one's genetic representation in the next generation, how can homosexuality be explained?[18] As is well known, homosexual couples commonly

---

[17]   This restriction is only for the numerically dominant Han people, and does not apply to any of the countries many ethnic minorities — or so I was informed on a recent trip by both government employees and westerners conversant with the internal affairs of China..

[18]   For that matter, how can sexual reproduction itself be explained — when it is only half as efficient as asexual reproduction in conveying copies of an organism's genes to the next generation? Of the variety

rear children — whether offspring of one of the partners, or wholly adopted. Such nurturing transcends the simple (though all-important) economic side of children's lives, and is a vital part of reproduction in the human social context.

Does reproduction have an effect on sex lives? Anyone with small children knows that it can indeed; there are, as well, purely physical reasons causing sexual behavior to be curtailed before and after childbirth. Then there is the all-too-common propensity for husbands to stray either while their wives are pregnant, or when they are mired at home with a number of small children.

2.3. Sex<----->Economics

Sex, of course, can be a business — as the comment on prostitution opening this section made clear. Pornography, too, is a business — and the prodigious sales of such material on Ebay and other channels on the Internet makes sex one of the "sales leaders" in the electronic economy. That the vector can run completely around the triangle is obvious: sales of pornography may well stimulate reproduction — but more likely through the economic success of the pornographer than through whatever sexually stimulating effect the product might have on the consumer.

Yet there are further and perhaps more interesting links between sex and economics. If economic success is only tenuously tied to reproductive success in humans (at least when measured in sheer numbers of copies of an individual's genes left to the next generation), economic success is closely linked with sexual success — at least in the public imagination. "Romance without finance" — pronounced (by Charlie Parker) to be a "drag" in the lyrics to the 1940s bebop song of that title — bespeaks the importance that economic power can have in conducting a sex life — a connection that can even go so far as marriage and kids: reproduction. But that final vector is, of course, only a partial outcome of the more general game of sex — a game that, like everything else in life (human and otherwise), needs "economics" simply to keep it running.

Sex in the workplace (again, in industrialized societies, though Wrangham's reports of bonobo behavior also come to mind) is also notoriously more about power than it is about reproduction. Though sometimes office affairs lead to marriage and kids, (or even just kids), and (perhaps more often) to the dissolution of marriages (and therefore perhaps the economic degradation of families, hence of kids), the primary goal of such arrangements is generally not reproductive.

Suffice it to say, there are independent, interactive links between the three categories of sex, economics and reproduction in human life. At the very least, we have to concede that sexual intercourse among humans — consenting or not — is not automatically "about" reproduction. Nor, for that matter, can any item of human behavior be taken for granted as a mechanism to spread genes. I say this not just

---

of answers posed to this question, most take the form that some functional advantage (such as availability of gene repair) inherent in diploidy offsets the supposed evolutionary advantages of haploidy. Insofar as homosexuality is concerned, its mere existence throughout recorded human history should be sufficient to cast doubt on the efficacy and wisdom of taking a hard ultra-Darwinian line on explaining human behavior!

because I have argued against the central ultradarwinian notion that an organism's behavior as manifested in its economic life is really "all about" the spread of its genes, but specifically because of the still greater subtlety and complexity of human behavior occasioned by the unique decoupling of sex and reproduction in human evolution. How long this has been true of human behavior is another issue. The presence of some form of sexual activity year round in all great apes, especially in the continual sexual receptivity reported in bonobos, with its non-reproductive consequences — seems to presage our own dramatic decoupling of sex and reproduction, perhaps implying a very ancient pedigree. Some authors (e.g. Fisher, 1982) have argued that the very basis of human social organization represents a form of "sex-for-food" tradeoff — one that may well be present in rudimentary form in surviving bonobo society today.

3.   MORE HUMAN UNIQUENESSES: ECOLOGICAL ASPECTS OF HUMAN EVOLUTION

I said at the outset of this paper that little evolution occurs in the absence of regional ecological upheaval sufficiently severe to cause the extinction of a significant percentage of pre-existing species. This claim is based on the repeated pattern of what Vrba (1985) has called "turnover pulse" events. Typically, regional biotas — both ecosystems and the species occurring within a region — exhibit profound "stasis": in the marine realm, for example, species typically remain stable for 5-10 million years. But it is a striking pattern: different, unrelated species, many appearing at about the same time, persist for millions of years relatively unchanged; then, abruptly, many species disappear (either through habitat tracking as environments change, or via true extinction), and are replaced by species either newly arrived or newly evolved. The pattern is as typical of Cambrian marine trilobite faunas, as it is of Mesozoic dinosaur faunas, as it is of Tertiary mammalian faunas. This includes late Tertiary African assemblages — and that means that the pattern includes the early phases of hominid evolution (see Eldredge, 1999, for details).

    Vrba's (1985) original example of a "turnover pulse" was, in fact, the global cooling event that climaxed at about 2.5 million years ago. The vegetation pattern of eastern and southern Africa rather abruptly changed from wet woodlands with interspersed grasslands, to a drier, grassland-dominated, more open savannah setting. Among all the mammalian species to disappear around 2.5 million years ago was the southern African species *Australopithecus africanus*. Very quickly it was replaced by not one, but two hominids representing separate lineages: (1) the obligate herbivore *Paranthropus* (i.e. robust australopithecine species), and (2) the omnivorous *Homo* (in the form of the early species *Homo rudolfensis* and *Homo habilis* — see Tattersall and Schwartz, 2000 for a review of these and all other known hominid species).

    Significantly, stone tools show up in the archeological record for the first time right at this 2.5 million year datum. Thought to have been made by the earliest members of our *Homo* lineage, these tools are the first definitive evidence of a shift away from pure anatomy and physiology in the hominid approach to economic life;

they bespeak (in their undeniably crude way) of the importance of learned and regularized behavior — of culture — in our ancestor's economic behavioral repertoires.

I believe a case can be made that culture has progressively taken hold of the human approach to economic life over the past 2.5 million years (see arguments to that effect, for example, in Eldredge, 1998). The very last time when there seems to have been a direct relationship between global climate change and an event in human evolution was arguably ca. 1.7 million years ago — when another global cooling pulse produced the earliest known Pleistocene glacial ice sheets on North America and Eurasia, and when *Homo ergaster*, precursor to the (later) Asian species *Homo erectus*, first appeared.

But consider the events surrounding the advent of the *second* major Pleistocene glacial advance — at about .9 million years ago. There were no documented extinctions, or appearance of new species, in the hominid lineage to accompany this global climatic event. But there *was* an ecological event involving these hominids that, insofar as I know, was unprecedented in the prior 3.5 billion year history of life: Coincident with this glacial pulse, hominids left Africa for the first time in sufficient numbers to leave their tools and bones as common elements in the sedimentary record. It is highly unusual for a species to dramatically expand the range of environments it can tolerate — and it is more than likely that never before did a tropical species come to occupy regions in higher latitudes, especially during a period of global cooling and glaciation! Though this is inferential, the betting must be that this significant ecological shift occurred because of culture — and *not* through some newly evolved physiological or anatomical features. African *Homo ergaster,* for example, was known to have had the use of fire — as well as a more sophisticated stone tool tradition than the earlier species of that genus.

Thus the relative importance of culture in human ecology, I firmly believe, has been on the rise for millions of years before our own species appeared. This, of course, is unique — though, once again, adumbrated by behaviors seen in various great ape species today (e.g. Goodall, 1992). But hominid species, up to and including our own, still maintained the 3.5 billion year old relationship that all organisms have with biological economic systems: all species are broken up into local populations ("avatars"), forming a part of the local ecosystem. And it is worth reiterating at this juncture that this is the context where the vector of natural selection takes shape.

All that changed with the invention of agriculture, independently in a number of regions, beginning about 10,000 years ago. I (Eldredge, 1995b, 1998) have concluded that this was no mere change in the human ecological niche, but rather a revolution unprecedented in the 3.5 billion year history of life: for the first time, a species — *our* species, *Homo sapiens* — stopped living as avatars within local ecosystems[19]. Rather, we superposed ourselves on top of these systems, and indeed even declared war on them as we began converting terrestrial systems to the

---

[19]   The exception, of course, are the various hunter-gathering peoples, who up until recently did in fact maintain the primordial relation to local ecosystems. There are no such peoples left, at least in a form untouched by post-Agricultural, post-Industrial humanity.

monocultures of agriculture. And it has been successful: our population, estimated to be about 5 million a scant 10,000 years ago, now stands at 6 billion at the millennium. Talk about economic success affecting reproductive success!

Yet there is still a third major aspect of human ecological history — one that, along with the invention of culture, then the invention of agriculture, is also utterly unique in the history of life. With our communications and trade networks linking up all humanity globally, we have recently emerged as the first *economically* integrated species — exchanging over $1 trillion in goods and services among ourselves globally every day (Kennedy, 1993). Moreover, we are the first species in the history of life to act as a concerted economic entity (see above) — not, of course, within any single local ecosystem, but rather in relation to the entire (global) biosphere.

I realize that these latter two changes, radical as they are, are so recent that they cannot have affected the course of human biological evolution — including the sort of evolution of behaviors that forms the subject matter of evolutionary psychology. But they are the outcome of a 2.5 million year process that saw the rise of culture as the dominant avenue of human economic life — the source of the adaptations (or, really, adoptions) in behavior that informed the human approach to the physical and biological environment.

And so the questions become: how long has it been that sex, economics and reproduction have been separate, yet intertwined, themes in hominid life? And for how long, and to what extent, has learned behavior dominated innate behavior in hominid life?

4.   A TEST CASE: RAPE AS ADAPTATION

Everyone agrees that humans — and human behavior — have had an evolutionary history. I have claimed that narrow evolutionary psychology — and its forerunner, sociobiology — is based on the central tenets of ultradarwinian evolutionary biology: viz., that natural selection (viewed, in its strongest form, as a process of genic competition for representation in the next succeeding generation) is not only necessary, but also quite sufficient, to explain evolutionary change through time. Narrow evolutionary psychology claims that most aspects of human behavior are adaptations for the spread of genes — adaptations, moreover, evolved in remote times in circumstances rather unlike those in which the vast majority of modern humanity now lives.

I agree with all other evolutionary biologists that there must be an evolved, adaptive component to many if not all aspects of human behavior — adaptations shaped by natural selection. I have raised a number of points about biological systems generally, and human social structures specifically, that, severally and together, indicate that processes underlying evolutionary stasis and change are invariably a great deal more complex than such a simple application of ultradarwinian theory to human behavior would allow. I have reported that most evolutionary change in the last .5 billion years of Metazoan history is patently concentrated in cross-genealogical "turnover" events triggered by physical environmental change — thus effectively falsifying the central ultradarwinian tenet that evolution   simply, and exclusively, arises as an inevitable outcome of a competitive race among genic variants within species as time goes on. With reference to the dual hierarchical systems of economics and genealogy, arising from the two classes of organismic behavior generally, natural selection emerges (as Darwin originally said) as the effect that relative economic success has on reproductive success. Natural selection occurs in local populations in the context of local ecosystems — and here my analysis actually lends a point of credence to another common supposition of narrow evolutionary psychology: that the "selective pressure" that forged adaptations in the past may well no longer obtain in the modern world. The agricultural revolution removed all but a few remnant hunter-gatherers from that local ecosystem context.

But I have also argued that social systems are complex amalgams of reproductive and economic adaptations, effectively reintegrating the otherwise separate themes of survival ("making a living") in local ecosystems, and the task of reproducing. Adumbrated in the biology and behavior of various great ape species, social behavior in humans to a very great extent hinges on the "decoupling" of sex from reproduction: there is sex for pleasure, sex for power, sex for economic gain along with sex for reproduction.

Evolutionary psychologists ignore these nuances at their peril. Consider, for example, one of the strongest claims to be found in the evolutionary psychological literature: the hypothesis that rape is an adaptation, one forged long ago in human evolutionary history (see especially Thornhill and Palmer, 2000). It is a strong claim because it seems, given the underlying assumptions of narrow evolutionary psychology, to be of necessity true.

Others — including biologists and social scientists from many disciplines — object to seeing rape as arising from our genetic makeup, an ineluctable urge that arose long ago as an adaptation for the spread of genes, and an urge that cannot simply be willed, or legislated, away (see, for example, de Waal, 2000). The narrow evolutionary psychological view of rape patently views this form of violent, coerced sex to have been originally, at least, all about the spread of the rapist's genes. Sex, at least in this corner of evolutionary biological thinking, is all about reproduction. Yet there is a rich literature suggesting that rape, and the rage with which rape is closely associated, is far more about power (or, rather, powerlessness) than it is about making babies, in the psyche of the rapist.

To the objection that rape in complex, industrialized society is a distant echo of the day when rape evolved as an adaptation for the spread of genes — and absent a fossil record of rape behavior — the question naturally arises: how can we test the notion that rape originally evolved to maximize the spread of the rapist's genes? The traditional, and eminently practical, answer in evolutionary biology generally is to perform comparative studies on extant organisms — as is routinely done, for example, in systematics to judge the distribution of evolutionarily derived characteristics and thus the pattern of genealogical relationships among the organisms/taxa under study. The same principle applies when, for example, the antiquity of a human characteristic — behavioral or otherwise — is assessed in part by comparing human behavior with that of great ape species, or perhaps Primates more generally. For example, as briefly discussed above, the striking decoupling of sex and reproduction in human behavior is developed to a lesser extent in bonobos — and hinted at to a still lesser extent in the behaviors of other great ape species.

And so, in this spirit, it makes abundant sense to examine the nature and extent of rape in surviving hunter-gatherer societies. Though none persist in wholly "untouched" form, fortunately detailed ethnographies written before extensive western-world contact exist. Here, with data on the lives of contemporary hunter-gatherers, I would contend, the a priori claim that what was adaptive a million years ago is no longer so has considerably less force than when the same claim is made with respect to the very different ecological conditions experienced by post-Agricultural Revolution humanity.

And so we ask — what *is* the nature and significance of rape as documented in the ethnographies of hunter-gatherers? I make no claims of professional expertise in ethnology — nor have I performed an exhaustive search of the ethnographic literature in preparation for this paper, but what I have encountered so far offers little support to the notion that rape is an important means of spreading male genes in these societies. If anything, rape seems to occur less frequently, and to be tolerated even less, in hunter-gatherer societies than it is in modern, industrialized social systems[20].

The great problem in evolutionary biology is the convincing demonstration that a structure or an item of behavior is really an adaptation for its perceived function (Williams, 1966; Gould and Vrba, 1982). When we misconstrue the function itself — as when it is simply assumed that all forms of sexual behavior in humans is really about the spread of genes — as a corollary of the still deeper assumption that *all* behavior reflects, at base, a competitive race to leave copies of genes to the next generation, we reveal much more about the control of a priori theory over evolutionary analysis than we do about evolution itself.

American Museum of Natural History, New York

---

[20]   The frequency of rape, how much or little it is tolerated, and the extent to which rape leads to the production of children are key questions to be asked in a forthcoming comparative analysis of hunter-gatherer, pastoralist and agriculturally-based societies based on the Human Relations Area Files at Yale University. Pending the results of that study, my comments here are of necessity preliminary.

5. REFERENCES

Damuth, J. (1985). Selection among "species": A formulation in terms of natural functional units. *Evolution, 39*, 1132-1146.

Darwin, C. (1859). *On the Origin of Species.* London, Eng.: John Murray.

Darwin, C. (1871). *The Descent of Man, and Selection in Relation to Sex.* London, Eng.: John Murray.

Dawkins, R. (1976). *The Selfish Gene.* New York: Oxford University Press.

de Waal, F.B.M. (2000, April 2). Survival of the rapist. *New York Times Book Review,* 24-25.

Dobzhansky, T. (1937). *Genetics and the Origin of Species.* (Reprint ed., 1982). New York: Columbia University Press.

Eldredge, N. (1985). *Unfinished Synthesis. Biological Hierarchies and Modern Evolutionary Thought.* New York: Oxford University Press.

Eldredge, N. (1986). Information, economics and evolution. *Annual Review of Ecology and Systematics, 17*, 351-369.

Eldredge, N. (1995a). *Reinventing Darwin: The Great Debate at the High Table of Evolutionary Theory.* New York: John Wiley and Sons.

Eldredge, N. (1995b). *Dominion.* New York: Henry Holt and Co.

Eldredge, N. (1998). *Life in the Balance.* Princeton, N.J.: Princeton University Press.

Eldredge, N. (1999). *The Pattern of Evolution.* New York: W.H. Freeman and Co.

Eldredge, N. (in press). The sloshing bucket: How the physical realm controls evolution. In J.P. Crutchfield and P. Schuster (Eds.), *Evolutionary Dynamics—Exploring the Interplay of Selection, Neutrality, Accident and Function.* New York: Oxford University Press.

Eldredge, N. and Grene, M. (1992). *Interactions: The Biological Context of Social Systems.* New York: Columbia University Press

Fisher, H. (1982). *The Sex Contract.* New York: W. Morrow.

Goodall, J. (1992). *The Chimpanzee: The Living Link Between 'Man' and 'Beast': The Third Edinburgh Medal Address.* Edinburgh, Scotland: Edinburgh University Press.

Gould, S. J. and Vrba, E.S. (1982). Exaptation -- a missing term in the science of form. *Paleobiology, 8*, 4-15.

Hamilton, W.D. (1964a). The genetical evolution of social behavior, I. *Journal of Theoretical Biology, 7*, 1-16.

Hamilton, W.D. (1964b). The genetical evolution of social behavior, II. *Journal of Theoretical Biology, 7*, 17-52.

Kennedy, P. (1993). *Preparing For the Twenty-First Century.* New York: Random House.

Malthus, T.R. (1798/1826). *An Essay on the Principle of Population.* London, Eng.: J. Murray.

Mayr, E. (1942). *Systematics and the Origin of Species.* New York: Columbia University Press.

Paterson, H. E. H. (1985). The recognition concept of species. In E. S. Vrba (Ed.), *Species and Speciation. (Transvaal Museum Monograph # 4*, pp. 21-29). Pretoria: Transvaal Museum.

Pick, J. and Anderton, M. (1999). *Building Jerusalem: Art, Industry and the British Millennium.* Amsterdam, The Netherlands: Harwood Academic Publishers.

Salthe, S. N. (1985). *Evolving Hierarchical Systems.* New York: Columbia University Press.

Sherman, P. W., Jarvis, J.U.M. and Alexander, R.D. (Eds.). (1991). *The Biology of the Naked Mole-rat.* Princeton, N.J.: Princeton University Press.

Tattersall, I. and Schwartz, J.H. (2000). *Extinct Humans.* New York: Westview Press.

Thornhill, R. and Palmer, C.T. (2000). *A Natural History of Rape: Biological Bases of Coercion.* Cambridge, MA.: MIT Press.

Vrba, E. S. (1985). Environment and evolution: Alternative causes of the temporal distribution of evolutionary events. *South African Journal of Science, 81*, 229-236.

Williams, G. C. (1966). *Adaptation and Natural Selection: A Critique of Some Current Evolutionary Thought.* Princeton, N.J.: Princeton University Press.

Williams, G. C. (1992). *Natural Selection: Domains, Levels, and Applications.* New York: Oxford University Press.

Wilson, E. O. (1975). *Sociobiology.* Cambridge, MA.: Harvard University Press.

Wilson, E.O. (1998). *Consilience.* New York: Alfred A. Knopf.

Woolfenden, G.E. and Fitzpatrick, J.W. (1984). *The Florida Scrub Jay: Demography of a Cooperative-Breeding Bird.* Princeton, N.J.: Princeton University Press.

Wrangham, R.W. (1986). Ecology and social relationships in two species of chimpanzees. In D.I. Rubenstein and R.W. Wrangham (Eds.), *Ecological Aspects of Social Evolution: Birds and Mammals* (pp. 352-378). Princeton, N.J.: Princeton University Press.

Wright, S. (1931). Evolution in Mendelian populations. *Genetics, 16,* 97-159.

Wright, S. (1932). The roles of mutation, inbreeding, crossbreeding, and selection in evolution. *Proceedings of the Sixth International Congress on Genetics, 1,* 356-366.

SARAH BLAFFER HRDY

THE OPTIMAL NUMBER OF FATHERS

Evolution, Demography, and History in the Shaping of Female Mate
Preferences

1. MODELS THAT ASSUME "ARDENT" MALES AND "COY" FEMALES

According to Darwin's theory of sexual selection, males compete among themselves
for access to females, and then females choose the one best male. As Darwin put it,
the female "with the rarest exception, is less eager (to mate) than the male...." The
female generally "requires to be courted; she is coy, and may often be seen en-
deavoring for a long time to escape..." (Darwin, 1871, p. 273). A century later,
textbooks with chapter titles like "The Reluctant Female and the Ardent Male"
(Daly & Wilson, 1978) perpetuate this essential dichotomy between the sexes.
Because sperm-producing males invest less in offspring than ovulating and
gestating females do, and because of the time that must elapse between female
conceptions, males benefit from mating with as many partners as they can and are
naturally eager to do so, while females cannot benefit from philandering and extra
fertilizations in this same way (Trivers, 1972). This presumption of monandrous
females coupled with males who ranged from monogamous to polygynous shaped
our reconstructions of early hominid mating systems.

       To this day, it remains axiomatic in many circles that females do not
benefit from multiple partners — especially not in humans where male protection
and provisioning are essential for offspring survival. It is assumed that mothers
lose, and cannot possibly gain from behaviors that reduce male certainty of
paternity (e.g., see Symons, 1982, p. 299 for an explicit statement of this widely
held assumption often left unstated). This is why it is often assumed that men must
have an insatiable desire for sexual variety, in contrast to women, who should be
indifferent to it (Pinker, 1997, p. 473). The reason men desire many partners —

Steven J. Scher & Frederick Rauscher (Eds.). Evolutionary Psychology: Alternative
Approaches, 111-133

Reprinted with Permission from D. LeCroy & P. Moller (2000). (Eds.).
Evolutionary Perspectives on Human Reproductive Behavior (Annals of the New
York Academy of Sciences, v. 907).

while women desire only one — is that supposedly a prehistoric man "who slept with fifty women could have sired fifty children," while a woman who slept with many partners "would have no more descendants than a woman who slept with one" (Pinker, 1998, p. 30).

At one level, such arguments are indisputable. No one can reasonably deny a generalized male eagerness to mate evident in many different species, nor fail to note that some females are sexually discriminating, even to the point of being obligately monandrous. The pronghorn antelope provides the very model of a sexually selected Darwinian mammal. Having scrutinized the performances of males in her vicinity, the female pronghorn makes sure that she is in the custody of the most vigorous male available during the brief period when she is ready to conceive, and then mates just once, only with him (Byers, 1997, especially pp. 214-230). After all, she descends from a long line of ancestresses who had one clear priority: to produce offspring capable of outrunning the cheetah that once coursed across North America, and exercised a voracious selection pressure on pronghorns.

Longstanding selection pressures that favor the most viable offspring explain why females "free" to choose (*sensu* Gowaty) among progenitors should be more fertile and have more viable offspring. In the clearest demonstration to date, Marion Petrie has shown how peahens comparison-shop and then mate with the peacock whose train is most elaborate (Petrie, 1994). Chicks sired by the male with the largest eyespots grew larger and survived better. Since peacocks contribute nothing to offspring beyond their genes, the most plausible interpretation is that the fanciest males also provided the most viable genes — as predicted by sexual selection theory. The problem does not reside with Darwin's theory, but with the practice of generalizing from the female pronghorn or peafowl (females with clear priorities and quite a few options) to females generally, including females whose options are more constrained (Gowaty, 1996; Gowaty, 1997a, 1997b). Hence, when we presume that women are modest and sexually discriminating because "that's the way all females are...." we close the case too soon, leaving out history relevant to both the evolution and also the development of the behavior we are studying, in particular all the tactics and stratagems both by males (and also by other females) that interfere with female choice or create circumstances that override a straightforward quest for good genes.

It should not surprise us therefore to learn about another of Marion Petrie's research findings: across a broad sample of birds that live in socially monogamous pairs rates of extra-pair paternity (based on DNA matching) were highest in populations with the most genetic variation between males (Petrie, Doums & Moller, 1998). Populations with the highest incidence of "infidelity" were those in which outside partners were likely to be most genetically different from the female's mate. Being paired with an individual who, from the female's perspective, is a suboptimal male — whether it is because he is genetically "inferior," immunologically inappropriate, too close a relative, or whatever — is one obvious rationale for a female to seek extra-pair copulations. And, indeed, once researchers started to look, sperm competition turned out to be widespread (Baker & Bellis, 1995; Eberhard, 1996; Smith, 1984; Thornhill & Gangestad, 1996). What is often overlooked, however, is that without selection pressure on females to mate polyandrously, strong selection pressures on males to produce voluminous and competitive sperm would never have been at work in the first place. Indeed, one of the more plausible rationales for the rare evolution of intromittent penises in a species of weaverbird is that selection for this mode of sperm delivery was produced by polyandrous mating by the anything-but-coy females in that species (Winterbottom, Burke & Birkhead, 1999). If this hypothesis holds up, it would be ironic that penises — viewed by many as the essence of ardent maleness — would have evolved to help males cope with the challenges generated by female promiscuity.

In what follows, I first summarize comparative evidence across animals that illustrates why when females can *not* have their first choice (which would be freedom to choose the father with the most viable genes in a world where the mother and her offspring are kept safe and guaranteed access to the resources they need), they resort to "Female Plan B," seeking benefits available from mating with a range of males. Next, I return to the primate order to examine specific problems female primates have in exercising free mate-choice, and to features of female sexuality (defined here as readiness to copulate) that I assume evolved to counteract and overcome these obstacles. In particular, 1 will argue that polyandrous mating was an important element in the strategic repertoire primate mothers use to keep their infants alive, and that a polyandrous (as opposed to monandrous or "coy") heritage is central to the psychophysiological legacy that our prehominid ancestors brought to the hominid experiment. Finally, I review ethnographic evidence demonstrating that polyandrous tendencies are more widely expressed in the human species than is apparent from cross-cultural surveys taken from the ethnographic present.

Instead of attributing monandrous mate preference in women to some essential female nature, this alternate view of female primate sexuality requires us to consider recent history (measured in thousands and hundreds of years) as well as the evolutionary history of those populations.

2.   BENEFITS OF POLYANDRY: COMPARATIVE EVIDENCE

Once sociobiologists began to consider seriously the possibility that females might benefit from polyandrous mating, one of the first stereotypes to crumble was the assumption that males are unique in seeking sexual variety for its own sake (again see Symons, 1979 for a clear statement of that widely held assumption). Recent experiments with pseudoscorpions (*Cordylochemes scorpiodes*) reveal females actively seeking sperm from sequential partners. Typically, females paired with the same male prefer a respite one-and-a-half hours after mating, and then are eager to resume mating after 48 hours. Given a chance to mate with a different male, however, the proportion of females accepting sperm from an additional male was as great after an hour-and-a-half as after 48 hours. No comparable quest for novelty was detected for males. Males remained eager to mate again and again with the same female (Zeh, Newcomer & Zeh, 1998). Furthermore, subsequent experiments demonstrated that females receiving sperm from two different males had a significantly higher reproductive success than did females receiving an equivalent number of sperm packets *all from the same male*, probably due to increased genetic compatibility between partners (Zeh, Newcomer & Zeh, 1999).

Similar preferences for "novel" (read outbred?) males are reported for free-ranging primates (Hrdy, 1977; Small, 1993 p. 166ff). As early as the 1970s genetic studies using protein polymorphism data to perform paternity exclusions for a troop of Japanese macaques revealed that 29% of infants were sired by males from outside the troop. Similarly, among chimps at the Tai site in Cote d'Ivoire, some seven percent of infants were sired by males from other communities. Reports from chimps in Tanzania and Guinea confirm this pattern of occasional extra-community paternity. Apparently, furtive matings permit female Japanese macaques (Hrdy, 1977, p. 137, n 13) and chimps (Vigilant, Hofreiter, Siedel and Boesch, 2001) to circumvent constraints of breeding options imposed by cliques of locally dominant males. New genetic evidence for hominoid primates reveals that proteins linked to sperm production have evolved faster in humans and chimpanzees than among gorillas, suggesting that sperm competition characterized our hominid ancestors as well as the ancestors of modern chimps (Wyckoff, Wang & Wu, 2000). If human ancestors were characterized by sperm competition it strengthens the likelihood that early human females were mating polyandrously. But why? Let us first consider comparative evidence for other animals.

Abundant evidence now exists for a wide range of animals that females free to mate with a range of males are more fertile and their offspring more viable (Hoogland, 1998; Madsen et al, 1992; Zeh et al, 1998). Among prairie dogs, for example, females who escape being monopolized by a single male, and manage to mate with three or more males, are more fertile and produce significantly larger litters than do mothers who mated with only one male (Hoogland, 1998). Because prairie dog litters may be sired by multiple progenitors, such litters will be genetically more diverse with attendant protection against lineage extinction (due to parasites, for example) (Baer & Schmid-Hempel, 1999). Maternal fecundity is correlated not only with the number of males the female mates with, but also correlated with the mother's body size. Maternal body size is a factor not just because big mothers are more fertile, but also because, as Hoogland points out, large females are better at avoiding domination by males who might otherwise constrain their mate choices (Hoogland, 1998).

In line with conventional Darwinian thinking, a prairie dog male benefits from monopolizing access to a female. But there is an added twist. The male's mate does not always benefit from being so managed. Discrepant interests between males and females explain why females able to resist male control should be more fertile or produce more viable offspring. But improving their odds in the genetic lottery of sexual recombination is not the only incentive for mothers to engage in polyandrous matings. Females also benefit in ways that have nothing to do with which sperm actually fertilizes her egg. Other-than-genetic benefits include the chance to exchange sexual access for immediate benefits — such as nutrients — or for future benefits such as eliciting male protection, support, or tolerance for subsequently born infants. In order for polyandrous tendencies to evolve, benefits must on average outweigh costs in terms of energy, exposure to sexually transmitted diseases or punishment by possessive mates.

A classic example of immediate benefits from mating *other* than fertilization, would be katydids, where males squeeze out a large sperm packet full of nutrients and then transmit it to the female who converts those resources into progeny. Other exchanges of sex for resources (or social support) can be widely documented among primates, both in primates like chimps and humans, where males hunt, and in those like bonobos, where hunting is rare (deWaal & Lanting, 1997; Knight, 1991).

But can sexual relations with a female alter a male's behavior toward offspring she subsequently bears? In many primates (34 different species, so far) infanticide is one of the more toxic effects of sexually selected competition between males. Among langur monkeys, for example, males who enter the breeding system from outside may kill unweaned infants (Hrdy, 1979). Over an 18-year-long study of langurs at Jodhpur, in the largest such study ever undertaken, Sommer (1994) reports that 33% of all infants die by being killed when their mothers are intercepted by males they have never mated with. Infanticide effectively cancels the mother's last mate choice, distorts her options for scheduling the next conception, and imposes pressure on her to conceive after a shorter interval than might otherwise be physiologically optimal for her, constraining her to breed with the male at hand rather than waiting for a better alternative. Recent DNA evidence collected by Carolla Borries and colleagues in the first langur field study to ascertain paternity reveals that none of the victims were attacked by genetic fathers. Males who either were or might be the father (this based on both DNA evidence and behavioral observations to ascertain which males mated with the mother when she was fertile) refrain from attacking offspring of that female. At Borries's site, where males are sometimes able to remain near the mother, possible fathers actually help her to protect her infant. Since all mothers mate with multiple males, none of the protectors could be certain of paternity, yet a possibility of paternity was sufficient to alter the male's subsequent behavior towards her offspring (Borries et al, 1999; Launhardt et al, 1998), presumably because past sexual history with the mother provides some sort of cue that elicits tolerant versus destructive behavior towards her infant.[1] Because there are both practical and ethical constraints on doing such experiments with primates, the only rigorous research on cues that

---

[1] The best evidence for this is that even a strange infant, temporarily kidnapped from another troop, is not attacked so long as it remains in the possession of a female who is familiar to the male.

promote switches from infanticidal to nurturing behavior in males has been done with rodents (Perrigo & vom Saal, 1994). Although we are ignorant of the exact processes involved in the case of monkeys, it seems unlikely that the transformation in male behavior is due to any conscious decision.

Langurs are not the only primates where males with only a fractional probability of paternity help protect a former mate's offspring. Some savanna baboon males who mate with a female subsequently stay close. These "possible fathers" look out for their offspring and intervene if an infant, possibly theirs, is threatened by another male (Palombit, 1999). I believe that sexual swellings actually evolved among primates precisely to facilitate breeding with several "possible fathers."

Just how effective male proximity is for keeping babies alive is hard to quantify. The task is simplified when, as in humans and some birds, males provision, because observers can measure how much food is brought to immatures cached in a centralized homebase or nest. The best evidence for how mothers benefit from manipulating information about paternity derives from a type of European sparrow known as the dunnock (*Prunella modularis*). Dunnock females are typically polyandrous, males (if they can be) are polygynous. Alpha and beta males calibrate the number of mouthfuls of food they bring chicks in accordance with how often they managed to copulate during the period when the female was fertile (Burke et al, 1989; Davies, 1992). As predicted by the hypothesis that females manipulate the information available to males about paternity (Hrdy, 1979, pp. 32-35), DNA fingerprinting revealed that dunnock males were often, but not always, accurate in their paternity "assessments."

The most striking similarity with primates, however, is found in a close relative of dunnocks (*Prunella collaris*) that also lives in multi-male, multi-female breeding groups. These birds have converged upon a baboon-like solution for making sure that fertile females mate with several males. The female's cloacal region protrudes and turns scarlet, increasing the odds that multiple males will be drawn into the web of possible paternity (Nakamura, 1990). The more males — up to three — provisioning chicks, the larger the number of chicks surviving to fledge (Nakamura, 1998a, 1998b).

3. TRAITS FACILITATING POLYANDROUS MATING ARE PROMINENT IN PRIMATES

In the Primate order, sexual swellings have evolved at least three different times, and characterize some 25 species. "No case," Darwin wrote, "interested and per-plexed me so much as the brightly colored hinder ends and adjoining parts of certain monkeys" (Darwin, 1876, p. 18-19). I doubt, however, that Darwin would have remained puzzled for long if he had read recent accounts of chimp and bonobo sexual behavior (Parish & deWaal, 2000). A maximally swollen female chimp mates 1-4 times an hour with thirteen or more partners. Over her lifetime, she will engage in some six thousand or more copulations (Wrangham, 1993) with dozens of partners, in order to produce no more than five or so surviving offspring (Wallis & Almasi, 1995).

Let us assume that sexual swellings did evolve to insure that female primates mate with multiple partners. Some years ago, I attempted to make sense of the confusing diversity of sexual patterns in Old World monkeys and apes — both those with and those without sexual swellings — by substituting this new assumption for the old assumption that each female was selected to mate with the one best male (Hrdy, 1986, 1997). I assumed that by and large these females were resorting to a different strategy. The "goal" for them was to mate polyandrously with a range of partners. How to manage this became the "problem" females had to "solve." Exactly how they solved it depended on phylogenetic constraints, current mating system and demographic conditions.

Where multiple males are permanently in residence, the most efficient solution is for females to compress mating into a discrete period around ovulation and to conspicuously advertise estrus so that males have to follow the female around and compete among themselves for the opportunity to mate, and then their "goal" accomplished, to return to business as usual, namely, foraging. In most primates, however, one dominant male excludes competing males; females have only occasional (often furtive) opportunities to mate with subordinate or outside males. Under these circumstances, one way for females to solve the problem of mating with a range of males is to exhibit the same midcycle peak in libido universally found in primates, but to also solicit sex on a less cyclical, more "situation-dependent" basis.[2] The absence of any discrete signal of ovulation visible at a distance would be an asset under such circumstances.

When ovulation is not advertised by conspicuous swellings, only a resident male able to monitor a female across cycles has reliable cues (olfactory as well as visual?) as to when she is actually fertile. Among langur monkeys, for example, there is no conspicuous visible sign at ovulation. Instead females present their rumps and shudder their heads with variable and idiosyncratic intensity. Most solicitations occur at midcycle, but females have the potential to also solicit males and mate on a situation-dependent schedule (cf., Andelman, 1987; Buchanon-Smith & Jordan, 1992; Palombit, 1992; Takahata, 1980; van Noordwijk, 1985). Some years ago, Kim Wallen reviewed experimental results that provide indirect support for the hypothesis that there is more to primate mating than conception. When groups of macaque females (who do not exhibit discrete sexual swellings at

---

[2.] Libido is an old psychological term for sexual drive; primatologists prefer "sexual proceptivity." Such desire is presumed to have evolved because it increased a fertile female's chances of conceiving. However, many primates (not only women) exhibit "proceptive behavior," actively solicit males, or copulate even at times when they are not ovulating. This flexible capacity to mate on a situation dependent basis across the cycle leads to a great deal of nonconceptive sexual behavior between potentially fertile males and females who are not currently fertile. Given this situation, it is the biological equivilent of apples versus oranges to compare the "sex drive" of a potentially fertile male with a nonovulating female, or to assume that the urge to mate derives from the same "motivation" or evolved for the same reason in both sexes.

midcycle as chimps do) were caged with a single male, they basically played the game by the endocrinological book. Female proceptivity peaked at midcycle, and mating was confined to this midcycle period of "estrus." However, when females were caged with multiple males, the patterning of sexuality in these macaques became more flexible and they solicited sex across the follicular phase of the cycle, with dominant females taking precedence over subordinates in mating with the most males (Figure 4 in Wallen, 1990). (See Bercovitch, 1999, for discussion of the especially variable and complex expression of sexual swellings in the genus *Macaca*, which includes interesting exceptions to general patterns described here).

Extraordinarily enterprising bonobo females combine elements of both visible swellings plus periods of sexual receptivity that last for weeks. But it is human females who (like langurs) do not have a conspicuous physical sign around ovulation, who fall at the extreme edge of the primate continuum of flexible receptivity. Women exhibit a midcycle peak in libido but are capable of copulating throughout the cycle (Stanislaw & Rice, 1988) (for broader literature review see Table 3 in Hrdy, 1997). Not only does human female behavior and the cues that she exhibits to males change, but even the criteria by which females assess males over the menstrual cycle change, so, for example, women prefer men with more "masculine" faces at midcycle, more "feminized" faces at other endocrinological phases (see Penton-Voak et al., 1999, and the references therein).

Many people still assume that our hominid ancestors had sexual swellings that were lost over the course of human evolution, some say to promote pair bonding (Lovejoy, 1981). In fact, swellings are more likely to have been independently evolved in the line leading to chimps and bonobos. Sexual swellings are scarcely detectable in the other Great Apes or among the last surviving relics of the genus *Homo* — modern humans. "Concealed ovulation" (or more accurately, ovulation without advertising) in our own species is not so much a new trait as an extreme manifestation of an old one.

4.   WHY IS POLYANDRY SO RARE IN HUMANS — OR IS IT?

Wherever primates are well studied, there turn out to be remarkably few populations where females do not, when feasible, solicit strange or "extra-group" males (van Noordwijk & van Schaik, 2000). Even in famously monogamous species like titi monkeys or siamangs, females solicit outsiders when they can (Mason, 1966; Palombit, 1999). From the sexual swellings and prominent clitoris of a chimpanzee, to the semi-continuous, situation-dependent receptivity of a tamarin, female primates apparently evolved to draw multiple males into the web of possible paternity when feasible. When, in 1981, I proposed that such a polyandrous tendency (however subdued) was part of the legacy that prehominid females brought to the human experiment, the idea was rejected not only by feminists uncomfortable at the prospect of assigning biologically based predispositions to either sex, but also by evolutionary psychologists, who deemed the idea of polyandrous potentials in human females impossible on theoretical grounds because paternal provisioning was viewed as essential to female reproductive success, and males capable of assessing the mother's recent sexual history ought to "diminish their parental investments as their confidence in paternity wanes" (Symons, 1982, p. 299). "Why," Don Symons (1982), a founding father of evolutionary psychology, inquired, "should a female be better off with ... three males, each of which invests one-third unit [than] with one male which invests one unit?" He concluded that there is only "dubious evidence that this [assertively sexual female] nature exists and no evidence that women anywhere normally tie up multiple male parental investments by confusing the issue of paternity..." (p. 299).

Across cultures, formal polyandrous marriages are indeed exceedingly rare (fewer than 2% of human cultures are so classified). But informally, polyandrous arrangements are far more common due to extramarital affairs, to a shortage of women or inability of one man to provide security (Smedley, 1980), to a husband's "sharing" his wife with kin, age-mates or allies (which by some estimates is found in one-third of all human cultures) (Broude, 1994, p. 334), or due to women who take up with sequential mates over a lifetime (Guyer, 1994; Sangree, 1980). Because so little attention has been focused on these topics, however, it can be difficult to learn from the ethnographic record whether a woman was seduced, raped, complicitous, or the initiator, or whether the husband was duped or supportive. For husbands are not always prohibitively jealous of their wives (e.g., see Smedley, 1980, for an African case study and Crocker and Crocker, 1994, for a South American one). That is, mothers — and sometimes husbands as well -- behave as if they were aware that male solidarity could be critical to their well being, or that having several "fathers" could promote the survival of offspring that statistically are more likely to have been sired by a woman's husband (or by his kin) than by an unrelated progenitor.

All foragers, and hence all early humans, were cooperative breeders in the sense that no mother could hope to successfully rear successive children unless she had direct and substantial assistance from others (Hrdy, 1999). In this respect, humans are different from other extant apes, for whom provisioning (mostly by mothers) ends at weaning. In humans, by contrast, provisioning goes on and on, long past weaning, sometimes past adolescence, past marriage, and even past the time that an offspring begins to breed. Among many hunter-gatherers, youngsters 18 years and older are still consuming more calories than they collect (Kaplan, 1997). Mothers by themselves — especially if they have new infants — cannot successfully rear offspring without assistance from others. Not all of this assistance comes from husbands, or even necessarily from men. Caretaking assistance by pre-reproductive group members and provisioning help from other mothers and especially post-reproductive kin (often referred to as "grandmothers" since mother's mother, mother-in-law or aunt sometimes provide critical help) is increasingly well documented for foraging societies (Hawks et al, 1998; Hill & Hurtado, 1996; Hrdy, 1999).

What is important about "polyandrous motherhood"[3] is not just the spectacle of women "having fun," but the more enduring vision of mothers making do. My goal here is not to rewrite ethnography in the wake of our society's changing attitudes towards female sexuality, but to point out how new assumptions about the potential benefits of polyandry (some of them introduced into evolutionary biology by feminists) can increase our awareness of female strategies. Once we broaden our definition of polyandrous behavior to include situations where one mother is linked to several men — husbands, fathers, and possible fathers — polyandry is not so rare after all (see Tew, 1951; Smith, 1953; Muller, 1980; and Guyer, 1994, pp. 231-252, for both pre- and postcolonial West African societies; Hakansson, 1988, for densely populated areas of East Africa; Crocker and Crocker, 1994; Hill and Hurtado, 1996; and Beckerman et al., 1998 for tribal South America; pre-twentieth century ethnographic accounts like those for the Huron, cited in Hartung, 1985, for North America; Berndt and Berndt, 1951, for aboriginal Australia; Befu, 1968; and Shih, 1993 for traditional societies in Central Japan and southwestern China; as well as Hrdy, 1999, for additional examples from contemporary mother-centered families in rural and urban Africa and the Americas, as well as the Caribbean). Wherever power relations between the sexes permit it — which among humans is more likely to be the case among matrilocal women, who tend to have greater reproductive autonomy — and wherever ecological or economic circumstances make polyandrous matings more beneficial than monandrous pairing, we would expect mothers to hedge their bets by trading off certainty of paternity for the advantages to be obtained from "several fathers."

Take the Ache of eastern Paraguay (Hill & Hurtado, 1996, pp. 229ff.). At any one time, the majority of marriages are monogamous. Yet each of these unions at some point is likely to be polygynous or polyandrous. For marriage among foragers is inherently unstable, especially when unions are passing through a polygynous or polyandrous phase. The marriage dissolves from internal tensions due to male jealousy or to intolerance between co-wives. Sixty percent (11 of 18) of a sample of men interviewed about the period prior to contact with Westerners, had been in a polyandrous marriage at least briefly. Over their lives, most Ache women have children with two or more men, a pattern found in many traditional societies (e.g., Sangree, 1980). Ultimately, in spite of the obvious commonalities of interest between a husband and a wife and in spite of all the efficiencies that trust and long-term pair bonds can offer, these unions are perpetually at risk due to tensions between the preoccupations of fathers, whose top priority is often access to a new mate (hence quantity of offspring sired), compared to the concerns of mothers whose top priority is more often the quality and the prospects for those offspring they commit to (discussed further in Hrdy, 1999).

[3.] *Polyandrous motherhood* is a relatively new term used by anthropoligists (Guyer, 1994) to cope with the discrepancies between formal marriage labels and the actual lives of women rearing children fathered by different men, or children whose genetic paternity is unclear. A woman may be married to a man other than the genetic "father" of a given child or find herself eliciting assistance from several men — not necessarily her husband.

This does not mean that fathers are unimportant. Far from it. The record on that is all too clear: children without male protection and provisioning suffer terrible costs from malnutrition, infanticide, and pedicide (Hill & Hurtado, 1996). This is not an "anti-family" message. To my knowledge, monogamy, with its emphasis on shared interests between the sexes, has always provided the best antidote to the more toxic effects of sexual selection. For a mother with the luxury of choosing her mate, under circumstances where both parents are likely to be committed to investing in the offspring, monogamy may well be the woman's optimal strategy.

The point is not that males don't matter, but rather that there was never much evidence or a very strong theoretical basis for assuming that mothers in the Pleistocene could count on fathers to give a higher priority to provisioning children they already have rather than seeking additional mates any more than mothers today can count on them to do so. Instead, what impresses behavioral ecologists like Kristen Hawkes, James O'Connell, and Nicholas Blurton-Jones is how often men today (in the case of their studies of hunters among African foragers) seem more interested in maximizing prestige (which translates into more sexual partners) than in actually provisioning families. They emphasize the impracticality of foraging decisions, particularly men's obsession with large and prestigious prey like eland, even when higher returns in terms of protein can be obtained by targeting more abundant, but less prestige-enhancing small prey (Hawkes et al, 1998; Hawkes, O'Connell & Blurton-Jones, n.d.). It is telling, for example, that among people like the Ache, hunters lose interest in their wives right after birth — at just the time when a women most needs to be provisioned. In the pungent idiom of the Ache, men don't like being around new mothers because "their bodies smell (of milk)..." (Hill & Hurtado, 1996). While men tend to find very pregnant and postpartum wives less sexually attractive, women have increased libido in the first and second trimesters of pregnancy (Masters & Johnson, 1966) but reduced libido in the months post partum. (e.g., Barrett et al, 1999) — just when they presumably (especially in foraging societies) are *most in need of provisioning*. In other words, nothing about this pattern conforms to predictions generated by the model that either women's sexuality (willingness to engage in sex) or their sexual attractiveness evolved to insure male provisioning after birth.

If paternal provisioning were absolutely essential for survival of offspring, fathers themselves should have been selected long ago to find babies and new mothers irresistibly attractive. But there is little evidence that they do. Rather, it is just when mothers need protection and provisioning most that men seem sexually least interested in wives and most likely to seek new sexual partners. The unreliability of some (many?) fathers[4] would be a compelling reason for women who anticipate unpredicatable provisioning to hedge their bets by lining up support from an array of allomothers (individuals other than the mother who help care for

---

[4] This paper focuses on maternal rather than paternal perspectives; I do not discuss variation in parenting behavior by men.

her offspring). Such allomothers might include her own kin as well as "possible" fathers and their kin.

Is there, then, never any reason — apart from capture, cloistering, clitoridectomies, constant surveillance, or monopolization of the resources women need to reproduce — for a woman to freely choose to remain with one man and be faithful to him? Of course there is: when spouses are compatibly matched, when the man is committed to staying, and especially when shared stakes in offspring or other endeavors are high enough. This is one reason why rates of DNA-detected misattributed paternity are inversely correlated with socioeconomic status (Baker, 1999; Cerda-Flores et al, 1999).

There are also internalized reasons for women — even those without these incentives — to behave modestly. In many societies, a girl is taught that her status and that of her children depends on her "reputation" (one reason, other than claustration, why rates of misattributed paternity would be so low in populations such as orthodox Jews [Boster, Hudson & Gaulin, 1999]). So too do women behave modestly when they are convinced from an early age that demons, damnation, or other punishments await those who transgress normative sex roles (Hrdy, 1999). But otherwise (especially in societies that are matrilocal, bilocal, or neolocal, but even occasionally in those that are patrilineal), informal polyandry is more common.

At this point, some readers may be wondering about the bottom line: can polyandrous matings and confusion of paternity ever increase a woman's reproductive success? To date, the best-documented cases derive from lowland South America. In this part of the world there is a commonly accepted belief that fetuses are "built up" in a woman by multiple applications of semen from several different men (a biological fiction known to anthropologists as *partible paternity* [Beckerman et al, 1998]). A belief in partible paternity characterizes societies ranging over a vast area from central and eastern Brazil (the Mehinacu, the Kaingang, the Arawete, and the Curripaco) northeastward to the Bari and Yanomana of Venezuela, east to the Matis of Peru, all the way south to the Ache of Paraguay. A belief in partible paternity encompasses people belonging to at least six different language groups, tribes separated by thousands of miles, who presumably diverged from one another long ago. Such a belief, where it exists, reduces potential costs to mothers from polyandrous mating (Beckerman et al, 1998).

Among the matrilocal hunter-gatherer-horticulturist Canela, virtually every child has several co-fathers. Indeed, the Canela are unusual for casting the web of possible paternity across more than a dozen different candidates since women engage in publicly sanctioned unions with many men, often having sexual intercourse with them as part of a designated ceremony (Crocker & Crocker, 1994). Virtually every Canela child born has more than one possible father. Elsewhere in this "partible paternity zone," children are more likely to have only a couple of possible "fathers" or else only one. In these cases, it is possible for researchers to compare the survival chances of children who have attributed to them different numbers of possible fathers.

Behavioral ecologists Kim Hill and Magdalena Hurtado (1996, p. 444) report that 63% of Ache children from their demographically reconstructed (pre-contact) forest sample had one or more secondary fathers. Children with one primary and one secondary father had the highest survival rates, while those with only one, or with more than two (i.e., too many possible fathers), survived less well. Among the Bari, 80% of children (156 out of 194) with paternity ascribed to several "fathers" survived to age fifteen, compared to only 64% (404 out of 628 of children) with only one father a difference significant at the 0.001 level (Beckerman, 1999). Beckerman et al (1998) attribute this greater survival to the gifts of food co-fathers provide.

Having several presumptive fathers is likely to be especially advantageous where one man may not be able to reliably provision a family, or where fathers are critical for offspring-survival but are also likely to die. (Throughout this area fatherless children are less likely to survive). Other demographic contingencies — such as a shortage of wives — can also increase pressure for polyandrous unions. Consider for example a case reported among the Yanomana, a people famous for the polygynous marriages of powerful males who accumulate many wives. Napoleon Chagnon's research provides sociobiologists their "chestnut" case for a traditional society in which a man's dominance status corrclates with his reproductive success. What is often overlooked, however, is that (as with the Ache) a comprehensive view of Yanomana family systems must also include not only a wife's extra-pair matings, but also occasional polyandrous phases in the family dynamic. During the years just after the anthropologist John Peters contacted the Shirishana Yanomana, a period characterized by a shortage of women, there were nine polyandrous marriages and five monogamous ones. (Peters & Hunt, 1975; Peters, 1982) (Although all the relevant parties lived together, these polyandrous marriages were informal and transient, so that the distinction between polyandrous marriage and polyandrous mating is not clear-cut.) All marriages begin monogamously. Thereafter, an extra wife will be added if such a woman is available and the husband prevails. But if wives are in short supply, it may be that an extra husband (who presumably has no better option than to marry polyandrously) is added. Furthermore it must be noted that if the first husband has a good chance of being the father of offspring sired and the additional father enhances the probability of their survival, or if the first husband benefits from the alliance with another man, paternal as well as maternal interests may be served by this arrangement. No doubt the belief in partible paternity facilitates such polyandrous unions. Nevertheless, monogamy among these people, was the most stable marital form, an uneasy compromise between maternal and paternal interests.

Everywhere, polyandrous unions and communal sharing of wives are fragile arrangements, especially after contact with outside groups. Among the

Canela, there were both internal and external pressures that discouraged their persistence (e.g., disapproval by outside government agents and domestic changes within families as Canela men obtained jobs in the wage economy). It is unusual in any traditional society for publicly sanctioned informal polyandry to survive contact with economic systems that produce competition for defensible resources. Even among people who persist in believing that paternity is partible among a wife's different sexual partners, patrilineal ownership of the means of production (probably a relatively recent innovation in the Amazonian partible paternity zone) can lead to a new puritanism. As ethnographer Paul Valentine describes for the Curripaco, these people continue to believe that infants are composites built up by multiple inseminators. Yet patrilineal ownership of productive land along the river has since developed among these people, making husbands increasingly intolerant of infidelity by wives — which persists, but in secret. At the root of this change, I suspect, is newly valuable property and the patrilineal transmission of this property. A desire to avoid confusion or conflict over patrilineal resources provides one reason why, if a Curripaco man dies, his widow is supposed to remain chaste or else marry a kinsman from the husband's patrilineage (Valentine, 1999).

Across cultures, polyandrous matings range from the extremes of publicly sanctioned ritual couplings among the Canela, or the wife-sharing of clan-based groups like the Masai, to the furtive unions that characterize all but the most coercively patriarchal societies. Through time and across space a broad range of female predispositions can be documented in ethnographic, historical, and even pre-historic accounts that linger on as folklore about the Maenads and their ilk. Species differences notwithstanding, across primates and across populations, the main factors determining how monandrous primate females are have less to do with the fact that they are the ovum-producing sex, than with their ecological and historical circumstances. Key variables include how much autonomy the female's local alliances permit her, and how successful males in her population are (and have traditionally or historically been) in excluding rivals and controlling female movements. A reliable generalization across primates, including humans, is that females who remain among their kin in female philopatric (or "matrilocal") arrangements have greater autonomy than those who live patrilocally (Hrdy, 1981; Ross, 1986).

Until recently, I, like most sociobiologists, assumed that the female philopatry typical of social mammals, including most species of Old World monkeys, had been replaced by male philopatry among apes, and that this patrilocal way of life was "species-typical" and "universal" among both chimps and humans. (Wrangham & Peterson, 1996, p.125) Many of those applying evolutionary perspectives to human behavior still take it for granted that in almost all traditional societies "sons stay near their families and daughters move away...." (Rodseth et al., 1991, p. 477) It is a conclusion that initially rested on two points: the importance of closely bonded male relatives in chimps and the finding that 70% of cultures in the ethnographic record are patrilocal (Witkowsi & Divale, 1996). Since 80% of patrilocal societies are polygynous, the presumption about male patrilocal residence seemed consistent with presumptions about uni-male polygynous family systems, and led to the conviction that early human mating systems could safely be assumed to be patrilocal and polygynous. Today, however, these assumptions are far from secure.

As evidence on chimp demography and genetics accumulates from long-term field studies, the residence patterns of chimps and other apes are looking a lot more complicated than previously assumed. If they can, female chimpanzees who find themselves on secure, food-rich territories stay near their mothers. Of 14 Gombe Stream females whose lives have been monitored since birth, six have remained, five transferred to new communities, and three have disappeared. Conversely, of 11 adult females present in 1995, five were natives and six were immigrants (see note 22 in Pusey et al., 1997). Furthermore, at the Tai field site (but not at Gombe), average degrees of genetic relatedness among adult males are no higher than among females. Perhaps more to the point for those interested in maternal strategies, philopatric females (who also tend to be socially dominant) breed at an earlier age, produce offspring after shorter intervals, and produce offspring with high survival rates. The all-time record for female reproductive success among wild chimps (seven offspring) is held by Flo's daughter Fifi, who inherited her mother's territory (Pusey et al., 1997; see also Harcourt et al., 1981, p. 267 for gorillas). The moral is clear: those who can, stay; those who can't, migrate away to breed.

When we turn to the human ethnographic record, patrilocal residence and polygynous marriages do indeed predominate. But this record post-dates massive population shifts caused by rapidly expanding populations of post-Neolithic agriculturists and herders. No doubt inter-group raiding for women pre-dated the Neolithic, but defensible land and other material resources along with increasing rates of population growth would have intensified the pressure on men to remain near kin, enhancing patrilocal allegiance and the formation of fraternal interest groups (Witkowsi & Divale, 1996). The need to defend local resources makes sons the sex with greater resource-holding potential, and in patrilocal situations, the sex with the most reliable allies. Male offspring are then the obvious candidates to receive resources that are transmitted across generations, eventually leading to patrilineal inheritance and the development of related patriarchal institutions (Hrdy & Judge, 1993).

Well suited to inter-group raiding, patrilineal groups expanded into areas that 10- and 20,000 years ago were occupied by hunter-gatherers living under variable conditions, often at very low densities. When anthropologist Carol Ember focused only on hunter-gatherer societies still living more nearly as Pleistocene foragers did (excluding groups that used boats or depended on horses to hunt), only 56% were patrilocal. The rest were matrilocal or, more commonly, bilocal (Ember 1978: Fig. 2). Indeed, according to Alvarez (in press) even these revised estimates

Table 1. Cross cultural surveys indicate that some 67% of societies sampled from around
the world exhibit patrilocal residence patterns (Ember & Ember, 1985). However, when
considering only foraging societies subsisting as our Pleistocene ancestors did this
proportion drops to 56%.

	Sample of World Societies	Foraging Societies Only (Omitting Those Using Horses or Boats)
PATRILOCAL	67%	56%
BILOCAL	7%	22%
MATRILOCAL	15%	20%
AVUNCULAR	4%	1%
NEOLOCAL/OTHER	7%	1%

are overly biased in favor of patrilocality. Alvarez's case-by-case analysis of the
original ethnographies from which Ember's codings were taken showed that bilocal
residence was the most prevalent pattern. Wherever foragers live at low densities,
or in unpredictable environments (e.g., with variable rainfall), kin ties are utilized
to migrate away from adversity and to gravitate towards ecological, social, and
reproductive opportunities. Both men and women should prefer locales with
available resources. Mothers, however, might prefer groups offering allomaternal
assistance in childrearing, while fathers might have quite different priorities (e.g.,
availability of fertile women).

I do not doubt that some early hominids lived patrilocally, relied on male-
biased inheritance of status and hunting grounds, and developed many of the
essential ingredients of patriarchal mindsets. But more and more I am impressed by
how flexible and opportunistic many primates, including human foragers, are.
What strikes me is how unwise it was to project a breeding system derived from one
type of patrilocal and patrilineal human society onto bipedal (and hence "hominid")
ancestors subsisting primarily on seeds and fruits 4 million years ago, or onto
anatomically modern members of the genus *Homo* hunting and gathering and
beginning to move out of Africa 100,000 years ago, or beginning to people the
Pacific land masses and the New World 50- to 20,000 years ago. I can not think of
any reason why the mating systems and preferences of these people would be less
variable and less flexible than those of foragers today, or less variable than other
"weedy" or highly adaptable primates like baboons, langur monkeys, or
chimpanzees (formerly far more widely spread across Africa than they are today). If
anything, greater control over their environment should have made humans more
variable.

5.   AS POWERFUL AS EVOLUTIONARY THEORY IS, WHY DO WE STILL
NEED HISTORY?

Why does history matter for reconstructing the mating preferences of our ancestors? There are several reasons. Across primates, whether a female lives matrilocally or migrates out to breed has important implications for her freedom of movement and reproductive autonomy (Hrdy, 1981; Smuts, 1992). In matrilocal societies with bilateral inheritance like the Canela have, the mother's brother figures more importantly in the lives of young people than does their genetic father. Property passes through the mother to her brother's sons, rather than from a father to his own son. Although it has become virtually dogma among those applying evolutionary theory to human behavior that matrilineal arrangements developed as cultural adaptations to protect lineages from the consequences of female infidelity, I now think it likely that we had the sequence backwards. Uncertain paternity, we all assumed, promoted the development of matrilineal inheritance in the 15% or so of human societies in the world today where that system still prevails (see Hartung, 1985, for a classic treatment; see also p. 272 in Daly and Wilson, 1978, and p. 432 in Pinker, 1997). But matrilocal residence is a necessary precondition for the development of matrilineal systems (Aberle, 1961), and if (as I am now convinced) women in matrilocal societies have the most social leverage and reproductive autonomy, the opposite scenario seems just as plausible: women would be most likely to mate polyandrously with several men where support from matrilineal kin (including help provisioning young) provided them the social leverage to do so. Since I assume such patterns were more common prior to the Neolithic than afterwards (meaning prior to the introduction of herding, agriculture, settled living, higher population densities, and the greater emphasis on defendable property that these entail), history is essential to this interpretation.

In a species as opportunistic as human primates are, with outcomes so often dependent on which individuals happen to have the most leverage at the moment, history is enormously relevant for explaining phenomena like female mate preferences. Consider the case of women's preferences for "wealthy" providers, by now widely documented. It is often claimed that such preferences reflect innate female proclivities and supposedly evolved in their current form during humanity's "Environment of Evolutionary Adaptedness" (Buss, 1994). But are these preferences really innate? Or do they reflect women's adjusting to their circumstances? If the former, we have to explain why females evolved a preference for "wealthy" men (i.e., men with more resources than other men), a status that men in African foraging societies (like the !Kung San or the Hadza) scrupulously avoid. Furthermore, in sedentary, nonforaging societies, where wealth may indeed be a factor in women's choice of husband, wealth tends to be accumulated over time and thus concentrated in the hands of older men. How then to explain an evolved preference in women for older men who, even if still potent, might deliver along with their sperm an added load of genetic mutations (Crow, 1999)? Simplistic assertions about females preferring wealthy or dominant males to the contrary, we know a great deal more about how males compete with one another for access to mates than we know about the underlying criteria for female mate preferences, especially in situations where female choices are not constrained by male monopolization of resources. If, on the other hand, preferences for wealthy men are viewed as opportunistic (and quite possibly recent) adjustment to circumstances (discussed as the "patriarchal constraints" hypothesis in Hrdy, 1997), we acknowledge that under some ecological, demographic, and historical circumstances women prefer men with access to the most resources without claiming to have demonstrated the existence of innate universal preferences. For, if preferences for men with resources is a response to patriarchal social structures (meaning patrilocality, patrilineal inheritance and institutions, and belief systems biased in favor of male reproductive interests and control of resources), and if patriarchal social organizations are only one possible type of human social arrangement, it does not follow that those same preferences will be found in societies where historically women's choices have been less constrained.

Supposedly evolutionary psychologists have already taken my challenge into account:

> An obvious retort is that women value wealthy and powerful men because it is the men who have the wealth and power. In a sexist society women have to marry up to get them. That alternative has been tested and refuted. Women with large salaries, postgraduate degrees, prestigious professions, and high self-esteem place a *greater* value on wealth and status in a husband than other women do. So do the leaders of feminist organizations. Poor men place no higher value on wealth or earning power in a wife than other men do. Among the Bakweri in Cameroon, the women are wealthier and more powerful than the men, and they still insist on men with money (Pinker, 1997, p. 482, emphasis in original).

In other words, Pinker claims that data from the Bakweri provide the test case demonstrating an innate preference of women for men with property, as opposed to good genes, good sense, dependable character, or some other trait. So what is known about the Bakweri? Few cases would serve better to make my point that we can not claim to understand women's mate choices without taking into account the context — economic and historical — in which female mate preferences were expressed. For the Bakweri, as was also true in much of the U.S. until the 1870s and in England even later, are characterized by patrilineal inheritance of property. A woman's status and that of her children were largely determined by the status of the man she married. As late as the 1960s when this report on Bakweri land tenure was published:

> [a Bakweri] woman could not inherit land, nor could land used by her be inherited by anyone other than a male member of her husband's lineage ... (Ardener, Ardener & Warmington, 1960, p. 319)

Bakweri women had the right to work the land, and may in fact do most of the work, but ownership depended on a woman's husband's holdings. Even though a woman was able to earn in her own right, she might well perceive that she and her children had a stake in her husband's holdings. So far, the only thing the

Bakweri case demonstrates is that there is a longstanding legal tradition in place that improves the odds that women continue to choose males on the basis of wealth.

From the perspective of men able to hold onto property, patrilineal inheritance has obvious reproductive advantages. It may even serve maternal interests if bands of related men protect her and her children from marauding males from other groups. But it is a way of life built around the assumption that the optimal number of "fathers" for any infant born to his mate will always be the same, just one — him. For women, however, not only the identity of the father, but the optimal number of "fathers" depends on circumstances. Whenever extensive and exclusive paternal investment is essential to produce quality offspring of enviable status, or where harsh penalties attend adultery, the mother's optimal number of fathers is likely to be the same as his, but otherwise, not necessarily.

The question then becomes: at what points in human evolution and history did patrilineal interests start to prevail? Are the consequences now inscribed in the genome of our (by bonobo standards) relatively chaste and extremely modest species? Or did evolution produce females more sensitive in this respect so that they could adapt quickly to local circumstances and customs that have long varied, and still do vary? This is one of the areas of mate preferences that we know least about, all too often overlooked in our eagerness to document essential male-female differences or to demonstrate just how "natural" patriarchal arrangements are. Yet just as social scientists can not hope to understand human affairs without taking into account evolution, I am convinced that evolutionists cannot do so without taking into account history.

University of California-Davis

6.   ACKNOWLEDGMENTS

I am indebted to human behavioral ecologists Kristen Hawkes and Steve Beckerman, as well as to all those who participated in the 1999 AAAS conference entitled *Partible Paternity* organized by S. Beckerman and P. Valentine. I am also thankful to fellow sociobiologist P.A. Gowaty for inspiring me to think about constraints on female choice in new ways. And I thank A. Harcourt, J. Hartung, D. Hrdy, D. Judge, M. Borgerhoff-Mulder, R. Hames, W. Skinner, R. Stallman, and M. Towner for valuable discussion and criticism.

7.   REFERENCES

Aberle, D.F. (1961). Matrilineal descent in cross-cultural perspective. In D. M. Schneider & K. Gough, (Eds.) *Matrilineal Kinship*. (pp. 666-727). Berkeley, CA: University of California.

Altmann, J. (1980). *Baboon Mothers and Infants*. Cambridge, MA: Harvard University Press.

Alvarez, H. (in press). Residence groups among hunter-gatherers: A view of the claims and evidence for patrilocal bands. In B. Chapais and C. Berman (Eds.). *Kinship Behavior in Primates*. Oxford, Eng.: Oxford University Press.

Andelman, S. (1987). Evolution of concealed ovulation in vervet monkeys (*Cercopithecus aethiops*). *American. Naturalist. 129*, 785-799.

Ardener, E., Ardener, S., & Warmington, W.A. (1960). *Plantation and Village in the Cameroons: Some Economic and Social Studies*. Oxford, Eng.: Oxford University Press. Oxford, England. [Published for Nigerian Institute of Social and Economic Research.]

Baer, B. & Schmid-Hempel., P. (1999). Experimental variation in polyandry affects parasite loads and fitness in a bumblebee. *Nature, 39*, 151-153.

Baker, R.R. & Bellis, M.A. (1995). *Human Sperm Competition: Copulation, Masturbation and Infidelity*. London, Eng.: Chapman and Hall.

Baker, R.R. (1999, January 24). *Sperm wars: A study of multiple mating in Britain*. Paper presented at the AAAS Meeting, Anaheim, CA.

Barrett, G., Pendry, E., Peacock, J., Victor, C., Trakar, R. & Manyonda, I. (1999). Women's sexuality after childbirth: A pilot study. *Archives of Sexual Behavior, 28*, 179-191.

Beckerman, S. (1999, January 24). *The concept of partible paternity among native South Americans*. Paper presented at AAAS Meeting, Anaheim, CA.

Beckerman, S., Lizarralde, R., Ballew, C. Schroeder, S., Fingelton, C., Garrison, A., & Smith, H. (1998). The Bari partible paternity project: preliminary results. *Current Anthropology, 39*, 164-167.

Befu, H. (1968). Origins of large households and duo-local residence in Central Japan. *American Anthropologist, 70*, 309-319.

Bercovitch, F. B. (1999). Sex skin. In E. Knobil & J.D. Neill (Eds.). *Encyclopedia of Reproduction* (v. 4, pp. 437-443). San Diego, Ca.: Academic Press.

Berndt, R.M & Berndt, C.H. (1951). *Sexual behavior in Western Arnhem Land*. (*Viking Fund Publications in Anthropology*. No. 16). NY: The Viking Fund.

Borries, C., Launhardt, K., Eppeln, C., & Winkler, P. (1999). DNA analyses support the hypothesis that infanticide is adaptive in langur monkeys. *Proceedings of the Royal Society of London. B266*, 901-904.

Boster, J. S., Hudson, R.R., & Gaulin, S.J.C. (1999). High paternity certainties of Jewish priests. *American Anthropologist, 100*, 967-971.

Broude, G.J. (1994). *Marriage, Family and Relationships: A Cross-Cultural Encyclopedia*. Santa Barbara, Ca.: ABC-CLIO.

Buchanon-Smith, H. & Jordan, T.R. (1992). An experimental investigation of the pair bond in the Callitrichid monkey. *International Journal of Primatology, 13*, 51-72.

Burke, T., Davies, N.B, Bruford, M.W., & Hatchwell, B.J. (1989). Paternal care and mating behaviour of polyandrous dunnocks *Prunella modularis* related to paternity by DNA fingerprinting. *Nature, 338*, 249-251.

Buss, D. (1994). *The Evolution of Desire*. NY: Basic Books.

Byers, J.A. (1997). *American Pronghorn: Social Adaptations and the Ghosts of Predators Past*. Chicago, IL: University of Chicago Press.

Cerda-Flores, R.M., Barton, S.A., Marty-Gonzalez, L.F., Rivas, F. & Chakraborty, R. (1999). Estimation of non-paternity in the Mexican population of Nuevo Leon: A validation study with blood group markers. *American Journal of Physical Anthropology, 109*, 281-283.

Crocker, W. & Crocker, J. (1994). *The Canela: Bonding through Kinship, Ritual and Sex*. Fort Worth, Tx.: Harcourt Brace.

Crow, J. (1999). The odds of losing at genetic roulette. *Nature, 397*, 293-294.

Daly, M. & Wilson, M. (1978). *Sex, Evolution and Behavior*. North Scituate, MA: Thompson/Duxbury Press.

Darwin, C. (1871) [1974 reprint]. *The Descent of Man and Selection in Relation to Sex.* Detroit, MI: Gale Research Co.

Darwin, C. (1876). Sexual selection in relation to monkeys. *Nature 15,*18-19.

Davies, N.B. (1992). *Dunnock Behaviour and Social Evolution.* Oxford, Eng.: Oxford University Press.

de Waal, F.B.M. & Lanting, F. (1997). *Bonobo: The Forgotten Ape.* Berkeley, Ca.: University of California Press.

Eberhard, W.G. (1996). *Female Control: Sexual Selection by Cryptic Female Choice.* Princeton, NJ: Princeton University Press.

Ember, C. (1975). Residential variation among hunter-gatherers. *Behavior Science Research, 3,* 199-227.

Ember, C. (1978). Myths about hunter gatherers. *Ethnology, 17,* 439-558.

Ember, C. and Ember, M. (1985). *Cultural Anthropology.* (4th ed.) Englewood Cliffs, NJ: Prentice Hall.

Gagneux, P., Woodruff, D.S., & Boesch, C. (1999). Female reproductive strategies, paternity and community structure in wild West African chimpanzees. *Animal Behaviour, 57,* 19-32.

Gowaty, P.A. (1996). Battles of the sexes and origins of monogamy. In J.M. Black (Ed.) *Partnerships in Birds: The Study of Monogamy.* (pp. 21-52). Oxford, Eng.: Oxford University Press

Gowaty, P.A. (1997). Sexual dialectics, sexual selection, and variation in reproductive behavior. In P.A. Gowaty (Ed.). *Feminism and Evolutionary Biology.* NY: Chapman and Hall.

Gowaty, P.A., Ed. (1997). *Feminism and Evolutionary Biology: Boundaries, Intersections and Frontiers.* NY: Chapman and Hall.

Guyer, J. (1994). Lineal identities and lateral networks: The logic of polyandrous motherhood. In C. Bledsoe and G. Pison (Eds.). *Nuptiafity in Sub-Saharan Africa -- Contemporary Anthropological and Demographic Perspective* (pp. 231-252). Oxford, Eng.: Clarendon Press.

Hakansson, T. (1988). *Bridewealth, Women and Land: Social Change among the Gusi of Kenya. (Uppsala Studies in Cultural Anthropology 10).* Philadelphia: Coronet Books.

Harcourt, A., Harvey, P.H., Larson, S.G., & Short, R.V. (1981). Testis weight, body weight and breeding system in primates. *Nature, 293,* 55-57.

Hartung, J. (1985). Matrilineal inheritance: New theory and analysis. *Behavioral and Brain Sciences, 8,*661-688.

Hawkes, K., O'Connell, J.F., & Blurton-Jones, N.G. (n.d.). *Hadza hunting and the evolution of the nuclear family.* Unpublished ms., Salt Lake City: University of Utah.

Hawkes, K., O'Connell, J.F., Blurton-Jones, N.G., Alvarez, H. & Charnov, E.L. (1998). Grandmothering, menopause, and the evolution of human life histories. *Proceedings of the National Academy of Sciences (USA), 95,* 1336-1339.

Hill, K. & Hurtado, A.M. (1996). *Ache Life History: The Ecology and Demography of a Foraging People.* NY: Aldine de Gruyter.

Hoogland, J. (1998). Why do Gunnison's prairie dogs copulate with more than one male? *Animal Behaviour, 55,* 351-359.

Hrdy, S.B. & Judge, D.S. (1993). Darwin and the puzzle of primogeniture: An essay on biases in parental investment after death. *Human Nature, 4,* 1-46.

Hrdy, S.B. (1977). *The Langurs of Abu: Female and Male Strategies of Reproduction.* Cambridge, MA: Harvard University Press.

Hrdy, S.B. (1979). Infanticide among animals: A review, classification and examination of the implications for the reproductive strategies of females. *Ethology and Sociobiology, 1,* 3-40.

Hrdy, S.B. (1981). *The Woman that Never Evolved.* Cambridge, MA: Harvard University Press.

Hrdy, S.B. (1986). Empathy, polyandry and the myth of the coy female. In R. Bleier (Ed.). *Feminist Approaches to Science.* NY: Pergamon Press.

Hrdy, S.B. (1997). Raising Darwin's consciousness: Female sexuality and the prehominid origins of patriarchy. *Human Nature, 8,* 1-49.

Hrdy, S.B. (1999). *Mother Nature: A History of Mothers, Infants, and Natural Selection.* NY: Pantheon.

Kaplan, H. (1997). The evolution of the human life course. In K. Wachter and C. Finch (Eds.). *The Biodemography of Longevity: Between Zeus and the Salmon* (pp. 175-211). Washington, D.C.: National Academy Press.

Knight, C. (1991). *Blood Relations: Menstruation and the Origins of Culture.* New Haven, CT: Yale University Press.

Launhardt, K., Epplen, C., Epplen, J.T., & Winkler, P. (1998). Amplification of microsatellites adapted from human systems in faecal DNA of wild Hanuman langurs (*Presbytis entellus*). *Electrophoresis, 19,* 1356-1361.

Lovejoy, O. (1981). The origins of man. *Science, 211,* 241-250.

Madsen, T., Shine, R., Loman, J., & Hakansson, T. (1992). Why do female adders copulate so frequently? *Nature, 355,* 440-441.

Mason, W. (1966). Social organization of the South American monkey, *Callicebus moloch*: A preliminary report. *Tulane Studies in Zoology, 13,* 23-28.

Masters, W.H. & Johnson, V.E. (1966). *Human Sexual Response.* Boston, MA: Little, Brown.

Muller, J.C. (1980). On the relevance of having two husbands: Contributions to the study of polygynous-polyandrous marital forms on the Jos Plateau. *Journal of Comparative Family Studies, 11,* 359-369.

Nakamura, M. (1990). Cloacal protuberance and copulatory behavior of the alpine accentor (*Prunella collaris*). *The Auk, 107,* 284-295.

Nakamura, M. (1998). Multiple mating and cooperative breeding in polygynandrous alpine accentors. I. Competition among females. *Animal Behaviour, 55,* 259-275.

Nakamura, M. (1998). Multiple mating and cooperative breeding in polygynandrous alpine accentors. II. Male mating tactics. *Animal Behaviour, 55,* 277-289.

Newcomer, S., Zeh, J. A., & Zeh, D.W. (1999). Genetic benefits enhance the reproductive success of polyandrous females. *Proceedings of the National Academy of Sciences (USA), 96,* 10236-10241.

Palombit, R. (1992). *Pair bonds and monogamy in wild siamangs* (Hylobates syndactylus) *and whitehanded gibbon* (Hylobates lar) *in northern Sumatra.* Unpublished Doctoral Dissertation, University of California, Davis, CA.

Palombit, R. (1999). Infanticide and the evolution of pair bonds in nonhuman primates. *Evolutionary Anthropology, 7,* 117-129.

Parish, A.R. & de Waal, F.B.M. (2000). The other "closest living relative": How bonobos (*Pan paniscus*) challenge traditional assumptions about females, dominance, intra- and intersexual interactions, and hominid evolution. In D. LeCroy and P. Moller (Eds). *Evolutionary Perspectives on Human Reproductive Behavior (Annals of the New York Academy of Sciences, v. 907).* (pp. 97-113) New York: NYAS.

Penton-Voak. I.S., Perrett, D.I., Castes, D.L., Kobayashi, T., Burt, D.M., Murray, L.K. & Minamisawa, R. (1999). *Menstrual cycle alters face preference. Nature, 399,* 741-742.

Perrigo, G. & vom Saal, F. (1994). Behavioral cycles and the neural timing of infanticide and parental behavior in male house mice. In S. Parmigiano & F. vom Saal, (Eds). *Infanticide and Parental Care* (pp. 365-396). Chur, Switzerland: Harwood Academic Publishers.

Peters, J.F. & Hunt, C.L. (1975). Polyandry among the Yanomana Shirishana. *Journal of Comparative Family Studies, 6,* 197-207.

Peters, J.F. (1982). Polyandry among the Yanomana Shirishana Revisited. *Journal Comparative Family Studies, 13,* 89-95.

Petrie, M. (1994). Improved growth and survival of peacocks with more elaborate trains. *Nature, 371,* 598-599.

Petrie, M., Doums, C. & Moler, A.P. (1998). The degree of extra-pair paternity increases with genetic variability. *Proceedings of the National Academy of Sciences (USA), 95,* 9390-9395.

Pinker, S. (1997). *How the Mind Works.* NY: Norton.

Pinker, S. (1998, February 9). Boys will be boys: An evolutionary explanation for presidents behaving badly. *New Yorker,* 30-31.

Pusey, A., Williams, J. & Goodall, J. (1997). The influence of dominance rank on the reproductive success of female chimpanzees. *Science, 277,* 828-831.

Rodseth, L., Wrangham, R.W., Harrigan, A., & Smuts, B.B. (1991). The human community as a primate society. *Current Anthropology, 32,* 221-254.

Ross, M.H. (1986). Female political participation: A cross-cultural explanation. *American Anthropologist, 88,* 843-858.

Sangree, W.H. (1980). The persistence of polyandry in Irigwe, Nigeria. *Journal of Comparative Family Studies, 11,* 335-343.

Shih, C.K. (1993). *The Youngning Moso: Sexual union, household organization, and ethnicity in a matrilineal duo-local society in southwest China.* Unpublished Doctoral Dissertation, Stanford University, Stanford, CA.

Small, M. (1993). *Female Choices: Sexual Behavior of Female Primates.* Ithaca, NY: Cornell University Press.

Smedley, A. (1980). The implications of Birom ciscisbeism. *Journal of Comparative Family Studies, 11,* 345-357.

Smith, M. G. (1953). Secondary marriage in northern Nigeria. *Africa: Journal of the International African Institute 23,* 298-323.

Smith, R. (1984). Human sperm competition. In R. L. Smith (Ed.), *Sperm Competition and the Evolution of Mating Systems,* 601-609. NY: Academic Press.

Smuts, B. (1992). Male aggression against women: An evolutionary perspective. *Human Nature 3,* 1-44.

Sommer, V. (1994). Infanticide among the langurs of Jodhpur: Testing the sexual selection hypothesis with a long-term record. In S. Parmigani & F. vom Saal, (Eds.), *Infanticide and Parental Care.* Chur, Switzerland: Harwood Academic Publishers.

Stanislaw, H. & Rice, F.J. (1988). Correlation between sexual desire and menstrual cycle characteristics. *Archives of Sexual Behavior, 17,* 499-508.

Symons, D. (1979). *The Evolution of Human Sexuality.* Oxford, Eng.: Oxford University Press.

Symons, D. (1982). Another woman that never existed. *Quarterly Review of Biology, 57,* 297-300.

Takahata, Y. (1980). The reproductive biology of a free-ranging troop of Japanese monkeys. *Primates, 21,* 303-329.

Tew, M. [subsequently Douglas, M.J.] (1951). A form of polyandry among the Lele of the Kadai. *Africa: Journal of the International African Institute, 21,* 1-12.

Thornhill, R. & Gangestad, S.W. (1996). The evolution of human sexuality. *Trends in Ecology and Evolution, 11,* 98-102.

Trivers, R. (1972). Parental investment and sexual selection. In B. Campbell, (Ed.). *Sexual Selection and the Descent of Man.* Chicago, IL: Aldine.

Valentine, P. (1999, January 24). *Fathers that never exist: Exclusion of the role of shared father among the Curripaco of the Northwest Amazon.* Paper presented at AAAS meeting, Anaheim, CA.

Van Noordwijk, M. & Van Schaik, C. (2000). Reproductive patterns in mammals: Adaptations against infanticide? In C. van Schaik & C. Janson, (Eds.) *Infanticide by Males and Its Implications.* Cambridge, Eng.: Cambridge University Press.

Van Noordwijk, M. (1985). Sexual behaviour of Sumatran long-tailed macaques (*Macaca fascicularis*). *Zeitschrift für Tierpsychologie, 70,* 177-196.

Vigilant, L, Hofreiter, M., Siedel, H. & Boesch, C. (2001). Paternity and relatedness in wild chimpanzee communities. *Proceedings of the National Academy of Sciences (USA), 98,* 12890-12895.

Wallen, K. (1990). Desire and ability: Hormones and the regulation of female sexual behavior. *Neuroscience and Biobehavioral Review, 14,* 233-241.

Wallis, J. &. Almasi, Y. (1995, June, 23). *A survey of reproductive parameters in free-ranging chimpanzees (*Pan troglodytes*).* Paper presented at the 18th Annual Meeting of the American Society of Primatologists.

Winterbottom, M., Burke, T. & Birkhead, T.R. (1999). A stimulatory phalloid organ in a weaver bird. *Nature, 399,* 28.

Witkowsi, S. R. & Divale, W.T. (1996). Kin groups, residence and descent. In D. Levinson & M. Ember (Eds.), *Encyclopedia of Cultural Anthropology (*Vol. 2., pp. 673-680). NY: Henry Holt.

Wrangham, R. & Peterson, D. (1996). *Demonic Males: Apes and the Origins of Human Violence.* Boston, MA: Houghton Mifflin.

Wrangham, R. (1993). The evolution of sexuality in chimpanzees and bonobos. *Human Nature, 4,* 447-480.

Wyckoff, G.J., Wang, W., & Wu, C-I. (2000). Rapid evolution of male reproductive genes in the descent of man. *Nature, 403,* 304-309.

Zeh, J.A., Newcomer, S.D. & Zeh, D.W. (1998). Polyandrous females discriminate against previous mates. *Proceedings of the National Academy of Sciences (USA), 95,* 13732-13736.

KAROLA C. STOTZ AND PAUL E. GRIFFITHS

DANCING IN THE DARK

Evolutionary Psychology and the Argument from Design

1. EVOLUTIONARY PSYCHOLOGY AND ITS CRITICS

1.1. Convenient Enemies

The *Narrow Evolutionary Psychology Movement*[1] represents itself as a major reorientation of the social/behavioral sciences, a group of sciences previously dominated by something called the 'Standard Social Science Model' (SSSM; Cosmides, Tooby, and Barkow, 1992). Narrow evolutionary psychology alleges that the SSSM treated the mind, and particularly those aspects of the mind that exhibit cultural variation, as devoid of any marks of its evolutionary history. Adherents of narrow evolutionary psychology often suggest that the SSSM owed more to ideology than to evidence. It was the child of the 1960s, representing a politically motivated insistence on the possibility of changing social arrangements such as gender roles:

> Not so long ago jealousy was considered a pointless, archaic institution in need of reform. But like other denials of human nature from the 1960s, this bromide has not aged well (Stephen Pinker, endorsement for Buss, 2000)).

This view of history does not ring true to those, like the authors, who have worked in traditions of evolutionary theorizing about the mind that have a continuous history through the 1960s and beyond: traditions such as evolutionary epistemology (Stotz, 1996; Callebaut and Stotz, 1998) and psychoevolutionary research into emotion (Griffiths, 1990, 1997).

---

[1] EDITOR'S NOTE: In this book, the term 'narrow evolutionary psychology' signifies the approach to evolutionary psychology developed by Cosmides, Tooby, Buss, et al. This term was chosen not to imply that this approach has an inappropriately narrow point of view, but merely to suggest that the approach adopts a narrower range of assumptions than 'broad evolutionary psychology' (or, just 'evolutionary psychology'). This latter term signifies evolutionary psychology generally, practiced with any of a very broad range of assumptions possible within the general framework of evolutionary approaches to psychology. For more detail on this terminology, see the editor's introduction, p 1

Steven J. Scher & Frederick Rauscher (eds.). Evolutionary Psychology: Alternative Approaches, 135-160

The two research traditions that look most like the supposedly dominant SSSM are behavior analysis in psychology and social constructionism across the social and behavioral sciences generally. Behaviorism was indeed a dominant paradigm in the classic sense until the late 1950s, but it has been in continuous retreat ever since. Social constructionism has excited widespread interest ever since its origins in the work of Peter Berger and Thomas Luckmann (Berger and Luckmann, 1967), but it has only ever been the received view in sub-fields of certain disciplines, such as cultural anthropology. In experimental psychology and cognitive science, the two fields that narrow evolutionary psychology is most concerned to reform, social constructionism has never achieved any kind of dominance. Furthermore, contrary to the impression given by narrow evolutionary psychology, the tradition of psychoevolutionary research in the social and behavioral sciences is a more or less continuous one leading back through the sociobiology and Darwinian anthropology of the 1970s to the longstanding program of human ethology whose approach was laid down by Konrad Lorenz and Niko Tinbergen and whose best known representative is perhaps Irenaus Eibl Eibesfeldt. Thus, what narrow evolutionary psychology represents as monolithic 'old' and 'new' approaches to the mind are better seen as longstanding oppositions between and within various disciplines and sub-disciplines in the human sciences. The central feature of the SSSM, the idea that most psychological mechanisms are 'general-purpose' or 'content-independent', is something many earlier theorists have criticized. Contrary to its publicity, narrow evolutionary psychology is not 'the new science of the mind': the inevitable result of finally putting Darwinism to work in the realm of human affairs. Instead, it is the conjunction of two longstanding research traditions, neither of which is the only viable option in its own field. These traditions are the classical, representational program in cognitive science (Marr, 1982; Fodor, 1983) and the adaptationist form of neo-Darwinism that informed '70s sociobiology and was popularized by Richard Dawkins (Dawkins, 1976).

In this paper we argue that narrow evolutionary psychology inherits the worst failings of both of its constituent programs. Its methodology is unsuitable either for making heuristic predictions about mental structure that can guide psychological research or for providing deep, naturalistic explanations of mental structure. On a more optimistic note, we offer a more workable alternative way to garner the heuristic benefits of a biological perspective for psychological research and sketch some of the elements that will have to be added to the version of evolutionary theory favored by narrow evolutionary psychology in order to construct fully naturalistic explanations of mental structure.

1.2. The Evolution of Cognition: A Commitment to Darwinism

One result of the historical story that accompanies narrow evolutionary psychology is an unfortunate tendency to treat all critics of the movement as opponents of evolutionary psychology in general, or even of the theory of evolution itself. We want to make it clear that we are neither. We are committed to seeking a *naturalistic* account of cognition, one that makes mental processes part of the natural world and their investigation part of natural science. This implies that cognition must have evolved like any feature of living systems. A fully naturalistic perspective, however, requires more than mere consistency with some model of evolution. Naturalism requires that both the model of cognition and the model of evolution are themselves devoid of any essential commitments that cannot be given a natural explanation. The models must be:

1.1.1. Mechanistic

The entities and processes postulated by the models must be either processes that feature in lower-level ('physical') theories, or emergent, system-level properties whose emergence can be causally explained in terms of lower-level processes. A good example of this second sort of explanation is the emergence of structure, such as attractors and bifurcations, in the dynamics of complex systems. This structure is emergent in the sense that it cannot be predicted from or reduced to regularities governing the activity of the systems components. The fact that an unpredictable dynamical structure emerges, however, can be fully explained in terms of regularities governing the system components. No mysterious extra ingredient is required. In the present context, a key implication of mechanism is that functional and design language must be able to be exhaustively 'discharged' in mechanistic terms. That is, the fact that biological systems can be discussed in those terms must be mechanistically explained in much the same way that system dynamics can be mechanistically explained.

In the context of biology and cognition, it is also critical to notice that the quest for explanatory continuity does not imply the traditional 'reduction' of the social to the individual and the individual to its parts. The contextual conditions under which systems operate are as legitimate a source of explanation as the intrinsic properties of system components. The tendency of an asexual species to remain in one region of phenotypic space, for example, can be explained in terms of the canalized developmental structure of individual organisms or, equally legitimately, in terms of the constraints imposed on the species by selection. The more 'internal' explanation is not intrinsically preferable to the more contextual explanation. In the same way, human development proceeds in a rich, 'developmental niche' constructed by previous generations, and the constraints imposed by this niche are a legitimate source of explanation of species-typical traits.

1.1.2. Historical

Naturalistic models of cognition and other features of biological form must be consistent with the historical emergence of these features over time. Historical explanations that depend on the presence of unique sets of conditions presented in the correct sequences are not less satisfactory than explanations using general laws that apply across a wide range of initial conditions. In fact, the nature of biological systems provides reasons to expect historical explanations to be prevalent. Biological species are historical lineages capable of unlimited evolutionary change, not natural kinds of organisms, and so do not feature in traditional, universal laws of nature (Hull, 1984; Griffiths, 1999). The best candidates for traditional laws in evolutionary theory are ecological generalizations in which species and populations figure only as instances of ecological kinds, such as 'primary producer' or 'current occupant of patch' (Hull, 1987). But the output of processes governed by these ecological laws and generalizations is typically sensitive to the initial conditions of the process, so the resultant explanations are likely to be historical in nature (O'Hara, 1988).

1.1.3. Developmental

A naturalistic model of an evolved trait must allow a mechanistic understanding of the development of that trait both in ontogeny and in its original occurrence as an 'evolutionary novelty'. It has been recognized since Darwin himself that the theory of natural selection requires a theory of heredity and variation. We argue below that a mere reference to gene transfer and random mutation fails to discharge this explanatory obligation. Reference to genetic information and a genetic program are still less satisfactory, since the literal genetic code is only concerned with protein structure and the broader uses of these terms are nothing more than a promissory note to be paid later with a full, mechanistic account of developmental biology. That is why molecular genetics and molecular developmental biology are important to contemporary evolutionary theory: they supply elements of the evolutionary process that have previously had to be assumed. As well as filling a gap in our understanding of evolution, the particular way in which the gap is filled will have implications for evolutionary theory, as is manifest in the upsurge of interest in 'evolutionary developmental biology'.

A dominant theme of the rest of this paper will be the need to consider organisms as situated in a natural environment. In different ways, this is the key to meeting all three of the obligations we have outlined. Mechanistic explanations of complex systems typically require as much attention to the constraints imposed on those systems by their context as to the constraints imposed by their constituents. The sorts of historicized evolutionary explanations that we have described above are contextual in this way: they attend to the historical conditions in which the organism evolved. Finally, the explanatory strategy in developmental biology most likely to leave promissory notes scattered about is one that localizes control of development in a single material resource. Single causes in development derive their specific effects from the context in which they operate. While it can be a useful experimental tactic to treat this context as given, this tactic achieves experimental tractability precisely by sacrificing explanatory completeness.

In the next section we outline the problem that narrow evolutionary psychologists suggest is the primary impediment to progress in cognitive science and the solution that they offer to this problem. In Section 3 we argue that this solution is unlikely to work and that a more promising alternative is readily available. In Section 4 we turn to the account of evolution presupposed by narrow evolutionary psychology and argue that it needs to be enriched in various respects before genuinely naturalistic explanations of mental processes are possible.

2.   COGNITIVE SCIENCE IN THE DARK?

But in many branches of the psychological and behavioral sciences it is today quite usual to devise, out of hand, some sort of experimental procedure, apply it to a highly complicated system about which next to nothing is known, and then record the results. Of course, information can be, and has been gathered by this method... However... we prefer to have results before the present interglacial period comes to an end. That is why ethology emphatically keeps to well-tried Darwinian procedures (Lorenz, 1966, p. 274).

Practitioners [of anthropology, economics, and sociology have to] realize that theories about the evolved architecture of the human mind play a necessary and central role in any causal account of human affairs. ...Cognitive scientists will make far more rapid progress in mapping this evolved architecture if they begin to seriously incorporate knowledge from evolutionary biology and its related disciplines ... into their repertoire of theoretical tools, and use theories of adaptive function to guide their empirical investigations. (Tooby and Cosmides, 1998, p. 195)

In essence, the critique of current cognitive science offered by narrow evolutionary psychology is the same as Konrad Lorenz's earlier complaint against what he liked to call 'the American behaviorists'. A complex device like the human brain exhibits an extraordinary number of regularities, but only some of these can properly be construed as facts about how the mind *works*. The vast majority of regularities are mere side effects and are not useful entry points to a systematic understanding of the principles according to which the system operates. Without an evolutionary perspective, psychological science is groping in the dark. It does not know what it is looking for and when it finds something it does not know what it is looking at. To Lorenz, the laboratory-based search for laws of behavior seemed as misguided as dropping automobiles from buildings under controlled conditions in order to 'discover the principles governing their operation'. In the same vein, advocates of narrow evolutionary psychology argue that empirical psychology without an evolutionary perspective has no way to determine whether it is studying meaningful units of behavior or mental functioning. The fundamental idea behind narrow evolutionary psychology is that the natural way to classify behavior and the cognitive functioning that underlies behavior is in terms of adaptive design:

The intellectual payoff of coupling theories of adaptive function to the methods and descriptive language of cognitive science is potentially enormous. By homing in on the right categories — ultimately adaptationist categories — an immensely intricate, functionally organized, species-typical architecture can appear ... Just as one can flip open *Gray's Anatomy* to any page and find an intricately detailed description of some part of our evolved species-typical morphology, we anticipate that in 50 or 100 years one will be able to pick up an equivalent reference work for psychology and find in it detailed information-processing descriptions of the multitude of evolved species-typical adaptations of the human mind, including how they are mapped onto the corresponding neuroanatomy and how they are constructed by developmental programs (Tooby and Cosmides, 1992, p. 68-69).

2.1. Narrow Evolutionary Psychology: The Past and the Present

The form of evolutionary theory that figures in narrow evolutionary psychology is continuous with that which gave rise to sociobiology, but the emphasis on cognitive mechanisms, as opposed to behavior, is new. In fact, sociobiologists criticized the earlier ethological tradition for explaining human behavior as the result of evolved mechanisms rather than focusing on the direct predictions of evolutionary theory about behavior itself. The latter approach had been adopted with considerable success by behavioral ecology during the 1960s, just as the ethologists' 'hydraulic model' of mental mechanisms was falling into disrepute. In behavioral ecology, behaviors were interpreted as evolutionarily stable strategies in competition between and within species. Models of these competitive interactions between organisms could be constructed using the new techniques of evolutionary game theory and the predictions of these models tested against actual behavior. Sociobiology simply sought to extend this successful approach to humans. It was argued that sociobiology was superior to ethology because it made predictions about behavior and tested them rather than merely describing behavior and explaining it. This led to the hope that evolutionary models could guide psychological research and point it towards important phenomena that would otherwise be misunderstood or overlooked. The advocates of this new approach and proponents of these arguments included leading figures in today's narrow evolutionary psychology, such as Jerome Barkow (Barkow 1979). Narrow evolutionary psychology has retained the idea that evolutionary theory can make predictions to assist the process of psychological discovery, but has become strongly critical of the sociobiological emphasis on behavior. According to narrow evolutionary psychology, the current human environment is so different from that in which humans evolved that current behavior is unlikely either to be the same as the behavior produced in the past or to have the same effects on biological fitness. For these reasons, narrow evolutionary psychology does not use evolutionary theory to predict which behaviors will be observed today or which behaviors will be adaptive today. Instead, evolutionary theory is used to predict which behaviors would have been selected in postulated ancestral environments[2]. Current human behavior is to be explained as the output of the mechanisms that evolved to produce those ancestral behaviors when these mechanisms operate under modern conditions. Narrow evolutionary psychology also adopts the idea that apparently very diverse behaviors may be the manifestations of a single, evolved rule under a range of local conditions, an idea which originated in 'Darwinian anthropology' (Alexander 1979; Alexander 1987). Refocusing research on the 'Darwinian algorithms' that underlie observed behavior, rather than the behavior itself lets the evolutionary psychologist 'see through' the interfering effects of environmental change and cultural differences to an underlying human nature (Figure 1).

---

[2] The simple contrast between earlier sociobiology and today's evolutionary psychology suggested here is a caricature that does not do justice to the earlier researchers, who were often very well aware of the point about environmental change. For an account of the historical development of sociobiological methods, see chapter 13 of Sterelny & Griffiths (1999).

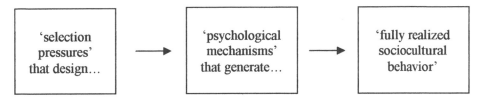

Figure 1. Psychology as the 'Missing Middle.' (See Cosmides et al., 1992, p. 6)

Narrow evolutionary psychology argues that psychological mechanisms must be described using the representational, information-processing language of classical cognitive science. Behavioral descriptions cannot be used, for the reasons described above. Neurophysiological descriptions are an obvious alternative, as they correspond to the morphological descriptions given to other, evolved features of human anatomy; but the form of evolutionary theory preferred by narrow evolutionary psychology will not predict anything about 'mechanisms' in this literal sense. The models used in behavioral ecology predict which behaviors will be selected but do not predict anything about how those behaviors will be produced. If we accept the conventional view in cognitive science that indefinitely many different neurological mechanisms could potentially support the same behavior, behavioral ecology predicts nothing about neurological structure apart from its output when supplied with input of the kind it received in the evolutionary past:

> When applied to behavior, natural selection theory is more closely allied with the cognitive level of explanation than with any other level of proximate causation. This is because the cognitive level seeks to specify a psychological mechanism's function, and natural selection theory is a theory of function. (Cosmides and Tooby, 1987, p. 284)

What narrow evolutionary psychology refers to as theories about 'psychological mechanisms' are more accurately described as theories of cognitive functioning — theories about the performance profile of the mind.

This fact about the output of adaptationist reasoning fits together neatly with the idea, usually attributed to David Marr (1982), that explanation in cognitive science should proceed simultaneously at three, mutually illuminating levels (Figure 2). The highest level concerns the tasks that the cognitive system accomplishes — recovering the shape and position of objects from stimulation of the retina, for example. The lowest level concerns the neurophysiological mechanisms that accomplish that task — the neurobiology of the visual system, in our example. The intermediate level concerns the functional profile of those mechanisms, or as it is more usually described, the computational process that is implemented in the neurophysiology. The two higher levels of analysis are irreducible because each level is multiply realizable at lower levels: the same task can be accomplished by different algorithms and the same algorithm can be implemented on different hardware. Redescription at a lower level thus results in a reduction in generality.

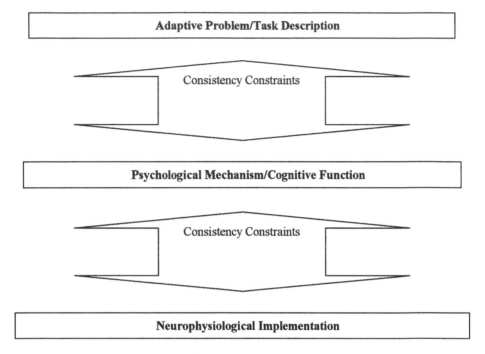

Figure 2. The Three 'Marrtian' Levels of Analysis in Cognitive Science.

Marr argued that adjacent levels of analysis are mutually illuminating and that research should be pursued simultaneously at all three levels. Hypotheses about the neural realization of the computational level constrain hypotheses about computational processes to those that can be realized by the proposed neural systems. Conversely, hypotheses about computational processes guide the interpretation of neural structure. It makes sense to look for structures that could perform the tasks that need to be performed. Similar relations of mutual constraint hold between the level of task description and the computational processes. But there remains something of a puzzle as to how the highest level, the task description, is to be specified, other than by stipulation. It seems obvious that the task of vision is to reconstruct the surrounding objects but why is this the right answer? Why is color vision an aid to object recognition, rather than the overall aim of vision being aesthetic experience and object recognition only a means to that end? Why are visual illusions not the *non plus ultra* of visual well-functioning? This is essentially the problem of providing a natural taxonomy of cognitive function that was encountered above. The value of evolutionary theory to cognitive science has been described in many ways in the narrow evolutionary psychology literature, but all of these come down to the same thing: it provides the task description and thus constrains lower-level hypotheses (Figure 3). The purpose for which an organism has been designed by natural selection is the task description of that organism and the sub-tasks correspond to separate adaptive challenges posed by the ancestral environment:

Evolutionary psychologists expect to find a functional mesh between adaptive problems and the structure of the mechanisms that evolved to solve them (Cosmides, et al., 1992, p. 7).

Because the enduring structure of ancestral environments caused the design of psychological adaptations, the careful empirical investigation of the structure of environments, from a perspective that focuses on adaptive problems and outcomes, can provide powerful guidance in the exploration of the mind (Tooby and Cosmides 1992, p. 72).

2.2. Massive Modularity

One of the best-known aspects of Narrow Evolutionary Psychology is the 'massive modularity thesis', according to which the mind has few if any domain general cognitive mechanisms. Instead, the mind is a collection of separate 'modules' each designed to solve a specific adaptive problem, such as mate-recognition or the enforcement of female sexual fidelity. The massive modularity thesis is the result of reasoning from a very general claim about selection pressures to a very general conclusion about the structure of the mind. Narrow Evolutionary Psychology claims that evolution would favor multiple modules over domain general cognitive mechanisms because each module can be fine-tuned for a specific adaptive problem. Hence, it is argued, cognitive scientists should look for domain specific effects in cognition and should conceptualize their work as the search for and characterization of mental modules.

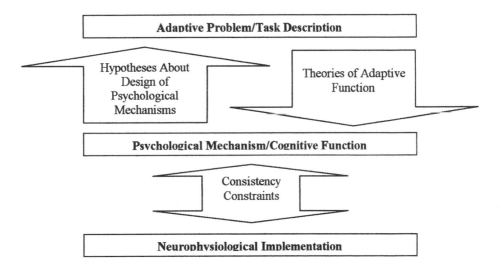

Figure 3. Evolutionary Reasoning from One Marrtian Level of Analysis to Another. (Adapted from Cosmides et al., 1992, p. 10, & Tooby and Cosmides 1997, p. 2).

3.   ENLIGHTENMENT FROM EVOLUTION?

In this section we argue that the proposed evolutionary heuristic for cognitive science — the use of evolutionary task descriptions to constrain theories of cognitive function — is unworkable. Fortunately, another heuristic, familiar from actual practice in other areas of functional anatomy, is available.

The idea that knowledge of evolutionary functions can act as a guide to research into cognitive functioning faces an obvious objection. It would seem at first glance that knowledge of the selection pressures in distant evolutionary episodes is even harder to come by than knowledge of current cognitive functioning. Evolutionary function is an epistemically demanding concept, one whose disciplined application requires considerable research and which, even then, typically remains highly inferential and subject to frequent reappraisal (Brandon, 1990, Ch. 5; Lauder, Armand, & Rose, 1993). The actual functioning of cognitive systems, however, is an empirical matter about which we can gain experimental knowledge. Moreover, evolutionary functions are *unusually* hard to establish in the case of cognitive functioning. As described above, narrow evolutionary psychology denies that current behaviors and their ecological effects are good evidence for the evolutionary functions of the mechanisms that underlie those behaviors. Thus, while most behavioral ecologists can conduct empirical tests of fit between observable behavior and the predictions of an evolutionary model, narrow evolutionary psychology is forced to interpose between the observation and the prediction a model of the psychological mechanism that produced the ancestral behavior. This second, psychological model is used to predict which behavior will occur under modern conditions. It is this prediction that is tested against empirical data. A huge hypothetical apparatus thus separates the data from the model under test and, as always, the test is only as reliable as the assumptions that went into building that apparatus. A further difficulty is that behavioral ecologists are typically able to base their evolutionary models on empirically derived knowledge of the relevant ecology. Narrow evolutionary psychology must base its models on reconstructions of past ecologies from paleontological and comparative data.

There is a still deeper problem, which we believe is more or less fatal to the proposed evolutionary heuristic. Narrow evolutionary psychology presumes that evolutionary theory can guide psychological research because it can model the selection pressures that led to the evolution of traits about which we lack current descriptive knowledge. But, as we will now show, the ability to model selection pressures is directly proportional to current descriptive knowledge of the form of trait. The heuristic will only work where it is not needed! Narrow evolutionary psychology argues that knowledge of evolutionary function is a guide to the actual form of the mind because:

> In evolved systems, *form follows function*. The physical structure is there because it embodies a set of programs; the programs are there because they solved a particular problem in the past (Tooby and Cosmides, 1997, p. 13, our emphasis).

The idea is that evolutionary theory can reconstruct the niche in which the human mind evolved and predict how the mind will be structured to fit that niche. More precisely, the evolutionary theorist will take the complex property of occupying the niche and conduct a functional analysis of that property akin to the functional analysis of the mind described above. The property of occupying the niche can be thought of as the organisms 'lifestyle' (e.g., living in a tropical forest eating insects that live under the bark of trees). This lifestyle consists of separate tasks (getting up the trees, finding the insects, extracting the insects, and so forth). Having created this task description the theorist can predict that the organism will have mechanisms that allow it to get up the tree, mechanisms that allow it to find the insects and mechanisms that allow it to extract them from under the bark. In the same way, it is proposed, we can take the niche that the human mind evolved to occupy and functionally analyze the property of occupying that niche in order to determine the (functional) structure of the mind.

The trouble with this proposal is that it assumes that we can reconstruct the niche while we are ignorant about the structure of the mind. The problem facing narrow evolutionary psychology is quite unlike that facing the student of tropical woodpeckers, who can identify the relevant niche empirically. It is also unlike that of the paleontologist, who knows the form of the woodpecker from the fossil record. What psychologists pursuing the narrow evolutionary psychology research program propose to do is more like a paleontologist who has found fossil birds with no skulls and proposes to reconstruct their feeding mode by thinking about the niche they occupied. The problem, of course, is that the best way to reconstruct their niche would be to look at their beaks and determine for what tasks beaks like that are good. Narrow evolutionary psychology has overlooked the conceptual relationship between an evolutionary niche and the organism that fills it. An evolutionary niche is a hyperspace whose axes are ranges of tolerance for ecological parameters, parameters that range from rainfall to predator density. A simple volume of physical space contains innumerable, overlapping niches. To determine the niche of any given species it is necessary to know what ecological parameters the species responds to and in what range of those parameters a population of that species can maintain itself. The more that is known about an organism, the more precisely it is possible to state the dimensions and extent of its niche. The 'woodpecker' niche described above is laughably underspecified if the aim is to explain form. It is indeed occupied by woodpeckers in Borneo and Sumatra, but in New Guinea this niche is occupied by arboreal marsupials (Brandon, 1990, p. 67-68). If our evolutionary predictions about cognitive function are so imprecise as not to distinguish the psychological equivalents of flying and climbing they will not be of any great value to cognitive science. We will suggest in Section 4 that in order to make evolutionary predictions of the necessary precision it would be necessary to know not just a great deal about form, but also a great deal about development, since development determines the class of 'solutions' that are available for selection.

Given the difficulty of analyzing evolutionary function in the absence of descriptive anatomy, it is reassuring to note that structural anatomy, and to a lesser but still considerable extent functional anatomy, made great strides before Darwin. In his work on the emotions, for example, Darwin relied on knowledge of the function of the facial muscles in emotional expression derived from the longstanding study of facial anatomy by artists and physicians. Functional anatomy is an important comparison case for narrow evolutionary psychology, as it is the equivalent for other organs of the cognitive level of analysis of brain function that narrow evolutionary psychology aims to bring into being. Functional anatomy describes the specific tasks performed by anatomical structures, tasks that could, at least in principle, be performed by other physical structures. Even after the widespread acceptance of Darwin's theory it is unclear that evolutionary functional analysis has played a major role in functional anatomy. That is not to say that an evolutionary perspective has not been important. The comparative method has been recognized as one of the keys to progress in anatomy since the renaissance, and this method is on a firmer footing once taxonomy is based on evolutionary relationships. There are other relevant aspects of an evolutionary perspective too, as we will show below. But the predominant notion of function in functional anatomy does not seem to be evolutionary function (teleonomy). One observation in support of this idea is that scientists elucidating anatomical and physiological function do not experience a major discontinuity in their research practice when they move from those features that can plausibly be supposed to be adaptations to those that are "nothing but spandrels, chemistry and entropy" (Tooby and Cosmides, 1998, p. 195). For example, some of the pairings between codons and amino acids that make up the genetic code and its variants are probably the result of selection for error minimization, whilst others are vestiges of chemical affinities in the RNA world and others reflect the temporal sequence in which new amino acids became available for inclusion in polypeptides (Knight, Freeland, & Landweber, 1999). Yet exactly the same research practices will reveal the function of all these codons — what they code for — because a codon's function is a matter of what the codon actually does and not why it does it. Similarly, anatomists do not usually withdraw claims about the functions of anatomical structures when presented with evidence that these are not the functions in virtue of which the structure was selected. The distinction between functions and mere effects, so critical to the evolutionary concept of function, does not seem critical for the practice of functional anatomy and physiology, or to the anatomical/physiological concept of function. This should not be surprising, since the evolutionary notion of function actually presupposes that the same functions can be identified in a way that says nothing about their evolution. The evolutionary functions of a trait are the ways it contributed to the fitness of ancestral organisms, that is to say, they are the functions assigned to the trait by a causal functional analysis of how those ancestral organisms survived and reproduced (Griffiths, 1993). The causal functional analysis of fitness is no different from the causal analysis of any other property of an organism, such as disease susceptibility: it merely identifies what the parts do in the overall causal mechanism. Ronald Amundson and George Lauder have discussed these issues in more detail and conclude that the predominant notion of function in the anatomical sciences is causal role function: the contribution made by a part of a mechanism to the causal capacity of the mechanism of which it is a part (Amundson and Lauder, 1994).

We have argued that evolutionary functional analysis is too epistemically demanding to provide a short cut to understanding cognitive function and that other fields of functional anatomy do not rely on evolutionary functional analysis. But the problem identified by narrow evolutionary psychology, and by ethologists like Lorenz, remains. The mind is an unusually complex system whose structure-function relationships are hard to determine. It would be profoundly useful to have a natural taxonomy of cognitive function to constrain hypotheses about function and to provide a structure within which to place empirical findings about function. Fortunately, there is an alternative source of such a natural taxonomy and, indeed, it is the one the ethologists originally had in mind.

Niko Tinbergen famously proposed that there were four questions that could be asked about any behavioral trait (Tinbergen, 1963):

1. What is the evolutionary history of the behavior?

2. What is the current use of the behavior in the life of the organism?

3. How does the behavior develop over the life of the organism?

4. What psychological and other mechanisms control the behavior?

The four questions correspond to four explanatory projects in biology. The first, evolutionary, question is answered by phylogeny reconstruction and evolutionary modeling. The second question is an ecological one: it asks how the trait contributes to the organisms' capacity to occupy its niche. There is a third question for developmental biology and a fourth for the cluster of anatomical and physiological disciplines, a cluster that includes experimental psychology and cognitive science.

We have described the similarity between narrow evolutionary psychology and Lorenz's view that the units of behavior studied by behavior analysis in the first half of the twentieth century were biologically meaningless and thus not a useful guide to the principles according to which the mind works. Unlike narrow evolutionary psychology, however, Lorenz did not suggest that psychologists tackle Tinbergen's first question and try to reconstruct evolution. He suggested that psychology tackle the second question and try to understand the ecological significance of behavior. In the context of animal behavior studies this amounted to studying behavior in something approximating a natural setting so as to be able to devise 'ecologically valid tasks' for later, controlled experimentation. In effect, the ethologists recommended using an ecological taxonomy of behavior to structure research on behavior. We suggest that an ecological taxonomy of cognitive function can play the same role for cognitive science. The study of cognitive functioning can be illuminated by the causal functional analysis of the capacity of the mind to occupy its *current* niche. Interestingly, this comes close to some of the methodological practices adopted by current research in situated activity or 'embodied mind' research (Hendriks-Jansen, 1996, Chapter 14).

We expect that adherents of narrow evolutionary psychology will regard this as a ridiculous proposal — surely any meaningful account of an organism's relations with its environment must classify the animals' activities in terms of their adaptive function! But a moment's thought reveals that this picture is back-to-front. Theories of adaptive origins are generated by conducting a causal functional analysis of the capacity of the organism to survive and reproduce in an ancestral environment.

The adaptive function of a trait *is* the function it is assigned in that analysis of *pure causal* function. If organism-environment relations cannot be understood unless the traits of the organisms are classified in terms of their adaptive function, then the entire enterprise of adaptive explanation cannot get started. So a purely causal analysis of the ecological function of behavior *must* be possible without knowing its adaptive function. But the idea that there are coherent concepts of function other than evolutionary adaptive function seems to be very hard for narrow evolutionary psychology advocates to assimilate.

4. A STEP-BY-STEP NATURALIZATION OF EVOLUTIONARY PSYCHOLOGY

The model of evolution used by narrow evolutionary psychology is the received view that came out of the 'modern synthesis' of Mendelian genetics and natural selection (Figure 4). This section attempts to enrich the model of evolution employed by narrow evolutionary psychology by adding some basic ingredients of naturalism to make it mechanistic, historical, and developmental (see Section 1.2, above).

We discuss a number of respects in which the traditional neo-Darwinian model of evolution fails to meet these desiderata. 1) It talks about form without having a theory of its genesis. 2) It expects a smooth fitness landscape for the mechanisms of mutation, sexual recombination, and selection to work upon, but has no explanation of the landscape itself. 3) It neglects important aspects of inheritance and makes the fact that humans have a high degree of cognitive flexibility and a complex system of cultural inheritance into an anomaly to be explained away. Finally, 4) it insists on selection as the 'sole anti-entropic force in nature' and ignores the other, well-established anti-entropic forces whose existence is a precondition for selection to produce order.

4.1. *Variation: The Origin of Form and Novelty in Evolution*

> Natural selection depends on sorting through variants. Central to this kind of explanation is the historically realized sequence of variants. Selection shares explanatory force with the dynamics of variation (Ahouse, 1998, p. 372).

> Darwin's theory of evolution is a theory of descent with modification. It does not explain the genesis of form, but the trimmings of the form, once they are generated (Kauffman, 2000, p. x).

There is a glaring gap in Figure 4: there is no reference to developmental biology or a theory of organization. Until this gap is filled, the model lacks an account of where phenotypes come from — an "evolutionary biology of organismic design" (Wagner, 1994, p. 276). In the adaptationist tradition, phenotypic variation is recognized as one of the main requirements of evolution, but its existence is rarely questioned or problematized. The capacity of developmental systems to generate variant forms that can solve adaptive problems enters the model only at the genetic level with the

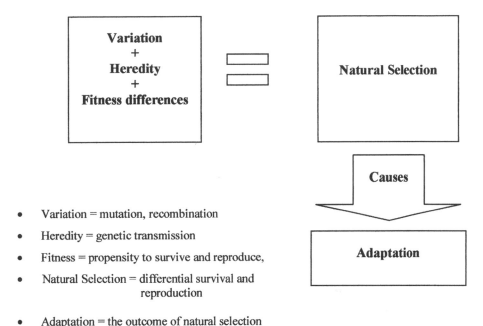

- Variation = mutation, recombination
- Heredity = genetic transmission
- Fitness = propensity to survive and reproduce,
- Natural Selection = differential survival and
        reproduction

- Adaptation = the outcome of natural selection

Figure 4. The Received View of Evolution By Natural Selection

reference to mutation and recombination. There are well-known historical reasons for this. The 'modern synthesis' of Mendelian genetics and natural selection that put so many of the biological sciences on a common theoretical basis failed to include the science of developmental biology (Hamburger, 1980). The synthetic theory bypassed what were at the time intractable questions of the actual relationship between stretches of chromosome and phenotypic traits. Although it was accepted that genes must, in reality, generate phenotypic differences through interaction with other genes and other factors in development, genes were treated as 'black boxes' that could be relied on to produce the phenotypic variation with which they were known to correlate. The black-boxing strategy allowed the two tractable projects — theoretical population genetics and the study of selection at the phenotypic level — to proceed. Population genetics, the mathematical core of the modern synthesis, could postulate genes corresponding to phenotypic differences and track the effect of selection on these phenotypic variants at the genetic level. Selection could be studied at the phenotypic level on the assumption that variant phenotypes were generated in some unknown way by the genes and that phenotypic change would be tracked by change in gene frequencies. Within this framework, the only account that can be given of phenotypic variation is that it corresponds directly to mutation and recombination at the genetic level. Any actual structure to development, resulting from the processes hidden in the 'black box,' will reveal itself only in the failure of selectionist reasoning based on the 'null hypothesis' that no such structure exists. Like other pure adaptationist research programs, narrow evolutionary psychology uses development only in this way, post hoc, to explain the lack of fit between a selective model and the data.

The continued exclusion of developmental biology from the evolutionary synthesis in favor of the genetic program metaphor, however, can only be regarded as a 'theoretical error of the first order' (Strohman, 1997). The methodological limitations that necessitated the black box approach to the gene have now been overcome, largely as a result of the molecular revolution. The vibrant field of evolutionary developmental biology has created a positive role for developmental biology in evolution: developmental biology explains where phenotypes come from and, in doing so, reveals the natural units of biological form. As empirical research on the formation and transformation of body plans has shown, ontogenetic pathways are not necessarily conserved along with the adult body plan (Raff, 1996). The same seems to be true with respect to genetic mechanisms, which often fail to provide a reliable basis for a homology concept because of their loose correlation to morphological variation. It seems that structural homologues exist quasi-independently from their genetic and developmental causes (Wagner, 1994, 1995). Conversely, dramatic evolutionary changes in phenotypes can appear despite highly conserved patterns of genetic expression and processes of developmental organization (Mueller and Wagner, 1996). These findings support a view of homologies as "emergent stable patterns that can not be explained by stability at a more elementary level" (Wagner, 1995, p. 283). There seems to be a growing recognition that genomic sequence information is insufficient to determine the way gene products (proteins) interact to produce a mechanism. In other words, genes in isolation contain insufficient information to determine gene function (Strohman, 1997).

The main focus of current research in evolutionary developmental biology is on major structural features of the body. In principle, however, the exact same approach should be applicable to the evolution of the mind. There have been some attempts to explore this possibility in the recent literature. Experiments and statistical analyses in neurogenesis conducted by Barbara Finlay and her colleagues (2001) found that few direct links could be made between the size of different brain structures and differences in behavior between species. Their findings suggest that, contrary to the widespread assumptions of structure/function relationship, increases in the size of individual structure may not be closely related to special behavioral capacities. The most useful predictor of structure sizes of individual brain structures is the sizes of other brain structures, with some additional minor effects of taxonomic relationship and overall brain and body size, suggesting that selection is, indeed, 'attacking a broader front'.

> Even a complete analysis of the adult brain, using the full array of current techniques in neuroscience, will leave unexamined central questions about the essential relationship between structure and function. The study of development promises unique insights into the nature of functional architecture. Likewise, patterns of comparative brain evolution show structure/function links in a different light than that cast by any one species. The problem we concern ourselves with here, then, is establishing the precise developmental substrate on which brain evolution selects. Do the brain and its information-gathering

organs divide themselves up in evolution into components, modules, or circuits that can be the independent objects of special selection...? Or does selection attack a broader front, working change by adjusting the parameters of a "standard" developmental program? (Finlay, Darlington, & Nicastro, 2001, pp. 267-268)

We have referred to some of the new approaches to evolutionary explanation that are emerging from evolutionary developmental biology. The lesson to be drawn from these new approaches for evolutionary psychology is that the 'natural kinds' of behavior it seeks — and which narrow evolutionary psychology claims to have found in innate and content rich, domain-specific modules — must be defined developmentally as well as functionally. Evolutionary psychology needs to account for the generation and fixation of traits. The real lesson which evolutionary theory has for psychology is that a synthesis is needed between behavioral ecology and developmental psychology — not evolutionary psychology, but evolutionary developmental psychology.

4.2. Evolvability Conditions: Quasi-Independence and Continuity

The mechanisms of generation and fixation (or integration) are two steps in the direction of building stable units of characters. However, they are only two steps in the production of natural units of biological form. An essential third step in the production of *adaptive* developmental organization is the decoupling of previously integrated parts into quasi-autonomous units:

[The phenomena of adaptation] can only be workable if both the selection between character states and reproductive fitness have two characteristics: continuity and quasi-independence. Continuity means that small changes in a characteristic must result in only small changes in ecological relations: a very slight change in fin shape cannot cause a dramatic change in sexual recognition or make the organism suddenly attractive to new predators. Quasi-independence means that there is a great variety of alternative paths by which a given characteristic may change, so that some of them will allow selection to act on this characteristic without altering other characteristics of the organism in a countervailing fashion; pleiotropic and allometric relations must be changeable. Continuity and quasi-independence are the most fundamental characteristics of the evolutionary process. Without them organisms as we know them could not exist because adaptive evolution would have been impossible. (Lewontin, 1978, p. 230)

Empirical evidence has shown that structurally or phylogenetically homologous characters can be the outcome of quite different developmental pathways (Hall, 1994; Wagner, 1994,1995; Wray & Raff, 1991; Bolker & Raff 1996). Even if we find similar patterns of ontogeny across different taxa these might turn out to be nothing more than 'crossing nodes' of developmental pathways coming from and going in quite different directions. Striking examples come in the form of directly developing amphibians that 'leap over' the usual larval stage or the apparent ease with which genus *Patriella* starfish species switch from producing small pelagic larvae to producing larger, directly developing benthic offspring (Palumbi, 1997). The concept that makes such phenomena consistent with the equally compelling evidence that developmental structure shapes variation is *developmental modularity*. Development is an integrated and integrative process as much as structures are interactively and hierarchically organized; yet structures as well as their underlying mechanisms can be decomposed into dissociable 'building blocks' (Brandon, 1999).

Two aspects are of importance, the *individualization* of characters allowing the free combination between individualized building blocks, and *constraints* acting against the variation of the character. The operational problem with separated body parts is how to distinguish between an adequate and a less or inadequate 'atomization' of the organism. This problem is at the center of organismic or morphological biology. What is being sought are mechanisms responsible for the creation and maintenance of the evolutionary units in questions. These are locally acting self-regulating mechanisms during the development of the organism that cause the differentiation of the organs. Most of them are well known: self-assembly, fixation of temporal patterns, and spontaneous pattern formation. Interestingly, these mechanisms differ in their causal role for constructing and maintaining organismic features. There are passive structures as well as actively maintained ones, determined by different causal factors. These results of developmental biology have led to the proposal that there are two quite different regulatory processes responsible for the construction of organic characters and the determination of their structural identity in spite of developmental perturbations: *morphogenetic* and *morphostatic* cellular mechanisms. Research on developmental modularity can explain how to pick the right traits out of such a complex organization as organisms; how, so to speak, to carve nature at its joints.

These results are able to reconcile the existence of apparently solid developmental constraints with apparently variable developmental pathways and are a big step towards a theory of morphological evolution. The modularity concept[3] provides an answer to the problem of how genotypic conditions are represented at the phenotype level (the genotype-phenotype map), and how phenotypic conditions are represented at the level of the organism's fitness (the phenotype-fitness map). Hence the concept of developmental modularity explains how continuity and quasi-independence are achieved, but only, of course, by characters that reflect the real, modular structure of development. Once again, the moral is that a genuinely evolutionary psychology cannot focus on the adaptive advantages of certain phenotypes and leave the genes to take care of the rest. Understanding how the mind grows is critical to determining how it might have evolved.

---

[3] It is ironic that two such closely related fields as narrow evolutionary psychology and evolutionary developmental biology should make such different uses of the concept of 'modularity'. NEP has a theoretical argument for the existence of modules: it would be difficult to optimize a mind for any one adaptive problem if the same mind is used to solve many problems. NEP modules are postulated on the basis of thinking about the structure of ancestral environments and evidence for their existence is provided by domain specific effects in cognitive performance. EDB has its own theoretical argument: modules explain how structures can be altered one at a time. But these structures need not (although they can) correspond to single adaptive functions and so must be discovered empirically, rather than via 'adaptive thinking'. Evidence for specific modules can take the form of 'developmental constraints' inferred from comparative biology or of direct evidence about how the phenotype develops. The EDB view of modules makes it obvious that the modular structure of the organism shapes the course of evolution, as well as being shaped by it, whereas the NEP view overlooks this fact, as discussed in Section 3 above.

4.3. Extended Inheritance

What we can conclude from the preceding section is that developmental mechanisms, which are to a certain degree *emergent* mechanisms with respect to their genetic basis, determine where one, quasi-independent evolutionary character ends and the next begins. That leads us to the question of the heritability of such mechanisms: their stability and reliable presence at the next generation. Have we not all learned that only genetic variations are of any interest to evolution since these are the ones that can be picked out by natural selection? How does this leave us with respect to the interaction of evolution and development?

Cosmides and Tooby give a suitably interactivist description of the relationship between genes and environment:

> The cognitive architecture, like all aspects of the phenotype from molars to memory circuits, is the joint product of genes and environment... [Evolutionary psychologists] do not assume that genes play a more important role in development than the environment does, or that "innate factors" are more important than "learning". Instead, [evolutionary psychologists] reject these dichotomies as ill-conceived (Tooby and Cosmides, 1997, p. 16).

So far so good. But in practice, this partnership can be very one sided:

> The genes *allow* the environment to influence the development of the phenotype [...] genes are simply regulatory elements, *molecules that arrange their surrounding environment* into an organism... To learn, there must be some mechanism that causes it, the mechanism that causes it must itself be unlearned — must be "innate" (Tooby and Cosmides, 1997, pp. 17-18, our emphases).

One needs to go a bit further to do justice to gene-environment interaction. Obviously, talk of 'innate mechanisms' only disguises the fact that the mechanism itself has to develop. Even the most fundamental mechanisms have to be constructed by the controlled expression of gene products. That expression relies on a wide range of causal factors, which is why normal development can be so easily perturbed. (Of course, most such perturbations are pathological, but so are most perturbations due to mutation.) It is commonly argued that the presence of the right genes must be what explains evolved traits, because genes are the only things organisms inherit from their ancestors. But a principled definition of inheritance does not yield this result (Griffiths and Gray, 2001). Organisms inherit an extended range of resources that interact to reconstruct the organism's life cycle. Some of these resources are familiar — chromosomes, nutrients, ambient temperatures, childcare. Others are less familiar, despite the recent explosion of work on "epigenetic inheritance" (Jablonka and Lamb, 1995). These include chromatin marks that regulate gene expression, cytoplasmic chemical gradients, and gut- and other endosymbionts.

Another important topic in recent biology is the participation of the organism in the construction of its niche (Odling-Smee, 1996). Hence a further aspect of inheritance is the local physical environment, altered by past generations of the same species and other species as well as the organism's own activities. Many of these inherited resources have distinctive roles. DNA is unique in acting as templates for protein synthesis. Membranes are unique in acting as templates for the assembly of proteins into more membrane. Chemical traces from foraging play a characteristic role in diet choice in many rodents. These empirical differences between what DNA does and what other factors do are real and important, but do not map onto any deeper, more metaphysical distinctions, such as that between form and matter or, as Cosmides and Tooby suggest, between factors which do the arranging and factors that are arranged.

4.4. Development as Adaptation, or Giving Genes a Break

Extended inheritance is an important element of the explanation of evolved traits. But it also serves to break down unnecessarily sharp distinctions between evolutionary adaptations and ontogenetic adaptation to the current environment. Narrow evolutionary psychology claims to have done this too, via the idea that development explores a tree of possibilities encoded in the genes, but this simply creates a sharp dichotomy between encoded outcomes triggered by the environment and outcomes that are not encoded and hence not subject to evolutionary explanation at all. The role of development in narrow evolutionary psychology is little more sophisticated than it was in the 'open program' model of the 1940s: Genes do not just code for a suitable reaction to a particular stimulus, they code for an 'open' program that has a range of suitable reactions, each adapted to one of several previously experienced environments. The 'program' must foresee all possible problems with ready solutions as appropriate reactions. If that were what cognitive development is like, then we would have a new evolutionary paradox: why did evolution invent complex and costly features like a mind and an extended period of post-natal development, while making no more use of them than to detect a few cues and respond with predetermined solutions to previously solved problems?

In the human case, we are dealing with the evolution of 1) a massively extended period of development — *childhood*, 2) an extended organ for the processing of ad hoc information — *cognition*, 3) the ability to form and perform complex social interaction — *sociality*, and 4) the capacity to produce a new kind of environment made out of rites, public knowledge and tradition and preserved by new ways of transmission — *culture*. According to narrow evolutionary psychology, or at least according to its oft-proclaimed account of the role of genes and environment in development, these processes do not allow humans to cope with genuinely novel environments at all — they merely serve to choose from a suite of pre-specified adaptations on the basis of environmental cues.

In contrast to narrow evolutionary psychology, the traditional view is that the function of these processes is to react to all sorts of 'adaptive problems' on the spot without the necessity to wait for multi-generational feedback to build another option into the developmental program. Development, cognition, and culture, it is argued, have been adapted for creating novel *adaptive* behavior. But traditionally, this new domain of adaptation has been seen as isolated from explanation by natural selection, as narrow evolutionary psychology constantly points out and rails against. Embracing extended inheritance and a richer model of the role of non-genetic resources in development makes it possible to accept the traditional view of the role of cognition and culture without drawing a sharp line between adaptation by natural selection and adaptation via cognition and culture. The new mechanisms of adaptation can be 'tweaked' and biased in all sorts of ways by adaptive evolution, as in, to choose the simplest example, the phenomenon of 'prepared learning' (Seligman and Hager, 1972). Evolution for flexibility can interact with evolution for bias and for stronger forms of canalization in many combinations, and evolutionary explanations of cognitive traits can take equally many forms.

4.5. Selection, Order and Adaptation

> Adaptations are the accumulated output of selection, and selection is the *single significant anti-entropic ordering force* orchestrating functional organic design (Tooby and Cosmides, 1992, p. 55, our emphasis).

> Thus, chance and selection, the two components of the evolutionary process, explain different types of design properties in organisms, and all aspects of design must be attributed to one of these two forces. *Complex functional organization is the product and signature of selection* (Tooby and Cosmides, 1992, p. 63, our emphasis).

These are typical statements of the idea that order must either be explained by selection or put down to mere chance. Random mutation and natural selection are the only possible explanations of order. Sometimes, this seems to be a sort of definition. If a trait's function is the role for which it has been selected and an adaptation is an outcome of natural selection, then it is trivially true that natural selection is the sole explanation of function and adaptation in nature. But this is an empty victory, since on these definitions there is much order (negentropy) in nature that is not obviously 'functional' or 'adaptive'. Narrow evolutionary psychology tries to obscure this by redefining negentropy itself as functional design (!), but this is profoundly unhelpful in understanding either negentropic processes in general or natural selection in particular. In this section we argue that not only do other negentropic forces exist, their existence is part of what makes possible natural selection and the further order that it produces.

The claim that nature is mainly entropic is a common prejudice and rests on a simple misinterpretation of the second law of thermodynamics. The growing science of complexity and complex adaptive systems has taught us that only *closed* systems are progressively chaotic (equilibrated), whilst *open* systems (including all living systems) are far-from-equilibrium and dissipative. The main neg(ative) entropic force in nature is *self-organization*, the exploitation of external energy for the production of order. The main mechanism is the production of energy gradients and the constrained release of energy: critically interacting components naturally tend to self-organize, and many of these self-organizing systems are able to perform physical work by means of internal *constraints* on the release of energy. Constraints are hyperstable structures sensitive to — and hence containing information about — relevant displacements from equilibrium that can be useful sources of energy from which work can be extracted (wind blowing or water flowing in one direction, concentrated heat sources like the sun, food as high-energy cluster of matter, etc.). They allow the constrained or directed release of this energy into a small number of degrees of freedom for the production of order (for example further constraints).

Hence *constraints in general are anti-entropic forces in nature,* and natural selection — or external constraint — is just one of them.

Natural selection occurs whenever there are individuals with differential fitness. The causal processes involved here, obviously, are the systematic contributions of heritable traits to the reproduction of individuals. So natural selection is the overall outcome of a range of causal processes taking place at the level of the organism and causing survival and reproduction. Selection itself — differential survival and reproduction — is a widespread phenomenon not only in biology but also in the physical, chemical or cultural realms, but it rarely seems to lead to the increasing adaptive complexity that is so striking in the biological realm. So the question arises: what is so special about organisms that selection upon them results in adaptive evolution? First, they are open, dissipative systems extracting order from the environment by means of self-organization that allows them to maintain and at the same time adapt themselves to internal and external perturbation, and to reproduce themselves. These distinctive capacities are those that several recent authors have claimed as the defining properties of *living* systems (Christensen and Hooker, forthcoming; Kauffman, 1993; Hooker, 1995; Weber and Depew, 1996). From this perspective, self-organization is not an alternative force competing with natural selection but the complementary force that creates systems capable of achieving adaptive complexity through evolution by natural selection. Self-organization can act locally as a force that resists selection — an internal fitness function drives the system to a particular attractor in its state space and holds it there in the face of mutation, thus preventing a response to selective forces. But when we look at the process on a larger scale, natural selection, by maximizing some external fitness function, is acting to move a population of systems in a population-level state space by choosing between individuals sitting at different attractors. Selection requires alternative, stably self-organized systems to choose between on the basis of the resultant (phenotypic) properties. Applying external fitness criteria is certainly important in producing what we call complex adaptation. However, at that stage a lot of necessary work on the way to a functioning organism has already been done by internal fitness criteria guiding the process of self-organization. These internal organizational processes are negentropic, not entropic, contrary to the frequent assertions of narrow evolutionary psychology:

> Finally, of course, *entropic effects of many types* act to introduce functional disorder into the design of organisms. They are recognizable by the lack of coordination that they produce within the architecture or between it and the environment, as well as by the fact that they frequently vary between individuals. Classes of entropic processes include mutation, evolutionary unprecedented environmental change, individual exposure to unusual circumstances, and developmental accidents (Tooby and Cosmides, 1992, p. 63, our emphasis).

Applying this line of reasoning to classic examples in developmental biology produces quite bizarre results. On what possible account of 'entropy' does perturbing Drosophilia development to produce the bithorax phenotype, either by mutation or by developmental shock, increase the entropy in the system? A bithorax Drosophila is at least as highly ordered as a wild-type Drosophila. The answer, of course, is an account that mixes up adaptive function and entropy in the phrase 'functional disorder'. But this redefinition is profoundly unhelpful. Selection can sometimes favor increased disorder, as in the evolution of vestigial traits, and order can arise without selection, as complexity theory amply demonstrates. There are any numbers of sound theoretical reasons to keep the concepts of order and functional design distinguished and no reasons we can see to run them together like this.

The application to evolution of complexity theory with its focus on systems dynamics and self-organization could shift our view from natural selection to a more inclusive vision of 'natural construction' by offering tools to integrate organizational dynamics into evolutionary theory. We can re-conceptualize natural selection as a result of the *interaction* of system and environment, and adaptation as the mutual *interactive construction* of the organism and its environment. Evolution can then be understood as change in the constitution and distribution of developmental systems. The developmental system is an organism-environment complex that changes over both ontogenetic and phylogenetic time. There is no need to attribute so much power to an external mover (natural selection) or to an independent internal force (genes and their mutations) that you deprive the organism of all its active control (Oyama, 1992; Stotz, 1999). This makes possible the re-interpretation of organisms as the active source of the emergent properties of life by means of interaction and construction, and marks a shift from focusing on the *products* of processes (like genotypes, traits, or gene frequencies) to the *processes* themselves.

5.   CONCLUSION: NATURALISM AND 'DESIGN'

There is nothing wrong with focusing on the concept of function. The possession of function and functional organization is indeed a paradigmatic property of living beings. Function, however, treated as a serious theoretical concept rather than a rhetorical frill, has remained the exclusive domain of biology, psychology and sociology and, of course, the study of human artifacts. This suggests that function is an *emergent property* in need of explanation in terms of more basic organizational principles. A major point of the last section was that function in biology cannot simply be reduced to random mutation and natural selection. It is the role of development to supplement those basics to give an adequate account of the origin of adaptive complexity. Development is needed because the design analogy mischaracterizes evolution. Here lies the deep commonality in the shortcomings of the explanatory strategies of evolutionary theory and traditional cognitive science, and therefore of the narrow evolutionary psychology that brings these two traditions together — they have bypassed development with its nonrandom and contingent processes of organization. Evolution and development are based on nonrandom physical processes that are able to link matter, energy and information to perform autocatalysis, reproduction, and physical work. Like evolution, development is a contingent, historical processes in which one step sets the stage for the next without going beyond that to determine the eventual outcome. This outcome will be the result of an *interactive* and *constructive* process of a system in its relation to its environment.

A properly epigenetic perspective on evolution and cognition should not presuppose the existence of any property that should rather be the subject of explanation. This implies the definition of mind-like behavior without ultimate reference to internal representation, and the definition of life without ultimate reference to teleological function. There is neither a natural designer who predefined the function or meaning of behavior, nor a last representational homunculus at the very end of the process of reference. Life processes are to be explained without reference to an ultimate, teleological function, just as intentionality is to be explained as emerging out of non-intentional processes.

University of Pittsburgh

6.   REFERENCES

Ahouse, J. C. (1998). The tragedy of a priori selectionism: Dennett and Gould on adaptationism. *Biology and Philosophy 13*, 359-391.

Alexander, R. (1979). *Darwinism and Human Affairs.* Seattle: University of Washington Press.

Alexander, R. (1987). *The Biology of Moral Systems.* New York: De Gruyter.

Amundson, R. & Lauder, G.V. (1994). Function without purpose: The uses of causal role function in evolutionary biology. *Biology and Philosophy, 9 ,* 443-69.

Barkow, J. H. (1979). Human ethology: Empirical wealth, theoretical dearth. *Behavioral and Brain Sciences, 2,* 27.

Berger, P. L. & Luckmann, T. (1967). *The Social Construction of Reality: A Treatise in the Sociology of Knowledge.* Garden City, N.Y.: Anchor Book.

Bolker, J. A., & Raff, R. A. (1996). Developmental genetics and traditional homology, *Bioessays, 18,* 489-494.

Brandon, R. (1990). *Adaptation and Environment.* Princeton, N.J.: Princeton University Press.

Brandon, R. N. (1999). The units of selection revisited: The modules of selection. *Biology and Philosophy, 14,* 167-180.

Buss, D. M. (2000). *The Dangerous Passion: Why Jealousy is as Essential as Love and Sex.* New York: Simon and Schuster.

Callebaut, W. & Stotz, K. (1998). Lean evolutionary epistemology. *Evolution and Cognition, 4,* 11-36.

Christensen, W. D. &Hooker, C.A. (forthcoming). The ascent of endogenous control: Autonomy-theoretic foundations for biological organization and evolutionary epistemology. Paper presented at *Bringing Life to Mind, 2nd Altenberg Workshop in Theoretical Biology,* Konrad Lorenz Institute, Alternberg, Austria, July, 1996.

Cosmides, L. &Tooby, J. (1987). From evolution to behaviour: Evolutionary psychology as the missing link. In J. Dupre (Ed). *The Latest on the Best: Essays on Optimality and Evolution* (pp. 277-307). Cambdrige, MA: MIT Press.

Cosmides, L., Tooby, & Barkow, J.H. (1992). Introduction: Evolutionary psychology and conceptual integration. In J.H. Barkow, L. Cosmides, and J. Tooby (Eds.).   *The Adapted Mind: Evolutionary Psychology and the Generation of Culture.* (pp. 3-15). New York: Oxford University Press

Dawkins, R. (1976). *The Selfish Gene.* Oxford, Eng.: Oxford University Press.

Finlay, B., Darlington, R. B., Nicastro, N. (2001). Developmental Structure in brain evolution. *Behavioral and Brain Sciences, 24,* 263-308.

Fodor, J. A. (1983). *The Modularity of Mind: An Essay in Faculty Psychology.* Cambridge, MA: Bradford Books/MIT Press.

Griffiths, P. E. (1990). Modularity & the psychoevolutionary theory of emotion. . *Biology & Philosophy 5,* 175-196.

Griffiths, P. E. (1993). Functional analysis & proper function. *British Journal for Philosophy of Science 44,* 409-422.

Griffiths, P. E. (1997). *What Emotions Really Are: The Problem of Psychological Categories.* Chicago: University of Chicago Press.

Griffiths, P. E. (1999). Squaring the circle: Natural kinds with historical essences. In R.A. Wilson (Ed.). *Species: New Interdisciplinary Essays.* (pp. 208-228.) Cambridge, M.A:MIT Press.

Griffiths, P. E. & Gray, R.D. (2001). Darwinism and developmental systems. In S. Oyama, P.E. Griffiths, and R.D. Gray (Eds.). *Cycles of Contingency: Developmental Systems and Evolution.* (pp. 195-218) Cambridge, MA: MIT Press.

Hall, B. K., Ed. (1994). *Homology: The Hierarchical Basis of Comparative Biology.* Academic Press.

Hamburger, V. (1980). Embryology and the modern synthesis in evolutionary theory. In E. Mayr and W.B. Provine (Eds.). *The Evolutionary Synthesis: Perspectives on the Unification of Biology; with a New Preface by Ernst Mayr.* (pp. 97-112). Cambridge, MA: Harvard University Press.

Hendriks-Jansen, H. (1996). *Catching Ourselves in the Act: Situated Activity, Interactive Emergence, Evolution and Human Thought.* Cambridge, MA: MIT Press.

Hooker, C. A. (1995). *Reason, Regulation and Realism: Towards a Regulatory Systems Theory of Reason and Evolutionary Epistemology.* Albany, NY: State University of New York Press.

Hull, D. (1984). Historical entities & historical narratives. In C. Hoowkay, (Ed.). *Minds, Machines & Evolution* (pp. 17-42), Cambridge, Eng.: Cambridge University Press.
Hull, D. (1987). Genealogical actors in ecological roles. *Biology & Philosophy, 2,* 168-184.
Jablonka, E. & Lamb, M.J.(1995). *Epigenetic Inheritance and Evolution: The Lamarkian Dimension.* Oxford, Eng.: Oxford University Press.
Kauffman, S. A. (1993). *The Origins of Order: Self-Organisation and Selection in Evolution.* New York: Oxford University Press.
Kauffman, S. A. (2000). *Investigations.* Oxford, Eng.: Oxford University Press.
Knight, R. D., Freeland, S.J., and Landweber, L. F. (1999). Selection, history and chemistry: The three faces of the genetic code. *Trends in Biochemical Sciences, 24,* 241-247.
Lauder, G. V., Armand, M.L., and Rose, M. R. (1993). Adaptations and history. *TREE, 8,* 294-297.
Lewontin, R. C. (1978). Adaption. *Scientific American, 239,* 212-230.
Lorenz, K. (1966). Evolution of ritualisation in the biological and cultural spheres. *Philosophical Transactions of the Royal Society of London, 251,* 273-284.
Marr, D. (1982). *Vision.* New York: W.H. Freeman.
Mueller, G. B. &Wagner, G.P. (1996). Homology, *Hox* genes and developmental integration. *American Zoologist 36,*4-13.
Odling-Smee, F. J. (1996). Niche-construction, genetic evolution and cultural change. *Behavioural Processes 35,*196-205.
O'Hara, R. J. (1988). Homage to Clio, or towards an historical philosophy for evolutionary biology. *Systematic Zoology, 37,* 142-155.
Oyama, S. (1992). Ontogeny and phylogeny: a case of metarecapitulation?, P.E. Griffiths (Ed.)*Trees of Life: Essays in Philosophy of Biology,*(pp. 211-240). Dordrecht, The Netherlands: Kluwer Academic Publishers.
Palumbi, S. R. (1997, Dec. 11). A star is born. *Nature, 390,* 556-557.
Raff, R. (1996). *The Shape of Life: Genes, Development and the Evolution of Animal Form.* Chicago: University of Chicago Press.
Seligman, M. E. P. & Hager, J.L. Eds. (1972). *Biological Boundaries of Learning.* New York: Appleton, Century, Crofts.
Sterelny, K. & P. E. Griffiths (1999). *Sex and Death: An Introduction to the Philosophy of Biology.* Chicago: University of Chicago Press.
Stotz, K. (1996). The psychology of knowledge in the context of evolutionary theory: Reflections on the link between cognition and sociability. *Evolution and Cognition, 2,* 22-37.
Stotz, K. (1999). *Interaction and Construction: Organizational Constraints in Evolution and Cognition.* Ph.D. Thesis. University of Ghent, Belgium.
Strohman, R. C. (1997). The coming Kuhnian revolution in biology. *Nature Biotechnology, 15,* 194-200.
Tinbergen, N. (1963). On the aims and methods of ethology. *Zietschrift für Tierpsychologie, 20,* 410-433.
Tooby, J. &Cosmides, L. (1992). The psychological foundations of culture. In J. H. Barkow, L. Cosmides and J. Tooby. (Eds.). *The Adapted Mind: Evolutionary Psychology and the Generation of Culture.* (pp. 19-136) Oxford, Eng.: Oxford University Press.
Tooby, J. &Cosmides, L. (1997). Evolutionary Psychology: A Primer. [On-line] Available: *http://www.psych.ucsb.edu/research/cep/primer.html.*
Tooby, J. &Cosmides, L. (1998). Evolutionizing the cognitive sciences: A reply to Shapiro and Epstein. *Mind and Language, 13,* 195-204.
Wagner, G. P. (1994). Homology and the mechanisms of development. In B.K. Hall (Ed.). *Homology: The Hierarchical Basis of Comparative Biology.* (pp. 273-299). New York: Academic Press.
Wagner, G. P. (1995). The biological role of homologues: A building block hypothesis. *Neues Jahrbuch der Geologischen und Paläontologischen Abhandlungen, 195,* 279-288.
Weber, B. H. &Depew, D.W. (1996). Natural selection and self-organisation. *Biology and Philosophy, 11,* 33-65.
Wray, G. A., & Raff, R. A. (1991). The evolution of developmental strategy in marine invertebrates, *Trends in Ecology and Evolution,6,* 45-50.

DOMINIC MURPHY

ADAPTATIONISM AND PSYCHOLOGICAL EXPLANATION

1.   INTRODUCTION

The research program of narrow evolutionary psychology[1] is most closely associated with the work of Cosmides, Tooby and Pinker (Barkow, Cosmides, and Tooby, 1992; Cosmides and Tooby, 1992, 1994, 1997; Baron-Cohen, 1995; Pinker, 1994, 1997; Tooby and Cosmides, 1992, 1995; Wright, 1994). Evolutionary psychology in this sense combines a highly modular view of the mind with the claim that natural selection designed human psychology to solve adaptive problems. It is the meeting of sociobiology and traditional cognitive science: of E. O. Wilson and Noam Chomsky (although Wilson does not seem quite as fond of 'selfish genes' as some of the people who have sought to apply his ideas). Of course, many people working in psychology who do not share the assumptions of the Cosmides-Tooby program nonetheless take evolution seriously. They write books or papers such that if you didn't know what evolutionary psychology was *supposed* to be, you'd think they were doing it (e.g., Allman, 1999; Atran, 1990; Frank, 1988; Griffiths, 1997; Griffiths & Stotz, 2000; Godfrey-Smith, 1996; Hauser and Carey, 1998; Kitcher, 1990; Sober and Wilson, 1998).

Much of what I have to say applies to the latter theorists also, but I focus on the Cosmides-Tooby program initially, since one of my themes is the relation of adaptationism to cognitive architecture and this shows up most clearly in their work. I will ask what adaptationism can tell us about our psychology, and conclude that even though it can be of at least heuristic value when it comes to uncovering behavior, it cannot license conclusions about cognitive architecture.

Godfrey-Smith (2001) distinguishes three adaptationist positions. First, *empirical adaptationism* asserts the ubiquity of design in nature and the pre-eminence of natural selection as the cause of evolution; second, *explanatory*

---

[1] EDITOR'S NOTE: In this book, the term 'narrow evolutionary psychology' signifies the approach to evolutionary psychology developed by Cosmides, Tooby, Buss, et al. This term was chosen not to imply that this approach has an inappropriately narrow point of view, but merely to suggest that the approach adopts a narrower range of assumptions than 'broad evolutionary psychology' (or, just 'evolutionary psychology'). This latter term signifies evolutionary psychology generally, practiced with any of a very broad range of assumptions possible within the general framework of evolutionary approaches to psychology. For more detail on this terminology, see the editor's introduction, p 1

Steven J. Scher & Frederick Rauscher (eds.). Evolutionary Psychology: Alternative Approaches, 161-184

adaptationism asserts that the really significant question in evolutionary biology is: what can explain complex design in nature? Natural selection may be the only natural cause of complex design even if it is only one weak cause of evolution as a whole. Third, *methodological adaptationism* recommends adaptationist reasoning as the strategy for organizing biological research. All three adaptationist variations are discernible in most evolutionary psychology, but when I discuss adaptationism in what follows it is methodological adaptationism that I have in mind.

Psychologists pursuing narrow evolutionary psychology contend that the mind is adapted to solve the problems humans faced in that long stretch of time during which we lived as hunter-gatherers. They refer to this period as the Pleistocene or "environment of evolutionary adaptedness" (EEA). In fact, many of our psychological capacities (like the visual system) comfortably pre-date the Pleistocene (Hauser & Carey, 1998); the main point is that narrow evolutionary psychology looks for problems that needed adaptive solutions in the past. Narrow evolutionary psychology is often criticized on this score for making untestable speculations about cognitive adaptations that depend on claims about a long-vanished environment. I argue that this objection can be met if we distinguish between *forward-looking* and *backward-looking* adaptationism. In Section 2 of this paper I defend the distinction between forward-looking and backward-looking adaptationism and give an example of testable forward-looking adaptationism. I go on to defend forward-looking adaptationism as a perfectly commonplace form of scientific explanation that is of considerable heuristic value but can also furnish causal explanations of the present in terms of historical processes.

Evolutionary psychologists of this school turn to natural selection to explain the cognitive modules underlying human behavior. Their notion of a module, however, is laxer than Fodor's original idea (Fodor, 1983). There are two main criteria of modularity in narrow evolutionary psychology. First, modules are special-purpose, or *domain-specific*, computational mechanisms. Domain-specificity is supposed to capture the idea that natural selection designed each module to deal with a particular problem our ancestors faced. What counts as a domain is seldom cashed out explicitly, with many theorists (not only in evolutionary psychology, by any means) preferring to rely on examples to convey an intuitive sense of a domain. There could, for example, be separate specialized systems dedicated to choosing mates, choosing food and choosing a place to live. The second main characteristic that narrow evolutionary psychology attributes to modules is *informational encapsulation*. Less than all the information in the mind is available to a module. It will typically have its own internal database (innate or acquired) that it alone consults, and a restricted range of inputs from elsewhere in the system, typically the outputs of other modules. (Even this second requirement is sometimes dropped, erasing the line between modularity and domain-specificity.)

Tooby and Cosmides capture the picture of the mind obtained by uniting modularity and adaptationism in the following passage:

> [O]ur cognitive architecture resembles a confederation of hundreds or thousands of functionally dedicated computers (often called modules) designed to solve adaptive problems endemic to our hunter-gatherer ancestors. Each of these devices has its own agenda and imposes its own exotic organization on different fragments of the world.

There are specialized systems for grammar induction, for face recognition, for dead reckoning, for construing objects and for recognizing emotions from the face. There are mechanisms to detect animacy, eye direction, and cheating. There is a "theory of mind" module ... a variety of social inference modules .... and a multitude of other elegant machines (Tooby and Cosmides, 1995, p. xiii-xiv).

In Section 3, I argue against this picture: evolutionary considerations tell us very little about cognitive architecture. Evolutionary hypotheses in psychology can be confirmed only at the level of task-description: a psychological competence or capacity that discharges a cognitive task. It is unclear what this unearthing of a competence tells us about the underlying cognitive mechanisms.

The stress on modularity and the assumption that modules evolved in the EEA are the main advertised differences between narrow evolutionary psychology and sociobiology, which looked for adaptive explanations of even contemporary behavior and had nothing to say about mechanisms (Symons, 1987; Wilson, 1978). However, the difference between old-style sociobiology and new-fangled evolutionary psychology is in danger of collapsing, and the reason for the collapse is that even verified evolutionary claims do not support conclusions about cognitive architecture. The testability objections I begin with can only be met by insisting on experimental psychological work. But experimental results that verify evolutionary claims can often only uncover behaviors, not underlying architecture (for other arguments along these lines, see Samuels, 1998). This brings up my second point: to really do serious evolutionary psychology we need to integrate developmental psychology into the picture. Only through the study of development can we find out about cognitive architecture. The connection between adaptationism and cognitive architecture is development.

2.   ADAPTATIONISM IN PSYCHOLOGY

2.1. The Time Machine Objection — Is Narrow Evolutionary Psychology Untestable?

Evolutionary psychologists following the Tooby-Cosmides program maintain that selection pressures in the EEA designed our modules. Critics of narrow evolutionary psychology reply that we cannot know very much about what happened in the EEA without getting into a time machine, and since we don't have a time machine it is impossible to gather the evidence needed to confirm hypotheses about any selection pressures in the EEA. The conclusion is that any adaptationist hypothesis about the likely psychological effects of natural selection is a "just-so story" — an untestable speculation.

Alison Gopnik, for instance, (Gopnik, 1996, p. 173) complains explicitly that narrow-school evolutionary psychologists are the heirs of Kipling rather than Darwin;

In fact, the evolutionary arguments for modularity are typically of an extremely weak kind. They are, in fact, the very weakest kind of evolutionary argument, simply that a particular trait might be helpful to an organism in an environment, or, even worse, in a hypothetical past environment for which we have only the scantiest evidence. They are just-so stories. None of the evidence that typically is required to support evolutionary arguments in biology . . . are ever presented. This is not too surprising, of course. Given the very uniqueness of most human cognitive abilities, this kind of evidence is, by and large, simply not available.

Gopnik is far from the only person to have made this complaint. Stephen Jay Gould (1997, p 51) makes the same point with even more conviction;

Evolutionary psychologists have gained some sophistication in recognizing that they need not postulate current utility to advance a Darwinian argument; but they have made their enterprise even more fatuous by placing their central postulate outside the primary definition of science — for claims about an EEA usually cannot be tested in principle but only subjected to speculation about . . . how can we possibly know in detail what small bands of hunter-gatherers did in Africa two million years ago?

The fundamental contention of Section 2 of this paper is that the time machine objection rests on a missed distinction. Claims about evolved psychological capacities can be confirmed by empirical research on modern humans, just like any other psychological hypothesis. To see why, one needs to understand the distinction between backward-looking and forward-looking adaptationism.

Lewontin summarizes the different types of explanation as follows (Lewontin, 2000, p.46-47):

Adaptive explanations have both a forward and a backward form. In the forward form, usually invoked for extant species, a problem for the organism is described on the basis of knowledge of or supposition about what is important to the organism. Then some anatomical, physiological, or behavioral feature of the species is proposed as the organism's solution to the problem. The backward form, usually used for extinct species known from fossil material, starts with a trait as a solution and searches for the problem that it has solved.

All an evolutionary psychologist needs to add to this summary is the claim that cognitive features can serve as putative solutions to adaptive problems.

Backward-looking adaptationism is perhaps the most familiar kind of adaptationist explanatory strategy, and it is what discussions about testability tend to assume is at stake. It uses adaptationist hypotheses to explain observed behavioral and morphological traits. Biologists frequently observe a novel and complex trait or feature in an organism. They try to understand the function the trait performs which has led to its presence in the population under study.

One type of inquiry that arises when evolution enters psychology is recognizably backward-looking. It is the attempt to construct and confirm evolutionary explanations for the existence of the mental modules which we think we know about and/or the mental and behavioral capacities to which they give rise. However, there is another adaptationist strategy that does not work that way. *Forward-looking adaptationism* attempts to use information about the EEA to generate predictions about the mental or behavioral capacities of contemporary organisms and/or the mental modules that subserve them. By theorizing about the context in which selection pressures arose we form hypotheses about what those pressures would most likely have been, given, in Lewontin's terms, our background knowledge or suppositions about what is important to the human organism. Having generated hypotheses about selection pressures we can make inferences about adaptive solutions to the problems the organism faced. So far this may all sound like a guessing-game, since we are discussing the generation of hypotheses; what counts is how we go about confirming these hypotheses. Here's the point: forward-looking adaptationist hypotheses in narrow evolutionary psychology are hypotheses suggesting the existence of specific psychological capacities in modern humans. We can look for these capacities quite directly. The confirmation of forward-looking adaptationist hypotheses depends on the existence in modern humans of the psychological traits that the hypotheses predict; it does not depend on finding out about events in the EEA. In order to find a psychological capacity we devise experiments to test modern humans, or otherwise gather appropriate data. In other words, evolutionary hypotheses can be tested using the same methods we would use to test any hypothesis about the minds of modern humans. We predict the existence of some psychological capacity, and devise tests to find it.

Backward-looking adaptationism takes a trait as given and looks for an adaptive explanation for it. Forward-looking adaptationism conjectures that a species has faced an adaptive problem and then looks for the trait that evolved to solve that problem. The two strategies are plainly distinct and only confusion can result from mistaking one for the other. It is also important to see that they are not incompatible. Indeed, I shall suggest later that they provide mutual support.

Once the distinction is in hand, we can see how it undermines Gopnik's objection. Gopnik seems to overlook the difference between forward-looking and backward-looking adaptationism. Hypotheses about the adaptive value of a module in the EEA make predictions about our *current* psychological endowment and these can be directly tested. If the trait is there we should be able to find it. Gopnik's mistake is to interpret a hypothesis about the EEA as the conclusion of an argument about the adaptive value of existing behavior rather than the premise of an argument about the pressures that led to the formation of a module. Gopnik confuses the starting-point of a forward-looking argument with the conclusion of a backward-looking one. Gould's mistake is similar: even if we have a hypothesis about what was designed in the EEA, we do not need to go to the EEA to test it. The claim that can be tested — on modern humans — is a claim about what we are left with as a result of those selection pressures, not the details of what small bands of hunter-gatherers were up to.

The search for adaptationist rationales of traits that currently exist has drawn little criticism compared to the attacks mounted on forward-looking work. I will not discuss backward-looking adaptationism here in detail, since a substantial literature already exists on the promises and pitfalls of developing an adaptationist account of existing traits (e.g Griffiths, 1996; Harvey & Pagel, 1991; Kitcher, 1990; Ridley, 1983). The points I raise in Section 3, though, are relevant to backward-looking adaptationist theses in psychology: we may come up with a compelling adaptationist story about current psychological traits, but that does not mean that conclusions about cognitive architecture are justified; nor, I shall suggest, will comparative analysis — an important adaptationist tool — work at the subpersonal level to justify architectural claims.

To develop the account of forward-looking adaptationism, and answer the time-machine objection at greater length, I turn now to an illustrative example of forward-looking adaptationist reasoning that has paid off in the form of testable hypotheses. The time machine objection can be met by drawing attention to forward-looking adaptationism, and since that objection is my focus at the moment I will concentrate my remarks on doing that.

2.2. Trivers-Willard

Fisher long ago explained why we should expect to see 50/50 sex ratios (Fisher, 1930). The failure of numerous insect lineages to conform to these expectations was addressed by Hamilton and others in the sixties. Trivers and Willard (1973) argued that even in non-insects there are certain circumstances in which organisms that are in good physical condition or are well provided for in other ways should invest heavily in male offspring, since these will inherit their parents' advantages, making them more likely to be chosen as mates by female conspecifics. This should provide the original parents with more grandchildren. On the other hand, females can generally mate much more easily, so less robust parents, or parents endowed with fewer resources, will get more grandchildren if they favor daughters over sons. We should expect to see the Trivers-Willard effect, then, when it pays parents to invest differently in male or female offspring depending on parental condition.

It turns out that there is good evidence for the effect in several species, the most famous example being that of red deer on the Isle of Rhum. There, year after year, mothers in better condition had more sons and less flourishing mothers gave birth to a disproportionate number of daughters. Another study found that female opossums given extra rations during pregnancy produced one and a half times as many sons as did females who were fed normally. Females fed less than normal rations were twice as likely to bear female offspring (Hrdy, 1987; Allport, 1997).

Trivers and Willard suggested that one of the species where the conditions obtain — and therefore one in which we could look for the effect — was our own. In humans, as in some other primate species, reproductive success depends not just on size but on other factors which lead to greater access to resources. In humans this might include status and income differences. And indeed, there is convincing evidence for a mild effect in humans that shows up where one would expect it: at the ends of the spectrum of social class. Research has borne out the expectation that higher status parents invest more in sons and lower status parents invest more in daughters. This occurs not just among elite families, but throughout the classes. Research on the demographics of early modern Portugal found that Grandees had more sons who reached adulthood and petty nobles more daughters (Boone, 1986). In eighteenth-century Schleswig-Holstein, farming families with more land invested more heavily in sons whereas landless peasants invested more heavily in daughters (Voland, 1984).

There is little evidence that humans give birth to more sons or daughters depending on their resources. However, the concept of parental investment ranges more widely than just birth numbers. The measure of parental investment in the work of Boone and Voland is differential survival to adulthood of sons and daughters. Using that evidence to search for a Trivers-Willard effect in a modern western society is likely to be inconclusive, because improvements in nutrition and medical care mean that survival to adulthood now has more to do with wider social factors and less to do with parental investment. However, the most startling evidence for a Trivers-Willard effect among humans used a different measurement of parental investment.

Gaulin & Robbins (1991) found that in lower-income families (< $10,000 per annum) more than half of the daughters were breast-fed, and fewer than half of the sons. In higher-income families (>$60,000 per annum) the rates of nursing were reversed; some 60% of the daughters were breast-fed, but almost 90% of the sons. Furthermore, parental investment in this study also showed up when different-sex siblings, who compete for parental attention, were added to the family. Affluent parents who had a son first waited on average some 3.9 years to add to the family. If they had a daughter first they produced another child in less than 3.2 years. The figures for lower-income families were 3.5 and 4.3 years, respectively.

Gaulin and Robbins took presence or absence of a male parent in the household as another measure of resources. It turned out that women without a male to share the child-rearing breastfed girls for about 8.5 months and boys only about a third as long, whereas boys were nursed longer by mothers who had a man around. The general picture emerges from Gaulin & Robbins' work of a conditional bias to invest differentially that reverses itself at extremes of parental condition, as Trivers and Willard expected.

Evolutionary approaches to the mind are often accused of making few interesting hypotheses and predictions. However, evidence that we are apparently able to compute Trivers-Willard and invest in offspring depending upon status supports a   highly counter-intuitive prediction.   Moreover, even though the hypothesis depends on a piece of adaptationist speculation, the evidence for a Trivers-Willard effect comes from the demography and child-rearing of modern humans, not allegedly pointless conjectures about the EEA.

Trivers and Willard are forward-looking adaptationists. They began with apparent conflicts between the general logic of sex ratios in mammals and some apparent counter-evidence, and made predictions about parental investment based on hypotheses about what would be adaptive in a given set of circumstances. Then they *predicted* that the same pattern should exist in humans. The argument is that an ability to invest differentially in offspring depending on one's status, resources and physical condition would be a good adaptation to have, consistent with our knowledge of general evolutionary factors. To test this theory, one doesn't need to tell a story about the distant past, because the evidence should be available among existing populations, or populations for whom we have ample historical records.

The same applies to other forward-looking hypotheses. They may be based on general points about what could have been adaptive in past environments, or they may be based on much more general adaptationist ideas considered in the light of background knowledge about humans.[2] The latter, one suspects, is often what narrow-school evolutionary psychologists are talking about when they mention the EEA, and their position might in fact be strengthened if they dropped the pretense that they are discussing a real place. Theorists who are less invested in the marriage of sociobiology and MIT cognitive science often make similar arguments, as when Sober and Wilson appeal to the anthropological record to support their claims about the circumstances in which altruism should be adaptive for human groups (Sober and Wilson, 1999).

2.3. History, Explanation, Confirmation

So far, we have seen that forward-looking adaptationist claims can be tested in the contemporary world. I now turn to the question of exactly what is confirmed when we find a psychological capacity as predicted. Obviously the claimed capacity is there, but what else have we discovered?

We can distinguish a strong and a weak claim about what a confirmed forward-looking prediction shows. The weak claim is just that in these cases forward-looking adaptationism proves its worth as a heuristic that generates interesting claims about contemporary minds or cultures. These are just predictions about the modern mind and are open to straightforward testing. The strong claim is that confirming a forward-looking adaptationist hypotheses uncovers some of the causal-historical structure of the world. Past conditions caused the psychology of humans alive today to have one form rather than another. By investigating historical conditions, then, we make predictions about the present state of the world, confirm those predictions and conclude that we have uncovered a causal relation between events in the past and what we now see around us. This idea stresses not just the heuristic value of forward-looking adaptationist thinking, but its status as a form of causal explanation.

The commonest objection to the strong claim is that there are just too many other possible explanations for a present-day state of affairs that the alleged explanation appeals to (Fodor, 1998). Some of these may be non-selectionist or otherwise ahistorical explanations. It is important to see that these may not be incompatible with evolutionary explanations; they may, for example, be about proximate psychological mechanisms rather than ultimate evolutionary causes (Mayr, 1976; Kitcher, 1990). However, some alternative ahistorical explanations may be incompatible with evolutionary explanations. I will address this problem in a moment. Whatever one's view of ahistorical explanatory alternatives, however, one may still think that too many alternative historical explanations can be cooked up. Current evidence is compatible with indefinitely many alternative historical scenarios, and once we have the evidence we can invent some alternative histories to

---

[2] There is an obvious concern that "background knowledge" about humanity will too often take the form of crackpot biases and vested interests. This is an entirely general worry about the behavioral sciences, which we should certainly take seriously. The only direct response I can think of is to rigorously test the predictions that are generated. As time goes by we can hope that better theories will lead to better background knowledge.

our hearts' content. Again, without a time-machine we cannot discriminate among alternative histories. Perhaps we can demonstrate the heuristic value of forward-looking adaptationism, but we cannot accept the strong claim.

I defend the possibility of the strong claim, although one will not always be in a position to make it at the conclusion of a piece of research. To defend it in principle, though, I will try to deflect the objection just outlined. I will discuss the seemingly reasonable idea that there are too many other possible explanations for a trait's function. Then I will look at the specific claim that the historical causal structure of the world is simply inaccessible.

In a particular case the force of the objection comes not from general considerations but from the availability of incompatible alternatives. It is not enough just to say that there must *be* some alternative explanations. They should be stated, they should have testable consequences of their own, and preferably they should make some additional predictions.

With respect to some forward-looking claims it may be easy to envisage decent alternative explanations. In other cases it is not. No other line of inquiry has predicted or explained the Trivers-Willard effect in the full range of species it applies to, let alone in humans. If we cannot imagine any alternative explanation of the evidence we have good reason to believe the explanation that Trivers and Willard provided. At the very least, our confidence that we have found the cause of the Trivers-Willard effect should be raised.

The more general problem with the objection from the excess of possible histories is that it applies to other sciences with wholly unacceptable results. Cosmologists, for one distinguished instance, have confirmed predictions about the big-bang by using our current particle physics and by studying the available contemporary astronomical evidence. They have not traveled back in time to see what happened in the first seconds of the universe.

Cosmologists rely on the assumption that the effects of the big-bang are still with us. They argue that by using contemporary evidence such as the existence of background radiation, or the distribution of cobalt atoms, we are able to suggest and confirm hypotheses about the effects of the big-bang, and hence uncover some of the history and structure of the universe. This pattern of reasoning is the same as the one I attributed to makers of the strong claim about forward-looking adaptationism. The reasoning is common throughout the historical sciences, although it has attracted little philosophical attention.

Now, I daresay that we could come up with alternative histories that explained the distribution of cobalt atoms differently. Perhaps there was no big-bang, but there is a hitherto undiscovered source of cobalt somewhere in the universe. This objection would have little force if delivered at a meeting of astrophysicists. Why should evolutionary psychologists be worried by its analogue? All manner of historical sciences rely on the idea that by hypothesizing about past conditions we can develop stories about how that past caused the conditions we now see. A well-confirmed evolutionary claim in psychology is, in principle, as credible as any other historical claim, and there are effective ways of using historical evidence to discriminate between adaptive histories (Griffiths, 1996, 1997).

The real force of forward-looking explanations comes if we can integrate them with backward-looking explanations in a mutually supporting structure. We might start with some known facts and develop an explanation about how those facts might have originated; this is backward-looking adaptationism. Then this historical explanation could be a source of new, testable hypotheses. The important difference between them lies in their different confirmation relations, but this is no bar to their being integrated into a mutually supporting, bootstrapping structure.

The mutual articulation of forward- and backward-looking strategies shows one way in which we can confirm evolutionary hypotheses in psychology. Each strategy can suggest fruitful lines of inquiry that the other can exploit. If we develop a powerful pattern of explanation and predictive success like this we can be confident that we are on the right lines. Like forward-looking explanations in general, this bootstrapping is found outside psychology. For example, the theory that an asteroid impact explains the extinction of the dinosaurs was motivated by facts about the distribution of iridium. First, geologists and physicists worked backwards to uncover an historical explanation for the observable traces of the past that they had found. Generating the hypothesis about a meteor impact led to, in the second place, several predictions about evidence which should be present today — an impact crater, for example, and shocked quartz deposits (Alvarez, 1997). That second round of reasoning worked *forward* from an hypothesis about the past to the existence of present-day evidence which can confirm the hypothesis.

Both forms of reasoning, backward-looking and forward-looking, exist in the historical sciences, and one should not impugn them *a priori* unless one thinks that all historical science is suspect. No one should want to declare so much good science off-limits, so the onus is on skeptics about the strong claim in psychology to explain why it is impermissible in that one case. Evolutionary psychology should not be set rules different from those to which other historical sciences conform.[3]

I conclude that the popular "time machine" objection has been overhyped. If it is bad science to make claims about the causal influence of the past, then the objection miscarries because it would render a great deal of perfectly good science inadmissible. If the point is a narrower one, that forward-looking methods cannot be applied in psychology to produce testable results, then it seems to fall foul of the several research programs that have developed testable hypotheses and sought to confirm them and rule out competitors. Forward-looking adaptationism is not going to solve all psychology's problems. The extent to which it can deliver useful results is obviously an empirical matter. But it is important to note that it *is* empirical, and that *a priori* objections based on the epistemic accessibility of the past can be answered.

---

[3] The same point can be made about similarities between adaptationist reasoning and reasoning in the social sciences. Economists, for example, often explain behavior via models that appear to attribute an implausible amount of knowledge about the economy or one's psychology or future habits. These models are defended on the grounds that they should be judged by their consequences rather than their assumptions. This point about modeling is germane to adaptationist models too and is another instance of the way in which arguments about evolutionary reasoning are continuous with wider scientific methodology. Methods should be judged across the board, not singled out for ridicule in one context.

That concludes my defense of adaptationist methods in psychology. The other face of narrow evolutionary psychology is a theory of psychological mechanisms. Unlike some critics, I think that the problems with narrow evolutionary psychology lie as much, if not more, with the psychology as with the evolution — or rather, with the connections between them. There is a persistent tendency to treat evolutionary considerations as supporting the position narrow evolutionary psychology takes on cognitive architecture. Evolutionary psychologists with a general commitment to modularity write as though the discovery of a discrete psychological capacity shows us that a domain-specific module has been discovered. This step is far too quick, as I shall now try to show. Once we appreciate this, we will have a better grasp of the limitations of evolutionary considerations in psychology.

3. COGNITIVE ARCHITECTURE

3.1. Three Questions

We can distinguish three questions about the relation between capacities we uncover and the architecture underlying them. First, we can ask whether we are dealing with (for example) a Trivers-Willard *module* at the computational level. That is, is there a domain-specific, encapsulated computer underlying Trivers-Willard behavior or, for example, a set of mechanisms which evolved to do other tasks but can be pressed into service for this one? Second, how does the computational mechanism discharging a cognitive task actually work? For example, is it a set of stored rules or a connectionist network? Third, is the computational system shared across species? The alternative is that there are different responses to similar adaptive pressures on different lineages, implemented by different systems. A Trivers-Willard effect is found in many species besides humans, but the nature of the effect varies across cases. All the species can do the job, but they might do it very differently. This puts important obstacles in the way of generalizing from comparative research.

The first question, whether we have found a module when we find a psychological capacity, is the one that is most relevant to narrow evolutionary psychology in general, and there are strong suggestions in the literature that many evolutionary psychologists think the answer is "yes". I will look at the first question in some detail, first saying why I think we can attribute this affirmative answer to narrow evolutionary psychology, and then giving some reasons for skepticism about their answer. Then I will deal with the second and third questions much more briefly. Finally, I will look at developmental perspectives that hold out promise of integrating evolution and development without prejudging the issue of modularity.

3.2. Is the Capacity Realized in a Distinct Computational Module?

Tooby and Cosmides argue that evolutionary considerations *imply* that modules exist. They argue that general-purpose architectures "could not have evolved, survived or propagated because they are incapable of solving even routine adaptive problems" (Cosmides and Tooby, 1994, p. 58). They sometimes concede that there are general-purpose psychological systems (Cosmides and Tooby, 1997), although they seem to think that a general-purpose device would be of little use and could not have evolved to solve specific adaptive problems, because "[g]eneral-purpose mechanisms can't solve most adaptive problems at all, and in those few cases where one could, a specialized mechanism is likely to solve it much more efficiently" (1994, p. 58). Symons is just as severe: "Each kind of problem is likely to require its own distinctive kind of solution . . . There is no such thing as a 'general problem solver' because there is no such thing as a general problem" (1992, p. 142). Cosmides and Tooby (1994, 1997; see also Pinker, 1997) argue that the same principle — a different system for each problem — applies also to the human body. They urge that we have no reason to expect the mind/brain to be any different.

The conclusion being drawn, then, is that evolutionary considerations compel us to believe in modularity. We could not have evolved without solving adaptive problems and we cannot solve adaptive problems without specialized domain-specific systems. The passages I have cited claim that the mind grows piecemeal by developing discrete specialized structures in response to particular adaptive problems. If this is right, we have strong reason to expect that in discovering a psychological capacity we also discover the module designed to discharge that capacity. In other words, the whole tenor of narrow evolutionary psychology suggests that one should answer yes to the question whether a given psychological capacity is realized in a distinct computational module.

These arguments notwithstanding, the connection between behavior and underlying mechanism is not transparent. From the verified prediction that a certain capacity is found in a population, we cannot simply conclude that we are dealing with a discrete module that evolved to discharge the capacity we have found. This problem should be distinguished from Shapiro's (1999) discussion of what he calls the BTM ('behavior-to-mind') inference, which is the inference to the presence of psychological mechanisms on the basis of observed behavior. Shapiro is correct to point to the ubiquity of this inference among narrow evolutionary psychologists, but he goes wrong by assuming that the question whether the BTM inference is warranted is a matter of "when some bit of behavior is likely to implicate the presence of mind" (p. 86) and treating this as a biologicized version of the problem of other minds: under what circumstances are we justified in saying that a behaving organism has a mind at all? However, the sin committed by evolutionary psychologists taking the narrow approach cannot be that of inferring from human behavior that we have minds. Nor is their sin that of trying to figure out what our psychological endowment is based on our behavior, since all cognitive psychology does that. The unwarranted inference these psychologists are prone to is different. They assume that when we have identified a type of human behavior we are justified in positing the existence of a module that underwrites it — it is the existence of modules, not the existence of mentality, which is under supported by the behavioral evidence.

Very extravagant modularity should be optional even if one views the mind as an evolved computational organ, since the connections between function and structure may be very indirect. This indirectness seems to be the correct lesson to take to psychology from evolutionary theory, and not the very bold claim that evolutionary logic means that the mind is massively modular. One reason for the indirectness is that natural selection must work within pre-existing constraints, modifying pre-existing structures and pressing them into new uses. Evolution has no foresight, and so these structures will have been previously designed for other uses. The problem of modifying or re-arranging a lot of existing systems is a different kind of design task from that of simply coming up with a design to solve a problem.

Faced with the problem of re-configuring the mind to deal with a new set of problems, natural selection might indeed come up with novel modules. There are clearly other possibilities, however. An existing system could be pressed into service for a new use, perhaps abandoning the old use. That would leave us with a new module, albeit not quite a purpose-built one. Maybe, though, the module could discharge the new task as well as the old one. We would now have one system, with two functions. Another possibility is that a collection of pre-existing systems might meet the new challenge without registering the costs of building a new system. Lastly, the much-despised domain-general systems might actually be good for something after all.

These considerations let us distinguish three ways in which we might answer the first of our questions, whether a given capacity is realized in a distinct computational module. If the capacity is indeed realized in a distinct module we have a *module-specific* computational explanation. This kind of explanation correlates a psychological capacity, or a distinguishable component thereof, with a computational module responsible for its implementation. It identifies features of the computational system with components of the behavior.

However, we should not expect even module-specific computational explanations to invariably correlate modules one-to-one with adaptive psychological capacities. Even if we can identify a capacity with an underlying module, there remains the complication that the module might implement more than one capacity. There are clear precedents from physiology for this, despite the argument of narrow-school evolutionary psychologists that the body relies on dedicated structures. Excretion and reproduction look like pretty good candidates for distinct adaptive capacities, but they share physical machinery in half our species; one structure, two functions. Of course, each capacity draws on further mechanisms with only one job (testes, bladder), but the output goes through the same structure.

A different case would be one in which a set of modules evolve to do their respective jobs, but in aggregate enable further capacities to be discharged. A theory of how the mind implements a capacity via the interaction of a collection of modules gives us a second sort of explanation, which we might call a *multiple-module* computational explanation. Rather than having an identifiable psychological competence realized by a module designed for that purpose, we would be faced with the simultaneous employment of several mechanisms, each with its peculiar adaptive history. The interaction among these mechanisms explains how a psychological capacity can be realized without the design of a new purpose-built computational system. We can envisage a competence using a collection of mechanisms designed for other purposes. Many behaviors may require multiple-domain explanations. They are not correlated with modules built to implement them, but they are the by-product of the joint workings of systems for which different, module-specific, adaptive explanations may in turn be possible. (Of course, we must also be open to the possibility that some of the components may not have adaptive explanations at all.)

The third kind of relation between function and structure appeals to domain-general mechanisms. A *domain-general* explanation does not involve modules at all, either singly or in concert. As we have seen, narrow evolutionary psychology seems committed to the idea that only modules can solve adaptive problems. Much strife has arisen on this point, so I will belabor it a little.

As with module-specific explanations of functions that share structure, we can envisage a physiological analogue to domain-general cognitive architecture. Again, the argument for domain-specificity from analogy with physiology appears to fail, even if we leave aside the problem of how to identify "domains" in physiology. If you don't think that there are physical organs that can carry out a wide variety of tasks then I invite you, as G.E.Moore did, to hold up your hands. Hands are distinct, identifiable bodily structures. And they have an indefinite number of functions (Hull, 1989). If it makes sense to talk about domains in physiology, then hands are domain- general bodily structures [4].

Tooby and Cosmides do have a stronger argument against the idea that domain-general psychological systems are of adaptive importance. This is the idea that the domain-general systems fail solvability tests — models using general purpose algorithms, it is claimed, are unable to solve adaptive problems that humans can solve (Cosmides and Tooby, 1994; Tooby and Cosmides, 1992). There are two problems with this argument. First, when it comes to the performance of complicated cognitive tasks we aren't exactly inundated with successful computational models of any kind, including domain-specific ones. In areas where there are some respectable models, such as face-recognition or memory, the performance of models using domain-general learning algorithms (usually connectionist ones) has often been lauded unduly, but it is unclear that they are doing noticeably worse than domain-specific systems.

Second, Cosmides and Tooby (1994) themselves draw attention to the fact that, traditionally, computational models have been applied to problems that are psychologically unrealistic — tractable in the laboratory, but unlikely to carve the mind at its joints. This complicates the solvability argument, for the poor performance of these systems as psychological models may be attributable to the problems they are working on, rather than the methods they use.

---

[4] Replying to a question on this point following a talk at Rutgers, Pinker argued that although we can do lots of things with our hands, they are in fact adapted for one function - manipulation (as opposed to the hands of Australopithecines, which were adaptations for tree-climbing). This is not a good response, though, because a foe of modularity could suggest, by parity of reasoning, that if our multi-purpose hands are adaptations for manipulation, then our brains are adaptations for learning, and although we can learn lots of things with them, that does not add up to their having numerous different special functions. This exchange shows that the physiology-psychology analogy is probably no use at all, as well as reinforcing how hard it is to establish just what a domain is, such that a module can be specific to one.

This is especially salient once we take learning into account. Narrow evolutionary psychology is sometimes written as though the superiority of domain-specific systems is in principle a matter of their special-purpose algorithms, but they sometimes say that the crucial edge comes from having more knowledge about the problem. It makes a big difference which claim is their actual one. In the following passage, for example, methods and knowledge are more or less completely confounded: "The difference between *domain-specific* methods and *domain-independent* ones is akin to the difference between experts and novices: Experts can solve problems faster and more efficiently than novices because they already know a lot about the problem domain" (Cosmides & Tooby, 1997, p. 83, italics in original). Surely, though, an expert can *know* more about a problem domain than a novice without using different *methods*. Faced with the problem of explaining the resurgence of the French monarchy in the thirteenth century I would bet against myself and back a medieval historian — not because she knows some special method that I don't, but because she knows a lot more pertinent facts than I do.

If solving an adaptive problem can simply depend on becoming expert via the acquisition of knowledge, then it seems that a general-purpose system with a powerful learning algorithm could well do so, especially if it were given many years to learn the information, as might happen for humans with the acquisition of social information during childhood. Faced with an adaptive problem, natural selection might design a new module, but it might do just as well by relying on an existing domain-general system with lots of time to learn about the problem.

Ultimately, of course, it is an empirical question whether one should prefer, in a given case, module-specific explanations, multiple-module explanations or domain-general explanations. I hope to have shown, though, that narrow evolutionary psychology tends to assume the first with undue confidence, based merely on discoveries about the existence of psychological capacities. Forward-looking adaptationist reasoning discovers psychological capacities or traits, not the architecture underlying them. The move from function to structure is likely to be very complicated for any theoretically interesting partition of behavior. Despite the apparent beliefs of some thinkers, there is no warrant for inferring the presence of a module from the presence of an adaptation at the level of task-description. This also suggests narrow evolutionary psychology is less clearly distinct from human sociobiology than one might have thought, since the former's claims to focus on cognitive architecture rather than behavior turn out to rely on questionable inferences about the logic of adaptationist thinking in psychology.

That we can't make conclusions about underlying structure on the basis of observed behavior or overall functioning is hardly a surprising point. Indeed, it would be surprising if this were not true, for surely it is not generally the case that one can predict an organism's innards from its functional capacities. Knowing that an organism can deal with toxins in its environment, for example, doesn't tell us anything about the workings of the organs it uses to do that. We know what they can do, not how they do it.

3.3. How Does the Computational Module Work?

The answers to the second and third questions I posed are shorter. I turn now to the question of how modules work, and then look briefly at the question whether shared adaptive capacities across lineages are evidence for shared mechanisms.

Let's assume that we have identified an adaptive capacity. Further, let's assume that we have good reason to believe that we are dealing with a computational module. We can imagine that we are able to base this conclusion on the sorts of general psychological theories and strategies that are standardly taken to isolate computational modules. We are still not justified in making particular claims about the workings of the module. We might be able to understand perfectly well what a system does without grasping the underlying engineering. There are different ways to build a device to carry out a particular function. Knowing what a module was designed to do is a matter of understanding a distinct psychological competence, perhaps by isolating it from others via empirical evidence such as dissociations, which leave the competence intact while causing deficits in other areas. Understanding the engineering, however, is a matter of finding out exactly how a device is built to discharge the competence. This cannot just be read off evidence that the competence exists.

The significance of this for the evolutionary perspective on psychology is that an underlying module might realize a particular psychological capacity even though it has no resources designed expressly to realize that capacity. It is always possible that existing resources have been co-opted for a new use. So even if we have evidence that a discrete module exists we are still not justified in assuming that the module is an adaptation designed to discharge a particular cognitive task.

Hauser and Carey (1998) review studies showing that rhesus monkeys and cotton-top tamarinds share with human infants the fundamentals of numerical representation. The original studies on infants (Wynn, 1992) convinced many people, including the editor of *Nature*, that human infants can count. However, as Hauser and Carey note, the existence of a capacity to distinguish between one, two or more different entities is compatible with a number of underlying representational structures.

One possibility is Gelman and Gallistel's (1978) suggestion that there is a mentally represented list of symbols ("numerons") which can be put in a one-to-one correspondence with the entities that are being tracked. Roughly, numerons are numerals in the language of thought. A second possibility is Meck and Church's (1983) Accumulator Model. This assumes that the nervous system keeps track of energy pulses emitted at a constant rate when the animal is engaged in counting behavior. The total energy emitted is an analog representation of number.

The third possibility Hauser and Carey entertain, based on work by Claudia Uller, is that no symbolic representation of number is involved at all. Instead, the animal opens a distinct "object file" for each individual it is attending to. The animal represents number by having a mental model that includes the separate entities being attended to. However, no actual numerical symbol is employed.

These are three very different representational systems. Tests can be devised to distinguish between them, but we cannot tell which, if any, is correct merely by reflection on the capacity that we have uncovered. The interesting point is that if the third explanation is correct then there is a competence in numerical representation shared by monkeys and human infants that uses no representational resources peculiar to counting. The Object File model employs only a capacity to distinguish between objects and track them. A species can distinguish between one or more objects without evolving a dedicated counting module. According to this third view, organisms that develop a capacity to open object files could employ them as surrogates for numerical symbols and hence count without growing a module to represent numbers.

3.4. Are the Modules Shared Across Species?

I conclude my tour of the problems we face making adaptationist inferences about psychological mechanisms by examining comparative tests. To use comparative data productively in psychology we need to be very clear about what work on related species shows about our own. We may make a prediction based on forward-looking adaptationist hypotheses and take that prediction, interpreted as a claim about how our minds got to be the way they are, to be supported by comparative evidence that we share a competence with close relatives. Again, though, we have not shown anything about the way the competence is realized in humans, even if we figure out the mechanisms by which another species does the job. It is hard to know when we share a competence with another species, and even when we succeed in showing this it still does not follow that we share a mechanism with that species, even if it is a closely related one. (For a very clear survey of some of these problems in the context of comparative studies of speech perception, see Trout, 2001.)

Suppose we assume that the Object File model is the best explanation for the shared counting capacities of the human infant and various related species. It is in that case likely that human adults have a competence that adults of other species lack. It is likely that human adults have the competence that is subserved by the Object File model, but we have another one as well, and this additional competence is not shared by beasts or babies. The number of object files which can be kept open simultaneously depends on short-term memory and may be as low as three. This is consistent with the profile of results obtained from testing infants, but human adults, even English majors, can count to more than three. Comparative studies may suggest that infants have a capacity that is phlyogenetically quite venerable, but this may not be a good model of adult human mechanisms.

Hauser and Carey review experiments that show how hard it can be to establish which mechanisms carry out a cognitive task. I said earlier that the most that a forward-looking adaptationist explanation could do is uncover a competence and not a mechanism. I take the work on counting to show that comparisons across lineages need to made with great care too.

Even if we are clear about the stage of development at which we are making the comparison, the most that we can show from comparative data is that humans share capacities with other species at the level of task-description. There is no inference from the fact that one species has a computational system that subserves a competence to the conclusion that we share that mechanism because we are related and we share the competence. Even if the competence was inherited from a common ancestor, we cannot conclude that related species realize it via the same mechanism. Shared competences are not enough. Although comparative data can be suggestive, we must look at our own species to see what computational mechanisms we may have.

3.5. Development as the Missing Link

All this architectural uncertainty places limits on the psychological payoff of adaptationism. There may be good reasons for believing in modularity, but adaptationism alone isn't one of them. Why then, has narrow evolutionary psychology been so quick to seize on modularity? Well, it is noteworthy that, as construed by narrow evolutionary psychology, modules have many of the properties ascribed to genes by some of the more prominent selfish gene theorists. More generally, there is a recurrent attraction to the idea that the genome is a blueprint or instruction book specifying the endpoint of development. I think this picture of the evolutionary process has had a profound effect on the way cognitive evolution has been conceived of by this group of evolutionary psychologists — as essentially accretion of and change in modules. Modules, on the view I have been attributing to narrow evolutionary psychology, are essentially bodies of information, as genes are in Williams' later work (Williams, 1997); Tooby and Cosmides (1992) claim that "any time the mind generates any behavior at all, it does so by virtue of specific generative programs in the head" (p. 39). To be sure, Tooby and Cosmides admit that cognitive development depends on the environment, but they insist that cognitive development is guided by "programs in the head" just as the developmental process in general is guided by "developmental programs" that are regulated by genes (p.78). The blueprint model of the gene imagines genes as bodies of information specifying traits. That is, genes are domain-specific; they work to produce their proprietary piece of the phenotype, so the standard picture in narrow evolutionary psychology envisages domain-specific modules causing a particular psychological capacity to develop. Modules are handed down in fixed form across the generations and as such they are responsible for the psychological phenotype — they disaggregate and recombine and the information they carry survives the brains they live in just as genes, in the Dawkins story, replicate and outlive their vehicles. For this analogy to work, modules had better be innate, otherwise they may accrue features in each generation that cannot be passed on to succeeding generations, and their role as fixed evolutionary replicators will be jeopardized. So development becomes "like data decompression triggered by outside events" (Glymour, 2000, p. 57); modular programs unfold in response to stimuli, and development is this unfolding of programs in the head, as the evolved cognitive architecture of our species grows in our minds. Just as genes need to be discrete, stable and replicable bodies of information in order to play the role foisted on them by the gene's-eye view of evolution, so too must modules be discrete, stable and replicable bodies of information if they are to guide and constrain development, according to this view of the relation of development to evolution — the unfolding of adaptive programs. However, this view of development is entirely optional, and we can dispense with the analogy. A better view of development severs the connection between adaptationism and massive modularity and installs a different view of psychological ontogeny.

Narrow evolutionary psychology has a view of modules that ascribes to them the role in development that genes play in gene-centered views of development — repositories of information that guide ontogeny and represent its outcome. But this argument for modularity is no better than the others we have looked at. The analogy is mistaken. Genes do not guide or represent development in the appropriate way, and neither do modules.

3.6. Interactionist Perspectives on Development

The last few years have seen diverse perspectives on development emerge which share a skepticism about the idea of cognitive ontogeny as the unfolding of an innate program. In the last section I noted the similarity between narrow evolutionary psychology's construal of modules and the conception of genes as blueprints. The move away from that understanding of genes has seen the rise of Developmental Systems Theory (DST) (Griffiths & Gray, 1994; Oyama, 2000a, 2000b). A developmental system is "a heterogeneous and causally complex mix of interacting entities and influences that produces the life cycle of an organism" (Oyama 2000b, p.1).

DST blurs a number of traditional distinctions; it denies that there is a clear difference between replicators and interactors, it refuses to draw a sharp line between biological and cultural evolution, and it is most vehement about the senselessness of the nature/nurture distinction. Timothy Johnston (1988), for example, calls the distinction between the learned and the innate "invidious" (p. 629). (Note that such attacks on the intelligibility of learned/innate distinction do not just threaten nativist positions in the "new rationalism" [Fodor, 2000]. If positions like Johnston's are correct in general they undermine the whole conceptual apparatus of rationalism versus empiricism.) The main controversy over DST has concerned its claim that the units of evolution are in fact developmental systems, whole life cycles of organisms, plus the resources (such as nests) that are replicated along with organisms across the generations, and even, in some views, the enduring features of the world (for example, sunlight), which persist across generations and are exploited by the developing organism (Griffiths and Gray, 1994). My concern here, however, is what DST says about development.

Proponents of DST are fond of "causal parity" arguments which stress that considerations adduced to support the idea that genes are privileged factors in development can equally be adduced to support the privileging of other factors, such as aspects of the environment: so that if "some aspect of an organism is deemed to have a 'biological base' because its variants are correlated with genetic variation in a particular population at a particular time, then one ought also to be willing to call something 'environmentally based' if it is correlated with variations in the surround" (Oyama, 2000b, p.124). DST is less a scientific theory than a philosophical or metascientific position, which denies causal priority to any of the components necessary to build an organism. In the case of DST the denial is directed chiefly at the role of genes, but similar arguments can be used against the view of development as merely the unfolding of modules.

DST is only one of a number of views that are inclined to stress the interaction, in development, of the growing organism and its surroundings, as well as the action of evolution on development events (see also Deacon, 1997). DST shares the same side in this debate with a number of other positions, including perspectives on evolution and development that are less radical than full-blown DST. Schaffner (1998), for example, endorses a view of development according to which, "epistemically and heuristically, genes do seem to have a primus inter pares status" (p. 234). He notes that several adherents of DST would dissent from this view. On the other hand, his parting line is: "[t]he melody of behavior represents no solo performance — it is [the] outcome of an extraordinarily complex orchestra — and one with no conductor" (p. 249); this final flourish leads Griffiths and Knight (1998) to say that Schaffner is in fact a developmentalist. Whether or not this is true of Schaffner, it is not always easy to see where the borders are between DST and other approaches to development that do not share the gene-centered view but do not agree with DST about the units of evolution (e.g., Lewontin, 2000; Sterelny, Smith and Dickison, 1996). Typically, these other views do draw attention to the variety of resources that are involved in normal development.

These perspectives lie on a spectrum with DST at the extreme end, and they come from biology. They have converged with a number of other approaches drawn from the cognitive sciences. (For an overview see Griffiths and Stotz, 2000). These include neural constructivist/connectionist and other neo-Hebbian approaches (Elman et al., 1996; Lotto and Purves, 2000; Quartz and Sejnowski, 1997) and views which regard the mind as essentially embedded in the surrounding environment and relying on environmental scaffolding to develop (Clark, 1997). We might also include views according to which children's minds grow by theorizing, since theorizing is an activity that depends on there being an environment to theorize about that can provide feedback (Gopnik and Meltzoff, 1997).

These differently motivated "interactionist" views on development draw on a huge array of studies that together decisively refute the idea of development as simply the unfolding of modular databases. A conception of innate psychology is still feasible in the light of this work, if "innate" in some contexts means, as Fiona Cowie (1998) has suggested, that explaining why babies are born with certain dispositions or even with domain-specific innate knowledge is not psychology's job. What seems untenable is the view that innate modules are simply prodded into unfolding, controlling cognitive development as the blueprint model thinks of genes controlling ontogeny in general.

To become psychologically plausible, any evolutionary perspective on psychology must take development into account. A plausible view of cognitive architecture must attend to development, since — as we have seen — adaptationist and comparative theses alone are insufficient to justify architectural claims. The "time machine" objection fails to distinguish forward-looking and backward-looking adaptationism. The distinction allows for a range of explanatory strategies that can support each other. These can be integrated with existing psychological research. However, the logic of adaptationist psychology does not imply that results at the level of task-description show anything of much interest about computational systems. However, the integration of psychology and evolutionary biology requires more than just taking existing cognitive psychology and subjecting its results to adaptationist thinking; nor is it enough to come up with forward-looking hypotheses about human behavior and trying to ground them within a presupposed modular architecture. Real integration requires taking development seriously.

California Institute of Technology

4.   ACKNOWLEDGMENTS

I should thank Steve Stich for helpful comments on earlier versions of this paper; I owe a lot also to conversations with Richard Samuels at an early stage. Some of the ideas were tried out in a talk given by Stich, Chris Knapp and the author at the 1998 meeting of the Society for Philosophy and Psychology. I have also been helped by conversations with Mike Bishop, Fiona Cowie, Shaun Nichols, Steve Quartz, Jesse Prinz and Jim Woodward.

5.   REFERENCES

Allen, C & Cummins, D. (Eds). (1998). *The Evolution of Mind*. Oxford, Eng.: Oxford University Press.
Allman, J. (1999). *Evolving Brains*. San Francisco: W. H. Freeman
Allport, S. (1997). *A Natural History of Parenting*. New York: Random House
Alvarez, W. (1997). *T. Rex and the Crater of Doom*. Princeton: Princeton University Press
Atran, S. (1990). *Cognitive Foundations of Natural History*. Cambridge, Eng.: Cambridge University Press.
Barkow, J., Cosmides, L. & Tooby, J. (Eds.). (1992). *The Adapted Mind*. Oxford, Eng.: Oxford University Press
Baron-Cohen, S. (1995). *Mindblindness*. Cambridge, MA: MIT Press
Boone, J. L. (1986). Parental investment and elite family structure in pre-industrial states. *American Anthropologist, 88,* 859-878
Carruthers, P & Chamberlain, A. (Eds.). (2000). *Evolution and the Human Mind*. Cambridge, Eng.: Cambridge University Press.
Carruthers, P. & Smith, P.K. (Eds.). (1996). *Theories of Theories of Mind*. Cambridge, Eng.: Cambridge University Press.
Clark, A. (1997). *Being There*. Cambridge, MA: MIT Press.
Cosmides, L. (1992) Cognitive adaptations for social exchange. In J. Barkow, L. Cosmides, & J. Tooby (Eds.).*The Adapted Mind* (pp. 163-228). Oxford, Eng.: Oxford University Press
Cosmides, L. & Tooby, J. (1994) Beyond intuition and instinct blindness: Towards an evolutionarily rigorous cognitive science. *Cognition, 50,* 41-77.
Cosmides, L. & J. Tooby (1997) The modular nature of human intelligence. In A.B. Scheibel & J.W.Schopf (Eds.). *The Origin and Evolution of Intelligence* (pp. 71-101). Sudbury, MA: Jones & Bartlett.
Cowie, F. (2000). *What's Within?* New York: Oxford University Press.
Deacon, T. W. (1997). *The Symbolic Species*. New York: W. W. Norton.
Elman, J.L., Bates, E.A., Johnson, M.H., Karmiloff-Smith, A., Parisi, D., & Plunkett, K. (1996). *Rethinking Innateness: A Connectionist Perspective on Development*. Cambridge, MA: MIT Press.
Fisher, R.A. (1930). *The Genetical Theory of Natural Selection*. Oxford, Eng.: Clarendon Press
Fodor, J. A. (1983). *Modularity of Mind*. Cambridge, MA: MIT Press
Fodor, J.A. (1998). *In Critical Condition*. Cambridge, MA: MIT Press.
Fodor, J. A. (2000). *The Mind Doesn't Work That Way*. Cambridge, MA: MIT Press.
Frank, R.H. (1988). *Passions Within Reason*. New York: W.W.Norton
Gaulin, S.J.C. & Robbins, C.J. (1991). Trivers-Willard effect in contemporary North American society. *American Journal of Physical Anthropology, 85,* 61-69
Gelman, R & Gallistel, C.R. (1978). *The Child's Understanding of Number*. Cambridge MA: Harvard University Press
Glymour. C. (2000). Android epistemology for babies. *Synthese, 122,* 53-68.
Godfrey-Smith, P. (1996). *Complexity and the Function of Mind in Nature*. Cambridge: Cambridge University Press
Godfrey-Smith, P. (2001). Three types of adaptationism. In S. Orzack & E.Sober (Eds). *Optimality & Adaptationism* (pp. 335-357). Cambridge, Eng.: Cambridge University Press.
Gopnik, A. (1996). Theories and modules: Creation myths, developmental realities, and Neurath's boat. In P. Carruthers & P.K. Smith (Eds.). *Theories of Theories of Mind* (pp. 169-183). Cambridge, Eng.: Cambridge University Press.
Gopnik, A. & Meltzoff, A.N. (1997). *Words, Thoughts, and Theories*. Cambridge, MA: MIT Press.
Gould S. J. (1997, June 26). Evolution: The Pleasures of Pluralism. *New York Review of Books, XLIV*(11), 47-52.
Griffiths, P. E. (1996). The historical turn in the study of adaptation. *British Journal for the Philosophy of Science, 47,* 511-532.
Griffiths, P. E. (1997). *What Emotions Really Are*. Chicago: University of Chicago Press.
Griffiths, P. E. & Gray, R. (1994). Developmental systems and evolutionary explanations. *Journal of Philosophy, 91,* 277-304.

Griffiths, P. E. & Knight, R.D. (1998). What Is the developmentalist challenge? *Philosophy of Science, 65*, 253-258.

Griffiths, P. E & Stotz, K. (2000). How the mind grows: A developmental perspective on the biology of cognition. *Synthese, 122*, 29-51.

Harvey, P & Pagel, M. (1991). *The Comparative Method in Evolutionary Biology*. Oxford, Eng.: Oxford University Press.

Hauser, M. & Carey, S. (1998). Building a cognitive creature from a set of primitives. In C. Allen & D. Cummins (Eds.). *The Evolution of Mind* (pp. 51-106). Oxford, Eng.: Oxford University Press.

Hrdy, S. B. (1987). Sex-biased parental investment among primates and other mammals: A critical evaluation of the Trivers-Willard hypothesis. In R. Gelles & J. Lancaster (Eds.). *Child Abuse and Neglect* (pp. 97-147). Hawthorne, N.J.: Aldine De Gruyter

Hull, D. (1989). On human nature. In D.Hull, (Ed.). *The Metaphysics of Evolution*. Albany, N.Y.: SUNY Press

Johnston, T. (1988). Developmental explanation and the ontogeny of birdsong: Nature-nurture redux. *Behavioral and Brain Sciences, 11*, 617-663.

Kitcher, P. (1990). Developmental decomposition and the future of human behavioral ecology. *Philosophy of Science, 57*, 96-117.

Lewontin, R. (2000). *The Triple Helix*. Cambridge, MA: Harvard University Press.

Lotto R. B. & Purves, D. (2000). An empirical explanation of color contrast. *Proceedings of theNational Academy of Sciences (USA), 97*, 12834-12839.

Mayr, E. (1976). Cause and effect in biology. In *Evolution and the Diversity of LIfe; Selected Essays* (pp. 359-371). Cambridge, MA: Harvard University Press.

McGuire, M. & Troisi, A. (1998). *Darwinian Psychiatry*. Oxford, Eng.: Oxford University Press

Meck, W.H. & Church, R.M. (1983). A mode control model of counting and timing processes. *Journal of Experimental Psychology: Animal Behavior Processes, 9*, 320-334

Nesse, R. & Williams, G.C. (1994). *Why We Get Sick*. New York: Times Books.

Oyama, S. (2000a). *The Ontogeny of Information* (2nd ed.) Durham, NC: Duke University Press

Oyama, S. (2000b). *Evolution's Eye: A Systems View of the Biology-Culture Divide*. Durham, NC: Duke University Press

Pinker, S. (1994). *The Language Instinct*. New York: Harper

Pinker, S. (1997). *How the Mind Works*. New York: W.W. Norton

Pinker, S. & Bloom, P. (1990). Natural language and natural selection. *Behavioral and Brain Sciences, 13*, 707-727.

Ridley, M. (1983) *The Explanation of Organic Diversity*. Oxford, Eng.: Blackwell Scientific Publications.

Samuels, R. (1998). Evolutionary psychology and the massive modularity hypothesis. *British Journal for the Philosophy of Science, 49*, 575-602.

Schaffner, K. (1998). Genes, behavior and developmental emergentism: One process, indivisible? *Philosophy of Science, 65*, 209-252.

Segal, G. (1996). The modularity of theory of mind. In P. Carruthers & P.K. Smith (Eds.). *Theories of Theories of Mind* (pp. 141-157). Cambridge, Eng.: Cambridge University Press.

Shapiro, L. (1999). Presence of mind. In V. G. Hardacstle (Ed) *Where Biology Meets Psychology: Philosophical Essays*. Cambridge, MA: MIT Press, 83-98.

Sober, E. & Wilson, D.S. (1998). *Unto Others: The Evolution and Psychology of Unselfish Behavior*. Cambridge, MA: Harvard University Press.

Sterelny, K., Smith, K.C., and Dickison, M. (1996). The extended replicator. *Biology and Philosophy, 11*, 377-403.

Symons, D. (1987). If we're all Darwinians, what's the fuss about? In C. B. Crawford, M. F. Smith & D. L. Krebs (Eds.). *Sociobiology and Psychology: Ideas, issues and applications* (pp. 121-146). Hillsdale, NJ: Lawrence Erlbaum Associates.

Symons, D. (1992). On the use and misuse of Darwinism in the human sciences. In J. Barkow, L. Cosmides, & J. Tooby (Eds.).*The Adapted Mind* (pp. 137-159). Oxford, Eng.: Oxford University Press

Tooby J. & Cosmides, L. (1992). The psychological foundations of culture. In J. Barkow, L. Cosmides, & J. Tooby (Eds.).*The Adapted Mind* (pp. 19-137). Oxford, Eng.: Oxford University Press.

Tooby, J. & Cosmides, L. (1995). Foreword. In S. Baron-Cohen (Ed.). *Mindblindness* (pp. xi – xviii). Cambridge, MA: MIT Press

Trivers, R. (1971). The evolution of reciprocal altruism. *Quarterly Review of Biology 46*, 35-57

Trivers, R. (1985). *Social Evolution*. Menlo Park, Ca.: Benjamin/Cummings

Trivers, R. & Willard, D. (1973). Natural selection of parental ability to vary the sex ratio of offspring. *Science, 179*, 90-91.

Trout, J. D. (2001). The biological basis of speech: What to infer from talking to the animals. *Psychological Review, 108*, 523-549.

Quartz, S. R. & Sejnowski, T.J. (1997). The neural basis of cognitive development: A constructivist manifesto. *Behavioral and Brain Sciences, 20,* 537-596.

Voland, E. (1984). Human sex-ratio manipulation: Historical data from a German parish. *Journal of Human Evolution, 13*, 99-107.

Williams, G. C. (1997). *The Pony Fish's Glow*. New York: Basic Books.

Wilson, E.O. (1978). *On Human Nature*. Cambridge, MA: Harvard University Press.

Wright, R.P. (1994). *The Moral Animal*. New York: Pantheon

Wynn, K. (1992). Addition and subtraction by human infants. *Nature, 358,* 749-750

STEVEN R. QUARTZ

TOWARD A DEVELOPMENTAL EVOLUTIONARY PSYCHOLOGY

Genes, Development, and the Evolution of the Human Cognitive Architecture

1.   RETHINKING THE RELATIONSHIP BETWEEN DEVELOPMENT AND EVOLUTION

1.1.   The Modern Synthesis and What Was Left Behind

After a century of intermittent dialogue between psychology and evolutionary biology, the outline of a synthesis between the two disciplines now appears to be emerging. The current form of this synthesis, referred to here as narrow evolutionary psychology[1] (Barkow et al., 1992; Buss, 1999), is the union of two specific frameworks from evolutionary biology and psychology. Specifically, narrow evolutionary psychology brings together the Modern Synthesis of evolutionary biology, which views evolutionary change primarily in terms of changes in gene frequency, with a nativist cognitive psychology, which views the mind as a collection of relatively autonomous, specialized processors, or modules (Hirschfeld & Gelman, 1994). As I outline in more detail below, both strands of evolutionary psychology are largely adevelopmental. There is accumulating evidence, however, that both evolutionary and psychological theory must incorporate a developmental perspective in order to construct successful theory. For example, it is now well established that a major route to evolutionary change is via alterations in developmental programs. If this is indeed the case, then evolutionary change must act in accordance with the range of possible changes to these programs, which in the

---

[1] EDITOR'S NOTE: In this book, the term 'narrow evolutionary psychology' signifies the approach to evolutionary psychology developed by Cosmides, Tooby, Buss, et al. This term was chosen not to imply that this approach has an inappropriately narrow point of view, but merely to suggest that the approach adopts a narrower range of assumptions than 'broad evolutionary psychology' (or, just 'evolutionary psychology'). This latter term signifies evolutionary psychology generally, practiced with any of a very broad range of assumptions possible within the general framework of evolutionary approaches to psychology. For more detail on this terminology, see the editor's introduction, p 1

Steven J. Scher & Frederick Rauscher (eds.). Evolutionary Psychology: Alternative Approaches, 185-210

case of behavior and cognition involves alterations to the development of the brain. From a psychological perspective, it is increasingly clear that ontogeny plays a far more central role in shaping behavior and cognition than its marginalization in nativist cognitive psychology allows (Quartz & Sejnowski, 1997). Any evolutionary psychology integrative framework must therefore take development seriously.

In recent years, new evolutionary and psychological frameworks have emerged that are thoroughly developmental in perspective. In evolutionary theory, this developmental perspective is known as evolutionary developmental biology (Raff, 1996; Arthur, 1997; Hall, 1998); in psychology, this developmental perspective is known as developmental cognitive neuroscience (Elman et al., 1996; Quartz & Sejnowski, 1997). To date, evolutionary developmental biology and developmental cognitive neuroscience have not been brought together to construct an alternative evolutionary psychology framework that places development at its center to explicitly account for the evolution of cognition in terms of developmental alterations to neural structures. In this chapter, I present the preliminary outlines of such a view, which I refer to as "developmental evolutionary psychology." From this perspective, I will suggest that failing to take into account how evolution acts on developmental programs to regulate alterations in brain structure and function has resulted in a seriously distorted view of the evolution of cognition and the resulting human cognitive architecture; it has also contributed to a mischaracterization of the role of culture in human development and evolution. In contrast, I will suggest that developmental evolutionary psychology suggests an alternative view of the human cognitive architecture that replaces the highly modular view of narrow evolutionary psychology with a behavioral systems view. As I explore below, this perspective views the human cognitive architecture as a hierarchically organized control structure, where this hierarchical organization is evident both evolutionarily and developmentally. Additionally, this perspective provides a principled means of incorporating recent results from cognitive neuroscience, which have tended to be marginalized in narrow evolutionary psychology. This, then, furthers the naturalistic stance narrow evolutionary psychology advocates but falls short of achieving. Finally, I will present evidence from paleoclimatology that suggests the environment of evolutionary adaptation (EEA) was markedly different from the account most prevalent in narrow evolutionary psychology. This evidence suggests that the selective forces underlying the evolution of the human cognitive architecture were critically connected to highly unstable climes, as there is an intriguing temporal coincidence of rapid hominid encephalization and increasing ecological instability during the Middle Pleistocene (600-150 kyr BP; Ruff et al., 1997). Based on these considerations, I suggest that an important feature of hominid evolution was a process I have referred to as progressive externalization (Quartz & Sejnowski, 1997; Quartz, 1999), whereby the brain's development became increasingly regulated by extrinsic factors, likely mediated by heterochronic changes in neural development. I suggest that this process allowed for flexible prefrontally mediated cognitive function, particularly in the social domain, and underlies the capacity for rapid changes in social structure that was a response to the need for buffering ecological instability (see also Potts, 1996). The upshot of this process was symbolic culture, which plays a central role in shaping the structures underlying human cognition (Tomasello, 1999).

1.2. Taking Development Seriously

Both components of narrow evolutionary psychology, evolutionary biology and nativist cognitive psychology, are largely adevelopmental. Regarding the latter, Chomsky's work on language acquisition has been highly influential in the field of cognitive development. Chomsky's principal argument concerned the relative impoverishment of the environment as an informational source, which he argued was too barren to provide sufficient information for a child equipped only with general learning mechanisms to converge on a grammar that would underlie language competence (see Cowie, 1998). Aimed against B.F. Skinner's behaviorist analysis of language use, Chomsky argued that the child must bring certain knowledge of grammar to the task of language acquisition *a priori*. This knowledge took the form of a language organ, a structure containing domain-specific knowledge.

Although Chomsky hypothesized such a specialized structure only for language, his arguments proved compelling and resulted in a widespread adoption of domain-specific organs, or modules, for a variety of other cognitive capacities, such as social cognition (Brothers & Ring, 1992) and numerical cognition (Dehaene et al., 1999). This view has led to a widely adopted modular view of the mind (Fodor, 1983; Hirschfeld & Gelman, 1994). This, in turn, has had major consequences for the specific proposals of narrow evolutionary psychology regarding the structure of the mind and its development. In particular, Tooby and Cosmides' (1992, pp. 93ff.; Cosmides and Tooby, 1994) critique of the Standard Social Science Model echoed many of Chomsky's arguments against behaviorism's general learning strategies (for an evaluation of many of these arguments in their evolutionary context, see Fodor, 2000).

Although nativist cognitive psychology has been largely adevelopmental, the rise of cognitive neuroscience in recent years has spawned a growing interest in development. This work has in turn given rise to a growing developmental cognitive neuroscience (Elman et al., 1996; Johnson, 1997; Quartz, 1999). In contrast to nativist cognitive psychology, the cornerstone of developmental cognitive neuroscience is a series of new experimental results; the findings range from developmental neural plasticity at the systems level to single cell physiology, as I explore in more detail below. Together, these results indicate that human development is both more protracted and more sensitive to environmental signals than nativist cognitive psychology supposed; this makes it important to understand the implications of these results for an evolutionary psychology integrative framework.

As stated above, there is another source of narrow evolutionary psychology's adevelopmental perspective: the Modern Synthesis in evolutionary biology. Although embryology and evolution were considered together in the late

19th century, by the 1920s and 1930s Morgan, Dobzhansky, and others provided powerful arguments for why evolutionary biology should move away from the ties to embryology that Haeckel, Weissmann and others emphasized (for a review, see Gilbert et al., 1996). In place of embryology, the shapers of the Modern Synthesis argued that transmission genetics provided the most appropriate coupling with natural selection, culminating in the view that evolution is essentially changes in gene frequency. Despite the attempts of Goldschmidt in the 1930s, and Waddington in the 1940s and 1950s, to combine evolution and development, little progress was made integrating development into evolutionary theory until recently. Only with major advances in the molecular genetics of development, beginning in the 1980s, have inroads been made regarding adding a developmental perspective to evolutionary theory. Specifically, this work has begun to demonstrate the "deep structure" of development, beginning with fundamentally important insights into the homologous developmental pathways underlying a variety of embryonic processes from drosophilia to mammals. The cornerstone result of this work was the discovery of homeobox genes and their striking conservation (reviewed in Hirth & Reichert, 1999; Reichert & Simeone, 1999). Given the enormous differences in neuroanatomy between vertebrates and invertebrates, their brains were long thought to be unrelated with little obvious homology. However, at a deeper, molecular level they are remarkably similar in that homologous regulatory genes have been identified that control regionalization, patterning, and identity in embryonic brain development. So striking are these new results that it now appears unlikely that successful evolutionary theory can be constructed that does not have a prominent place for development. Based on such observations, the nascent field of evolutionary developmental biology has emerged (for a review, see Raff, 2000).

The emergence of developmental cognitive neuroscience and evolutionary developmental biology in recent years suggests a possible major reorientation of evolutionary psychology. As I have indicated, the major shortcoming of narrow evolutionary psychology is its marginalization of development, whose incorporation now appears essential to any satisfactory account of an evolutionary framework for human cognition and behavior. In what follows, I will sketch the outlines of such an approach that begins to integrate developmental cognitive neuroscience and evolutionary developmental biology into a view I refer to as developmental evolutionary psychology. As I explore, this approach adds an additional important constraint. Whereas both the Modern Synthesis and nativist cognitive psychology largely treat the brain as a black box, both evolutionary developmental biology and developmental cognitive neuroscience explicitly address the issue of neural structures and mechanisms. This, then, allows developmental evolutionary psychology to further the naturalistic perspective narrow evolutionary psychology advocates but falls short of by relegating neuroscience to a minor role (e.g., Tooby & Cosmides, 1992). Because developmental evolutionary psychology is explicit about the mechanisms and structures underlying cognition and behavior, it examines the nature of the deep structure in the fundamental patterning of vertebrates that both constrains possible evolutionary changes and facilitates morphological alterations along certain routes. The central questions developmental evolutionary psychology asks, then, are, what alterations in developmental mechanisms and processes underlie the evolution of the structure and function of the brain and sensory systems, how are these reflected in the organization of the human cognitive architecture, and how do these generate human behavior and cognition?

In what follows, I sketch a response to these central questions that incorporates the insights of comparative neuroanatomy and the molecular genetics of development. Based on these results, I will suggest that narrow evolutionary psychology's model of the human cognitive architecture, one based on massive modularity, is inconsistent with the permissible mechanisms underlying evolutionary alterations to neural structures. I then present an alternative, hierarchical behavioral systems view of the evolved human cognitive architecture that is based on integrating developmental cognitive neuroscience and evolutionary developmental biology into a developmental evolutionary psychology. More specifically, in Section 2.1, I consider shortcomings in the trait-level analyses that have played a prominent role in adaptive thinking and the problematic inference to cognitive modules based on that level of analysis. To make this concrete, I examine Lovejoy et al.'s (1999) analysis of the hominid pelvis. This example demonstrates that relatively simple alterations in developmental programs can have a cascade effect and thereby alter systemic properties, such as the entire pelvic field, casting doubt on the sufficiency of trait level analyses. These considerations suggest that alterations in genomic regulatory systems is a key mediator of evolutionary change. Next, in Section 2.2, I consider this insight from the perspective of brain evolution. In particular, I examine the striking finding that, despite a 10,000-fold range in neocortex size across mammals, the relative size of many brain structures is highly correlated. I review evidence indicating that heterochronic changes in the duration of neurogenesis result in the coordinated pattern of brain size across a variety of mammalian species. These results suggest that neural systems highly covary with one another as a consequence of the restricted range of permissible alterations that evolutionary change can act upon. This makes the massive modularity hypothesis of narrow evolutionary psychology untenable. In Section 2.3, I then turn to consider whether these heterochronic changes may themselves reflect a deeper structure of biological design. I review evidence that demonstrates that much of the diversity of mammalian brains reflects the spatial organization of the neural tube. This suggests that the range of permissible changes to the relative size of brain structures must reflect this deep structure of neural development.

Based on this evidence, I conclude that, since evolutionary changes involve heterochronic alterations to developmental programs that result in systemic changes throughout the brain, narrow evolutionary psychology's modular account of the human cognitive architecture should be replaced by one that views the brain as a collection of behavioral systems. In Section 3, I present a proposal for one such behavioral systems view that is based on comparative work that identifies common design principles across a wide variety of nervous systems. This behavioral systems view places development at its center, suggesting an alternative evolutionary psychology framework that integrates developmental cognitive neuroscience and evolutionary developmental biology. In Section 4, I consider recent work in paleoclimatology that suggests that the ecological conditions that may have driven hominid brain evolution were markedly different from the proposals of narrow evolutionary psychology and accords better with the model of cognitive architecture I present. In Section 5, I examine this issue in more detail and consider how alterations in development may underlie the capacity for complex cultural learning that was a response to ecological instability.

2.   BUILDING BRAINS: DEVELOPMENT AND THE UNITS OF SELECTION

2.1. Traits, Genes, and the Morphogenetic Field

In narrow evolutionary psychology there is a deep connection between modules and genes (e.g., Pinker, 1997, p.32). An informal criterion of a module is that it has a semi-independent evolutionary account, which involves an analysis of genetic transmission under natural selection. As Sterelny and Griffiths (1999) note, narrow-school evolutionary psychologists follow the strategy of adaptive thinking in attempting to identify modules and their function. That is, a solution is inferred from the structure of a historical problem, which requires reconstructing the evolutionary context, or environment of evolutionary adaptation. This trait-level analysis of behavior depends on identified traits being separately heritable, corresponding to a module, so that evolution can act on the basis of that trait's variation. Such a view makes strong predictions regarding permissible evolutionary alterations to the substrates of cognition. Indeed, it is somewhat surprising that this modular account of the human cognitive architecture, and the evolutionary path to it via semi-autonomous selection of modules, has not been considered in terms of whether it is consistent with the emerging understanding of the paths to evolutionary change in nervous systems. There have, however, been many more general cautions regarding the functional identification of a trait and its putative separate heritability (Dobzhansky, 1956; Gould and Lewontin, 1979). Without additional constraints, a behavioral analysis can lead to behaviors being seen as composed of numerous characters, or modules; such trait atomization relies on the assumption of particulate inheritance. Put another way, the capacity to functionally dissect behaviors into component parts in no way entails that those components are mediated by modules with separable heritability.

Recently, Lovejoy et al. (1999) analyzed the mammalian postcranium from a developmental perspective and demonstrated that trait atomization could lead to a serious distortion of cladistic analyses. Their specific example involved the transformation of the common ancestral pelvis into that of early hominids. They suggest that the evolution of the pelvis may have involved the modification of the geometry of pattern formation, such as a progressive increase in the slope of molecular gradients in the limb bud, initiating a developmental cascade that would alter the entire pelvic field. Thus, although it is possible to identify separable traits at the morphological level – sacrum, platypelloid birth canal, pubic symphysis, superior and inferior pubic rami, obturator foramina — none of these may have a unique evolutionary history nor be under separate selective pressure. Rather, the entire pelvis may be systemically modified as a function of alterations in development.

Gilbert et al. (1996) similarly suggest that incorporating results regarding the deep structure of developmental programs results in a major modification of the units of selection. Rather than the gene, they suggest that the morphogenetic field is the basic unit of ontogeny whose alterations mediate evolution. Such a perspective leads naturally to the view that changes in genomic regulatory systems are the mediators of evolutionary change (Davidson, 2001). This observation merits further investigation, as it is of central importance to an evolutionary psychology perspective. That is, what is the range of permissible evolutionary alterations to nervous systems, and does analysis at a behavioral trait level result in a distorted account?

2.2. Scaling Brains

The first question to ask is, what processes underlie changes in the size of brain structures? The organization and neuropharmacology of the brain stem, which mediates basic homeostatic functions, appear to be highly conserved across species (Ross et al., 1984). In contrast, there is a 10,000-fold range in neocortex size across mammals. A uniquely mammalian structure, neocortex occupies a disproportionate percentage of total brain mass in anthropoid primates (monkeys, apes, and humans), from 60-80% of the total (Nieuwenhuys et al., 1998). The disproportionate increase in neorcortex size in anthropoid primates is believed to reflect important cognitive and behavioral skills that underlie complex social and cognitive functions. Indeed, this disproportionate increase is referred to as encephalization and is the basis for the important view that anthropoid evolution is in part characterized by the increasing cortical mediation of complex behavior and cognition.[2]

Given the enormous range of neocortex size across mammals in terms of both relative and absolute sizes, it is important to consider what mechanisms and processes determine these differences and along what dimensions these differences lie. Neocortex is not unconstrained to change across all dimensions. Indeed, the thickness and the general organization of neocortex differs relatively little across species.[3] Rather, neocortex across species is organized into radially oriented, vertically interconnected columns, and shares a horizontal organization into layers designated I-VI. Cortical circuitry also shares basic themes, with deep layers (VI and V) sending efferent to subcortical and cortical structures, the middle layer (IV)

---

[2] Although encephalization may underlie important cognitive differences among anthropoid primates, in general it is difficult to relate differences in brain size to cognitive differences across species; see Kaas (2000).

[3] There are some important exceptions. For example, Allman (1999) has recently demonstrated that anthropoid primates possess a special class of cells, known as spindle cells, whose physiology might underlie important elements of higher cognition. In addition, cortical thickness is twice as thick in human neocortex as it is in mice neocortex, largely a consequence of the increased need for connectivity.

receiving afferents from the thalamus, and with the upper layers (II and III) integrating information within the cortex. Phenotypic variability in the size, number, and interconnectedness of cortical areas thus underlie species differences in behavior and cognition.

Alterations in the size of neocortex appear to be mediated primarily by the number of neurons and their supporting elements. It is possible to increase the size of neurons, however this would require a complex recalibration of their physiological properties, which in turn would require novel biophysical mechanisms that instead appear to be highly conserved. Thus, while larger brains do tend to have larger neurons, this increased size is not highly significant and does not account for differences in brain size. Based on this and other considerations, a possible route to neocortical diversity is via evolutionary modifications of the program of cortical development. The fact that neocortex does not vary across all dimensions, but retains common organizational themes such as radial and laminar organization, suggests that only a portion of cortical development programs differ, making it possible to use a comparative methodology across species to assess alterations in cortical development programs. Combined with other experimental techniques, such as gene knockout experiments, it is possible to identify the processes underlying neocortical diversity.

One process underlying alterations in the size of body parts, including the brain, involves alterations to cell proliferation. The three-dimensional neuronal organization of the neocortex develops from a two-dimensional sheet of proliferating cells during a restricted period of early development (McConnell, 1995; Rakic, 1988). During early gestation, the anterior-most end of the neural tube expands outwards, forming a pair of telencephalic vesicles that become the cerebral hemispheres. Neurons are not generated in the region they will occupy in the mature organism. Instead, they are generated in the ventricular zone (VZ), a primitive epithelial sheet of dividing cells that line the cerebral ventricles. Prior to neurogenesis, these progenitor cells divide symmetrically to establish a precursor pool. The onset of neurogenesis is marked by the first postmitotic cells leaving the ventricular zone and migrating along radial glial fibers, eventually forming a structure known as the cortical plate. As more postmitotic cells migrate out into the cortical plate, they do so in an inside-out temporal sequence, generating the layers of the neocortex, with later migrating cells forming the more superficial layers.

One potential route to building specialized brain structures, such as modules, would be through modulating the process of neurogenesis, whereby specific precursor populations would be generated and migrate to a specific neocortical site. For such a strategy to be feasible, the process of neurogenesis would have to be dissociable and thus restricted phases of neurogenesis would be under natural selection. It is possible to investigate this possibility through a comparative method, as it makes a strong prediction: if natural selection operates on neurogenesis in this way, then the size of some individual brain structures in different species should diverge from the relative size of other structures. That is, the relationship among brain structures across species should not show strong signs of linked regularities.

Heinz Stephan and colleagues published a series of volumetric data sets for eleven brain divisions and for more discrete nuclei and zones for a large sample of insectivores, prosimians, simians, and bats (Stephen et al., 1981; Frahm et al., 1982) that has become a widely used dataset to analyze comparative brain structures. Using a factor analytic approach, Finlay and Darlington (1995) found that the size of various brain structures across 131 mammalian species was highly correlated, with the primary exception of the olfactory bulb. In general, the relative proportions of different brain structures can be highly predicted by overall brain size. Put another way, mammalian brains appear to scale in a highly coordinated fashion. These highly predictable relationships between the sizes of major brain structures indicate that diverse brains derive from a highly conserved homeotic starting point. Differences across species stem from alterations in global proliferative processes: heterochronic changes in the duration and/or rate of neurogenesis that result in linked regularities among brain structures. This suggests that restricted phases of neurogenesis are not independently under selective pressures. Further evidence to support this possibility stems from the striking finding that the order of neurogenesis — the order in which neuronal populations give rise to various brain structures — appears to be highly conserved across species (reviewed in Finlay et al., 2001). During neurogenesis, many progenitor cells continue dividing symmetrically, producing one postmitotic cell and one progenitor cell. Thus, the pool of progenitor cells grows exponentially. This suggests that later generated structures will get proportionally larger, largely as a consequence of the exponential nature of symmetric cell division, as indeed the linked regularities discussed above confirm. That is, Finlay and Darlington (1995) found that greater durations of neurogenesis were correlated with a proportional increase in overall brain size and differential effects on the size of brain components, with later generated structures growing in a predicable fashion. As Finlay and Darlington (1995) put it, late makes large.

2.3. Heterochrony, Segmental Models, and the Deep Structure of Development

Given the coordinated, predictable shift in relative neural structures, a key concept that emerges is that of heterochrony, the phylogenetic variation in the relative timing of major developmental events (for a recent review of the notion of heterochrony, see Gould, 2000). Does the fact that heterochronic changes in the duration of neurogenesis result in the coordinated pattern of brain size across a variety of mammalian species reflect something about the deep structure of development? These linked regularities might indeed reflect a deeper structure of development, whereby the highly conserved order of neurogenesis reflects the spatial organization of the neuroaxes of the neural tube, a highly conserved organization that likely precedes vertebrates. One of the most important insights from the molecular genetics of development regards the fact that conserved regulatory genes have highly restricted spatial patterns of activity, underlying the segmental patterning of body plans. Segmentation is best understood in *Drosophilia*, where the basic segmented body plan is specified by positional information laid down in the early embryo by an interacting group of regulatory genes (reviewed in Pick, 1998; for a computational analysis, see Reinitz et al., 1998). Under the sequential, hierarchical action of these genes, the embryo is subdivided into increasingly specified body regions along the anterior-posterior axis. Morphogenesis is thus specified by a progressively restricted subdivision of the embryo, including the action of homeotic genes that assign an identity to established regions.

The central nervous system is composed of four major subdivisions: the spinal cord, hindbrain, midbrain, and forebrain. The forebrain (prosencephalon) mediates most higher cognitive functions, and includes such structures as neocortex, archicortex, and thalamus. The forebrain was long thought to be an exception to segmental models, as its topography appeared non-segmental, making it unclear how topographically organized developmental programs would operate. Rubenstein and colleagues (Rubenstein et al., 1994) suggested that the vertebrate forebrain does follow a segmental model, and postulated that dorsoventral (D/V) and anteroposterior (A/P) patterning mechanisms subdivide the embryonic forebrain into longitudinal and transverse domains. According to their prosomeric model, the embryonic forebrain is a neuromeric structure subdivided into a grid-like pattern of histogenic domains defined by longitudinal and transverse boundaries, and so follows many of the deep developmental themes found in other segmental models.

Recently, Finlay et al. (1998; 2001) examined whether there was any relation between the conserved ordered of neurogenesis and the prosomeric model of brain organization. They found a strong relationship between position on the prosomeric axes and duration of neurogenesis. Specifically, more ventral and anterior regions have a more protracted period of neurogenesis, illustrating that the coordinated scaling of the relative size of brain structures is in part a reflection of the spatial organization of the neuraxes. This suggests that the range of permissible changes to the relative size of brain structures must reflect this deep structure of neural development. In particular, the exponential growth of neocortex relative to the rest of the brain may therefore be in part a consequence of its prosomeric location.

3. FROM MODULES TO BEHAVIORAL SYSTEMS: THE HIERARCHICAL ORGANIZATION OF BEHAVIOR AND ITS EVOLUTION

3.1. Common Nervous System Design Principles

The above considerations demonstrate that it is infeasible to view the neocortex as a collection of relatively autonomous modules. Rather, evolutionary changes in neural structures involve heterochronic alterations to developmental programs that result in systemic changes throughout the brain. As Finlay et al., (2001) state, "natural selection does not do its work on some equipotent substrate, but on a complex mechanism with a history of previous change that makes some adaptations more 'workable' than others." For these reasons, an analysis of the neural mediation of behavior, and the evolutionary paths available to alter such structures, requires abandoning a modular, trait atomistic view of the human cognitive architecture. In its place, I outline a model that is consistent with the results presented above. Specifically, I present a behavioral systems model that regards the brain as a hierarchical control structure, where this hierarchical organization is evident both developmentally and evolutionarily. This behavioral systems model places a premium on the complex interaction between developmental mechanisms and a structured environment, and, therefore, rests on the second component of developmental evolutionary psychology, namely developmental cognitive neuroscience.

The existence of highly conserved nervous system developmental mechanisms suggests that nervous systems, despite their apparent diversity, share a deep structure, or common design principles, just as the fact that two million distinct species share only 35 major body plans suggest that body plans share many common design principles. Even the simplest motile organisms require control structures to regulate goal-directed behavior necessary for survival in a variable environment (for discussion, see Allman, 1999). For example, although the bacterium *E. coli* does not possess a nervous system, it does possess control structures for sensory responses, memory, and motility that underlie its capacity to alter behavior in response to environmental conditions. The capacity to approach nutritive stimuli and avoid aversive stimuli in the maintenance of life history functions is the hallmark of behavioral systems across phyla. Whereas chemotaxis in bacteria involves a single step from sensory transduction to motor behavior, some multicellular organisms embody control structures that involve intercellular communication via hormonal signaling, while others possess nervous systems with control structures that add layers of mediating control between sensory transduction and motor behavior.

There are several alternative design possibilities for biological control structures. One is to make a closed system, in the sense of linking fixed behavioral patterns between internal goal states and their environmental targets. Although there are many examples of this strategy (Gallistel, 1992), there are more powerful and flexible control structures. One such strategy involves leaving the path from internal goal state to target state open and discoverable via learning. Principal among this latter design strategy are reinforcement-based systems that are capable of learning an environment's reward structure.[4]

3.2. The Ubiquity of Reward Structures in Nervous Systems

A variety of experimental techniques, ranging from psychopharmacology to neural imaging, has demonstrated the striking ubiquity and conservation of reward structures across species. At virtually all levels of the human nervous system, for example, reward systems can be found that play a central role in goal-directed behavior (Schultz, 2000). Here, I focus on one such system, the midbrain dopamine system (Figure 1). The midbrain dopamine system projects principally from the

---

[4] Although this strategy emphasizes learning, it is important to bear in mind that it requires a primitive set of target states that have intrinsic reward value to the organism (classically known as unconditioned stimuli).

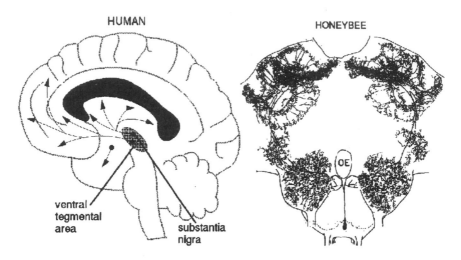

Figure 1. Neuromodulatory (octopamine) neurons in the bee brain and dopamine projections in the human brain play homologous roles. Neural activity in these neurons distributes information about expected reward.

ventral tegmental area to the nucleus accumbens and the temporal and frontal cortex. Studies utilizing self-stimulation paradigms revealed that activation of this system was highly reinforcing, often with laboratory animals preferring to self-stimulate this system than eat or copulate with a receptive partner (reviewed in Wise, 1996). Most addictive substances involve this system, giving rise to the hedonic theory of dopamine as the signal underlying pleasure (though see Garris et al., 1999).

Given what I have previously stated regarding the possibility that control structures are highly conserved, it is interesting to note, as Figure 1 illustrates, the striking homology between the dopamine system in humans and a reward system in the bumblebee. The bumblebee suboesophogeal ganglion contains an identified neuron, VUMmx1, which delivers information about reward during classical conditioning experiments via the neurotransmitter, octopamine, which is similar in molecular structure to dopamine (Hammer, 1993).

Both experimental and computational work on the role of VUMmx1 in bumblebee foraging has provided important insights into the signal carried by octopamine and the system's functional significance (Real, 1991; Montague et al., 1995). Rather than simply carrying information regarding reward, it appears that octopamine signals information regarding prediction errors. Whereas reward is traditionally a behavioral notion, prediction is a computational notion. The difference between certain rewarding outcomes and their predictions can be used to guide adaptive behavior. A system that learns through prediction learning need not have the path from goal to reward specified, in contrast to fixed behavioral patterns, such as stimulus-response learning. Instead, the path from goals to rewards may be left open and discoverable via learning, resulting in flexible action. Evolution, then, may shape the pattern of basic rewards animals are motivated to obtain, but the behavioral path is left open to discovery, as are more complex relations among predictors. In this sense, brains are prediction machines that use information gathered from past experience to predict future events important for survival (reviewed in Montague and Quartz, 1999).

Experiments utilizing neurophysiological recording in behaving monkeys by Schultz and colleagues demonstrate that the midbrain dopamine system plays an important role in prediction learning in the mammalian brain (Schultz et al., 1993). When these monkeys were presented with various appetitive stimuli, dopaminergic neurons responded with short, phasic activations, which typically lasted for only a few repeated presentations. In an important finding, however, Schultz and colleagues found that when the rewarding stimuli were preceded by an auditory or visual cue, dopamine neurons changed their time of activation to just after the time of cue onset. In contrast, when the reward did not follow the conditioned stimulus, dopamine neurons were depressed below their basal firing rate exactly at the time the reward should have occurred. These results indicate that the dopamine signal encodes expectations regarding the delivery of reward. That is, the output of dopamine neurons code for an error between the actual reward received and predictions of the time and magnitude of reward. Like the octopamine signal in the bumblebee, the dopamine signal codes a prediction error that can be used in learning and in action selection. This mode of action is equivalent to Temporal Difference learning, a thoroughly examined form of reinforcement learning (Sutton and Barto, 1998) that learns the predictive structure of an environment. Simulations demonstrate that despite the apparent simplicity of this model, it is a very powerful learner, capable of learning master level backgammon, for example (Tesauro, 1995).

A variety of evidence supports the notion that this system works in a similar fashion in humans (though it is important to point out that this in no way is meant to be the exclusive locus of behavioral choice). For example, it is possible to design reward functions where the computational model of dopamine will pursue sub-optimal strategies. Montague and Quartz (1999) found that human choice behavior in a simple two-card task followed these sub-optimal strategies when faced with these anomalous reward functions. Berns et al. (2001) have recently examined prediction learning directly with functional imaging, essentially replicating Schultz's monkey experiments in humans, and have found activation of the midbrain dopamine system. These results suggest that the midbrain reward system in the human brain shares common functional properties with homologous reward systems across a diverse array of species.

3.3. The Hierarchical Structure of the Human Behavioral System

It is deeply intriguing to note where the midbrain dopamine system projects to in the human brain. In particular, what is most intriguing is the fact that it projects to dorsolateral prefrontal, premotor, and parietal cortex, which are structures believed to mediate goal representations, and the orbitofrontal cortex, which is believed to mediate the representation of relative reward value and reward expectation (for a review, see Schultz, 2000). A great deal of attention has centered on the dorsolateral and orbitofrontal prefrontal cortex as structures implicated in crucial components of human cognition, particularly social cognition and theory of mind (Stone et al., 1998), symbolic learning (Deacon, 1997), representations of self (Craik et al., 1999), and executive function and behavioral inhibition (Norman & Shallice, 1986).

In an evolutionary context, it is important to ask, what is the functional significance of the fact that a phylogenetically old part of the brain projects to a relatively phylogenetic newcomer? According to the view of developmental evolutionary psychology, these structures constitute a hierarchically organized control structure, where additional layers of control have been added to the evolutionarily conserved dopamine system and where this hierarchical organization is evident developmentally as well. To see how, it is important to examine the developmental links between these components, as I explore in more detail below.

Diamond and colleagues (reviewed in Diamond, 1998) have demonstrated that a functional midbrain dopaminergic system is necessary for normal development of prefrontal functions. The most compelling evidence regarding this developmental dependence stems from studies of Phenylketonuria (PKU). Patients suffering from PKU do not naturally produce a particular enzyme, phenylalanine hydroxylase, which converts the essential amino acid phenylalanine to another amino acid, tyrosine, the precursor of dopamine; when untreated, PKU leads to severe mental retardation. Diamond and colleagues found that lowered levels of tyrosine uniquely affect the cognitive functions dependent on prefrontal cortex because of the special sensitivity of prefrontally projecting dopamine neurons to small decreases in tyrosine. In a 4-year longitudinal study, they found that PKU children performed worse than matched controls, their own siblings, and children from the general population on tasks that required the working memory and inhibitory control abilities dependent on dorsolateral prefrontal cortex. In contrast, these PKU children performed well on control tasks that were not mediated by prefrontal cortex (Diamond et al., 1997).

The hierarchical organization of the control structures that constitute the human cognitive architecture is apparent developmentally, with human cognition and behavior becoming increasingly mediated by frontal structures. In contrast to the early functional involvement of midbrain dopamine systems, prefrontal structures develop relatively late and exhibit a protracted development that continues into adolescence. Thus, behavior and cognition increasingly comes under the mediation of frontal structures from subcortical structures across development, a process sometimes referred to as frontalization of behavior (Rubia et al., 2000). For example, executive function is a control mechanism that guides, coordinates, and updates behavior in a flexible fashion, particularly in novel or complex tasks (Norman and Shallice, 1986). This requires that information related to behavioral goals be actively represented and maintained so that these representations may guide behavior toward goal-directed activities. In humans, executive function follows a special developmental trajectory, reflecting an evolutionary reorganization of prefrontal structures and their development. Between 7 ½ and 12 months of age, infants show a developmental progresson on A-not-B (Diamond, 1985), delayed response (Diamond and Doar, 1989), and object retrieval tasks (Diamond, 1988). There is substantial evidence that these tasks are mediated by dorsolateral prefrontal cortex and rely on working memory, neural representations of goal-related information, and behavioral inhibition (Goldman-Rakic, 1990; Petrides, 1995). Further, various sources of evidence indicate that dopamine is necessary for successful performance on these tasks (Sawaguchi and Goldman-Rakic, 1994).

3.4. Computational Links

Although there is strong evidence that an intact dopamine system is necessary for the developmental emergence of prefrontal functions, a largely unresolved question concerns the specific nature of this developmental link. One particularly intriguing possibility is that the dopamine signal serves as a learning signal that guides the construction of prefrontal structures during development. Computational work on the midbrain dopamine system suggests such a learning role with strong analogies to temporal difference learning, a form of reinforcement learning (Sutton & Barto, 1998). A key notion underlying reinforcement learning is that of learning through interacting with one's environment. For example, a major source of knowledge stems from an infant's interactions with its environment, which produces a wealth of information about cause and effect, about the consequences of actions, and about what to do in order to achieve goals—all without the need for an explicit teacher. (Of course, Piaget also emphasized the central importance of the developing child's agency and active exploration with its environment in his constructivist theory of cognitive development.)

Learning through interacting with one's environment requires structures that direct the system to its environment. According to the view I have been outlining here, this is mediated in part by the midbrain dopamine system. One clue for this role derives from studies of the neurobiology of personality, which view personality as deriving from motivational systems. From this perspective, the midbrain dopamine system constitutes a behavioral facilitation system that underlies fundamental properties of personality, specifically extraversion and positive emotionality (Depue & Collins, 1999). From a developmental perspective, this behavioral facilitation system appears to be operative at an early age and likely underlies major dimensions of temperament, along with other diffuse ascending systems, such as noradernergic and serotonergic systems. Thus, given this system's computational properties and its role as a behavioral facilitation system early in postnatal development, this system is ideally situated to be involved in the reinforcement or self-supervised construction of prefrontal structures underlying complex behavioral control.

This computational role can be illustrated by comparing reinforcement models of learning to models of self-organization, or unsupervised learning. The best-known account of unsupervised learning is Hebbian learning, which in its simplest form is:

$$\Delta w_{kj}(t) = \eta y_k(t) x_j(t)) \tag{1}$$

where a synaptic weight w_{kj} of neuron k with presynaptic and postsynaptic signals denoted by x_j and y_k respectively are altered at time step t and where η is a positive constant that determines the rate of learning. Algorithms such as equation 1 and a variety of modifications essentially find efficient representations of salient environmental information by implementing such data reduction strategies as principal component analysis. Such algorithms can be modified to become reinforcement learning algorithms by making weight updates dependent on the Hebbian correlation of a prediction error and the presynaptic activity at the previous timestep. This takes the following form:

$$w(i, t-1)_{new} = w(i, t-1)_{prev} + \eta x(i, t-1)\delta(t) \tag{2}$$

where $x(i, t-1)$ represents presynaptic activity at connection i and time $t-1$, η is a learning rate, and $w(i, t-1)_{prev}$ is the previous value of the weight representing timestep $t-1$. The term $\delta(t)$ is a prediction error term (see Figure 2) and is the difference between a prediction of reward and the actual reward, represented as the output of the dopaminergic projection to cortex in the simulation framework. The addition of this term changes the Hebbian framework to a Predictive Hebbian one (Montague & Sejnowski, 1994) and is the essential computed differential in the temporal differences method of reinforcement learning (Sutton & Barto, 1998) with close connections to dynamic programming (Bellman, 1957).

The developmental link between the midbrain dopamine system and prefrontal structures suggests that an explicit account of the developmental trajectory of cognitive skills is necessary; an account based on innately-specified modules is inadequate. According to this view, complex developmental skills decompose into developmental precursors, which may often be mediated by structures that are distinct from those mediating the mature state. For example, face processing is believed to be mediated by subcortical structures during early postnatal development, but it subsequently shifts to cortical sites (reviewed in Johnson, 1997). The model I have outlined above suggests a possible way of bootstrapping a system into such complex representations by biasing development by making the system selectively attentive to faces. An economical means of implementing such a strategy would be by making faces, or primitive template representations of them, rewarding to the system, thereby designing a system that preferentially attends to faces. It is clear that human infants possess such behavioral biases, which may be implemented through projections to midbrain dopamine systems that constitute unconditioned stimuli.

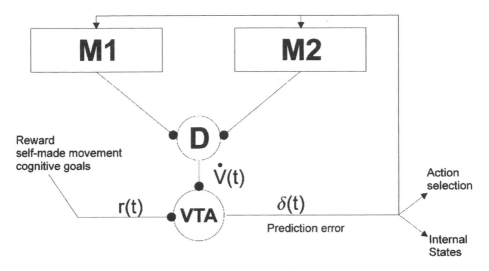

Figure 2. Architecture of Prediction learning. M1 and M2 represent two different cortical modalities whose output is assumed to arrive at the ventral tegmental area (VTA) in the form of a temporal derivative $\dot{V}$ (t). Information about reward r(t) also converges on the VTA. The VTA output is taken as a simple linear sum $\delta(t) = r(t) + \dot{V}$ (t). The output connections of the VTA make the prediction error $\delta(t)$ simultaneously available to structures constructing the predictions.

3.5. Protracted Development and Constructive Learning

These considerations suggest another important evolutionary alteration to developmental programs with important consequence for the evolution of human cognition. Above I highlighted evolutionary alterations in the duration of neurogenesis that appears to account for many aspects of increases in brain size. In addition, it appears that the human brain's development is also more protracted than other anthropoid apes. For example, the chimpanzee brain reaches 95% of its final mass by age two, whereas the human brain does not reach this milestone until the age of five. On many accounts, the protracted nature of human development has mainly negative consequences, such as extending the period of heightened vulnerability. Such accounts often regard protracted human development as a side effect of the constraints bipedalism placed on the design of the female pelvis, and thus on limits to the size of the birth canal.

The interpretation of protracted development as a liability stems in part from a view of development as largely a process of intrinsic maturation. Protracted neural development need not be viewed simply as a cost to the organism. Instead, under certain conditions extending development can result in powerful learning strategies. There are two requirements: first, development must not be simply a process of intrinsic maturation. Instead, it must be sensitive to environmental structure, in that activity emanating from the environment must play a role in the construction of neural circuits. Second, this developmental strategy can be enhanced if neural development is not concurrent across different regions of the cortex, but instead follows a hierarchical scheme. Viewed instead as a kind of learning, its protractedness takes on special, positive qualities. In previous work I outlined a view I refer to as neural constructivism whereby the functional properties of cortex are built from the dynamic interaction between neural growth mechanisms and environmentally-derived neural activity, acting hierarchically at the regional level and with high specificity at the cellular level (Quartz & Sejnowski, 1997; Quartz, 1999). Neural constructivism suggests that the interaction between processes traditionally described cognitively as learning interact in complex ways with their neural substrates to construct neural circuits.

The starting point for this work was an investigation into the relationship between developing neural structures and the learning properties of cortex. Since its beginnings, developmental neurobiology has been embroiled in debate over whether development is a progressive increase in neural structures or whether it essentially involves a selective elimination of exuberant structures (see Purves et al., 1996 for a summary of this debate). As this question has important consequences for the learning properties of cortex, I examined the developmental time course of synaptic numbers, axonal processes, and dendritic arbors and concluded that the bulk of the evidence favors progressive increases in these measures during development. In addition, I reviewed neurobiological results spanning over thirty years that support the role for activity-dependent mechanisms in the progressive construction of neural circuits. On the basis of this work, I suggested that cortical development is not characterized by an early overproduction of neural elements followed by selective elimination, nor is it one exhausted by mechanisms of selective elimination operating on transient, exuberant structures. Rather, neural development during the acquisition of major cognitive skills is best characterized as a progressive construction of neural structures, in which environmentally-derived activity plays a role in the construction of neural circuits. This revised view of the role of activity in the construction of neural circuits forms the basis for neural constructivism. From the perspective of cognitive development, I suggested that this far-reaching interaction between neural growth and environmentally-derived neural activity undermined the distinction between biological maturation and learning. In place of this dichotomy, I articulated a theory of "constructive learning" and suggested that it possesses more powerful acquisition properties than traditional accounts of cognitive development assumed.

In more recent work (Quartz, 1999; Quartz & Sejnowski, 2000) I have investigated the implications of two important advances for neural constructivism. Recent longitudinal studies of brain development using MRI have demonstrated pre-adolescent increases in cortical gray matter in all cortical lobes (Giedd et al., 1999; Thompson et al., 2000). In addition, this growth is heterochronic; that is, regions of cortex develop at different rates (Thompson et al., 2000). This is extremely significant for theories of cognitive development for the following reason. Although many features of Piaget's developmental view have come under extensive criticism, the core idea that development involves the expansion of hierarchically organized sequential operations, beginning with perceptual and sensorimotor functions and becoming more combinatorially complex, remains popular. These studies and others suggest that the brain develops hierarchically, with early sensory regions developing prior to more complex representations in association areas (Quartz, 1999). Given the influence of activity in this construction, it suggests a powerful hierarchical construction process whose acquisition properties remain essentially unanalyzed. Although MRI studies lack the spatial resolution to identify the cellular components of neuropil – neural processes and non-neuronal cells, or glia – responsible for increases in cortical gray matter, recent advances in microscopy that allow the continuous monitoring of cellular components at high resolution (Maletic-Savatic et al., 1999; Engert & Bonhoeffer, 1999; reviewed in Wong and Wong, 2000) have revealed a highly dynamic view of development at the cellular level. In particular, these studies demonstrate that activity is not simply permissive in its regulation of development. Rather, temporally correlated activity between pre- and post-synaptic elements that induces long-term potentiation results in the local sprouting of dendritic elements, in agreement with Hebb's original postulate in its developmental context (Hebb, 1949). These results are highly significant for theories of cognitive development, as they indicate that environmentally-derived patterned neural activity plays an instructive role in the construction of neural circuits, both within unsupervised and self-supervised modes.

Although prefrontal function has traditionally been most closely associated with purely cognitive functions, its central involvement in social cognition has become increasingly apparent in recent years. Indeed, one potential reason for protracted development lies in the difficulty of developing the social competence necessary for complex social life. There is now good evidence to indicate that one component of social competence, theory of mind, depends at least in part on the appropriate social exposure for its development, as many deaf children show delays on theory of mind tasks (Peterson & Siegal, 1995; Russell et al., 1998). This is believed to be due to the fact that parents of deaf children are typically naïve signers, and so household social interactions are limited by communicative ability.

Human social behavior becomes increasingly sophisticated over the developmental timecourse. In particular, over development individuals become increasingly skilled at reading subtle social cues and adjusting their behavior accordingly by applying appropriate behavioral schemes and norms to rapidly shifting contexts. Increasingly mature forms of social cognition involve a cognitive flexibility and the ability to match behavioral strategies with the contingencies of various situations. The developmental frontalization of behavior that underlies these capacities reflects a process I have referred to previously as progressive externalization (Quartz & Sejnowski, 1997). Progressive externalization refers to the process whereby neural development becomes regulated by environmental influences over longer periods of postnatal exposure. This emphasis on behavioral plasticity contrasts with the emphasis on evolutionarily-encoded behavioral strategies. Under what conditions did such capacities emerge?

4. THE ADAPTIVE HISTORY OF HOMINID EVOLUTION: RETHINKING THE ENVIRONMENT OF EVOLUTIONARY ADAPTATION

4.1. Beyond Directional Selection

A crucial assumption of any evolutionary psychology integrative approach is that human cognitive and behavioral capacities reflect our lineage's history. Without this assumption, there would be little impetus to understand the relationship between evolution and psychology. An analysis of the environment of evolutionary adaptation (EEA) plays an especially prominent role in narrow evolutionary psychology, as its adaptive thinking places a premium on inferring the mind's Darwinian algorithms from the nature of the enduring challenges confronting our ancestors.

The most prominent scenarios of hominid adaptation are habitat-specific. That is, a specific, stable ecological context is typically identified as the EEA. The most popular such account is the savanna hypothesis, according to which our ancestors lived as hunter-gatherers on the African savanna. According to some interpretations of this EEA, the ecological challenges confronting our ancestors were relatively minor, making the social environment the primary selective force, where a Machiavellian intelligence was most adaptive.

The notion that the EEA was characterized by a stable ecological context is complicated by recent work in paleoclimatology. Through painstaking analysis of ice cores, deep ocean cores, and land and lake sediments, climate scientists are piecing together a surprising history of the earth's climate (for a review, see Potts, 1996; Bradley, 1999). This research reveals that the last million years was a time of jarring climatic changes, the greatest period of climatic fluctuation since Lucy walked the planet 3.5 million years ago, and could be the period of the greatest climatic fluctuations ever registered on the planet. Often within the span of a decade, climates underwent dramatic alterations, from rain forest to arid savanna to steppe. The pressures ecological instability placed on species is evident by the pronounced reduction in biodiversity during this period, particularly with regard to species that were highly specialized for particular ecologies (Potts, 1996).

The notion of a long enduring EEA that remained stable enough for its problems to act on hominids over an evolutionary timescale is also complicated by the fact that for most of hominid evolution there was a statis in relative brain size. Indeed, between 1.8 and .6 million years ago, the brain scaled essentially as a straightforward function of body mass. Hominid encephalization appears to have occurred mostly within the last 600,000 years (Ruff et al., 1997).

It is intriguing to note that this fairly recent process of encephalization coincided with the period of unprecedented climatic instability I mentioned above. Although ecological instability certainly does not exclude a wide variety of enduring problems that likely remained stable across varying climes, it suggests that solutions to such problems alone cannot account for the evolution of human cognition. Rather, it suggests that human cognitive evolution was driven in part by environmental variance and the challenges such instability presented. This suggests a basic adjustment in how we ought to view the evolutionary pressures that helped shape human cognition. There are two possible responses to ecological instability. A species may attempt to track its preferred habitat, as appears to have been the case with chimpanzees, who might have taken shelter in rain forest refugia during glacial periods. An alternative response is open to those species that possess enough behavioral flexibility to adapt to differing ecological contexts. Potts (1996) contrasts the selective pressure of adapting to multiple ecological contexts, a pressure he refers to as variability selection, with the more traditional notion of directional selection, and suggests that variability selection was a major force in human origins.

5.   PROGRESSIVE EXTERNALIZATION AND THE ONTOGENIC ROLE OF CULTURE

5.1. The Progressive Externalization of Development

This perspective places a premium on behavioral flexibility. I have suggested that this behavioral flexibility is mediated by a human cognitive architecture that is a hierarchically-organized control structure, and which displays a developmental trajectory whereby behavior is increasingly mediated by prefrontal structures. Based on an increased encephalization, which appears to be a fairly recent process, it appears to be the product of heterochronic alterations in development that result in both increased neocortical volume and protracted development, reflecting a process I have referred to as progressive externalization.

Ecological instability suggests another possible response: the construction of buffers that make one less vulnerable to the immediate environment. One such buffer is novel forms of social organization, and ultimately symbolic culture. The cognitive structures that I have emphasized in developmental evolutionary psychology's model of the human cognitive architecture are those necessary for complex social life and symbolic culture. The process of progressive externalization, mediated in part by heterochronic changes in neural development, whereby the development of cognitive structures became increasingly dependent on prolonged environmental interaction, may thus have been the route to designing a cognitive architecture capable of the highly flexible and context-sensitive behavior necessary for participation in a complex culture. Symbolic culture, then, plays a central role in constructing the structures that make it possible.

California Institute of Technology

6.   ACKNOWLEDGMENTS

This research was supported by National Science Foundation Career Grant #0093757. I would like to thank the editors for their very helpful comments on an earlier draft of this chapter.

7.   REFERENCES

Allman, J. (1999). *Evolving Brains*. New York: Freeman.

Arthur, W. (1997). *The Origin of Animal Body Plans : A Study in Evolutionary Developmental Biology*. Cambridge, U.K. ; New York: Cambridge University Press.

Barkow, J.H., Cosmides, L., & Tooby, J. (Eds.). (1992). *The Adapted Mind: Evolutionary Psychology and the Generation of Culture*. New York, NY, US: Oxford University Press.

Bellman, R.E. (1957). *Dynamic Programming*. Princeton, N.J.: Princeton University Press.

Berns, G.S., McClure, S.M., Pagnoni, G., & Montague, P.R. (2001). Predictability modulates human brain response to reward. *Journal of Neuroscience, 21*, 2793-2798.

Bradley, R.S. (1999). *Paleoclimatology : Reconstructing Climates of the Quaternary* (2nd ed.). San Diego: Academic Press.

Brothers, L., & Ring, B. (1992). A neuroethological framework for the representation of minds. *Journal of Cognitive Neuroscience, 4*, 107-118.

Buss, D.M. (1999). *Evolutionary Psychology: The New Science of the Mind*. Needham Heights, MA.: Allyn & Bacon, Inc.

Cosmides, L., & Tooby, J. (1994). Origins of domain specificity: The evolution of functional organization, *Mapping the Mind: Domain Specificity in Cognition and Culture*. (pp. 85-116). New York: Cambridge University Press.

Cowie, F. (1998). *What's Within? : Nativism Reconsidered*. New York: Oxford University Press.

Craik, F.I.M., Moroz, T.M., Moscovitch, M., Stuss, D.T., Winocur, G., Tulving, E., & Kapur, S. (1999). In search of the self: A positron emission tomography study. *Psychological Science, 10,* 26-34.

Darlington, R.B., Dunlop, S. A., & Finlay, B.L. (1999). Neural development in metatherian and eutherian mammals: Variation and constraint. *Journal of Comparative Neurology, 411*, 359-368.

Davidson, E.H. (2001). *Genomic Regulatory Systems : Development and Evolution*. San Diego: Academic Press.

Deacon, T. W. (1997). *The Symbolic Species : The Co-evolution of Language and the Brain*. New York: W.W. Norton.

Dehaene, S., Spelke, E., Pinel, P., Stanescu, R., & Tsivkin, S. (1999). Sources of mathematical thinking: Behavioral and brain-imaging evidence. *Science, 284*, 970-974.

Depue, R.A., & Collins, P.F. (1999). Neurobiology of the structure of personality: Dopamine, facilitation of incentive motivation, and extraversion. *Behavioral & Brain Sciences, 22*, 491-569.

Diamond, A. (1985). Development of the ability to use recall to guide action, as indicated by infants' performance on AB. *Child Development, 56*, 868-883.

Diamond, A. (1998). Evidence for the importance of dopamine for prefrontal cortex functions early in life, *The Prefrontal Cortex: Executive and Cognitive Functions*. (pp. 144-164). New York: Oxford University Press.

Diamond, A., & Doar, B. (1989). The performance of human infants on a measure of frontal cortex function, the delayed response task. *Developmental Psychobiology, 22*, 271-294.

Diamond, A., Prevor, M.B., Callender, G., & Druin, D.P. (1997). Prefrontal cortex cognitive deficits in children treated early and continuously for PKU. *Monographs of the Society for Research in Child Development, 62*, 1-205.

Dobzhansky, T. (1951). *Genetics and the Origin of Species*. (3rd Ed.). New York: Columbia University Press.

Elman, J.L. (1996). *Rethinking Innateness : A Connectionist Perspective on Development*. Cambridge, Ma.: MIT Press.

Engert, F., & Bonhoeffer, T. (1999). Dendritic spine changes associated with hippocampal long-term synaptic plasticity. *Nature, 399*, 66-70.

Finlay, B.L., & Darlington, R.B. (1995). Linked regularities in the development and evolution of mammalian brains. *Science, 268*, 1578-1584.

Finlay, B.L., Darlington, R. B., & Nicastro, N. (2001). Developmental structure in brain evolution. *Behavioral & Brain Sciences, 24*, 263.

Finlay, B.L., Hersman, M.N., & Darlington, R.B. (1998). Patterns of vertebrate neurogenesis and the paths of vertebrate evolution. *Brain, Behavior and Evolution, 52*, 232-242.

Fodor, J.A. (1983). *Modularity of Mind : An Essay on Faculty Psychology.* Cambridge, MA.: MIT Press.

Fodor, J.A. (2000). *The Mind Doesn't Work That Way: The Scope and Limits of Computational Psychology.* Cambridge, MA.: The MIT Press.

Frahm, H.D., Stephan, H., & Stephan, M. (1982). Comparison of brain structure volumes in Insectivora and Primates. I. Neocortex. *Journal fur Hirnforschung, 23,* 375-389.

Gallistel, C.R. (1990). *The Organization of Learning.* Cambridge, Ma.: MIT Press.

Garris, P.A., Kilpatrick, M., Bunin, M.A., Michael, D., Walker, Q.D., & Wightman, R.M. (1999). Dissociation of dopamine release in the nucleus accumbens from intracranial self-stimulation. *Nature, 398,* 67-69.

Giedd, J.N., Blumenthal, J., Jeffries, N.O., Castellanos, F.X., Liu, H., Zijdenbos, A., Paus, T., Evans, A.C., & Rapoport, J.L. (1999). Brain development during childhood and adolescence: a longitudinal MRI study. *Nature Neuroscience, 2,* 861-863.

Gilbert, S.F., Opitz, J. M., & Raff, R.A. (1996). Resynthesizing evolutionary and developmental biology. *Developmental Biology, 173,* 357-372.

Goldman-Rakic, P.S. (1990). Cortical localization of working memory. In J.L. McGaugh, N.M. Weinberger, and G. Lynch (Eds.). *Brain organization and memory: Cells, systems, and circuits.* (pp. 285-298). New York: Oxford University Press.

Gould, S.J. (2000). Of coiled oysters and big brains: How to rescue the terminology of heterochrony, now gone astray. *Evolution and Development, 2,* 241-248.

Gould, S.J., & Lewontin, R.C. (1979). The spandrels of San Marco and the Panglossian paradigm: a critique of the adaptationist programme. *Proceedings of the Royal Society of London. Series B: Biological Sciences, 205,* 581-598.

Hall, B.K. (1998). *Evolutionary Developmental Biology.* New York: Chapman & Hall.

Hammer, M. (1993). An identified neuron mediates the unconditioned stimulus in associative olfactory learning in honeybees. *Nature, 366,* 59-63.

Hebb, D.O. (1949). *The Organization of Behavior: A Neuropsychological Theory.* New York: Wiley.

Hirschfeld, L.A., & Gelman, S.A. (Eds.). (1994). *Mapping the Mind: Domain Specificity in Cognition and Culture.* New York: Cambridge University Press.

Hirth, F., & Reichert, H. (1999). Conserved genetic programs in insect and mammalian brain development. *Bioessays, 21,* 684.

Johnson, M.H. (1997). *Developmental Cognitive Neuroscience: An Introduction.* Malden, MA.: Blackwell Publishers Inc.

Lovejoy, C.O., Cohn, M.J., & White, T.D. (1999). Morphological analysis of the mammalian postcranium: A developmental perspective. *Proceedings of the National Academy of Sciences (USA), 96,* 13247-13252.

Maletic-Savatic, M., Malinow, R., & Svoboda, K. (1999). Rapid dendritic morphogenesis in CA1 hippocampal dendrites induced by synaptic activity. *Science, 283,* 1923-1927.

McConnell, S.K. (1995). Constructing the cerebral cortex: Neurogenesis and fate determination. *Neuron, 15,* 761-768.

Montague, P.R., Dayan, P., Person, C., & Sejnowski, T.J. (1995). Bee foraging in uncertain environments using predictive hebbian learning. *Nature, 377,* 725-728.

Montague, P.R., & Quartz, S.R. (1999). Computational approaches to neural reward and development. *Mental Retardation & Developmental Disabilities Research Reviews, 5,* 86-99.

Montague, P.R., & Sejnowski, T.J. (1994). The predictive brain: Temporal coincidence and temporal order in synaptic learning mechanisms. *Learning and Memory, 1,* 1-33.

Nieuwenhuys, R., Donkelaar, H.J.T. & Nicholson, C. (1998). *The Central Nervous System of Vertebrates.* New York: Springer.

Norman, D.A., & Shallice, T. (1986). Attention to Action: Willed and Automatic Control of Behavior. In R. J. Davidson, G.E. Schwartz ,and D. Shapiro (Ed.), *Consciousness and Self-Regulation* (pp. 1-18). New York: Plenum Press.

Peterson, C.C., & Siegal, M. (1995). Deafness, conversation and theory of mind. *Journal of Child Psychology and Psychiatry, 36,* 459-474.

Petrides, M. (1995). Functional organization of the human frontal cortex for mnemonic processing: Evidence from neuroimaging studies. In J. Grafman, K. J. Holyoak, and F. Boller (Eds.), *Structure and Functions of the Human Prefrontal Cortex* (pp. 85-96). New York: New York Academy of Sciences.

Pick, L. (1998). Segmentation: Painting stripes from flies to vertebrates. *Developmental Genetics, 23*, 1-10.

Pinker, S. (1997). *How the Mind Works*. New York: Norton.

Potts, R. (1996). *Humanity's Descent*. New York: William Morrow.

Purves, D., White, L.E., & Riddle, D.R. (1996). Is neural development Darwinian? *Trends in Neurosciences, 19*, 460-464.

Quartz, S.R, & Sejnowski, T.J. (1997). The neural basis of cognitive development: A constructivist manifesto. *Behavioral & Brain Sciences, 20*, 537-596.

Quartz, S. R. (1999). The constructivist brain. *Trends in Cognitive Sciences, 3*, 48-57.

Quartz, S.R. & Sejnowski, T.J. (2000). Constraining constructivism: Cortical and subcortical constraints on learning in development, *Behavioral and Brain Sciences, 23*, 785-791.

Raff, R.A. (1996). *The Shape of Life: Genes, Development, and the Evolution of Animal Form*. Chicago: University of Chicago Press.

Raff, R.A. (2000). Evo-devo: The evolution of a new discipline. *Nature Reviews Genetics, 1*, 74-79.

Rakic, P. (1988). Specification of cerebral cortical areas. *Science, 241*, 170-176.

Real, L.A. (1991). Animal choice behavior and the evolution of cognitive architecture. *Science, 253*, 980-986.

Reichert, H., & Simeone, A. (1999). Conserved usage of gap and homeotic genes in patterning the CNS. *Current Opinion in Neurobiology, 9*, 589-595.

Reinitz, J., Kosman, D., Vanario-Alonso, C.E., & Sharp, D.H. (1998). Stripe forming architecture of the gap gene system. *Developmental Genetics, 23*, 11-27.

Ross, C.A., Ruggiero, D.A., Park, D.H., Joh, T.H., Sved, A.F., Fernandez-Pardal, J., Saavedra, J.M., & Reis, D.J. (1984). Tonic vasomotor control by the rostral ventrolateral medulla: Effect of electrical or chemical stimulation of the area containing C1 adrenaline neurons on arterial pressure, heart rate, and plasma catecholamines and vasopressin. *Journal of Neuroscience, 4*, 474-494.

Rubenstein, J. L., Martinez, S., Shimamura, K., & Puelles, L. (1994). The embryonic vertebrate forebrain: The prosomeric model. *Science, 266*, 578-580.

Rubia, K., Overmeyer, S., Taylor, E., Brammer, M., Williams, S.C.R., Simmons, A., Andrew, C., & Bullmore, E.T. (2000). Functional frontalisation with age: Mapping neurodevelopmental trajectories with fMRI. *Neuroscience & Biobehavioral Reviews, 24*, 13-19.

Ruff, C.B., Trinkaus, E., & Holliday, T.W. (1997). Body mass and encephalization in Pleistocene Homo. *Nature*, 387: 173-176.

Russell, P.A., Hosie, J.A., Gray, C.D., Scott, C., Hunter, N., Banks, J.S., & Macaulay, M.C. (1998). The development of theory of mind in deaf children. *Journal of Child Psychology and Psychiatry, 39*:, 903-910.

Sawaguchi, T., & Goldman-Rakic, P.S. (1994). The role of D1-dopamine receptor in working memory: Local injections of dopamine antagonists into the prefrontal cortex of rhesus monkeys performing an oculomotor delayed-response task. *Journal of Neurophysiology, 71*, 515-528.

Schultz, W. (2000). Multiple reward signals in the brain. *Nauret Review Neuroscence, 1*, 199-207.

Schultz, W., Apicella, P., & Ljungberg, T. (1993). Responses of monkey dopamine neurons to reward and conditioned stimuli during successive steps of learning a delayed response task. *Journal of Neuroscience, 13*, 900-913.

Stephan, H., Frahm, H., & Baron, G. (1981). New and revised data on volumes of brain structures in insectivores and primates. *Folia Primatologica, 35*, 1-29.

Sterelny, K., & Griffiths, P.E. (1999). *Sex and Death : An Introduction to Philosophy of Biology*. Chicago: University of Chicago Press.

Stone, V.E., Baron-Cohen, S., & Knight, R.T. (1998). Frontal lobe contributions to theory of mind. *Journal of Cognitive Neuroscience, 10*, 640-656.

Sutton, R.S., & Barto, A.G. (1998). *Reinforcement Learning: An Introduction*. Cambridge, MA.: MIT Press.

Tesauro, G. (1995). Temporal difference learning and TD-Gammon. *Communications of the ACM, 38*, 58-68.

Thompson, P.M., Giedd, J.N., Woods, R.P., MacDonald, D., Evans, A.C., & Toga, A.W. (2000). Growth patterns in the developing brain detected by using continuum mechanical tensor maps. *Nature, 404*, 190-193.

Tomasello, M. (1999). *The Cultural Origins of Human Cognition*. Cambridge, MA.: Harvard University Press.

Tooby, J., & Cosmides, L. (1992). The psychological foundations of culture. In J. Barkow, L. Cosmides, and J. Tooby (Eds.). *The Adapted Mind: Evolutionary Psychology and the Generation of Culture.* (pp. 19-136). New York: Oxford University Press.

Wise, R.A. (1996). Addictive drugs and brain stimulation reward. *Annual Review of Neuroscience, 19*, 319-340.

Wong, W.T. & Wong, R.O. (2000). Rapid dendritic movements during synapse formation and rearrangement. *Currint Opinion in Neurobiology, 10*, 118-124.

WILLIAM BECHTEL

MODULES, BRAIN PARTS, AND EVOLUTIONARY PSYCHOLOGY

The central focus in debates over broad evolutionary psychology is whether mental abilities can be understood as adaptive functions (Davies, 1996, p. 446). Narrow evolutionary psychology[1] further closely couples the claim that mental abilities are adaptive to a commitment to modularity of mental functions. This linkage is presented as quite direct — if the mind is comprised of discrete modules, then we can ask what are the selective factors that promoted each module. If, on the other hand, the mind is comprised of a single, fully integrated, general processor, then it would be much harder for natural selection to promote cognitive capacities individually.[2] And it would be much harder for us to give an explanation of the evolution of particular mental abilities. Cummins and Allen (1998, p. 3) provide a succinct account of the link between modularity and narrow evolutionary psychology:

> Taking an evolutionary approach to the explanation of cognitive function follows naturally from the growing body of neuroscientific evidence showing that the mind is divisible. The picture that is emerging from both noninvasive studies of normal brain function and from clinically defined syndromes resulting from brain damage from strokes, injury, and neurodevelopmental disorders is one of different substrates subserving different cognitive functions ... The Cartesian view of a seamless whole makes it hard to see how such a whole could have come into being, except perhaps by an act of divine creation. By recognizing the modularity of mind, however, it is possible to see how human mentality might be explained by the gradual accretion of numerous special function pieces of mind.

There is little doubt that contemporary neuroscientific evidence does repudiate the holism of Cartesian accounts of mind (the kind of holism grounded in the apparent unity of

---

[1] EDITOR'S NOTE: In this book, the term 'narrow evolutionary psychology' signifies the approach to evolutionary psychology developed by Cosmides, Tooby, Buss, et al. This term was chosen not to imply that this approach has an inappropriately narrow point of view, but merely to suggest that the approach adopts a narrower range of assumptions than 'broad evolutionary psychology' (or, just 'evolutionary psychology'). This latter term signifies evolutionary psychology generally, practiced with any of a very broad range of assumptions possible within the general framework of evolutionary approaches to psychology. For more detail on this terminology, see the editor's introduction, p 1.

[2] The difficulty seems comparable to that in a standard feedforward connectionist networks where acquiring a new input-output pattern disrupts already acquired ones unless the previously acquired ones are retrained along with the new one. This is known as the problem of *catastrophic interference*. Two ways connectionists have tried to respond to this difficulty is to provide a principled means of continually retraining on previously learning examples (McClelland, McNaughton, & O'Reilly, 1995) and by building in modules (Jacobs, Jordan, & Barto, 1991).

Steven J. Scher & Frederick Rauscher (eds.). Evolutionary Psychology: Alternative Approaches, 211-227

thinking and consciousness that motivated Flourens in his rebuttals of Gall in the 19th century and Lashley and others in the first half of the 20th century). But what kind of modularity does neuroscience really support? What sort of cognitive processes are carried out by the separable components of the brain? Most advocates of narrow evolutionary psychology identify modules at a fairly course grain. Modules are proposed for various tasks it is thought our ancestors needed to perform — reasoning about groups and coalitions, detecting cheaters, making risk aversive decisions, or interacting with other minds. The reason why psychologists advocating narrow evolutionary psychology seek modules responsible for whole tasks humans perform is clear — they match the proposed selection forces.[3] (These psychologists did not originate the search for modules at this level; the prototype of such modules is the language acquisition module advocated by Chomsky.) I will argue, however, that the sort of modules supported by neuroscience are at a far finer grain. They are involved with what Petersen and Fiez (1993, p. 513) characterize as elementary operations, not tasks:

> . . . elementary operations, defined on the basis of information processing analyses of task performance, are localized in different regions of the brain. Because many such elementary operations are involved in any cognitive task, a set of distributed functional areas must be orchestrated in the performance of even simple cognitive tasks ... A functional area of the brain is not a task area: there is no "tennis forehand area" to be discovered. Likewise, no area of the brain is devoted to a very complex function; "attention" or "language" is not localized in a particular Brodmann area or lobe. Any task or "function" utilizes a complex and distributed set of brain areas.

Many proponents of narrow evolutionary psychology (Cosmides & Tooby, 1994; Gigerenzer, 1997; Shettleworth, 2000) simply assume that the mind/brain is modular at the relatively coarse grain at which they work and focus instead on arguing for proposals for particular modules and accounts of their evolution. Most of the arguments for modularity have originated elsewhere, especially in computer science and neuropsychology. Accordingly, I begin with a review of those arguments. I then turn to current neuroscience to argue that the units of brain organization do not correspond to modules as conceived in narrow evolutionary psychology. Neural information processing units are both far more integrated into the overall neural system and operate at a far finer grain than supports the strategies used in narrow evolutionary psychology. Consequently, the task of developing an evolutionary account of cognitive function must be construed much differently than it is by current practitioners of this approach. I will sketch the alternative in the final section.

1.   MODULES: FODORIAN, COMPUTATIONAL, AND NEUROPSYCHOLOGICAL

At the center of most discussions of modularity is the account offered by Fodor (1983). For Fodor, the core mind (which he termed the *central system*, and which he construed as

---

[3] Cf. Cummins (1998, p. 31): "Structures evolve in response to environmental demands, demands that impact on survival rates and reproductive success." (See also Shettleworth, 2000).

engaged in inference and belief fixation) was not modular.[4] Rather, modules are found between transducers and the central system and have the task "to present the world to thought" (1983, p. 40). Although the modules for him are responsible for information processing, they do so in an automatic and autonomous manner. He characterizes the operation of the modules in terms of nine properties: they (1) are domain-specific, (2) are mandatory in their operation, (3) allow only limited central access to the computations of the modules, (4) are fast, (5) are informationally encapsulated, (6) have shallow outputs, (7) are associated with fixed neural architectures, (8) exhibit characteristic and specific breakdown patterns, and (9) exhibit a characteristic pace and sequencing in their development. Of these, Fodor places the primary emphasis on informational encapsulation, which requires that a module use only information encoded within it in its processing; in particular, a module cannot invoke information stored in other modules or in central cognition.[5] One thing that restricting the information available to a module does is make its processing task tractable. But it also prevents what is often referred to as *top-down* processing between modules — the use of later processing of higher-level cognitive information in lower-level processing.[6] Many accounts of perception allow top-down influences whereby what one sees is influenced by knowledge and expectations. Such accounts engender the view that perception is theory-laden and skeptical worries that we lack any independent, objective epistemic access to the world. Fodor offers it as a virtue of his approach that the output of modules are objective in the requisite sense (Fodor, 1984).

Fodor's account of modularity is extremely strong in the degree of isolation it creates between modules. One consequence of this is that processing within modules cannot exhibit much intelligence. Modules can perform complex manipulations of inputs, but because they are encapsulated and their operation is mandatory, they cannot respond flexibly by drawing upon other sources of information. Accordingly, Fodor's account does not lend itself to application to central processes. Evolutionary psychologists who draw on Fodor, however, "see cognition as modular right through from input to decision processes" (Shettleworth, 2000, p. 54). In many respects, Fodor's account of modules is the one narrow evolutionary psychology needs to embrace, since his modules are sufficiently autonomous to be potentially selected for independently. But the inability of such modules to accommodate intelligent processing would seem to make them of limited use to narrow evolutionary psychology. Fodor's is not the only account of modules narrow evolutionary

---

[4] Fodor's denial of modularity for the central system is a result of his construal of thinking as isotropic and Quinean. By *isotropic* he means that anything a person knows is relevant to determining whether to believe a given proposition, and by *Quinean* he means that the degree of confirmation of a belief depends on its relation to other beliefs. One may question how isotropic and Quinean human thought really is (see Waskan & Bechtel, 1997), but a main point to emphasize is that Fodor's rejection of modularity for central systems (and his accompanying law denying the possibility of cognitive science — see 1983, p. 107) is largely a result of his very strong conditions on what constitutes a module.

[5] Note that the notion of informational encapsulation is a strong notion. Fodor differentiates it from domain specificity, which many modular theorists employ: "Roughly, domain specificity has to do with the range of questions for which a device provides answers (the range of inputs for which it computes analyses); whereas encapsulation has to do with the range of information that the device consults in deciding what answers to provide" (1983, p. 103).

[6] See Appelbaum (1988) for a discussion of how this presents a problem for Fodor in analyzing data about speech perception.

psychology could draw on. Other accounts are found in computer science and neuropsychology, but as we shall see, these are event less suited to narrow evolutionary psychology's construal of modules as the units of evolution.

In computer science, ideas of modularity arose in the design of computer programs. By breaking complex tasks into components and developing subroutines for each, it became more efficient both to design and revise computer programs. But Herbert Simon argued that modularity was not just a consideration for programs. He argued that our ability to understand complex systems depended on them exhibiting what he called "near decomposability."[7] Simon imposed two conditions on near decomposability:

> (1) In a nearly decomposable system, the short-run behavior of each of the component subsystems is approximately independent of the short-run behavior of the other components; (2) in the long run the behavior of any one of the components depends in only an aggregate way on the behavior of the other components (Simon, 1969, p. 210)

Moreover, he advanced an argument that evolution could only have produced complex systems if the systems it produced were nearly decomposable; without the possibility of adjusting components piecemeal (and then composing them into wholes), complex structures could not have evolved in limited time. (Simon's conception of evolution also involves building complex assemblies out of nearly decomposable units. The hierarchical features of his account are not considered here. For a response to this argument, see Bechtel & Richardson, 1993.)

Another computer scientist (although originally a physiologist) who invoked a conception of modularity not just for computer programs but for the physiological systems he was modeling was David Marr (1982). He advanced a *principle of modular design* according to which the interactions between components in a system are weak and have limited effect on each other. This permits the isolation and independent study of the components. But for neither Simon nor Marr is such independence absolute. Simon speaks of *near* decomposability and Marr of organization being, to a *first approximation*, modular. Their conception of modularity is, accordingly, much weaker than Fodor's and less suited for the purposes of narrow evolutionary psychology.

With their qualifications, Simon's and Marr's conception of modular design seem entirely reasonable. Much of scientific practice since the 17th century has started by taking systems apart and attempting to understand how their parts behave (Bechtel & Richardson, 1993). This practice assumes there are parts and that they carry out operations on their own. But it is important to note that when this heuristic is adopted, it often succeeds only to a first approximation. Subsequent research frequently reveals complex modes of interaction between the components, which have the effect of severely modulating the behavior of the individual components. Second, the activities carried out by the parts of a system often do not perform functions that can be understood just from the framework of the activity of the overall system. Researchers sometimes begin by characterizing the

---

[7] The linkage between the assumption of modularity and scientific practice is also emphasized by Semenza, (1996, p. 481): "the value of the modularity principle probably transcends the likelihood of the nervous system implementing cognitive functions in a modular way. It seems, in fact, to honor a longstanding scientific tradition of decomposing complex entities into their basic functional components, a method that has often been successful in the physical sciences."

behavior of the parts from such a viewpoint. For example, once physiological chemists recognized that fermentation consisted of multiple chemical reactions, they first attempted to characterize the component reactions as themselves fermentations.   But only a reconceptualization of the component reactions in different terms (e.g., as oxidations, reductions, phosphorylations, transphosphorylations) allowed modern biochemistry to develop adequate mechanistic models of what components contributed and of the crucial interactions that allowed them together to carry out fermentation. I return to these considerations below, as they critically affect how we construe modular components in the mind.

Neuropsychology employs a notion of module that is closer to Simon's and Marr's than Fodor's. A major endeavor of neuropsychology has been to utilize the behavior of individuals with brain injury to make inferences about normal function. In its simplest version, one infers from a behavioral deficit in a patient that the area damaged in the patient's brain was responsible for the ability the patient has lost. Thus, Broca (1861) inferred from the Leborgne's deficit in articulate speech that an area in the frontal cortex that came to bear his name was the center of articulate speech. In the years since Broca, neuropscyhologists have identified a rich, often bewildering patterns of deficit in human patients.[8] Two important theoretical ideas began to bring order to the various findings of deficits in the mid-20th century. One was an emphasis on the association of deficits — by showing that different deficits generally appeared together, one could infer that each of the abilities in their normal manifestation depended on a common underlying process. The second was dissociation, especially double dissociations as developed and employed by Teuber (1955). The idea underlying double dissociation is that if one can find two patients or groups of patients, one of which exhibits diminishment of one capacity due to brain injury with much less or no diminishment of another capacity, and the other of which shows the reverse pattern, then the two capacities can be construed as relying, at least in part, on distinct brain processes. These dissociable components can be construed as modules (Shallice, 1988).

In the 1980s neuropsychology was partly transformed by adopting the information processing framework from cognitive psychology. Within cognitive psychology at the time information processing models were developed and evaluated almost exclusively in terms of behavioral data such as reaction times, but through sophisticated application of these techniques, psychologists began to identify component cognitive operations and develop models of how they interacted in achieving cognitive performance (Posner, 1978). The idea of processing information through different operations upon representations provided a powerful organizing principle for thinking about the deficits neuropsychologists had

---

[8] Until the 1980s, neuropsychology was pursued under three broad perspectives–the localizationist approach exemplified by Broca, the connectionist approach of Wernicke and Geschwind, and the holist approach of Head, Goldstein, and Lashley. The last proved dominant during the first half of the 20th century, but gradually lost sway, especially with the influence of Geschwind, the finding of anterograde and graded retrograde amnesia in H.M. following bilateral resection of his medial temporal lobe, and the studies on split brain patients by Roger Sperry and his collaborators.

identified.[9] Specifically, it enabled a shift into thinking about deficits from the point of view of underlying operations that were disrupted and not just localizing areas where lesions produced deficits:

> Traditionally, neuropsychologists studied the localization and functional organization of *abilities*, such as speech, reading, memory, object recognition, and so forth. But few would doubt that each of these abilities depends upon an orchestrated set of *component cognitive processes*, and it seems more likely that the underlying cognitive components, rather than the task-defined abilities, are what is implemented in localized neural tissue. The theories of cognitive psychology therefore allowed neuropsychologists to pose questions about the localization and organization of the components of the cognitive architecture, a level of theoretical analysis that was more likely to yield clear and generalizable findings (Feinberg & Farah, 2000, p. 16).[10]

Feinberg and Farah illustrate this shift with reading impairments. There are patients who can read non-words (*rint*) but not irregularly pronounced words (*pint*), and others who show the reverse pattern. This might suggest a center for non-word reading and another for irregular word reading, but an information processing account advances a different decomposition — one relying on a lexicon of words and another on grapheme-to-phoneme transition rules (Coltheart, 1987). In normal subjects, both support fluent reading, but when one or the other is impaired, one expects the pattern actually found in patients.[11]

For neuropsychology, then, the import of modularity is that the system is composed, at an appropriate grain, of components which can be studied in relative isolation and which carry out specific information processing operations. Thus, Shallice (1991, p. 431) describes the modularity assumptions operative in neuropsychology as follows:

1. The cognitive system being investigated contains a large set of isolable processing subsystems (in the sense of Posner, 1978) or modules (in the sense of Marr, 1982).

2. The modularity operates on a number of levels. As far as neuropsychology is concerned, however, there is a limit to the fineness of the grain of modularity.

3. Following Marr (1982), isolable processing subsystems may be viewed as having functions carried out by algorithms implemented by particular mechanisms.

The conceptions of modularity derived from computer science and especially neuropsychology already differ in a crucial respect from that operative in much of narrow evolutionary psychology. They do not offer a conception in which modules correspond to

---

[9] The availability of neuropsychological evidence for cognitive psychology was also important. By showing that different capacities were lost together (perceiving and mental imagery—see Farah, 1988; Kosslyn, 1994) or that some capacities were preserved in patients in whom others were lost (implicit memory in amnesics–see Schacter, 1987), neuropsychology could provide new sources of data about the nature of the information processing components.

[10] Cf., Semenza (1996, p. 481): "Without a theory of a given task, the principle of modularity applied to that task is conceptually empty and has no empirical ramification because anything may be viewed as a module."

[11] The dual-route model of reading has been challenged by neural network modelers who contend that a single pathway can account for reading and when lesioned generates both patterns of deficits (Plaut et al., 1996).

overall cognitive abilities that human agents possess. Rather, modules exist at a lower level, at the level of information processing operations which are recruited in various ways in realizing cognitive abilities. But the conception of modularity in neuropsychology retains the idea of relatively autonomous components. Does that square with the organization of the brain?

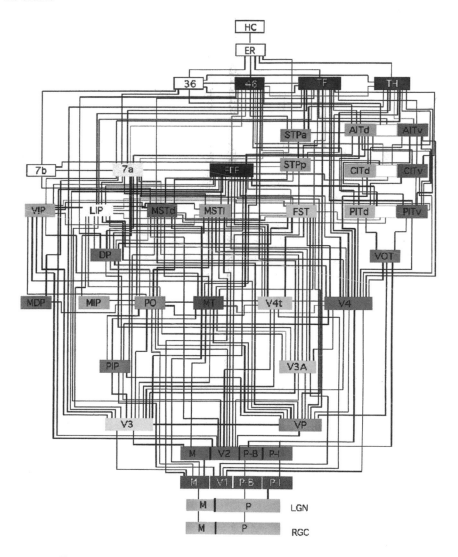

Figure 1. A Map of the Visual Processing Areas and their Interconnections in the Macque Brain. (From van Essen, Anderson, & Felleman, 1992).

2.   BRAIN CARTOGRAPHY AND MODULES

Clearly the brain is not an undifferentiated mass. Even a casual examination reveals fundamental differences. For example, it is not hard to differentiate the cerebral cortex from such other components as the brain stem, midbrain, and cerebellum. Within the cortex, major fissures mark out the four lobes. A natural assumption, and one that has guided much research, is that structural differences probably correspond to functional differences, although sometimes this heuristic may be misleading. The pattern of convolutions in the cortex is basically similar among members of a species, but it does not reliably map onto what are taken to be more basic functional units and more recent evidence suggests that it results from physical constraints on the developing brain rather than anything related to differences in function (Van Essen, 1997). The more micro-level decomposition into brain components, based on such factors as types of neurons present and their distribution between different laminae of the cortex, was begun by a number of early 20th century researchers, of whom Brodmann has had the greatest influence. The contemporary project of mapping the brain is fundamentally a continuation of Brodmann's, but carried out with additional resources. In addition to Brodmann's cytoarchitectural methods, researchers rely heavily on patterns of connectivity (as revealed, for example, through chemical tracers), the replication of topographical maps, and differences in function in delineating brain areas (Mundale, 1998). The result of this is a more fine-grained identification of brain areas and their connectivity. Although increasingly similar efforts are being made for other portions of the brain (see Carmichael & Price, 1994), the best exemplar of such brain mapping remains research on visual processing areas in the brain. Felleman and van Essen (1991) differentiate 32 visual processing areas in the macaque and 300 distinct pathways between them, yielding a picture of a complex, integrated system (see Figure 1).

For Brodmann, differentiating areas of cortex and mapping relations between them was not an end in itself. His assumption was that distinct areas would serve different functions: "It is a basic biological principle that the function of an organ is correlated with its elementary histological structure" (Brodmann, 1909/1994, p. 243). At Brodmann's time, however, the only tools for linking structures with functions were analyses of deficits after lesioning and responses to electrical stimulation. One of the most powerful tools during the 20th century in determining the function of neurons was single-cell recording. By determining the types of stimuli to which cells in different areas are responsive, researchers could begin to identify the kind of processing each was likely to be performing. While many details remain to be filled in, a basic outline of the steps in visual processing both in the ventral stream that results in object identification and in the dorsal stream that analyzes spatial relations and possibilities for action have been identified, largely on the basis of a combination of lesion studies and single cell recording studies (Bechtel, 2001).

When presented schematically, the organization of the processing streams seems to conform closely to models of information processing through sequential modules — information about wavelength, orientation, and spatial frequency is processed in the interblob areas of V1, from which the interstripe areas of V2 compute disparity and subjective contours, from which in turn V4 computes non-Cartesian patterns, and areas in inferotemporal cortex identify objects (van Essen & Gallant, 1994). But the details reveal a much more complex system. As Figure 1 exhibits, the different areas are multiply connected, including numerous lateral connections between different processing streams. On average, each visual area has ten distinct inputs and ten distinct outputs. Van Essen and DeYoe (1995) analogize the overall organization to a possible organization of a industrial factory, and describe design for a factory with merging and splitting of processing streams:

> The main disadvantage of this strategy is the need for complex links between modules. In exchange, there are two obvious advantages: It provides for efficient compartmentalization of function, insofar as each step of the manufacturing process can be assigned to a module well suited for that particular task; and it is inherently flexible, because each module can access whatever inputs it needs and can distribute its output as necessary to achieve the desired set of final products. A major thrust of this chapter will be to argue that similar principles apply to the overall design of the primate visual system (p. 384).

In the picture of cortical design van Essen espouses, the degree of autonomy of processing areas is significantly reduced. Each component still carries out its own information processing operation, but it is highly interconnected and responsive to other components.

An often noted important feature of cortical organization is that backwards projections are at least as numerous as forward projections. Nearly every forward projection has a corresponding backward projection. Although the function of the backward projections is still a matter of some dispute, one thing that is clear is that there are neuroanatomical differences between forward, backward, and lateral connections. Forward and backward projections both originate in either the superficial or deep layers,[12] but forward projections project to layer 4, whereas backward projections project to the superficial or deep layers. In contrast, lateral connections project to all layers of cortex (see Figure 2). (In large part, it was this distinctive pattern of forward and backward projections that enabled van Essen and his colleagues to place various cortical visual areas in the 10 different levels of the hierarchy shown in Figure 1.)

Although the details of brain anatomy and its relation to psychological function are best worked out in the case of vision, investigations on other brain areas suggest the same ideas apply elsewhere. The brain is comprised of different processing units, but the information processing operations they perform are at a quite micro-level of organization. Moreover, these units are highly interconnected. This description of neural organization might seem to be at odds with the popularized results of neuroimaging (to which Cummins and Allen allude in the quotation at the beginning of this paper). PET and many fMRI studies seemed to identify brain areas responsible for relatively macro-level tasks — word identification, face and object recognition, semantic processing, encoding and retrieval of semantic and episodic memories, etc. These seemed to be tasks close to the level proposed in narrow evolutionary psychology. But the identification of these tasks with one brain area is partly an artifact of the sensitivity of the instruments and the statistical measures invoked in early studies, which only revealed areas with the greatest increase in activation, and the use of the subtractive method. Employing the subtractive method, investigators used two

---

[12] If they originate in just one layer, though, forward projections originate in the superficial layer while backward projections originate in the deep layers.

tasks, which were thought to differ in one operation, and then subtracted the pattern of activation produced performing one task from that produced performing the other. The area(s) left after the subtraction were construed as performing the additional task. But many of the areas subtracted out might also figure in the new operation. For example, in evaluating Tulving's proposal that retrieval of episodic memories activates right prefrontal areas whereas retrieval of semantic memories activates left prefrontal areas, Buckner (1996) found that the left prefrontal areas and areas elsewhere in the brain were active above baseline in episodic retrieval as well, but camouflaged by the subtraction technique. The more common strategy in recent imaging studies is to identify networks of areas active in the performance of any task. The various components of these networks are thought to be interconnected, with each performing component subtasks of the overall cognitive activity. Increasingly, therefore, imaging is revealing highly interactive neural processing at a finer grain, a picture that coheres well with the neuroanatomy just discussed.

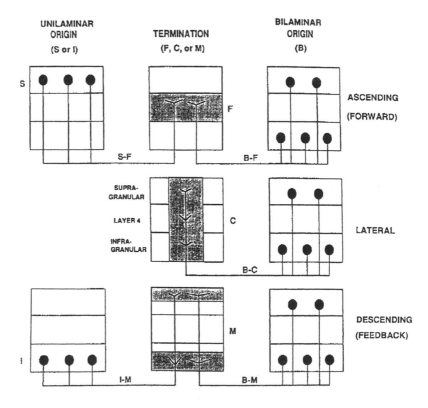

Figure 2. The Different Patterns of Connectivity Between Cortical Columns for Feedforward, Feedback, and Lateral Connections. (From Felleman & van Essen, 1991).

3.   CAN NEUROPSYCHOLOGY AND NEUROSCIENCE ACCOUNTS OF MODULES BE RECONCILED?

In the previous two sections I have contrasted the accounts of modules offered by neuropsychology and neuroscience, both in terms of the grain size of modules and especially in terms of their interconnectedness. Can these be reconciled? One force for doing so has been the development of connectionist or neural network modeling frameworks in psychology. Although typically such models do not intend to ground cognition directly in actual neural processing,[13] they do model cognitive processes at a far finer resolution than more traditional cognitive models (Smolensky, 1988). Recently, neural network modelers have simulated how neuropsychological deficits might result from lesioning such models (Hinton & Shallice, 1991; Plaut, 1995; Plaut, McClelland, Seidenberg, & Patterson, 1996). A not uncommon result is that simulated lesions at different sites in a highly interconnected network result in patterns of deficit similar to those exhibited by different patients. This suggests that the picture of highly interconnected micro-level modules resulting from neuroscience might also account for the patterns of deficits found in neuropsychology.

To show how this conception of highly interactive, fine-grained modules seems likely to gain further support in future psychological and neuropsychological research, I will focus on recent research on memory. It is common in memory research to distinguish between declarative and non-declarative memory, and, within declarative memory, to distinguish episodic and semantic memory (Cohen & Squire, 1980; Tulving, 1972). These distinctions were in large part motivated by the identification of patients who exhibited deficits in some memory abilities but not others. For example, HM, whose medial temporal lobe was resectioned by William Scoville in an attempt to reduce epileptic seizures, exhibits anterograde and graded retrograde amnesia for declarative memories, but retains the ability to develop non-declarative memories (e.g., exhibiting increased skill in a task with practice, with no recollection of having performed the task before — see Corkin, 1968). In contrast, KC, who became amnesic as a result of a motor cycle accident in the early 1980s, is able to develop new semantic memories, albeit with difficulty, but not episodic memories (Tulving, Heyman, & MacDonald, 1991).

One interpretation of these and other dissociations of memory capacities is that there are different systems responsible for the different types of memory (Tulving, 1984). One of the challenges faced by advocates of multiple memory systems is to clarify just what comprises a system. In Tulving's early conception, memory systems (a) are, in some sense, structurally distinct, (b) process different types of information and represent it differently, and (c) operate in accord with different principles (see also Sherry & Schacter, 1987). More recently Tulving (1999) has emphasized the type of information represented. He illustrates this idea in terms of three types of information provided when a person reads the sentence "aardvarks eat ants":

---

[13] Despite the fact that the units in such models are based in general features of neurons, most modelers do not treat that linkage very seriously. Rather, the units in the models are generally thought to represent interactive components in the neural system, perhaps more at the level of neural columns.

PRS, the perceptual representation system [an additional system Tulving introduced], encodes and stores information about the features of the visual objects represented by the letter strings AARDVARKS EAT ANTS. The semantic memory system, or a set of its (presumably numerous) subsystems, encodes and stores propositional information about the feeding habits of animals named aardvarks. The episodic system integrates, registers, temporally dates, and spatially localizes the rememberer's experience of the experience of being present and witnessing the sentence appearing on and disappearing from the screen (p. 20).

This proposal of different memory systems seems to fit well with the sorts of modules advocated by psychologists following the narrow evolutionary psychology program. But there has been a competing approach to studying such memory abilities which offers a quite different conception, one that emphasizes information processing procedures rather than systems. Roediger, Buckner, and McDermott (1999) characterize this approach as follows:

The hallmark of the procedural approach, harking back to Bartlett and Neisser, was that performance on memory tasks could be described as skilled performance and that one should look to the procedures of mind to explain cognitive performances. Many experiments can be interpreted as supporting the procedural approach, including several revealing dissociations in performance on tasks that all measured recognition of words. In particular, Kolers' experiments showed that transfer from one task to another benefitted to the degree that the procedures underlying performance on the two tasks were similar (p. 42).

The processing or procedural approach also employs dissociations to separate component processes, but is open to finding multiple processes within a purported memory system (such as the episodic memory system). The version of the process approach Roediger et al. embrace is *the components of processing framework*, developed by Morris Moscovitch. In this approach, different memory tasks may draw differentially upon different information processing procedures. When tasks are dissociated, that does not show that whole systems are separated, but that at least one component procedure figures differently in the two tasks (Hintzman, 1990).

In an illustrative example, Roediger et al. (1999) use a neuroimaging study to show how a multiple process model may be developed to account for abilities that would, in the systems approach, be assigned to different systems. In the baseline condition, subjects were just asked to complete a stem like COU____ with the first word that came to mind (a purely semantic memory task). In the other two conditions, the subjects first study a list of words. In the second condition, subjects are then given the same directions on the word stem completion task — complete the stem with the first word that comes to mind — while in the third condition, they were instructed to only complete the stem with a word they had just studied (an explicitly episodic memory task). In the first condition, word-stem completion with no previous exposure to words, increased activation was found in areas of visual cortex bilaterally, left frontal opercular cortex and supplementary motor areas, right premotor cortex and anterior cingulate. When the words were primed by prior exposure, the same areas were activated, but with reduced activations in visual areas. The researchers interpret this as evidence of incidental memory retrieval. When the instructions were added to complete the stems only with previously primed words, all the areas activated in the previous conditions were again activated, as well as two additional areas: anterior prefrontal cortex bilaterally and posterior medial parietal cortex. These are areas that have also been activated in other studies of episodic memory, but rather than construing this as evidence for a separate system for episodic memory, Roediger et al. interpret it as evidence for multiple components of a broader memory system that are recruited when the subject is asked to evaluate whether the items were previously encountered.

The *components of processing approach* thus identifies modules at a far smaller grain than the *memory system approach*, a grain congenial to mapping onto accounts of multiple brain areas differentially activated in performing different overall tasks. Although Roediger et al.'s account, as developed to date, does not emphasize the interactivity of the components, it is certainly compatible with discovering recurrent and collateral processing within the overall system in which the components are distinguished. It thus points the way to developing an account of interactive information processing modules at a much smaller grain size than is found in narrow evolutionary psychology.

4.   EVOLUTION WITHOUT FODORIAN MODULES

As I noted early in this paper, most advocates of narrow evolutionary psychology employ a notion of module that corresponds to overall abilities individuals exhibit. The claim is that these are the kinds of entities which evolution can promote. But I have been arguing that the sorts of modules neuroscientific evidence points to are at a much smaller grain size (one corresponding to information processing operations) and that these procedures are likely to be far more integrated through forward, backward, and collateral processing than those envisioned by these psychologists. Does the repudiation of these kinds of modules mean the demise of an evolutionary account of cognition? By no means, although it may spell the doom of narrow evolutionary psychology as currently practiced. I will conclude with a very brief sketch of what a broad evolutionary psychology perspective on cognition that is tied to interactive, smaller-grained modules such as are found in the brain might look like.

An important consideration is that evolution necessarily builds from what exists through small scale modifications. Sometimes the building results initially from duplicating existing parts, with each then becoming specialized for different operations that might be needed in carrying out different tasks. Other times the building results from developing new ways of relating the components that already exist. In either case, evolution begins with existing complex entities and modifies them. This is very different than a picture of developing new modules de novo. Moreover, it imposes an important constraint on evolutionary models — that they be grounded on information about phylogeny and the ancestral condition before the acquisition of a new ability.

Especially important for this alternative conception is the evolution of new cognitive abilities through new organization imposed upon pre-existing components. A speculative, but plausible, account of how linguistic abilities might have developed in this manner is advanced by Terrence Deacon (1997, 1998). Part of Deacon's analysis focuses on the overall character of the changes between the brains of apes and humans. The human brain is not just a general expansion of the ape brain, but a very selective expansion. The cerebral and cerebellar cortexes increase disproportionately to lower brain areas, and within the cerebral cortex, the frontal cortex has expanded much more than more posterior areas. Expansion of an area corresponds to increased number of neurons sending out projections. The connectivity patterns in mature brains are strongly influenced by the number of cells sending projections to various areas during early development and the ensuing competition between these projections for influence on the target area. Accordingly, the differential increase in the cerebral cortex results in its exercising greater control over lower level motor nuclei than the brain stem areas and midbrain areas responsible for stereotypic mammalian calls, accounting for the diminished call repertoire of humans and greater flexible control over voicing required for speech. In addition, the disproportionate increase in forebrain areas relative to the rest of cerebral cortex results in connections from it to many areas, including the motor areas controlling speech apparatus, winning out over connections from elsewhere.

Situating the inquiry into language processing in the context of such changes in brain organization raises an intriguing prospect. One can now try to examine the kinds of information processing performed in prelinguistic creatures by the areas from which increased projections in humans stem. Although the research is still in an early stage, it suggests that some prefrontal cortical areas in monkeys play an important inhibitory function, allowing animals to suppress previously learned associations and acquire new ones (Goldman-Rakic, 1987). Deacon offers intriguing suggestions as to how this inhibitory processing might constitute a primitive form of negation and how such negation is critical to establishing a true symbolic system, in which symbols have internal relations to one another as well as referential relations to things in the world.

This example from Deacon is intended simply as an illustration of how an evolutionary psychology might be developed without invoking the kinds of modules proposed within narrow evolutionary psychology. What is key to this approach is focusing on the information processing operations different brain areas are specialized for and analyzing how they are related to each other in normal processing. An important feature of this approach to broad evolutionary psychology is that, by positioning information processing operations in a phylogenetic lineage, the evolutionary analysis becomes a tool for advancing the decomposition of the overall ability into information processing operations. Once one has identified a brain area that is recruited to perform a task, one can hope to use information about the tasks the area is recruited for in other species as a clue to the type of information processing it supports. Thus, in Deacon's example, instead of just determining that a particular area plays a role in language processing, one can ask why a component that plays a different role in other species would be recruited for language processing in humans. Especially when this investigation is integrated with the developing information about brain anatomy and connectivity, the quest for discovering phylogenetic linkages can play a major heuristic role in determining what are the basic information processing operations that underlie cognitive performances. It is thus a heuristic for developing what Richardson and I call the decomposition of the performance, an important element in the quest for a mechanistic explanation (Bechtel & Richardson, 1993).

5.   CONCLUSION

I have argued that the conception of a module that figures in much narrow evolutionary psychology is not supported by what we know about brain organization and its contribution to cognition.   The brain does involve differentiated components, but these components perform fine-grained information processing operations, not whole tasks like cheater detection or reasoning about other minds.   These components, moreover, are highly integrated with each other, and are recruited into integrated networks to carry out the large-scale mental activities on which many evolutionary psychologists have focused. There is a motivation to link the sorts of information processing modules found in the brain to an evolutionary framework, but the emphasis is then on determining phylogenetic relations so as to utilize what is discovered about these modules in other species as clues about how they may contribute to cognitive tasks we perform.

University of California, San Diego

6. REFERENCES

Appelbaum, I. (1988). Fodor, modularity, and speech perception. *Philosophical Psychology, 11*, 317-330.

Bechtel, W. (2001). Decomposing and localizing vision: An exemplar for cognitive neuroscience. In W. Bechtel, P. Mandik, J. Mundale, & R. S. Stufflebeam (Eds.), *Philosophy and the Neurosciences: A Reader*. Oxford, Eng.: Basil Blackwell.

Bechtel, W., & Richardson, R. C. (1993). *Discovering Complexity: Decomposition and Localization as Scientific Research Strategies*. Princeton, NJ: Princeton University Press.

Broca, P. (1861). Remarque sur le Siege de la Faculte Suivies d' une Observation d' Aphemie. *Bulletins de la Societe Anatomique de Paris, 6*, 343-357.

Brodmann, K. (1909/1994). *Vergleichende Lokalisationslehre der Grosshirnrinde* (L. J. Garvey, Trans.). Leipzig: J. A. Barth.

Buckner, R. L. (1996). Beyond HERA: Contributions of specific prefrontal brain areas to long-term memory retrieval. *Psychonomic Bulletin and Review, 3*, 149-158.

Carmichael, S. T., & Price, J. L. (1994). Architectonic subdivision of the orbital and medial prefrontal cortex in the macaque monkey. *Journal of Comparative Neurology, 346*, 366-402.

Cohen, N. J., & Squire, L. R. (1980). Preserved learning and retention of pattern-analyzing skill in amnesia: Dissociation of knowing how and knowing that. *Science, 210*, 207-210.

Coltheart, M. (1987). Cognitive Neuropsychology and the Study of Reading. In M. I. Posner & O. S. M. Marvin (Eds.), *Attention and Performance* (Vol. XI, pp. 3-37). Hillsdale, NJ: Lawrence Erlbaum.

Corkin, S. (1968). Acquisition of motor skill after bilateral medial temporal-bole excision. *Neuropsychologia, 6*, 255-265.

Cosmides, L., & Tooby, J. (1994). Origins of domain specificity: The evolution of functional organization. In L. S. Hirschfeld & S. A. Gelman (Eds.), *Mapping the Mind* (pp. 85-116). Cambridge, Eng.: Cambridge University Press.

Cummins, D. D. (1998). Social norms and other minds: The evolutionary roots of higher cognition. In D. D. Cummins & C. Allen (Eds.), *The Evolution of Mind*. Oxford, Eng.: Oxford University Press.

Cummins, D. D., & Allen, C. (1998). Introduction. In D. D. Cummins & C. Allen (Eds.), *The Evolution of Mind* (pp. 3-8). Oxford, Eng.: Oxford University Press.

Davies, P. S. (1996). Preface: Evolutionary theory in cognitive psychology. *Minds and Machines, 6*, 445-462.

Deacon, T. W. (1997). *The Symbolic Species*. New York: Norton.

Deacon, T. (1998). Language evolution and neuromechanisms. In W. Bechtel & G. Graham (Eds.), *A Companion to Cognitive Science* (pp. 212-225). Oxford, Eng.: Basil Blackwell.

Farah, M. (1988). Is visual imagery really visual? Overlooked evidence from neuropsychology. *Psychological Review, 95*, 307-317.

Feinberg, T. E., & Farah, M. J. (2000). A historical perspective on cognitive neuroscience. In M. J. Farah & T. E. Feinberg (Eds.), *Patient-based Approaches to Cognitive Neuroscience* (pp. 3-20). Cambridge, MA: MIT Press.

Felleman, D. J., & van Essen, D. C. (1991). Distributed hierarchical processing in the primate cerebral cortex. *Cerebral Cortex, 1*, 1-47.

Fodor, J. (1984). Observation reconsidered. *Philosophy of Science, 51*, 23-43.

Fodor, J. A. (1983). *The Modularity of Mind*. Cambridge, MA: MIT Press.

Gigerenzer, G. (1997). The modularity of social intelligence. In A. Whiten & R. W. Byrne (Eds.), *Machiavellian Intelligence II. Extensions and Evaluation* (pp. 264-288). Cambridge, Eng.: Cambridge University Press.

Goldman-Rakic, P. S. (1987). Circuitry of primate prefrontal cortex and regulation of behavior by representational memory. In J.M. Brookhart, V.B. Mountcastle, and S.R. Greiger (Eds.). *Handbook of Physiology: The Nervous System* (Vol. 5, pp. 373-417). Bethesda, Md: American Physiological Society.

Hinton, G. E., & Shallice, T. (1991). Lesioning a connectionist network: Investigations of acquired dyslexia. *Psychological Review, 98*, 74-95.

Hintzman, D. L. (1990). Human learning and memory: connections and dissociations. *Annual Review of Psychology, 41*, 109-139.

Jacobs, R. A., Jordan, M. I., & Barto, A. G. (1991). Task decomposition through competition in a modular connectionist architecture: The what and where vision tasks. *Cognitive Science, 15*, 219-250.

Kosslyn, S. M. (1994). *Image and Brain: The Resolution of the Imagery Debate*. Cambridge, MA: MIT Press.

Marr, D. C. (1982). *Vision: A Computation Investigation into the Human Representational System and Processing of Visual Information*. San Francisco: Freeman.

McClelland, J. L., McNaughton, B. L., & O'Reilly, R. C. (1995). Why there are complementary learning systems in the hippocampus and neocortex: Insights from the successes and failures of connectionist models of learning and memory. *Psychological Review, 102*, 419-457.

Mundale, J. (1998). Brain mapping. In W. Bechtel & G. Graham (Eds.), *A Companion to Cognitive Science*. Oxford: Basil Blackwell.

Petersen, S. E., & Fiez, J. A. (1993). The processing of single words studied with positron emission tomography. *Annual Review of Neuroscience, 16*, 509-530.

Plaut, D. C. (1995). Double dissociation without modularity: Evidence from connectionist neuropsychology. *Journal of Clinical and Experimental Neuropsychology, 17*, 291-321.

Plaut, D. C., McClelland, J. L., Seidenberg, M. S., & Patterson, K. E. (1996). Understanding normal and impaired word reading: Computational principles in quasi-regular domains. *Psychological Review, 103*, 56-115.

Posner, M. I. (1978). *Chronometric Explorations of Mind*. Hillsdale, NJ: Lawrence Erlbaum Associates.

Roediger III, H. L., Buckner, R. L., & McDermott, K. B. (1999). Components of processing. In J. K. Foster & M. Jelicic (Eds.), *Memory: Systems, Process, or Function* (pp. 32-65). Oxford, Eng.: Oxford University Press.

Schacter, D. L. (1987). Implicit memory: History and current status. *Journal of Experimental Psychology: Learning, and Memory, 13*, 501-518.

Semenza, C. (1996). Methodological issues. In J. G. Beaumont, P. M. Kenealy, & M. J. C. Rogers (Eds.), *The Blackwell Dictionary of Neuropsychology*. Oxford, Eng.: Basil Blackwell.

Shallice, T. (1988). *From Neuropsychology to Mental Structure*. New York: Cambridge University Press.

Shallice, T. (1991). Precis of *From Neuropsychology to Mental Structure*. *Behavioral and Brain Sciences, 14*, 429-437.

Sherry, D. F., & Schacter, D. L. (1987). The evolution of multiple memory systems. *Psychological Review, 94*, 439-454.

Shettleworth, S. (2000). Modularity and the evolution of cognition. In C. Heyes & L. Huber (Eds.), *The Evolution of Cognition* (pp. 43-60). Cambridge, MA: MIT Press.

Simon, H. A. (1969). *The Sciences of the Artificial*. (2nd ed.). Cambridge, MA: MIT Press.

Smolensky, P. (1988). On the proper treatment of connectionism. *Behavioral and Brain Science, 11*, 1-74.

Teuber, H. L. (1955). Physiological psychology. *Annual Review of Psychology, 9*, 267-296.

Tulving, E. (1972). Episodic and semantic memory. In E. Tulving & W. Donaldson (Eds.), *Organization of Memory* (pp. 381-403). New York: Academic.

Tulving, E. (1984). Multiple learning and memory systems. In K. M. J. Lagerspetz & P. Niemi (Eds.), *Psychology in the 1990s* (pp. 163-184). North Holland: Elsevier.

Tulving, E. (1999). Study of memory: Processes and systems. In J. K. Foster & M. Jelicic (Eds.), *Memory: Systems, Process, or Function* (pp. 11-30). Oxford, Eng.: Oxford University Press.

Tulving, E., Heyman, C. A. G., & MacDonald, C. A. (1991). Long-lasting perceptual priming and semantic learning in amnesia. A case experiment. *Journal of Experimental Psychology, 17*, 595-617.

van Essen, D. C. (1997). A tension-based theory of morphogenesis and compact wiring in the central nervous system. *Nature, 385*, 313-318.

van Essen, D. C., Anderson, C. H. and Felleman, D. J. (1992). Information processing in the primate visual system: An integrated systems perspective. *Science, 255*, 419-423.

van Essen, D. C., & deYoe, E. A. (1995). Concurrent processing in the primate visual cortex. In M. Gazzaniga (Ed.), *The Cognitive Neurosciences* (pp. 383-440). Cambridge, MA: MIT Press.

van Essen, D. C., & Gallant, J. L. (1994). Neural mechanisms of form and motion processing in the primate visual system. *Neuron, 13*, 1-10.

Waskan, J., & Bechtel, W. (1997). Directions in connectionist research: Tractable computations without syntactically structured representations. *Metaphilosophy, 28*, 31-62.

JENNIFER MUNDALE

EVOLUTIONARY PSYCHOLOGY AND THE
INFORMATION-PROCESSING MODEL OF COGNITION

1.   INTRODUCTION.

Narrow evolutionary psychology[1] represents an integration of two disciplines which themselves are markedly interdisciplinary: evolutionary biology and cognitive psychology.   It thus inherits all the potential and vigor of a multidisciplinary hybrid. However, as William Bechtel and I have argued elsewhere, its integrative potential has not been fully developed (Mundale & Bechtel, 1996). This previous work focused on the obstacles for integration imposed by an ill-suited, computational view of function, and advocated its replacement with a more teleologically oriented view.   My concerns here are related, but focus on obstacles resulting from the particular information-processing (IP) model of cognition which dominates narrow evolutionary psychology.

As I discuss below, IP models as such need pose no difficulties for the progress of evolutionary psychology; however, the IP model which prevails in narrow evolutionary psychology is inspired by a functionalist theory of mind, and this construal brings serious complications with it.   I argue that the immediate implications of this model make for a stark contrast with the inherently integrative aims of evolutionary psychology, and are particularly obstructionist with respect to the integration of neuroscience.   This is not surprising, as functionalist approaches are, by design, intended to circumvent implementational relevance.   What is surprising is that this approach should be seen as the most appropriate vehicle by which to link cognitive-level domains with biological-level domains.   Furthermore, the functionalist information-processing model of cognition drags with it all the baggage of the multiple realizability argument, as I explain more fully below.   I also argue that a further consequence of this approach is that it weakens the case some evolutionary psychologists have made in favor of a new, integrated causal model (ICM) for the social sciences, as a replacement for the standard social science model

---

[1] EDITOR'S NOTE: In this book, the term 'narrow evolutionary psychology' signifies the approach to evolutionary psychology developed by Cosmides, Tooby, Buss, et al. This term was chosen not to imply that this approach has an inappropriately narrow point of view, but merely to suggest that the approach adopts a narrower range of assumptions than 'broad evolutionary psychology' (or, just 'evolutionary psychology'). This latter term signifies evolutionary psychology generally, practiced with any of a very broad range of assumptions possible within the general framework of evolutionary approaches to psychology. For more detail on this terminology, see the editor's introduction, p 1

Steven J. Scher & Frederick Rauscher (eds.). Evolutionary Psychology: Alternative Approaches, 229-241.

(SSSM).   Before turning to each of these difficulties I will first discuss the place of the IP model in contemporary narrow evolutionary psychology.

2.   THE ROLE OF THE INFORMATION-PROCESSING MODEL

Several figures have shaped the current state of evolutionary psychology, including Martin Daly, Roger Shepard, Don Symons, George Williams and others.   Some researchers have also begun to integrate the principles of evolutionary psychology with other fields.   Steven Pinker, for example, in *How the Mind Works* (1997) consolidates the case for combining evolutionary thinking with current research in the philosophy of mind and cognitive science.   Many would argue, however, that the most prominent figures in the field are Leda Cosmides and John Tooby. Their landmark anthology, *The Adapted Mind* (1992), remains the locus classicus for narrow evolutionary psychology, and for the last decade, they have been the most visible and outspoken champions of this field.   In light of their central and foundational roles, the work of Tooby and Cosmides will figure largely in the examples that follow.

Overall, the program of narrow evolutionary psychology represents an important, though incomplete step in closing a yawning explanatory chasm between high-level cultural and cognitive domains, on the one hand, and evolutionary theory, on the other.   To the extent that cognitive psychology enters into the integration of cultural phenomena and evolutionary theory, it represents an extension and refinement of sociobiology.   According to Tooby and Cosmides, it was partly the legacy of crude biological determinism which served to drive the social sciences into the isolationist, non-nativist stance which has long characterized them.   It is this stance that underlies what Tooby and Cosmides refer to as the Standard Social Science Model (SSSM), a model they reject in favor of their Integrative Causal Model (ICM).   In section III, I argue that the ICM presently shares many of the same weaknesses Tooby and Cosmides impute to the SSSM.   Next, I discuss the important features of the IP model of cognition for evolutionary psychology.

There are several varieties of IP views of cognition (Simon, 1969; Fodor, 1975; Pylyshyn 1980; Cummins 1983, and others), but the essential feature they share is that mind is to be understood as a device which receives, stores, computes, and otherwise processes information.   Additionally, the mind performs these information-processing operations in discernible, rule-governed ways.   For the present purposes, one of the most important features of IP models is the lack of implementational considerations.   What matters is the operational processes or "software" of the system, not how the processes are instantiated.   Thus, a given cognitive mechanism can be studied across a wide number of systems (whether organic or artificial), irrespective of the physical differences among those systems. This key feature, hailed by Pinker as "one of the great ideas in intellectual history" (1997, p. 24) has dominated cognitive psychology until quite recently.   In fact, IP models overall have had little competition in cognitive psychology, but the recent development of connectionist models has provided an alternative view of how information can be represented within a system.   Connectionist models are more biologically realistic, and place less emphasis on the rule-governed, explicit representation of information within a cognitive system. (see, for example, Rumelhart, McClelland, and PDP Research Group, 1986; Clark 1991).

Tooby and Cosmides are clear and forthright about their commitment to the IP model of the mind, and acknowledge its dismissive implications for neuroscientific and other implementational understanding. For example, in describing the psychological processes at work in the feeding behavior of a herring gull, they write:

> These descriptions of the herring gull's cognitive programs are entirely in terms of the functional relationship among different pieces of information; they describe two simple information-processing systems. Moreover, precise descriptions of these cognitive programs can capture the way in which information is used to generate adaptive behavior. Of course, these programs are embodied in the herring gull's neurobiological "hardware". Knowledge of this hardware, however, is not necessary for understanding the programs as information-processing systems. Presumably, one could build a silicon-based robot, using chemical processes completely different from those present in the gull's brain, that would produce the same behavioral output...in response to the same informational input.... (1992, p. 65)

Tooby and Cosmides repeatedly reject disciplinary isolationism and advocate the vertical integration of *all* sciences. Yet this is a useful illustration of how their particular deployment of the IP model of cognition discourages useful interaction with neuroscience and other lower-level sciences (sciences necessary for implementational understanding). Since knowledge of the hardware is deemed unnecessary for understanding the cognitive program, then, presumably, there is nothing urging us away from the disciplinary autonomy of cognitive psychology (at least as far as the more basic sciences are concerned).

Not only is information about the physical instantiation unnecessary in the IP model, but it is rendered nearly inapplicable as well. Cognitive processes are conceived at such a high, or "coarse-grained" level abstraction that the *correspondingly* coarse-grained analysis of the physical instantiation would be so general as to include a variety of physical realizers, including both biological and artificial systems. Tooby and Cosmides clearly acknowledge that their understanding of cognitive states involves their being multiply realizable (1992, p. 66). This, of course, raises the contentious doctrine of multiple realizability. As I will discuss in further detail below, claims about the multiple realizability of cognitive states are notoriously problematic and, along with the larger IP approach, carry further isolationist consequences with them.

Finally, Tooby and Cosmides' model illustration for how cognitive psychology is to be integrated with evolutionary biology provides us with yet another example of how disciplines at both lower *and* higher levels of explanation get left out of the picture. In this example, the integration consists of linking an evolutionary principle, Hamilton's rule (a rule used to determine the extent to which altruistic behavior among kin will be favored by natural selection) to the psychological mechanisms responsible for producing altruistic behavior.

Put simply, according to Hamilton's rule (Hamilton, 1964), altruism will be selected for when the cost to the individual of performing the altruistic act is less than the product of the following two factors: the amount of benefit to be derived by the beneficiary of the act, and a "relatedness" factor that represents the degree of kinship between benefactor and recipient. So, for example, a behavior that costs you relatively little but that proves to be very beneficial for a close relative is likely to survive natural selection. This rule has been variously expressed symbolically, but in the formulation Tooby and Cosmides use, altruism will be selected for when $C_i < r_{ij}B_j$, where C_i is the cost to the individual benefactor, r_{ij} is the degree of kinship between the benefactor and recipient, and B_j is the benefit to the recipient (1992, p. 67). All three of these (C_i, r_{ij}, B_j) are represented by a number between 0 and 1. The closer the degree of kinship, the higher the value of r_{ij}. Parents and children, for example, as well as full siblings, have a kinship value of .5, whereas the relation between grandparent and grandchild is .25.

The psychological mechanisms that produce the altruistic behavior are subject to the pressures of natural selection. The fitness of these psychological mechanisms is evaluated according to the regularity with which they produce altruistic behavior. In other words, "the more closely psychological mechanisms reliably produce behavior that conforms to Hamilton's rule, the more strongly they will be selected for" (Tooby & Cosmides, p. 67). The connection of these psychological mechanisms with the IP view of mind is also clearly specified, since, as they explain, "Under many ecological conditions, this selection pressure defines an information-processing problem that organisms will be selected to evolve mechanisms to solve" (p. 67).

Interestingly, as David S. Wilson (1989) and others have pointed out, altruistic behavior presents something of an evolutionary paradox: we see altruistic behavior in several species, but yet, altruistic acts (to the extent they detract from the altruist's survivability) would seem to be exactly the sort of behavior that would be selected against. Wilson argues that although altruism is not selected for at the level of the individual, it is nonetheless selected for at the group level. In other words, he argues that, if group A has more altruists than group B, then group A will be more favored by selection pressures than group B. Yet, at the level of the individual, if person A is more altruistic than person B, the selection pressures will favor person B. If this is so, then the selection of the cognitive mechanisms Tooby and Cosmides describe above will have to be understood to be selection pressures that are negative for the individual bearing the cognitive mechanism, yet positive for the groups which harbor those individuals. Presumably, then, Tooby and Cosmides would have to address more complex selection forces at work, factoring in some additional, group-dynamic consideration to account for the presence of altruistic behavior.

Though my focus here is on the integration of evolutionary psychology with lower-level sciences, this is an example of how the individual-cognizer perspective of the IP model inhibits integration with the cultural, anthropological, and perhaps even political theories required for understanding the group dynamics of altruistic selection.

With respect to lower-level sciences, in the model integration Tooby and Cosmides provide, we see another example of how preoccupation with the IP model of mind leads to a disregard for the implementational features of a system. As they admit, the selection process they confine themselves to is "'blind' to the specific physical implementation of their information-processing structure" (1992, p. 66), and they further acknowledge that the heuristic benefits of the integration they propose do not extend to the neurobiological levels which implement the IP mechanisms. Again, in failing to address the biological implementation of these psychological mechanisms, one loses the explanatory benefits of neurobiology. Furthermore, though the IP model is indifferent to the biological systems that instantiate a given psychological mechanism, evolutionary processes are not. If narrow evolutionary psychology can not accommodate a meaningful integration with the biological sciences, then it cuts itself off from the richer details of evolutionary theory, as well. I will return to this point in the next section.

In this section, I have described the information-processing view of the mind at work in Tooby and Cosmides' version of evolutionary psychology and have discussed some of its negative implications, particularly with respect to the integration of neuroscience. Next, I will discuss how the IP model weakens the case Tooby and Cosmides make for their model against the standard social science model.

3. THE CHALLENGE TO TRADITIONAL SOCIAL SCIENCE.

On the face of it, narrow evolutionary psychology (as a manifestation of Tooby & Cosmides' integrated causal model, or ICM) appears to avoid the weaknesses and failures of the SSSM, but in this section, I argue that, in fact, there are many shared weaknesses. Among Tooby and Cosmides' many criticisms of the standard social science model (SSSM), the following three, related charges are central: 1) it is isolationist, 2) it is particularly averse to biology, and 3) it requires an impossible psychology. It is isolationist in the sense that it has failed to integrate itself with other sciences, or even to acknowledge the need for general consistency and compatibility with other sciences. The neglect of biology found in the SSSM is motivated, in part, by moral and political considerations. These stem from the fact that biodeterminism and other forms of nativism have sometimes been used to justify racist and sexist agendas. Finally, the claim that it requires an impossible psychology derives in part from its isolationist stance; it posits theories of the human mind that can not account for abilities we are already known to possess, and that also never could have evolved. In order to see how narrow evolutionary psychology represents little, if any advantage over the SSSM with respect to the criticisms Tooby and Cosmides present, it is useful to take another look at how they frame the integration of cognitive psychology and evolutionary biology; this time, with an eye to its biological dimensions.

Although Tooby and Cosmides claim to be forging a link between cognitive psychology and evolutionary biology, the latter component isn't particularly "biological". Instead, it is an abstract principle of evolutionary theory (of the sort commonly found in sociobiological models) which, in their application, has little to do with either neurobiology or genetic theory. In order to see why this should be, it is useful to examine their view of biological systems:

An organism is a self-reproducing machine. All of the other properties of living organisms — cellular structure, ATP, polypeptides, the use of carbon's ability to form indefinitely large chains, DNA as a regulatory element — are incidental rather than essential, and the logic of Darwinism would apply equally to self-reproducing robots, to self-reproducing plasma vortices in the sun, or to anything else that reproduces with the potential for inheritable change (mutation) (Tooby & Cosmides, 1992, p. 50).

Unfortunately, it appears that their view of evolutionary biology, in so far as narrow evolutionary psychology is concerned, is as impoverished as the abstractly conceived, implementationally blind "logic of Darwinism" they describe above.

Tooby and Cosmides point to their model's integration of cognitive psychology and evolutionary biology to highlight the benefits of their integrated approach, but they also admit its limited contact with or relevance to neurobiology:

...this example illustrates how insights from evolutionary biology can bring functional organization into clear focus at the cognitive level, but not at the neurobiological level. Hamilton's rule immediately suggests hypotheses about the functional organization of mechanisms described in information-processing terms, but it tells one very little about the neurobiology that implements these mechanisms - it cannot be straightforwardly related to hypotheses about brain chemistry or neuroanatomy (1992, p. 68).

The integration just described should, of course, represent the first and most obvious departure from the isolationist stance of the SSSM. It should also be consistent with the integrative advantages they claim their model to possess; that is, a model which "makes progress possible by accepting and exploiting the natural connections that exist among all the branches of science" (1992, p. 23). Yet, at no point do they offer any real possibility for exchange between the cognitive domain of psychology and the implementational domains of biology, neuroscience, and other life sciences. The implications for the more basic sciences (e.g., physics, chemistry) are equally as bleak if their avenue of application is through the life sciences. If this is so, then narrow evolutionary psychology is isolationist with respect to all sciences below the level of cognitive psychology, and offers little, if any, advantage over the SSSM.

As noted above, some of the aversion to biology found in the SSSM has moral and political dimensions. Tooby and Cosmides admit that the appeal to biological explanations of human behavior has often been used to advance immoral, and often pseudo-scientific agendas; they insist, however, that these are not the inevitable results of a biologically informed approach. I agree with both these claims. But their version of evolutionary psychology is not an example of a model which can address these worries; instead of setting a positive example of biological integration, it simply avoids the issue by leaving biology out of the picture.

As to the third criticism that the SSSM "requires an impossible psychology" (1992, p. 34), the implementational blindness of narrow evolutionary psychology leaves Tooby and Cosmides open to the same charge. The focus of their criticism against the SSSM has to do with proposing psychological designs that could never have evolved. If their evolutionary theory is no richer than the Darwinian logic they describe above (conceived as an abstract set of rules applicable to any self-reproducing system capable of inheritable mutation), then any species-specific factors, (genetic, physiological, reproductive, or otherwise) fail to constrain. There are also other ways that psychological models can fail to be biologically realistic.

For example, as Bechtel and I noted in an earlier work (Mundale & Bechtel, 1996), a neuroscientifically informed perspective can be a check against proposing models which could never be realized within the human brain. Tooby and Cosmides clearly recognize the problem, but don't provide the sort of integration that can supply a solution.

4. WHY THE IP MODEL OF MIND FAILS EVOLUTIONARY PSYCHOLOGY

What we have here is a failure to integrate. Why, in spite of their often-repeated desire for full, scientific integration, do Cosmides and Tooby repeatedly fail to connect evolutionary psychology with the lower-level sciences? As I have been suggesting all along, the main obstruction lies with the IP model of mind coupled with the wider functionalist themes they adopt. This is not a framework which will support the sort of integration they envision, particularly with the neurobiological level. I will now discuss this claim in more detail.

In a typical functionalist package (e.g., Fodor, Putnam) one finds the following elements: an extremely coarse-grained, or abstract view of cognitive processes (as IP states); dismissal of implementational constraints or relevance (even with respect to organic vs. artificial distinctions); an isolationist psychology; and an allegiance to the multiple realizability argument (explained below). Now, none of these views logically entails the others. One can emphasize the information-processing features of cognitive states without committing to the claims of multiple realizability, and one can maintain a commitment to multiple realizability without thereby committing to isolationism. Richardson (1979), for example, shows how the multiple realizability of psychological (IP) states is compatible with their reduction to, and hence non-isolation from, physical states (Fodor and Putnam notwithstanding).

Though these functionalist elements can all be disentangled, nonetheless, they cohere well with each other and tend to be packaged together. As I have shown above, many of these elements appear in narrow evolutionary psychology as Tooby and Cosmides describe and exemplify it. By buying into the IP view of cognition, Tooby and Cosmides appear to have bought into the larger functionalist package as well. Given their oft-repeated goals for a scientifically integrated psychology, this is an odd combination of themes.

In order to see how and why the IP view tends to have these further obstructionist results, I will begin with the multiple realizability argument. Since the subject of multiple realizability is one that I have discussed elsewhere (Mundale, 1997; Bechtel and Mundale, 1999), I will be brief. The multiple realizability argument was first presented by Putnam (1967), as an attempt to defeat strong identity theory. Putnam interpreted strong identity theory as requiring one-to-one, or type-to-type correlations between mental states and brain states, and proposed that if he could find even a single instance in which the very same mental state is manifested by two different physical states, he would thereby have defeated strong identity theory. The example he took to fit this bill was hunger: an octopus can be hungry, and a human can be hungry, but their hunger correlates with two very different brain states. Therefore, strong identity theory is overthrown (supposedly). Many, including Fodor (who proposed similar versions of his own), thought this argument persuasive against type identity theory.

Bechtel and I have argued that multiple realizability fails to have any negative implications for identity theory because it is merely an artifact of mismatched levels of analysis. It is the coarse-grained, highly-generalized construal of mental states which allows for this sleight of hand; i.e., if mental states are cast at such a high level of abstraction, it is not appropriate or reasonable to expect that it should correlate with a fine-grained, physically specific implementation. And, of course, it is just this kind of high-level abstraction one finds in Tooby and Cosmides' IP account of mental states. What matters about mental states in this view is their causal relation to other informational inputs and outputs within the cognitive system; it is what they do, not how they are implemented that is taken to be important. As Tooby and Cosmides put it, "the same information-processing relationships can be embodied in many different physical arrangements"; all that matters is the stability of the functional relationships between information input and behavioral output (1992, p. 66). Given this framework, then, we should not expect that the sorts of high-level information-processing relationships that Tooby and Cosmides emphasize will correlate neatly with any micro-level, implementational details (indeed, they may not even be restricted to biological implementations).

From multiple realizability, the slide to isolationism may not be inevitable (again, Richardson, 1979, argues that it need not be), but nonetheless, the skids are greased. If IP domains cross-cut neurobiological domains (as they are wont to do, given the level at which functionalist IP domains are cast), then attempts at correlating the two are likely to prove fruitless, and if they prove fruitless, then there is no reason to try to integrate the two disciplines. This, in essence, is Fodor's argument for the disciplinary autonomy of psychology (1974). As discussed in section III above, Tooby and Cosmides often seem driven to isolationist results in the particular examples they cite, unable to find any heuristically useful correlations with implementational levels.

It is true that more recent work by Cosmides and Tooby (2000a; 2000b; Tooby and Cosmides, 2000) shows some attempts at engaging with neuroscience in their larger program. Most of their examples, however, are designed to showcase the benefits of the adaptationist program for neuroscience (primarily for computational neuroscience) in top-down explanations of neural architecture, not the other way around. The adaptationist program they recommend for neuroscience involves asking the following question: What adaptive information-processing problems did our minds evolve to solve? (2000b, p. 1261). Although they admit the possible benefits to be gained by bottom-up explanations involving neural constraint on cognitive design, they are generally dismissive of this approach, claiming that such benefits will only emerge in the long run, and that, in the meantime, the top-down approach "can be equally or more informative" (2000a, p. 1163) Straightforwardly neural or implementational features are also avoided by their emphasis on computational neuroscience. In this view, the brain is merely another computational system, and only incidentally neurobiological. Of course, there is nothing wrong in principle with viewing the brain this way; the problem is that by itself, it just doesn't represent anything that is particularly neuroscientific.

Their justification for this one-sided (merely top-down) strategy appears to be grounded, in part, by the following reasoning: There are many different cognitive systems that are realized in biological organisms. Yet, "the same basic neural tissue embodies all of these programs, and it could support innumerable others as well. Facts about the properties of neurons, neurotransmitters, and cellular development cannot tell you which of these billions of programs will develop reliably in the human (or, e.g., the rhesus) mind" (2000a, p. 1164). This sounds like a thinly veiled version of multiple realizability.   More commonly, one sees the version discussed above in which the same psychological state is said to be realizable in many different physical states.   But for the purposes multiple realizability serves, any apparent disruption of the one-to-one correspondence is considered suitable; thus, an alternative version of multiple realizability claims that the same physical substrate can realize many different psychological states.   Either way, the isolationist stance they are supporting here is similar to that of their earlier work; namely, that our understanding of cognitive (IP) mechanisms has little to gain from an understanding of the underlying neurobiological implementation.

Moreover, there is a strong hint of equipotentiationism in their statement above. Equipotentiationism is the view that all neural matter is "equipotent", or functionally equivalent. It is a view which has been seriously eroded as our understanding of different neuronal types has progressed, not to mention the progress that has been made in understanding the differential roles of various neurotransmitters and the transmitter-specific systems.   Though it is true, for example, that a given cluster of neurons may be multiply deployed in various processes, it does not follow that all neural tissue is basically the same, nor that information at the neuronal level is uninstructive with respect to functional processes.   To point to just one example, the density and distribution of different neuronal types (cytoarchitectonics) within the human cortex provided the foundation for our current understanding of the functional architecture of the human brain. The initial work of importance in this field was begun by Korbinian Brodmann early in the twentieth century, and cytoarchitectonics, along with many other modern techniques, remains in current use (see, for example, Mundale, 1998).

The notion of adaptiveness might be a useful way to narrow the pool of information-processing mechanisms one selects for further study; however, if the primary purpose of this adaptionist program is to elucidate the functional architecture of the brain, then it may narrow the pool in ways that are unnecessary and/or inappropriate. First, some of the cognitive functions in which neuroscientists are interested may not be adaptive. They could be either maladaptive (as with some forms of mental illness), or simply non-adaptive byproducts. The notion of a non-adaptive byproduct (what Stephen J. Gould and Richard Lewontin , 1979, famously dubbed a "spandrel") has been the focus of many heated and often acrimonious disputes in evolutionary circles, and I do not intend to be taking any particular stance within that larger arena. All I wish to point out is that not all of the functions we are interested in elucidating have clear adaptive status. On the other hand, mistaken attributions of adaptivity could send neuroscientists off on an architectural wild goose chase.

Certainly, some kind of constraint and refinement of how we understand cognitive IP mechanisms is necessary before one can expect them to be usefully integrated with neuroscience, but the adaptationist program alone, without any implementational constraints (such as biological realizability) seems unlikely to bridge the gap. Though the adaptionist program Cosmides and Tooby advocate may prove to be beneficial to neuroscience by highlighting important information-processing systems, the program is still too new to judge. Moreover, neuroscience already enjoys a long and sustained history of success in revealing the functional architecture of the brain and mind; so far, this has proceeded with minimal considerations about the adaptiveness of IP mechanisms. This is not to deny the role of evolutionary theory in neuroscience. It has and continues to play an important role, mainly in providing the underlying rationale for comparative brain anatomy across closely related species.

5. CONCLUSION: INTEGRATION AND THE IP MODEL OF COGNITION

As I have argued above, the IP view of cognition, coupled with other functionalist elements, fails to support the kind of scientific integration Tooby and Cosmides claim to endorse. Furthermore, it leaves narrow evolutionary psychology vulnerable to the same major criticisms they level against the Standard Social Science Model (SSSM). In this last section, I wish to suggest some ways in which a more benign IP model of cognition might be retained.

First, in spite of the functionalist thinking which dominates narrow evolutionary psychology, there is nothing about IP descriptions which requires that they be pitched at exclusively stratospheric levels. Though these levels are useful for purposes such as computer modeling, mathematical modeling, and simulation studies (and obviously should be retained for such purposes), they will not be useful for other forms of integration. But there are alternative levels at which the IP model can be cast, and IP descriptions need not preclude physicalist, or implementational descriptions.

As I have argued previously, the long history of brain mapping research, for example, requires that physical differentiation within the brain track coherently with functional differentiation (Mundale, 1998). IP descriptions can be had not only at the species-specific level, but also at such levels as specific brain systems, cortical layers, neural pathways, and even neurons themselves. The more fine-grained the IP description, the more closely it will correlate with its biological implementation. The more an IP description correlates with implementational structures, of course, the more it invites avenues of integration with neurobiological and other lower-level sciences. Nor, incidentally, need such integration necessitate a reductionist framework, as Bechtel and argued I argued previously (1996).

As Tooby and Cosmides are obviously aware, there are heuristically useful organo-specific IP mechanisms, for example, and below that, species-specific IP mechanisms, which would begin to offer some meaningful contact with biological levels of information. The insertion of several, additional layers of IP analysis, each at a different explanatory level, and each correlated with levels both above and below, would provide a reasonable way to extend the kind of interdisciplinary endeavor Tooby and Cosmides repeatedly advocate.

One way to conceive of extending the IP analysis is in terms Tooby and Cosmides already suggest. They argue that cognitive mechanisms need to be conceived of in more domain-specific ways, in contrast to the view of all-purpose, problem-solving cognitive mechanisms found in traditional cognitive science:

> Traditionally, cognitive psychologists have assumed that the human mind includes only general-purpose rules of reasoning and that these rules are few in number and content-free. But a cognitive perspective that is informed by evolutionary biology casts doubt on these assumptions. This is because natural selection is also likely to have produced many mental rules that are specialized for reasoning about various evolutionarily important domains such as cooperation, aggressive threat, parenting, disease avoidance, predator avoidance, object permanence, and object movement (1992, p. 179).

Hence, we should consider not just all-purpose IP mechanisms, but IP mechanisms which evolved in light of the forces of natural selection. They pry open this explanatory domain widely enough to insert evolutionary considerations, but the argument they make for inclusion could (and, I argue should) be extended further, to include even more explanatory constraints and heuristics. The more one specifies the nature of the problem to be solved, the more one is able to benefit from both higher and lower level disciplines.

To return to the example of the herring gull, though one could certainly analyze the gull's feeding program at the level of generality they describe (general enough so as to be implementable in a silicon-based robot), doing so would needlessly insulate our understanding of feeding behavior from what is distinctive of this *species'* feeding behavior. For that matter, it would not even capture anything specific about the feeding behavior of birds, nor even of vertebrates, or organic life forms. Yet, if the task is to understand the feeding behavior of the gull in terms of the sorts of problems its mental programs are adapted to solve (i.e., what sorts of inputs and outputs would be required in order to find sustenance), then those inputs and outputs would offer a richer, more detailed understanding of the *gull* if they were suitably constrained within its implementational, environmental, and informational context. For example: implementationally, the processing capabilities of a gull's brain are not those of a mammalian brain, nor of a reptilian brain, and likely not even the same as those of a hummingbird or owl; however, the number of ways a gull might attempt to solve the problem of acquiring food is seriously constrained by the processing limits of its brain. Just as Tooby and Cosmides condemn the Standard Social Science Model for positing theories about the human mind that never could have evolved, so they are vulnerable to positing IP models that never could be realized within the physical systems they address.

In sum, I have argued that the functionalist-flavored, IP model of the mind that is at work in narrow evolutionary psychology inhibits its possibilities for useful interaction with other sciences, particularly neuroscience. It also weakens its potential to provide a competitive alternative to the standard social science model. By abandoning certain functionalist commitments, however, the information processing model can be retained; primarily this would involve recasting IP descriptions to include more fine-grained, biologically specific levels of analysis.

In assessing the current, under-developed status of evolutionary psychology, it is perhaps wise to bear in mind the introductory statements by Barkow, Tooby and Cosmides:

> ...readers should bear in mind that none of these chapters are meant to be the last word "from biology" or "from psychology"; they are not intended to definitely settle issues. They are better thought of as "first words", intended to open new lines of investigation and to illustrate the potential inherent in this new outlook (1992, p. 4).

As such, these "first words" invite richly promising possibilities — possibilities which are best served by welcoming and facilitating the benefits of multi-disciplinary integration.

University of Central Florida

6. ACKNOWLEDGMENTS

I wish to thank my departmental colleagues at the University of Central Florida, particularly Ronnie Hawkins and Don Jones, for their kind support and helpful comments on earlier versions of this essay. I also wish to thank William Bechtel, at the University of California at San Diego, for his excellent suggestions and insights.

7. REFERENCES

Barkow, J., Cosmides, L. and Tooby, J. (1992). *The Adapted Mind: Evolutionary Psychology and the Generation of Culture.* New York: Oxford University Press.

Bechtel, W. and Mundale, J. (1999) Multiple Realizability Revisited: Linking Cognitive and Neural States, *Philosophy of Science, 66,* 175-207.

Clark, A. (1991). Systematicity, structured representations and cognitive architecture: A reply to Fodor and Pylyshyn. In T. Horgan and J. Tienson (Eds.), *Connectionism and the Philosophy of Mind* (pp. 198-218). Dordrecht: Kluwer.

Cosmides, L. and Tooby, J. (2000a). Introduction (to section on Evolution). In M. Gazzaniga (Ed.), *The New Cognitive Neurosciences* (pp. 1163-1166). Cambridge: MA, MIT Press/Bradford.

Cosmides, L. and Tooby, J. (2000b). The cognitive neuroscience of social reasoning. In M. Gazzaniga (Ed.), *The New Cognitive Neurosciences* (pp. 1259-1270). Cambridge: MA, MIT Press/Bradford.

Cummins, R. (1983). *The Nature of Psychological Explanation.* Cambridge, MA: MIT Press/Bradford Books.

Darden, L. and Maull, N. (1977). Interfield theories. *Philosophy of Science, 43,* 44-64.

Fodor, J. (1974). Special sciences, or the disunity of science as a working hypothesis. *Synthese, 28,* 97-115.

Fodor, J. (1975). *The Language of Thought.* New York: Crowell.

Gould, S.J., & Lewontin, R.C. (1979). The spandrels of San Marco and the Panglossian program: A critique of the adaptationist programme. *Proceedings of the Royal Society of London, 250,* 281-288.

Hamilton, W. D. (1964). The genetical evolution of social behavior, *Journal of Theoretical Biology, 7,* 1-52.

Mundale, J. (1997). *How Do You Know a Brain Area When You "See" One?* (Unpublished Ph.D. dissertation). Washington University, St. Louis, MO.

Mundale, J. (1998). Brain mapping. In W. Bechtel & G. Graham (Eds.), *A Companion to Cognitive Science* (pp. 129-139). Oxford: Basil Blackwell.

Mundale, J. and Bechtel, W. (1996). Integrating neuroscience, psychology, and evolutionary psychology through a teleological conception of function. *Minds and Machines, 6,* 481-505.

Pinker, S. (1997). *How the Mind Works.* New York: W. W. Norton and Co.

Pylyshyn, Z. (1980). Computation and cognition: Issues in the foundation of cognitive science, *Behavioral and Brain Sciences, 3,* 111-132.

Putnam, H. (1967). Psychological predicates. In W.H. Capitan and D.D. Merrill, (Eds.), *Art, Mind, and Religion* (pp. 37-48). Pittsburgh: University of Pittsburgh Press, 37-48.

Richardson, R. (1979). Functionalism and reductionism, *Philosophy of Science, 46,* 533-558.

Rumelhart, D., McClelland, J., and PDP Research Group. (1986). *Parallel Distributed Processing: Explorations in the Microstructure of Cognition.* (Vol. 1). Cambridge, MA: MIT Press/Bradford Books

Simon, H. (1969). *The Sciences of the Artificial.* Cambridge, MA: MIT Press.

Tooby, J. and Cosmides, L. (1992). The psychological foundations of culture. In J. Barkow, L. Cosmides, and J. Tooby, (Eds.), *The Adapted Mind: Evolutionary Psychology and the Generation of Culture* (pp. 19-136). New York: Oxford University Press.

Tooby, J. and Cosmides, L. (2000). Toward mapping the evolved functional organization of mind and brain. In M. Gazzaniga (Ed.), *The New Cognitive Neurosciences* (pp. 1167-1178). Cambridge, MA: MIT Press/Bradford.

Wilson, D. S. (1989). Levels of selection: An alternative to individualism in biology and the human sciences. *Social Networks, 11,* 257-272.

DOMENICO PARISI

EVOLUTIONARY PSYCHOLOGY AND ARTIFICIAL LIFE

1. EVOLUTIONARY PSYCHOLOGY AND NEURAL NETWORKS

In this chapter we outline a research perspective which shares the basic goal of narrow evolutionary psychology[1], that is, to develop a "psychology informed by the fact that the inherited architecture of the human mind is the product of the evolutionary process" (Cosmides, Tooby, & Barkow, 1992, p. 7), but approaches this goal using a theoretical and methodological framework very different from that of narrow evolutionary psychology. There are two main characteristics which distinguish our approach from narrow evolutionary psychology. First, narrow-school evolutionary psychologists tend to be cognitivists whereas the approach proposed here is connectionist. Cognitivism assumes that behavioral and mental processes can and should be studied at a functional or information-processing level without considering the physical structure of the brain. Cognitivists equate the mind with a computer's software, which is analyzed and designed by computer scientists who ignore the physics of the machine. In contrast, connectionism is the idea that behavior and mental processes are best studied using theoretical models such as neural networks which are directly inspired by the physical structure of the nervous system. Second, practicioners of narrow evolutionary psychology use a variety of methods and data for developing and testing hypotheses on the inherited features of the human mind and on the selective pressures that have caused the evolutionary emergence of these features: experiments on human subjects, anthropological data concerning different cultures, various types of evidence on past human behavior and societies (Buss, 1999). The approach proposed here uses computer simulation as the main methodology for developing hypotheses on the evolution of the human mind and for deciding if a proposed theory actually predicts/explains the empirical

---

[1] EDITOR'S NOTE: In this book, the term 'narrow evolutionary psychology' signifies the approach to evolutionary psychology developed by Cosmides, Tooby, Buss, et al. This term was chosen not to imply that this approach has an inappropriately narrow point of view, but merely to suggest that the approach adopts a narrower range of assumptions than 'broad evolutionary psychology' (or, just 'evolutionary psychology'). This latter term signifies evolutionary psychology generally, practiced with any of a very broad range of assumptions possible within the general framework of evolutionary approaches to psychology. For more detail on this terminology, see the editor's introduction, p 1

Steven J. Scher & Frederick Rauscher (eds.). Evolutionary Psychology: Alternative Approaches, 243-265

evidence. Neural networks are simulations, i.e., theoretical models expressed not using verbal or mathematical symbols, as traditionally in science, but as computer programs.

Why are neural networks better theoretical and methodological tools for studying the evolutionary shaping of the modern human mind than the cognitivist framework embraced by narrow evolutionary psychologists? One reason is theoretical. Neural networks complete the revolution in the study of the mind which began in the second half of the nineteenth century with the birth of scientific psychology. During the entire twentieth century psychology has remained a halfway revolution because, while it has adopted the experimental and quantitative methods of the natural sciences, it still uses a mentalistic explanatory vocabulary of belief, goal, intention, representation, rule, etc., derived from common sense and from the philosophical tradition, which is different from the conceptual vocabulary of the natural sciences that recognizes only physical causes producing physical effects. Neural networks complete the revolution because what takes place in the interactions between a neural network and the external environment and inside the neural network is nothing but physical causes producing physical effects. Since evolutionary psychology aims at "conceptual integration" (Cosmides, Tooby, & Barkow, 1992, p. 4) between psychology and the biological sciences, it is easier to attain conceptual integration if the fields to be integrated speak the same language. Neural networks speak the same language of the neurosciences and, if they are viewed as a chapter of Artificial Life, as we will explain in the next section, they also speak the same language of the other biological sciences, in particular of evolutionary biology.

Notice however that, notwithstanding their conceptual unification with the natural sciences, neural networks are not reductionist if by reductionism we mean that facts about behavior and mental life become facts about neurons and synapses. Nervous systems are complex systems in which a very large number of neurons interact locally, and from these interactions emerge the global properties that we call behavior and mental life. Behavioral and mental phenomena are caused by neurons and synapses but cannot be predicted or deduced from even a perfect knowledge of neurons and synapses. Furthermore, in the case of humans behavior and mental life are caused as much by the cultural environment that humans themselves create as they are by neurons and synapses.

The other reason why neural networks are to be preferred for studying the evolved basis of the human mind is methodological. Given the dearth of direct empirical evidence for testing hypotheses on the adaptive bases of human traits, evolutionary psychology tends to be limited to analysis and argument and its adaptive explanations often seem to be "just so stories". The causal history behind many evolved human traits is very complicated (and not necessarily adaptive) and it is often impossible to demonstrate to the satisfaction of everyone that a verbally expressed theory actually explains the human trait it is intended to explain. The author of the theory may claim that his/her theory explains the evolutionary origin of language or cooperative behavior but other people may remain unconvinced, and there may be no way to decide the issue if one can only discuss verbally if the theory actually explains the facts, i.e., if the facts "derive" from the theory. Verbally expressed theories, such as those of narrow evolutionary psychology, are likely to be incomplete, insufficiently precise and detailed, and possibly internally inconsistent, so that no one can really say that some particular theory actually predicts or explains what it purports to explain. On the other hand, if a theory is expressed as a computer program — i.e., it is a simulation — when the simulation runs in the computer the results of the simulation are the predictions derived from the theory and these predictions can be seen by everyone (literally, on the computer's screen). A theory expressed as a simulation must necessarily be complete, precise, detailed, and internally consistent because otherwise the program would not run in the computer or it would not generate the expected results. If the simulation results match the known empirical facts, the theory incorporated in the simulation actually explains the emprical facts. Furthermore, simulations function as virtual experimental laboratories in which the researcher can observe (simulated) phenomena in controlled conditions and can manipulate these conditions and determine the effects of the manipulations. This will strengthen our faith in the theory incorporated in the simulation. Hence, if one has a theory that claims to identify the evolutionary basis of some present human trait, one should incorporate his or her theory in a simulation and show that the simulation produces that human trait.

2.   NEURAL NETWORKS AS ARTIFICIAL LIFE

Neural networks are the main research instrument of the approach to studying the evolutionary bases of human mind proposed in this chapter. However, the neural networks that are appropriate for investigating the evolutionary bases of the human mind are not the "classical" neural networks of Rumelhart and McClelland (1986). If one wants to study how "the inherited architecture of the human mind is the product of the evolutionary process" one has to view and use neural networks in the broader perspective of Artificial Life. Artificial Life is the attempt to understand all the phenomena of the living world by reproducing these phenomena in a computer. Nervous systems, behaviors, and mental phenomena are part of the living world and therefore neural networks are part of Artificial Life. However, neural networks explicitly considered as Artificial Life (Artificial Life Neural Networks; ALNNs) are different from "classical" neural networks in the following respects (Parisi, Cecconi, & Nolfi, 1990):

- ALNNs have a physical body
- ALNNs live in a physical environment
- ALNNs have an inherited genotype
- ALNNs are members of biologically and, in the case of humans, also culturally evolving populations of networks.

A typical Artificial Life simulation aimed at behavioral and mental phenomena is a simulation of an entire population of organisms made up of successive generations of individuals. The population lives in an environment and the behavior of each individual in the environment is controlled by a neural network that simulates the individual's nervous system. In addition to the neural network, each individual has a body with given physical properties (size, shape, spatial arrangement and physical properties of sensory and motor systems, internal organs and systems in addition to the nervous system) and an inherited genotype. Each individual is born, develops, possibly reproduces, and dies. The birth of an individual is the creation of a new organism which inherits the genotype of its two parents (if reproduction is sexual). The inherited genotype interacts with the external environment (external to the genotype and external to the organism's body) to determine the phenotypical traits of the adult individual through a succession of developmental steps.

Evolution and genetic inheritance are intrinsic properties of Artificial Life simulations. Artificial Life uses genetic algorithms to model evolution. Individuals reproduce differentially, i.e., some individuals reproduce more than others, and reproduction is accompanied by the creation of new variants of genotypes due to random genetic mutations and to sexual recombination. Selective reproduction and the constant addition of new variants result in biological evolution, that is, changes in genotypes and, as a consequence, in phenotypes across a succession of generations. Inherited genotypes reflect the past history of adaptation to the environment of the species of which the individual organisms are members. Hence, ALNNs are ideal for studying the "inherited architecture" of the human mind which is the goal of evolutionary psychology. But actually doing simulations with even simple neural networks in simple environments shows that evolutionary change, and the inherited information which is its product, is not necessarily adaptive, as proponents of narrow evolutionary psychology tend to think, but can result from non-adaptive causes such as chance, historical contingency, continuing a previous evolutionary path, and developmental constraints. This is another difference between narrow evolutionary psychology and the approach described here.

A final difference is that while narrow evolutionary psychology stresses the role of evolution in shaping the human mind and downplays the role of individual learning, ALNNs are as much concerned with individual learning as with evolution. In fact, a crucial objective of many ALLN simulations is to study how evolution and learning interact in creating the adult phenotype. More specifically, since an important biologically evolved human trait is that most human behaviors are culturally learned, i.e., learned from others (Tomasello, 1999), ALLNs are as much concerned with cultural evolution as with biological evolution. Behaviors learned from others are transmitted from one generation to the next with selective reproduction of some behaviors and not of others and the addition of new variants due to learning and invention, imports from other groups, and random errors of transmission analogous to genetic mutations. In this case too, the selective reproduction of behaviors (and ideas, knowledge, value, artifacts) learned from others and the constant addition of new variants result in evolution, but it is cultural evolution rather than biological evolution. While in biological evolution "designs reproduce themselves through the reproduction of the individuals embodying them" (Cosmides & Tooby, 1992), in cultural evolution designs reproduce themselves in large measure independently from the reproduction of the individuals embodying them. Since humans are part of the living world, cultural transmission and evolution are among the phenomena exhibited by the living world and therefore they can be and are addressed using Artificial Life simulations. One important goal of the simulations is to study how biological evolution has created the pre-conditions for learning from others and for other human abilities that make cultural transmission in humans possible and how biological and cultural evolution interact in determining human behavior.

3.   WHAT IS GENETICALLY INHERITED REFLECTS ADAPTATION TO A PARTICULAR ENVIRONMENT BUT ALSO CHANCE AND PAST HISTORY

In Artificial Life simulations, populations of artificial organisms living in a particular environment inherit genetically transmitted information that reflects the properties of the environment and the task(s) the organisms must accomplish in order to survive and reproduce in the environment. The genetically inherited information can code for the morphology of the organisms' body as well as for their neural network and behavior. For example, if the coloration of the body of a population of artificial insects is encoded in the genotype and the insects are subject to predation from artificial birds that are more likely to capture a particular individual if the body coloration of the individual is very different from the color of the background environment, the simulation will show an evolutionary change in body color in the population of insects with a progressive assimilation of their body color to the color of the environment. If the environment's color suddenly changes — as actually happened in England at the end of the nineteenth century as a consequence of air pollution due to industrialization — individuals that were well-adapted to the previous environment become ill-adapted to the new environment and a new process of evolutionary change and adaptation begins (unpublished simulations with Andrea Di Ferdinando). (For other simulations of the evolution of both body morphology and behavior, cf. Sims, 1994)

But what is genetically inherited is not only an adaptation to the particular environment in which a species has evolved and reflects not only the properties of this evolutionary environment but it may also reflect chance and the particular past history of the species. This is shown by the following simulations (Lund & Parisi, 1996).

A population of artificial organisms that lives in an environment containing different types of food may evolve a generalist strategy of eating all food types if the energy value of the different food types is the same for the organisms and is fixed. However, if the energy value of the various food types co-evolves with the organisms and therefore it can change, the organisms tend to evolve a specialist strategy of eating only one type of food while ignoring the others. The genotype codes not only for the connection weights of the organisms' neural network but also for the manner in which the organisms process the different food types and extract energy from each of them. Hence, the quantity of energy the organisms extract from each food type can change, and can change in different ways for the various food types, during the course of evolution. In these circumstances evolution causes the emergence (co-evolution) of a better food-processing capacity for one of the food types together with a specialist strategy to eat that type of food in preference to the others.

But consider now what happens if the environment changes and the preferred food type gradually disappears from the environment. While the preferred food is still available, even if in reduced quantities, the population sticks to its specialist strategy. When the preferred food completely disappears while the other nonpreferred foods are still available, there is a sudden shift to a new specialist strategy of eating one of the previously nonpreferred foods. The genetically inherited food-processing capacity of the organisms changes in parallel, with the evolutionary appearance of a better food-processing capacity for the new preferred food.

But in addition to adaptation to the environment and the co-evolution of organisms' traits, it is chance that has a role in determining what emerges evolutionarily and is genetically inherited. One way in which chance enters into Artificial Life simulations is through the initial conditions of the simulation. Evolutionary simulations start with an initial population in which genotypes are randomly generated (from a 'seed') and different replications ('seeds') are used to obtain reliable results. Hence, chance can influence the course of evolution in any individual replication of the simulation and its eventual results. In the simulations just described the initial 'seed' can determine whether a specialist or a generalist strategy emerges evolutionarily when the capacity to process the different food types also evolves, even if with most 'seeds' it is a specialist strategy that emerges. But chance can influence the course of evolution in other ways. In one replication, chance can lead to a preference for one type of food while in another replication another type of food can emerge as the preferred one. Furthermore, when the environment changes and the preferred food gradually disappears, in one replication the initial preference for one type of food can persist until the preferred food completely disappears from the environment whereas in another replication a new preference for a different type of food starts to emerge as soon as the initially preferred food begins to become scarce.

The simulations we are describing also demonstrate the role of previous history and of pre-adaptation in evolution. The way in which a specialist strategy emerges in a population of organisms living in an environment with different food types varies as a function of the preceding history of the population. If we compare the emergence of a specialist strategy for some food type in a population with no previous history and in a population which already has evolved a specialist strategy for another food type and then has abandoned the former strategy because of a change in the environment, we see that the two populations are different in at least two ways. First, the emergence of the new strategy tends to be gradual in the former population and abrupt in the latter population. Second, the population with a previous evolutionary history outperforms the population with no previous history in total energy extracted from the environment. Both differences suggest an important role of pre-adaptation in evolution in that a population with a previous history of alimentary specialism appears to be pre-adapted to evolve a new kind of specialism. A detailed analysis of the activations of single units in the neural networks of the organisms of the pre-adapted population shows how this pre-adaptation is concretely realized in the genetic material and in the resulting phenotype (brain). (For details of this analysis, cf, Lund & Parisi, 1996. For another simulation in which evolutionary past history explains present adaptation, see Phelps & Ryan, 2000).

4.   EVOLUTION AND LEARNING COOPERATE TO PRODUCE ADAPTATION

Imagine a simulated organism that must explore as much of the environment as possible in order to find a target area which cannot be perceived by the organism from a distance (Nolfi & Parisi, 1997). The more of the environment the organism is able to explore the more likely the organism will end up in the target area. The organism is a physical robot with a cylindrical body, infrared sensors distributed on the anterior portion of the body, and two wheels that allow the robot to move around in the environment. The environment is rectangular and it has an outside wall that the robot can sense with its infrared sensors. There is a population of such robots that reproduce differentially as a function of two factors: (1) their ability to find the target area, and (2) their ability to avoid hitting the outside wall. The population evolves in an environment subject to variation between two states: light and darkness. In the lighted environment the robot can sense the wall with its infrared sensors from a greater distance than in the dark environment. The environment changes periodically with a temporal rhythm which coincides with the replacement of a generation by the following generation so that even generations of the population live in a lighted environment and odd generations in a dark environment. Although the organisms do not know if they are living in a lighted or in a dark environment since all they know is how distant they are from the wall at any given time, they behave differently in the two environments. In the dark environment, the organisms tend to include the space near the outside wall in their explorations because it is only when they are very near the outside wall that they can sense the wall. On the other hand, in the lighted environment the organisms are unable to explore the space near the wall because they sense the wall at a greater distance and they don't risk hitting the wall by approaching the wall further (Figure 1, top).

These results are obtained when the behavior (i.e., the connection weights) is entirely genetically inherited. If learning during life is added so that an individual can discover in which environment it is living, a different picture emerges. The connection weights which are genetically inherited by each individual are changed during an individual's life as a function of the experience of the individual in the particular environment. (Of course, these learned changes are not themselves inherited). Since the two environments cause different experiences in the organisms, the organisms now learn to distinguish between them. With learning the organisms' behavior changes. The organisms are less likely to explore the central portion of the

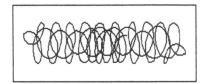 

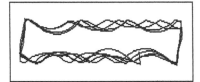 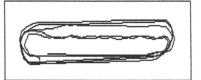

Figure 1. Behavior of two typical individuals of the population in a dark environment (left) and in a lighted environment (right). The top row represents an individual from a population without learning and the bottom row represents an individual from a population with learning. (From Nolfi & Parisi, 1997)

environment but they are able now to explore the environment near the wall even in the lighted environment because they now know that, when they first sense the wall in the lighted environment, the wall still lies at a distance (Figure 1, bottom).

This shows one way in which evolution and learning can cooperate to produce a different adaptation to the environment from that which results from evolution alone. In the simulations just described evolution and learning both operate on the connection weights of the neural networks. Evolution selects the initial genetically inherited weights, which already incorporate some useful knowledge about the environment, and learning refines those weights to add some new, more specific, knowledge about the specific environment in which the individual organism happens to live. (For other ways in which evolution and learning can cooperate to find the best connection weights in neural networks, see Nolfi, Elman, & Parisi, 1994; Belew & Mitchell, 1996; Floreano & Urzelai, 2000).

However, the behavior of an organism controlled by a neural network depends not only on the connection weights of the organism's neural network but also on the network's architecture, i.e., the particular pattern of connections specifying which unit is connected with which unit. Although evolution can produce genetically inherited constraints on the learned connection weights and learning can change not only the connection weights but also the architecture, one can advance the general hypothesis that evolution has a more important role in finding the best architecture for a particular type of organism in a particular environment while learning plays a critical role in finding the best connection weights for the genetically inherited architecture (Elman, Bates, Johnson, Karmiloff-Smith, Parisi, & Plunkett, 1996). In the next section, which is dedicated to another important issue dividing cognitivism and connectionism, the issue of modularity, we will describe a simulation in which evolution creates the network architecture and learning finds the appropriate connection weights for the genetically inherited architecture.

5.   MODULARITY OF THE MIND, MODULARITY OF THE BRAIN

Evolutionary psychologists taking the narrow approach tend to think that what is genetically inherited by humans is not just a nervous system and a general tendency/ability to learn but a set of specialized tendencies and abilities, called modules, somehow incorporated in the inherited nervous system. Connectionists, on the contrary, stress the role of learning and seem to think that not much more than a general tendency to learn from experience is genetically inherited. Most "classical" connectionist simulations are concerned with learning rather than with evolution and do not incorporate specific hypotheses about what is genetically inherited. Hence, connectionists tend to be described as anti-modularist.

ALLNs are different from "classical" connectionism in that ALLNs are not anti-modularist. However, the cognitivist perspective of narrow evolutionary psychology has a different conception of modules than the neural perspective of ALNNs. For cognitivists, modules tend to be components of the theories in terms of which empirical phenomena are interpreted and explained. A theory or model of some particular phenomenon can hypothesize the existence of different modules with different structure and/or function which by working together explain the phenomenon. Therefore, cognitive modules are postulated rather than observed entities. For example, in formal linguistics of the Chomskian variety syntax is considered as an autonomous module of linguistic competence in that empirical linguistic data (the linguistic judgements of native speakers) are interpreted as requiring this assumption. Or, in psycholinguistics, the observed linguistic behavior of adults and children is interpreted as requiring two distinct mental modules, one supporting the ability to produce the past tense of regular English verbs (e.g., *worked*) and the second one underlying the ability to produce the past tense of irregular verbs (e.g., *brought*) (Pinker, 1999). A third example of postulated modules is the notion of a module so precisely defined in Fodor's book *Modularity of Mind* (Fodor, 1983), one of the foundational books of cognitivism.

Neuroscientists also have a modular conception of the brain, but this conception is based on empirical observations of the anatomy and physiology of the brain rather than on theory. The brain is obviously divided up into a variety of 'modules' such as distinct cortical areas, different subcortical structures, interconnected systems such as the retina-geniculate-visual cortex or the basal ganglia-frontal cortex system. This rich modularity of the brain, both structural (anatomical and cytoarchitectonic) and functional (physiological), is evidenced by direct (instrumental) observation, by data on localization of lesions in various behavioral/mental pathologies and on neuropsychological dissociations, and more recently, and increasingly, by neuroimaging data.

Neural networks are theoretical models which, unlike cognitivist models, are directly inspired by the physical structure of the brain. In fact, neural networks are at the same time models of the brain and models of the mind. However, the neural networks used in most simulations described in the connectionist literature are nonmodular. They are homogeneous networks of units with minimal structure usually constituted by an input module (i.e., set of units), an output module, and (almost always) a single internal module in between. This is a serious limitation of current neural network models. The human brain's brilliant performances appear to be due not only to its being made up of one hundred billions of neurons (compared to the tens or hundreds of units of a neural network in a typical connectionist simulation) but also to its being not a homogeneous network of neurons but a very intricately interconnected system of distinct 'modules'. If neural networks claim to be inspired by the structure and functioning of brain, it is not clear how this rich brain modularity can remain absent from the neural networks used in the simulations. Nonmodular networks can illuminate important aspects of mind and behavior because they capture some of the basic physical properties of the brain as a network of units (neurons). However, it is almost inevitable that other important aspects of mind and behavior can only be accounted for if the simulations use modular neural networks that at least begin to match the rich modular structure of the brain.

However, modular networks should reflect the structure of the brain, not the "box-and-arrows" organization of cognitivist models. A module in a modular neural network is a (simulated) physical module, not a postulated theoretical construct. A neural module could be a sub-set of network units with more internal connections linking the units of the module among themselves than external connections linking the units inside the module with units outside the module. Or, more functionally, a neural network module could be an observed correlated activity in a sub-set of the network's units resulting from the pattern of connection weights, without 'anatomical' isolation of the sub-set of units. Neural modules in a neural network can be hardwired by the researcher or they can emerge as a result of evolution or development. If the modular structure is hardwired by the researcher, the researcher tends to be inspired by the actual modular structure of the brain rather than by theoretical considerations based on cognitive models. If the modules emerge spontaneously as part of the simulation, the researcher is interested in ascertaining if the emerging modular structure matches the known anatomical or physiological modularity of the brain.

The real contrast between neural network models and cognitive models, then, does not concern modularity per se but rather the nature of modules. Consider the cognitivist hypothesis that English speakers produce or understand the past tense of verbs using two distinct modules, one for regular verbs and the other for irregular verbs (Pinker, 1999). There appears to be some empirical evidence that these two modules may reside in separate portions of the brain. Patients with lesions in the anterior portion of the brain tend to fail to produce regular past tense forms while their ability to produce irregular past tense forms is preserved. In contrast, patients with lesions in the posterior portion of the brain tend to show the opposite pattern: they find it difficult to produce irregular past tenses but are able to produce regular ones (Ullman, Corkin, Coppola, Hickok, Growdon, Koroshetz, & Pinker, 1997). This may indicate that two distinct neural modules actually underlie past tense production.

This conclusion can be completely acceptable for a connectionist (at least for ALNNs). What separates the cognitive and the neural approaches to the treatment of past tense is the nature of the modules. Cognitivists claim that the regular past tense module is a rule-based module. To produce the past tense of the verb *to work* the brain applies the rule: "Add the suffix *-ed* to the verb root". In contrast, the irregular past tense module is an association-based module containing a finite list of verb roots each with its associated irregular past tense form. To produce the past of the verb *to bring* the brain just consults this list of associations, finds the appropriate verb root, and produces the associated past tense form. This theoretical interpretation of past tense behavior is rejected by a connectionist for the simple reason that his or her theoretical tools, i.e., neural network models, do not allow for this interpretation. Neural network models are inspired by the brain, and brains are physical systems made up of physical entities and processes in which all that can ever happen is the production of physico-chemical effects by physico-chemical causes. Hence, a neural network cannot appeal to a rule as an explanation of any type of behavior and cognitive ability. It is perfectly possible that distinct neural modules take care of regular and irregular past tense production but both modules would function in the same basic way, i.e., with neurons influencing other neurons through their synapses. This does not rule out the possibility that one can discover differences in the organization and functioning of the two different neural modules and of course one has to explain why the brain has found it useful to have two separate modules for controlling verb past tense behavior rather than just one, and, more generally, why evolved brains are modular rather than nonmodular.

One reason why the brain is modular might be that modularity solves the problem of neural interference. In most connectionist simulations there is only one task that the neural network must learn. Learning in neural networks consists of adjusting the value of the network's connection weights so that at the end of learning the network has a set of weights that allow the network to respond to each of the task's inputs with the appropriate output. Real organisms, however, must be able to accomplish not one single task but many different tasks in order to survive and reproduce. If a network has to learn more than one task and some particular connection is involved in more than one task, the problem of neural interference may arise. One task may require the weight value of that particular connection to be increased while the other task may require the same value to be decreased. Modularity solves this problem because it assigns separate sets of connections (modules) to each task. In modular neural networks connections are "proprietary" so that it never happens that one and the same connection receives contradictory commands to change its weight value.

Rueckl, Cave, & Kosslyn (1989) have shown that neural networks that have to learn to recognize both the identity of a visually perceived object and the object's location on the retina learn better if they have a modular rather than a nonmodular architecture. A modular architecture corresponds to the division in the brain between a ventral pathway for recognizing the identity of objects (*What*) and a dorsal pathway for recognizing their location (*Where*) (or for preparing a motor response with respect to the object [*How*]) (Ungerleider & Mishkin, 1982; Milner & Goodale, 1995). If one asks how this modular organization originates, evolution is likely to be the answer. In fact, if the network architecture varies from one individual to another individual, is genetically inherited, and a population of networks starts with randomly generated architectures encoded in the genotypes, it can be shown that a modular architecture emerges after a certain number of generations in the population (DiFerdinando, Calabretta, & Parisi, 2001). Furthermore, in the network architecture which emerges at the end of the simulation the neural module for the *What* task is larger (has more units) than the module for the *Where* task. This agrees with the results of Rueckl et al. (1989) who, in their simulations in which the network architecture is hardwired rather than evolved, have found that the best results are obtained when more hidden units are assigned to the *What* task than to the *Where* task because the *What* task is intrinsically more complex than the *Where* task.

These results are obtained if evolution finds the best network architecture but the organisms learn during life to recognize the identity and spatial location of objects. If both the network architecture and the connection weights are encoded in the genotype, there is no learning during life, and evolution must be able to find both the best architecture and the best connection weights. Under these circumstances, the results are much less good. The evolved organisms make errors in recognizing the spatial location and, especially, the identity of perceived objects, which appears to be due to the fact that the evolved architecture, although it is modular, assigns more hidden units to the easier *Where* task than to the more demanding *What* task. The organisms of the earlier generations tend to reproduce on the basis of their ability to locate the objects spatially (*Where* task) while their ability to identify the objects is not very good (*What* task) since recognizing the identity of objects is not necessary to have a competitive advantage in these early evolutionary stages. When later in evolution, competition becomes harsher and it would be useful to be able to recognize both the spatial location and the identity of perceived objects, evolution is unable to change the network architecture and to shift hidden units from the *Where* to the *What* task to reach higher overall performance levels.

The *What and Where* organisms must recognize the identity and the location of a perceived object at the same time. A real example is an animal which must be able both to approach prey and to escape from predators: in either case both the identity of the 'object' and its location must be recognized by the animal if the animal is to survive. In other simulations organisms have to accomplish two tasks to survive but in addition they have to be able to choose which of the two tasks to execute at any given time. Cangelosi, Parisi, & Nolfi (1994; see also Cecconi & Parisi, 1993) have simulated a population of organisms that live in an environment containing both food and water and they must be able to find food when they are hungry and to find water when they are thirsty. In any given moment the organisms are informed by their senses about both the location of the nearest food element and the location of the nearest water element and they must decide whether to approach food or water depending on their physiological state. The neural network which controls the behavior of the organisms is genetically inherited and the organisms eventually evolve a neural architecture which includes two modules, a food module and a water module, plus a third module encoding the motivational state of the organism and connected with both the food and the water modules. The motivational state (i.e., the activation pattern of the units constituting the motivational module) can be either hunger or thirst and it shifts to the alternative state after the organism has eaten a certain number of food elements or drunk a certain number of water elements. Based on its current state the motivational module gives control of the network's output to either the food module or the water module. Hence the evolved organisms can be seen on the computer screen to ignore water and approach food when they are hungry and to ignore food and approach water when they are thirsty.

How is the motivational module able to do this? In this architecture the food and the water modules are not entirely anatomical, as they were in the preceding simulation of the *What and Where* task, but they are at least partially functional. As can be seen from Figure 2, the food module and the water module share some of their units and connections. One can distinguish between a food module and a water module because when the motivational state is hunger only some of the network's units have an activation state which covaries with the sensory input (which encodes the location of both food and water) and these units constitute the food module, whereas when the motivational state is thirst these units are not sensitive to the input and it is the remaining units whose activation state covaries with the input. This is the water module. The motivational module, with its two different activation states encoding hunger or thirst, decides which portion of the sensory input has control of the network's output.

Another interesting result is evidenced by the evolved network architecture of Figure 2. If one looks at the evolutionary history that has eventually resulted in this network architecture one discovers that this particular population of organisms first evolves an ability to find food when hungry without a comparable capacity to find water when thirsty and only the later generations also evolve an ability to find water when thirsty. Since food and water are equally important for the survival of these organisms, this shows that what is genetically inherited does not reflect only adaptation but also historical contingency. Furthermore, this past evolutionary history, with its intrinsic contingency, has left a trace in the evolved network architecture. The two modules share some network units (unlike cognitive modules, neural modules are not necessarily neatly separated) but the food module which underlies an ability which has emerged earlier is smaller and simpler than the water module which underlies an ability which has emerged later and after the food module was already there. Since the food and water modules share some of their units, it seems as if the water module, when it emerges, co-opts some portion of the already existing food module, which can be interpreted as an example of exaptation (Gould & Vrba, 1982).

6.   EVOLVING SOCIAL BEHAVIORS

Many speculations of evolutionary psychology regarding the evolved bases of human behavior concern social behaviors, that is, behaviors elicited by conspecifics or having an effect on conspecifics. In Artificial Life simulations the environment can include nonbiotic elements and organisms of other species but it can also includeconspecifics and artifacts created by conspecifics. Therefore, ALLNs can be used to study the inherited architecture of the human mind as this inherited architecture is expressed in social behaviors.

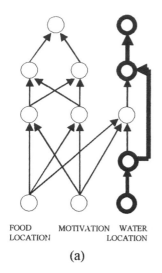

FOOD   MOTIVATION   WATER
LOCATION   LOCATION

(a)

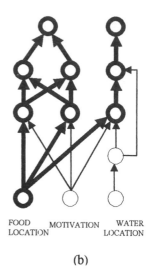

FOOD   MOTIVATION   WATER
LOCATION   LOCATION

(b)

Figure 2. Modular organization of a neural network with distinct modules indicated by thicker connections. (a) Food module. (b) Water module. (From Cangelosi, Parisi, & Nolfi, 1994.)

Consider the theory of kin selection (Hamilton, 1964) which assumes that evolution causes altruistic behaviors (behaviors that damage their author and benefit other individuals) to be infrequent if these behaviors benefit a nongenetically related individual, while these behaviors may be routinely exhibited by an individual if the benefit accrues to a genetically related individual. This can be simulated by having artificial organisms decide to give some of their resources to a conspecific as a function of whether the conspecific is genetically related or not. Sister neural networks in nonsexually reproducing populations are networks which are the offspring of the same parent and therefore they have the same connection weights, except for random mutations, and behave in similar ways. During its life an individual network can encounter both sister networks and other networks and the sensory input tells the network if the currently encountered individual is one of its sisters or an extraneous network. The network's output encodes a decision to give some of the network's resources to the other individual or to refrain from doing so. The results of the simulation show that the behavior predicted by inclusive fitness theory emerges evolutionarily. Evolved individuals give to sisters but not to nongenetically related individuals. By so doing they reduce their individual chances of surviving and reproducing but they increase the survival and reproductive chances of other individuals which have their same altruistic genes. Therefore, altruistic genes and altruistic behaviors directed to genetically related individuals do not disappear from the population.

This approach can be used to study the evolutionary emergence of parental love and filial love. Parental love is defined here as giving one's resources to one's offspring, filial love as the tendency to remain in proximity to parents in order to be able to receive resources from them. Parisi, Cecconi & Cerini (1995) have simulated a population of organisms in which sexually mature individuals (adults) and sexually immature individuals (children) live together. Adults and children exhibit different behaviors. Adults collect the food which is found in the environment while children follow their parents. Newborn individuals live for a fixed length of time as children and then they become adults. Each individual inherits two distinct neural networks, one controlling its behavior as a child and the other one controlling its behavior as an adult. The neural network controlling the behavior of the individual as an adult encodes the location of the single nearest food element as input and responds with a displacement of the individual in the environment as output. When the adult reaches a food element, the food element is captured. The individual's genotype encodes not only the connection weights of its neural network but also a 'parental care' gene which encodes the probability that the individual will eat the food element or give the food element to its offspring. Both the connection weights and the gene's value are inherited with random mutations that can change the connection weights or the gene value. The behavior of the individual as a child is controlled by a neural network with input units encoding the current location of the child's parent (the parent moves in the environment looking for food) and output units encoding a displacement of the child in the environment.

The behaviors that emerge evolutionarily are the following. Adults exhibit an ability to approach and find food in the environment. They eat part of the food they are able to find in the environment and give the remaining part to their offspring — which is the only way for a child to survive and reach maturity. This is parental love. Since food can only be received by a child if the child is sufficiently spatially close to its parent, children evolve an ability to follow their parents while their parents wander in the environment looking for food; therefore, they tend to remain in proximity to their parents. This is filial love or attachment (Bowlby, 1969). The simulation can be used to identify, given different environmental and other conditions, how much of their food adults tend to give to their already born offspring and how much they prefer to eat in order to survive and generate more offspring.

In these simulations age at maturity is fixed (hardwired). In other simulations one can study how this important developmental parameter can itself evolve and what are the causes and consequences of choosing an early or later age to cease to be a child and become an adult (Cecconi and Parisi, in preparation). In these simulations age at maturity varies from one individual to another individual, is encoded in the genotype and is genetically inherited from one's parents with mutations, and it therefore can change across generations. The results of the simulations show that, if nothing useful for the individual happens during childhood, age at maturity rapidly decreases evolutionarily (it almost goes to zero) so that childhood disappears as a developmental stage and the organisms are already adults when they are born. This results from the fact that only adults reproduce and therefore including a useless nonreproductive stage to one's life reduces the length of adult reproductive life and therefore the chances that one's genes will be present in the next generation.

However, if something useful for the individual happens during childhood, age at maturity stabilizes at some appropriate value and childhood continues to exist. In this variant of the simulation an immature individual learns some skill, say, some food processing ability, which will be used by the individual when it becomes an adult to increase the quantity of energy extracted from the food found in the environment. In this new condition the probability of an individual reproducing will depend not only on the length of its adult life (and, of course, on its ability to find food as an adult) but also on the length of its childhood — since a longer childhood will mean more time to learn to process food and therefore a better food processing ability to be used in adulthood. Again, the simulation can be applied to determine how the age at maturity which stabilizes after a while depends on various conditions which one can manipulate in the simulation.

But another interesting result of this simulation is the complex pattern of consequences that derive from having evolution determine age at maturity. One consequence is that population size is greater in the population with evolved age at maturity and a useful childhood compared with a population without childhood. Individuals that learn to process food when they are children extract more energy from the food they are able to capture in the environment when they become adults and this allows them to survive longer and have more offspring. (One offspring is generated each time the quantity of energy possessed by a given individual exceeds a given threshold. The individual gives half of its energy to the new offspring.) This causes an increase in population size.

Another consequence is that average life span is greater in the population with childhood than in the population without childhood. (An individual dies either because it has consumed all its energy or because it has reached a maximum age.) Notice that the population with childhood has a greater *adult* life span than the population without childhood, that is, its adult life span is longer, the addition of a childhood stage to the entire lifespan notwithstanding.

A third, perhaps surprising, consequence is that the individuals of the population with childhood are able to find fewer food elements when they become adults than the individuals of the population without childhood. This is not due to the fact that they are intrinsically less able to find food than the individuals of the population without childhood. When tested in identical (laboratory) conditions, the individuals of both populations exhibit similar levels of genetically inherited food finding ability. The individuals of the population with childhood are able to find fewer food elements because, as we have said, population size is greater in this population than in the population without childhood. Since the environment is the same for both populations, the environment is more crowded for the population with an evolved childhood and therefore each particular individual is able to capture fewer food elements than an individual living in the less crowded environment of the population without an evolved childhood. However, as we have seen, even if fewer food elements are found in the environment, the total quantity of energy extracted from food is greater because of the food processing ability learned during childhood.

The better global adaptation to the environment of the population with an evolved childhood compared to the population without childhood is demonstrated by a final set of simulations in which the two populations live in the same environment and compete for the same resources (food). In 10 out of 10 replications of the simulation in which the initial size of the population with childhood is the same as that of the population without childhood (500 individuals for each population), the population with childhood drives the population without childhood to extinction and it remains as the only surviving population. In another simulation in which the initial size of the population with childhood is half the size of the population without childhood (250 individuals vs 500 individuals), and therefore the former population is at a disadvantage compared to the latter, still the population with childhood outcompetes the population without childhood in 7 out of 10 replications of the simulation.

7. INTERACTION BETWEEN BIOLOGICAL AND CULTURAL EVOLUTION

Most human behavior is not only learned but it is learned from others (Tomasello, 1999). Since behavior learned from others is transmitted from one generation to the next and transmission is selective and accompanied by the constant addition of new variants of behavior, this results in cultural evolution, i.e., changes in behavior learned from others in a succession of generations of individuals. ALNN simulations are used to study cultural evolution as much as biological evolution, and how biological and cultural evolution may cooperate in determining human behavior.

A population of individuals lives in an environment that contains a certain number of resource elements. The behavior of each individual is controlled by a neural network with input units encoding the location of the nearest resource element and the output units encoding motor behavior that allows the individual to move in the environment. When an individual reaches a resource element, it captures the resource element and its fitness is augmented by one unit. At the beginning of the simulation the individuals' neural networks are assigned random connection weights. Therefore, the behavior of the individuals of the initial generation is rather inefficient from the point of view of resource procurement. These individuals tend to move randomly or stereotypically and, therefore, they are able to capture a very limited number of resource elements. However, for purely random reasons some individuals happen to have better connection weights than other individuals and these connection weights allow them to behave more efficiently, that is, to capture more resource elements than their less lucky conspecifics.

Just before the individuals of the first generation die (length of life is identical for all individuals and all individuals die at the same time), a second generation of individuals is created. These individuals are born with random connection weights like the individuals of the first generation but, at the beginning of their life, they are given a chance to learn to procure the resources by imitating the behavior of the individuals of the first generation (Figure 3).

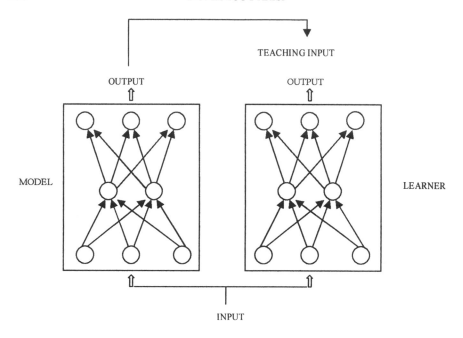

Figure 3. A simple model of learning by imitating another individual. Both the "learner" neural network (left) and the "model" neural network (right) are exposed to the same input and each responds by generating some output. The "learner" neural network learns by using the output of the "model" network as teaching input in the back-propogation procedure. The teaching input tells the "learner" network how to modify its connection weights in such a way that after a certain number of learning cycles the "learner" network responds to the input in the same way as the "model" network.

The best individuals of the first generation are selected as "models" of the individuals of the second generation and, furthermore, when an individual of the second generation learns the behavior of resource procurement by imitating its "model", some noise is added to the transmission process by slightly (randomly) modifying the teaching input. This noise has the consequence that in most cases a "learner" turns out to be less good at procuring the resources than its "model" but in a few cases a "learner" will outperform its "model". Of course, the individuals that happen to perform better than their "models" are more likely to be selected at the end of their life as the "models" of the individuals of the next generation.

The process is repeated for a certain number of generations. The capacity to procure the resources tends to increase with each successive generation and after a certain number of generations it reaches a steady state level which is clearly much better than the initial level (Denaro & Parisi, 1996).

In the simulation just described it is the researcher who selects the best individuals of each generation as the "models" of the next generation. In another simulation the individuals themselves evolve an ability to identify the best individuals of the preceding generation as "models" to be imitated. This ability to select the best individuals of the preceding generation as "models" is genetically inherited. The ability is encoded in the genotype of each individual as a number that measures the individual's level of ability in selecting good "models". An individual transmits this ability to its offspring. Biological reproduction is selective in that the individuals that are better at procuring resources (an ability culturally learned from "models") are more likely to have offspring than less able individuals. When an individual generates an offspring, the offspring inherits the same level of ability to select good "models" of its single parent (reproduction is nonsexual), with the addition of random genetic mutations which can either slightly increase or decrease the offspring's level of ability to select good "models" compared with its parent's level.

At the beginning of the simulation all individuals are assigned a random genotype, which means that the ability to select good "models" is not well developed in the initial population. Therefore, in the early generations not much is learned from the "models" since the "models" are not selected appropriately. However, because of the selective biological reproduction and the constant addition of random genetic mutations to the inherited genotypes the average ability to select good "models" progressively increases and at the end of the simulation it is much more developed than it was in the initial population.

The simulation just described is an example of cooperation between cultural evolution and biological evolution. The ability of resource procurement is culturally transmitted (i.e., learned from "models") whereas the ability to select good "models" is genetically transmitted (i.e., encoded in the inherited genetic material). The two types of evolution are in a reciprocal causal relation. The biological evolution of the ability to select good "models" is made possible by the cultural evolution of the ability of resource procurement. If there were no cultural transmission/evolution of the ability to procure resources, there would be no selective pressure for the evolutionary emergence of the genetically transmitted ability to select good "models". In fact, individuals that are born with a higher level of the ability to select good "models" are not, by this fact alone, more likely to reproduce. Being a good judge of the quality of potential "models" is of importance only because it allows an individual to learn more, that is, from better "models". On the other side, if there were no genetic transmission of the ability to select good "models", the culturally transmitted ability to procure resources would not emerge evolutionarily because individuals would not learn much from "models" because they would be unable to identify good "models". Hence, biological evolution causes cultural evolution or at least makes it possible.

Another example of an interaction (reciprocal causality) between cultural and biological evolution is the following one. Imagine that to learn by imitating another individual (the "model") it is necessary for the "learner" to be physically near the "model" — in order to be able to observe the behavior to be imitated. In this simulation each individual has two distinct neural networks. The first network is the network that allows the individual to find the resource elements present in the environment. As in the preceding simulations the connection weights of this network are randomly assigned at birth and the weights are gradually modified as the individual learns to procure the resource elements by imitating a "model". The second network also allows the individual to move in the environment but the input units of this second network encode the location of "models" rather then the location of resource elements. The connection weights of the second network are encoded in the inherited genotype and are not changed during an individual's lifetime. As in the previous simulation the individuals that collect more resources are more likely to have offspring and random mutations are added to the connection weights of the second neural network which are encoded in the genotype these individuals transmit to their offspring.

At the beginning of the simulation the connection weights of the second network are randomly assigned to all individuals. Hence, initially, the individuals are unable to move in the environment in such a way that they are able to remain in proximity to "models". The members of the initial generations tend to wander in the environment and to be removed from potential "models". Since in order to learn they must be physically near a "model", this implies that they cannot learn by imitating "models" and therefore they are not very good at procuring the resources. However, the connection weights of the second network are progressively changed by the selective biological evolutionary process and by the genetic mutations and, after a certain number of generations, the members of the population can be seen on the computer's screen to have a tendency to approach and remain in proximity to "models".

In this simulation, too, there is cooperation between cultural and biological evolution. The ability to approach and remain in proximity to a "model" does evolve genetically but not because approaching and remaining in proximity to "models" by themselves increase an individual's reproductive chances. The ability evolves genetically because of the pressure of cultural evolution. Approaching and remaining in proximity to a "model" makes it possibile for an individual to learn the capacity to procure resources by imitating the "model". Hence, genetic evolution is dependent on cultural evolution. However, cultural evolution is dependent on genetic evolution in that the culturally transmitted ability to procure resources would not evolve if individuals would not possess a genetically transmitted and evolved ability to approach and remain in proximity to "models" (Figure 4).

8.   SUMMARY

We have described an approach to the study of genetically inherited constraints on human behavior and of the past evolutionary pressures that have resulted in those constraints which differs from the approach of narrow evolutionary psychology in two main respects: the use of neural networks rather than cognitive models for interpreting and explaining human behavior and the adoption of computer simulation as a new way of expressing and testing theories on evolutionary scenarios. In this approach neural networks are viewed as part of Artificial Life, which means that, unlike "classical" neural networks, they have a body, live in an environment, have an inherited genotype, and are members of evolving populations of networks. This

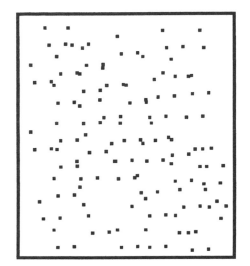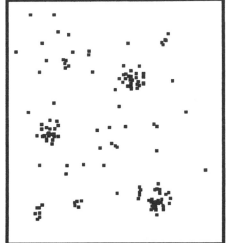

Figure 4. Spatial distribution of individuals at the beginning of the simulation (left) and after a certain number of generations (right). Individuals tend to aggregate in order to learn from "models".

approach implies a number of different emphases with respect to evolutionary psychology: (1) evolution is considered as only partially adaptive and the role of nonadaptive mechanisms in evolution emerges from the simulations; (2) the approach is modular in the sense that evolution creates specific adaptations and not only a general learning capacity but modules are physical (structural or functional) components of the brain rather than postulations of cognitive models, (3) learning, and not only evolution, is studied in the simulations, and special consideration is given to the various ways in which learning and evolution can cooperate to make behavior adaptive; (4) the past is important for humans — not only the biological past but also the cultural past; hence, what is simulated is not only biological but also cultural evolution, and their interactions.

The purpose of this chapter can be described as methodological rather than substantial. We have exemplified the approach by describing a number of simulations but these simulations in many cases address generic 'organisms' in generic 'environments' rather than specifically human organisms living in the human evolutionary environment. To make a more substantial contribution to the study of the specifically human adaptive pattern the simulations must address specifically human behaviors and capacities and they must recreate the specific human evolutionary environment.

National Research Council
Rome, Italy

9. REFERENCES

Belew, R.K. & Mitchell, M. (Eds). (1996). *Adaptive Individuals in Evolving Populations.* Reading, Ma.: Addison-Wesley.

Bowlby, J. (1969). *Attachment.* New York, Basic Books.

Buss, D.M. (1999). *Evolutionary Psychology: The New Science of Mind.* Boston: Allyn and Bacon.

Cangelosi, A., Parisi, D., & Nolfi, S. (1994). Cell division and migration in a 'genotype' for neural networks. *Network, 5,* 497-515.

Cecconi, F. & Parisi, D. (1993). Neural networks with motivational units. In J-A. Meyer, H.L. Roitblat, & S. Wilson (Eds), *From Animals to Animats 2.*(pp. 346-355). Cambridge, Ma.: MIT Press.

Cecconi, F. & Parisi, D. (in preparation). *Learning during reproductive immaturity in evolving populations of networks.*

Cosmides, L. & Tooby, J. (1992). Cognitive adaptations for social exchange. In . J. H. Barkow, L. Cosmides, & J. Tooby (Eds.), *The Adapted Mind: Evolutionary Psychology and the Generation of Culture* (pp. 163-228). New York: Oxford University Press.

Cosmides, L., Tooby, J. & Barkow, J.H. (1992). Introduction: Evolutionary psychology and conceptual integration. In J. H. Barkow, L. Cosmides, & J. Tooby (Eds.), *The Adapted Mind: Evolutionary Psychology and the Generation of Culture* (pp. 3-18). New York: Oxford University Press.

Denaro, D. & Parisi, D. (1996). Cultural evolution in a population of neural networks. In M. Marinaro & R. Tagliaferri (Eds), *Neural Nets. WIRN-96* (pp. 100-111). New York: Springer.

Di Ferdinando, A., Calabretta, R., & Parisi, D. (2001). Evolving modular architectures for neural networks. In R. M. French & J.P Sougne (Eds.). *Connectionist Models of Learning, Development and Evolution (Proceedings of the Sixth Neural Computation and Psychology Workshop)* (pp. 253-262). New York: Springer-Verlag.

Elman, J.L., Bates, E., Johnson, M.H., Karmiloff-Smith, A., Parisi, D., & Plunkett, K. (1996). *Rethinking Innateness. A Connectionist Perspective on Development.* Cambridge, Ma.: MIT Press.

Floreano, D. & Urzelai, J. (2000). Evolutionary robots with on-line organization and behavioral fitness. *Neural Networks, 13,* 431-443.

Fodor, J.A. (1983). *Modularity of Mind.* Cambridge, Ma.: MIT Press.

Gould, J.L. & Vrba, E. (1982). Exaptation, a missing term in the science of form. *Paleobiology, 8,* 4-15.

Hamilton, W.D. (1964). The genetical evolution of social behavior. *Journal of Theoretical Biology, 7,* 1-52.

Lund, H.H. & Parisi, D. (1996). Preadaptation in populations of neural networks evolving in a changing environment. *Artificial Life, 2,* 179-197.

Milner, A.D. & Goodale, M.A. (1995). *The Visual Brain in Action.* Oxford, Eng.: Oxford University Press.

Nolfi, S., Elman, J.L. & Parisi, D. (1994). Learning and evolution in neural networks. *Adaptive Behavior, 3,* 5-28.

Nolfi, S. & Parisi, D. (1997). Learning to adapt to changing environments in evolving neural networks. *Adaptive Behavior, 5,* 75-98.

Parisi, D., Cecconi, F. & Nolfi, S. (1990). Econets: Neural networks that learn in an environment. *Network, 1,* 149-168.

Parisi, D., Cecconi, F., & Cerini, A. (1995). Kin-directed altruism and attachment in an evolving population of neural networks. In N. Gilbert & R. Conte (Eds), *Artificial Societies. The Computer Simulation of Social Life* (pp. 238-251). London, Eng.: UCL Press.

Phelps, S.M. & Ryan, M.J. (2000). History influences signal recognition: Neural network models of túngara frogs. *Proceedings of the Royal Society, London, B267,* 1633-1639.

Pinker, S. (1999). Words and rules. The ingredients of language. London, Eng.: Weidenfeld and Nicolson.

Rumelhart, D.E. & McClelland, J.L. (1986). *Parallel Distributed Processing: Explorations in the Microstructure of Cognition. (Volume 1: Foundations).* Cambridge, Ma.: MIT Press.

Rueckl, J.G., Cave, K.R. & Kosslyn, S.M. (1989). Why are "what" and "where" processed by separate cortical visual systems? A computational investigation. *Journal of Cognitive Neuroscience, 1,* 171-186.

Sims, K. (1994). Evolving 3D morphology and behavior by computation. In R. Brooks & P. Maes (Eds), *Artificial Life IV. (Proceedings of the Fourth International Workshop on the Synthesis and Simulation of Living Systems)* (pp. 28-39). Cambridge, Ma.: MIT Press

Tomasello, M. (1999). *The Cultural Origins of Human Cognition*. Cambridge, Ma.: Harvard University Press.
Ullman, M., Corkin, S., Coppola, M., Hickok, G., Growdon, J.H., Koroshetz, W.J., & Pinker, S., (1997). A neural disassociation within language: Evidence that the mental dictionary is part of declarative memory and grammatical rules are processed by the procedural system. *Journal of Cognitive Neuroscience, 9*, 289-299.
Ungerleider, L.G. & Mishkin, M. (1982). Two cortical visual systems. In D.J. Jingle, M.A. Goodale, & R.J. W. Mansfield (Eds), *The Analysis of Visual Behavior*. Cambridge, Ma.: MIT Press.